GOING WILD
BOOK ONE OF THE ALASKA OFF GRID SURVIVAL SERIES

MILES MARTIN

ALASKA DREAMS PUBLISHING

Going Wild

By Miles Martin
Book One of The Alaska Off Grid Survival Series
©2021 Miles Martin
Artwork, Photos, Original Poetry ©2021
by Miles Martin, All rights reserved

This Book may not be re-sold or given away to others. All rights reserved, including the rights to reproduce this Book.

No part of this text may be reproduced, transmitted, downloaded, scanned, or copied in any form or means, whether electronic or mechanical, without the express written permission of the publisher.

Please purchase only authorized editions of this book and do not take part in or encourage piracy of copyrighted materials.

Published by:
Alaska Dreams Publishing
www.alaskadp.com
1st ADP Edition August 2021
PRINT PAPERBACK ISBN: 978-1-7359713-4-6
PRINT HARDCOVER ISBN: 978-1-7359713-5-3
This book was previously published by Miles of Alaska

Visit www.milesofalaska.com to find a bio of Miles, additional photos, stories, how-to videos, handmade artwork, and raw materials for sale.

Over the years, I have been asked about my life in the wilderness. I am asked about bears, building cabins, falling through the ice, sled dogs, and the whole lifestyle in general. How did I do it? What makes me tic? Why did I leave civilization? Many books have been written on the subject, along with famous movies. Very few are written by the one who did it, in the first person, at the time it is happening. This is such a story, the first book in the series.

I caught the fur, made the hat, jacket, knife, belt buckle, and built the black powder rifle.

FAMOUS?

In 1994, a world-famous photographer-reporter was sent by the New York Times to photograph and interview me on the Kantishna River, in the middle of the Wilderness, Alaska.

Max laughed. I asked what his problem was, and he said, "You are all alike!"

I asked, "And who am I supposed to be like?"

He told me, "All you famous people."

I reply, "Famous? Why? The more I learn, the less I know, and my life is filled with failed goals."

He laughed again and said, "John Lennon said exactly the same thing when I photographed him."

I give a sarcastic, "Yeah, right!"

He replied, "I'm one of the highest-paid photographers in the world. Do you think the New York Times would spend the money and send me out on a dead-end assignment, interviewing a nut, a loser, a false dreamer? You're the best in the world at what you do, just like John Lennon is the best there is at what he does. That's why I'm here."

There is no way I am in the same category as John Lennon.

This must be a line of bull, yet there must be some reason the New York Times would spend the money to send the best photographer in the world to the Alaska wilderness to see me.

A picture of me in 2001, taken in the village of Nenana where I still live in 2014. I'm wearing a cave bear tooth necklace I made.

CONTENTS

Map of the Area	8
The Interior of Alaska	9
Introduction	10
First Cabin	11
Chapter 1	13
New to Fairbanks, Alaska 1972	
Chapter 2	29
Into the Wild, Guns, Bears, Moose	
Chapter 3	51
Build Cabin, Learn Trapping, Marten, Wolves, Wolverine	
Chapter 4	76
The Dark, The Cold, Wolves, Fleas	
Chapter 5	112
Spring Ice Break up, More Bears, Eagle, Walk Out	
Photo Section	147
Chapter 6	152
Alaskaland, Railroad Job, First River Boat, Hard Time,	
Chapter 7	186
Yukon River, Second Cabin, Theft, Near Death, Rescue	
Chapter 8	225
Fur Buyer, Associated Press, Houseboat Plans, Mail Order Women	
Chapter 9	266
Houseboat Building, BLM Job, More Women, Big Plans	
Chapter 10	299
Fall, Jobs End, Finish Boat, Life on a Houseboat	
About The Alaska Off Grid Survival Series	313
Afterword	317
Magazine and News Stories	320
Other Titles Available From Alaska Dreams Publishing	322
Foot Notes	323

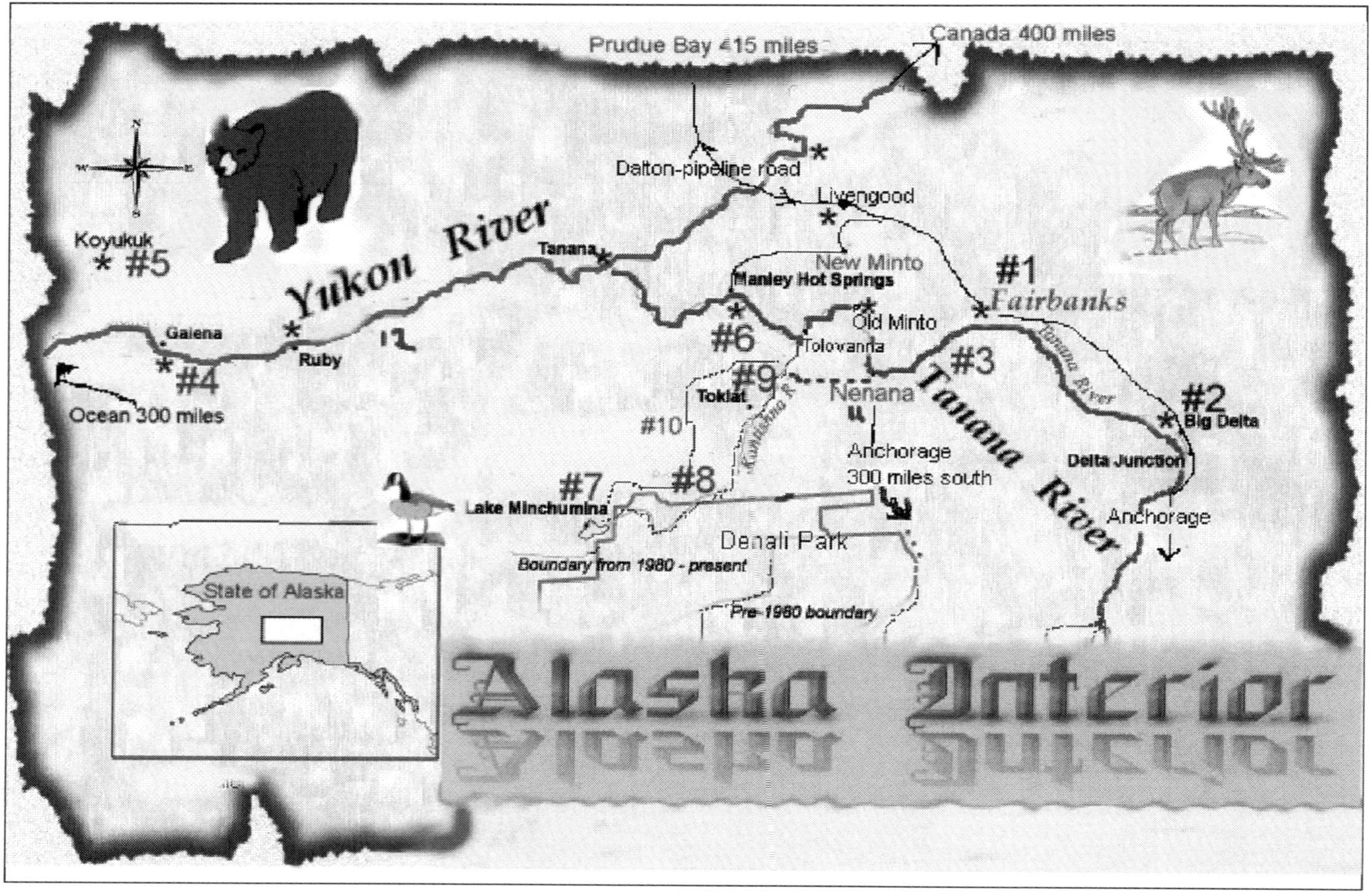
Alaska Interior
Prudue Bay 415 miles
Canada 400 miles
Dalton-pipeline road
Livengood
New Minto
Manley Hot Springs
Old Minto
Tolovanna
Nenana
Fairbanks
#1
#2
Big Delta
Delta Junction
#3
Tanana River
Anchorage
Anchorage
300 miles south
Denali Park
Boundary from 1980 - present
Pre-1980 boundary
Tanana
Yukon River
Koyukuk
#5
Galena
Ruby
#4
Ocean 300 miles
#6
#9
Toklat
#10
#7
#8
Lake Minchumina
State of Alaska

When you step into this map, you leave civilization. This area is so different from the civilized world that it is almost like coming to another planet. In an area that covers about 400,000 square miles (Alaska's Interior,) the largest community is Fairbanks. Fairbanks has a population of about 40,000. There are more communities on this map with under 100 people than over 100 people.

There are more bears than people on this map. More Salmon run upstream to spawn in a one month period than the number of tourists the entire state gets in ten years. If you were lost and lived long enough, it would be possible to spend the next twenty years walking and never see another human. This is a world where if you arrive without bug dope in the summer or mukluks in winter, it might cost you your life. This is a world where if you get in trouble, you don't dial 911, and the laws of nature, not man, rules supreme. Disobeying Man's laws can get you prison time. Disobeying Natures Laws can get you killed. The two sets of laws do not always agree.

The words on this map are not just words but dreams. The empty spaces between the words are a way of life, where we get berries, fish, hunt, trap, live, and die.

I have given numbers to the places various things happened that will be referred to throughout the book. You can come back to the map to see where that is.

#1 - I arrive in Fairbanks knowing of no other place.

#2 - I am flown into the wilderness to a fish camp on the Yukon.

#3 - I walk out to the Dalton Highway that's just being built and end up not far from Livengood.

#4 - I decide to build a houseboat and meet a builder in Big Delta.

#5 - I take off with the houseboat and end up in Fairbanks, where book #1 ends. The rest of the map will be relevant in books to follow.

INTRODUCTION

This is a true story, but not quite a biography, in that events did not necessarily happen in the exact order as told. Some of the names and exact details of some relationships, business dealings, and places have been changed to protect, um... I forget what I'm protecting. The truth, I guess. Most letters are real, but much of the conversation is spoken as best I can remember, following what they or I probably said. There is no deliberate attempt at deception. I'm just not a good, 'time-dates-numbers' person. I'm not good at following rules, so there may also be some 'missed grammar.' I may invent a word here and there. Think of this as a personal diary. Its value is meant to be its truth of soul and heart, and rawness-but not its perfection. Part of this story is about trying to live up to being perfect and never getting there.

There is a lot of fast action drama in a Jack London-Hemingway style. I also consider this a deep reading book that is hard to classify. This book is a psychological study. Many social issues are addressed, including society's views on guns, animal rights, laws, freedoms, racial issues, dreams, reality, rewards we reap, prices we pay for choices, and such matters. This book took almost twenty years to complete, originally with parts of it written with a pencil. I started over from scratch four times. This is not written as a memoir, but written in the present time as it was happening, as an ongoing diary.

The first cabin built.

After living an upper class educated life, of being used to playing tennis with my friends and talking to college professors, this is my new home. One room 8x6 ft, with a dirt floor, and seeing no human for eight months. One person's poison can be another's medicine. I find in this harsh life something that is missing elsewhere.

CHAPTER ONE

NEW TO FAIRBANKS, ALASKA 1972

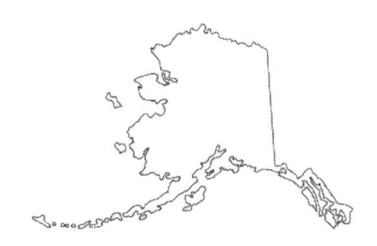

"I just want to get dropped off somewhere in the wilderness with my winter supplies. I've heard you might have a mail route that I could get dropped off along so the flight would be cheaper. I'm not particular where I get dropped. I'll build a cabin, trap, and walk out in the spring." I'm trying to sound more sure and more mature than my twenty-one-year age. The awkward silence that follows has me feeling defensive. I have no reason to feel this way because, after all, I've been in Alaska for three months now.

Piper Wright, the bush pilot, clears his throat. "Kind of spunky, aren't you?"

I shrug my shoulders, not knowing if this is a compliment, insult, or just a comment. I'm just closing a business deal, not looking for personal insights. The silence comes again, as I'm thinking I've heard how Alaskan winters are eight months long, and that's how long it would be before I could walk out. I've spent my life reading all the survival books, watching Walt Disney and such, so now it is time to make the move.

"You want to fly, or do I talk to another pilot?"

After another long pause, Piper says, "Feisty, too!" but he's smiling and seems to be contemplating an awkwardness, confirmed when I hear, "Problem is, it will take two flights for you and all your gear." I'm crestfallen, having only set aside enough money for one flight, until Piper adds, "However." Said as a one-word sentence. "I'll fly you if you work my fish camp on the Yukon River. I can bring all your supplies when I come to pick up the salmon strips you put up for me. I have camp gear, a boat, a motor, but I can't pay you. You can have half the fish, and you can build a cabin and trap there this winter."

"Sounds good to me!" is my happy reply. Piper and I shake hands, and that is that.

"Be ready to go in a week, meet me at the float pond, you'll know my plane, my name's on it, 7 a.m., July 5th."

With a new bounce to my walk, I leave the office, thinking how my plans have changed a little. At first, I wanted to live in a remote village in Canada. The hope was to do my art, photography, writing, hunting, and trapping. Canada hadn't worked out. Business there wasn't wrapped up yet, for…er…reasons I'd rather not think about. *Had to leave in a bit of a hurry.* Hopefully, the information will arrive in today's mail that will settle 'all that.' So I walk the length of Fairbanks to the post office.

Sitting in the sun on the post office steps, I read the letter I thought I was waiting for, having to do with my house and belongings I had to leave behind…

Hey Miles,
  Everything is pretty much the same here. Not much ever changes. You asked about your cats. The day after you left, Art set them up on the fence and shot them. I don't think anyone would have wanted them anyway. The guy who is buying your house doesn't want to send any more money, saying he doesn't have to pay an illegal alien. He says there was a flood in the basement. Something about the water pump and all your junk was hauled to the dump. I hope you're doing ok in Alaska. You should be a lot happier there in your own country. The guy getting the house says he found a needle full of drugs in the house, and if you come back, you'll be arrested. I know you don't use drugs, drink, or even smoke. Probably Art left the needle before the new owner moved in. Wish I had better news. Take care, **Chuck**

The forgotten letter falls in the street, to mix with the other trash, as my unfocused eyes stare inward. I kind of liked my cats. It looks like no money will be coming in from the house sale. This will be a loss of all that money I'd bought it with. I'd been so proud, twenty years old and owning my own house. A house that cost me all those extra hours on the carrier in the Navy. There were all those countries I never left the ship to see because I had a dream, a plan. Now all for nothing. Why hadn't my residency papers come through anyway? Dad wrote he was informed by the authorities I'd received papers denying residency, but I hadn't, so had the town set me up? Need I face why? My mind wanders. *The bitch is that I could have gone to Canada four years earlier and been accepted as a draft dodger, but I was unwilling to desert my country, that said it needed me.* The war was such a waste, and I wasn't needed in the least. Draft dodgers became the heroes. *Now almost everything I own is called 'junk'* at a dump in Canada. There is a family photo album, hundreds of paintings I'd done, the photographs I took, all the equipment, and my coin collection. Some of this wouldn't be damaged by water, so I doubt there was even a flood. Of course, I can't go back now to find out. Certainly, I can't afford an international lawyer."

A sigh comes forth unbidden. Doors are closing, bridges are burning behind me. Unable to ever turn back, my life is changing forever. "Do I choose to go into the wilderness? Or am I driven? All other options seem to be falling apart, so am I really as in control of my life as I think? What else is there for me? I've lost the option to go on in school in subjects of my choice because I didn't pass chemistry, a requirement for any direction I'd care to go in Biology. I had lost the choice of a military career because I never got along with officers. I don't seem qualified for any special occupation, and certainly, I will not settle for being a bum or for slave labor. I can't think of anything else that thrills me like the wilderness. Maybe my art or writing, but unless I'm in the top ten, I'm told these are not reputable occupations. They offer no future, no chance to be special or out from under someone's thumb. Trapping isn't reputable either, but at least it is exciting, and I think I'd be good at it. Mountain men are among my heroes. There are few heroes for the young among artists and writers, who are viewed as somewhat sissyish, to say the least.

Another sigh, for I'm not sure how much I'm fooling myself and everyone else. I've always been good with words, excuses, justifications. The result is that I look good to myself. Everyone else looks bad. Perhaps I'm really running away from my problems, as so many think. I turn over another letter I received. A whiff of her perfume brings memories.

Dearest Miles

Long time no hear from . . . you get lost in the woods? What's new in Canada? Will you be ending your letters as they talk there, with "aye?" As for me, I still cannot decide between Dave or Bill. Dave's really handsome, but Bill treats me so much better. I think I'm still looking for my frog, that I kiss and turn into a prince! College is ok; my grades are in the top ten (big deal). Because I still do not know what I want. I do miss you carrying my books to school and how you'd come across the street to my place to fix my breakfast because I'm always so late. Now, without you, I'm always late! Ha, ha, ha! So you think you'll ever come home?

Take care! **Love, Maggie**

This letter brings a smile and a flood of fond nostalgia. We've known each other since we were fourteen. I always had a crush on her. When I joined the Navy, our relationship could only be through the mail. Joining had been a hasty decision my father made. Dad had not noticed I had a girl I cared for. It seemed not to matter that my personal life was so affected. Having to tell Maggie I'm off to the military in a few days must have hurt her feelings. As if I did not care. These thoughts are rudely interrupted by a hail from the street.

"Hey, short shit, what's happening?" I turn to see my bunk partner from the Salvation Army greeting me. His head is bobbing, and he's asking, "Got any dope?"

I inwardly ask, "How long will it be before these bozos realize I want to be a mountain man and can't afford to mess up my mind. I'm interested in getting off on life, not dope!"

I reply to him with a straight face. "I got some battery acid if you got a needle, but you have to use it fast before it dissolves your needle." I watch his brain working, going

Hmm, battery acid, never heard of that one . . . pause, *Is this guy pulling my leg?* With no expression, I stand there until he says "No thanks" and walks away. Aimlessly I walk the street, in the general direction of the Salvation Army, deep in thought over my letters, my life, my goals, and deeply hurt, bitter, over the Canada thing, Viet Nam, the military in general, the loss of a chance for a normal life with someone I know and love.

Very few people are taking me seriously, I notice, but it doesn't matter. In the end, everyone has to be responsible for themselves. We can't worry about other people's opinions. This is a lonesome thought, with not one person believing in what I'm doing. *Wasn't it 'other people's opinion' that got me deported and losing everything I own...anyway?* Most people are talking about how I'll die out there in the wilds.

How can I ever go through life, never following through with a lifelong dream? As I walk along, my mind drifts off again. Never knowing if I 'could have, would have should have.' To be, or not to be, that is the question. A very old question. Should I risk dying while trying, or would I forever regret never having tried! Piper doesn't think I'm a loser, at least. He wants me to work in his fish camp. He trusts me, and I'll show him it wasn't a mistake!

I don't look forward to another week at the Salvation Army, waiting to get out to the wilderness. As I sit on my cot, listening to the drunks bicker, I consider how I'm not used to being seen as a bum. My life will be drastically changing soon; already has, and with no money and nothing to do, my mind drifts back in time.

Flash past[1] Was it Cleveland? Hawaii? LA? I know I was only four or five when I said I wanted to be a trapper. Someone is reading me, "Peter and The Wolf." Plans are not firm; come and go with other ideas. I did start collecting stories, articles, and bits of useful information for wilderness survival. There is a whole notebook full of written odds and ends. I've collected information on cabin building, making soap, tanning leather, and other useful wilderness skills. I never know what bit of information may be useful or might save my life, so I collect "everything." Likewise, I've watched every Rifleman and Gunsmoke episode "in awe."

My reverie of the past is brought abruptly to the present with, "Do you have a quarter?"

I respond, "No, I don't have a quarter...go get a job!" to the bum next to me. The bum mumbles something about my attitude problem and getting a life. My mind switches to thoughts of Fairbanks and how I arrived here, as

I continue to flash past. I arrived in Fairbanks three months ago, in April of 1973, and note it's called "A bustling city" of 70,000 people. The oil pipeline is starting to be built, and there are many transient people talking big money. I'm sorry to hear about the pipeline, and dislike oil, big business, and am here for other reasons. It doesn't take me long to surmise the situation here. Rooms renting for $50.00 a night is a couple of days' wages and turns out to be a mattress in someone's basement. Meals and rent are twice what they should be, which reminds me of the Soapy Smith days during the gold rush I'd read about. A world of swindles and con artists. The local people seem suspicious, on guard, or outright hostile to the big change. With only a few hundred dollars and a few belongings, I'd better get to the wilderness soon, or I'll miss the coming trapping season. I hate to put off my lifetime dream any longer and maybe get stuck in the rat race. I continue to remember how it was, coming to Alaska just a short time ago. I recall that first conversation that changed so much of how my future would go.

Still flashing past..."Yes, I hope to head out to the wilderness and trap, but I'm low on funds."

"Well," my companion says, "when in Rome, ya gotta do what da Romans do!" He goes on, "People in dis country travel in da kayaks, you read about dem? Well, that's what ya need ta do is get a-holt of one of them things."

"Maybe," I say, "But here I'm hoofing it, low on funds, no work, and no place to get such a craft. You see the price of a room? A guy could go broke here real fast! But if I had a boat of some kind, I think I could get a tent and some gear and go up this creek the town's on to where there's deserted places a guy could set up camp."

My companion grins, "That's what I was gonna tell ya. I god- a kayak I could a sell ya, deliver it right here to the river fer ya!" I'm all ears.

I pay $300.00 for a nice fiberglass kayak. After that, I get a tent, rifle, some food, and other gear I'd need to live in a camping situation. I have no money left, but I'm set with supplies to live a month or more. That's plenty of time to find work. Better yet, I might find a way to make a living in the wilderness! Everything gets loaded into the kayak. No one bothers telling me the water I see is running on top of the ice. The river hasn't broken yet. No one should be on the river now, not for at least a month yet. Nor does anyone tell me I don't need a 'kayak.' I could have got a nice brand new canoe for $200.00. Nor do they inform me that 'kayaks' are very tipsy and dangerous if you've never been in one before, especially when loaded as top-heavy as I have it.[2] "But Miles!" my conscience speaks to me, "Why don't we seek advice, listen to the right people. We could save a lot of heartaches, learning from other people's experience!"

"Um," I reply, "Let me think on that one…oh, I know. Because, for example, not one person told me I could have done what I've already done."

In the Navy, at home, among friends, co-workers, no matter whom I talked to, everyone said I couldn't do it! No one said, "Go for it," and it's no use getting local advice when you don't know what to ask when you don't know good advice from bad. Most people have an ulterior motive when they give you advice, such as they don't want you around, or they're trying to sell you something. Anyway, I don't like to bother people, ask silly questions, show off my ignorance, get laughed at, and be beholden to anyone for a favor. If I make a mistake, I'd rather it be my own, not someone else's. Then at least I can blame myself, correct it, and not be mad at someone else.

My conscience replies, "Well, Miles, You're certainly stubborn enough for the lifestyle!"

"Uh-huh," I answer, followed by, "What's this "you" stuff? What happened to 'we,' as in 'us.' "

As I launch my trusty sleek craft into my next adventure. I mumble to myself, "Gosh, she's tipsy."

Well, gotta learn how to do this sometime. I shove off into the wonderful world of kayaking. The black water pulls at my bright red kayak. It is pointy at both ends, round like a log, with just a little hole to sit in. A cold fog hugs the Chena River as I wobble this way, wobble that way.

How do the Eskimos do this? My conscience asks me, but I don't answer because I start to make headway and am getting the hang of it. If I had a tail, I'd wag it! *Here comes Miles, the mighty kayaker, stalking the tusky walrus.* Whoops! I dump her over, which becomes *Oh, burr,* as I enter the water. I'm not afraid, only cold. The water is knee-deep, which I hadn't realized. *Huh- ice under the water.* I thought ice belonged on top of the water. I'll be darn. Here and there, I step in a hole in the ice, with water going under that ice in whirlpools that I wouldn't want to be sucked into. It's slippery walking, as I feel the edge of the holes with my feet. All my heavy goods go down to the ice, get sucked into holes, and disappear. Most of the lighter things float away faster than I can retrieve them. There goes my sleeping bag. There goes my tent. I drag what I can ashore. My entire food supply has gone under the ice.

I had kayaked perhaps a mile upstream. I am in a thick birch thicket, not far from the Fort Wainwright gate. I've been in the freezing water for over half an hour and have been in the snow, soaking wet, sorting goods, with the air temperature hovering near freezing.

My conscience speaks, *We should have kept water-tight containers of matches and dry clothes.* Not bothering to answer, I walk to keep warm while shivering and turning blue. The sound of the traffic on Airport Road draws me, so I head for it. I don't know what to do. I'm down to my last quarter, with no place to stay, no friends, and no supplies, freezing to death.

My conscience whispers, *I see Street people on the porch of this building. This is the rescue mission.* I never in my life considered where 'street people' live or how they eat and sleep, but this is the answer. I'd seen it in a movie or read it in a book.

Squaring my shoulders, I walk in with as much dignity as I can muster. My soaking wet shoes go splash, splish, splosh, and I prepare myself to give some speech about how I've arrived here this way. *It's quite a long story, you must admit—and don't you have to qualify for a free place to stay? Like, you know, be an idiot or something? Do you think we can prove that we are an idiot and thus qualify for free stuff?*

"Sign here," I'm told, by the guy behind the desk, with hardly a glance up and no surprise on his face.

A place like this sees it all. Before I have time to open my blue lips, the Mission guy says,

"Here's your blanket, there's your cot, dinner's at 6:00, worship follows," sounding like it was said a hundred times a day, and probably does.

Flash past briefly ends.

From my cot at the Salvation Army, I smile at how it was. My first week at the Rescue Mission,

Flash past continues

My tongue is in the corner of my mouth as I concentrate on the delicate leaf of a flower. I'm working with watercolor paints on birch bark at the worktable in the mission.

"Huh, oh! Hi Sir." I always have trouble knowing how to address these stern-faced honchos. Should it be captain, deacon, pastor, your highness? I have an authority issue. One decides to sit next to me and discuss the salvation of my soul. My eyes and ears are all his, along with a pleasant smile, but my mind drifts off to "la la" land.

"And pray, and not be concerned with worldly goods…blah, blah, blah." The gist of which is my painting is frowned on. If I understand correctly, I should not be concerned with worldly affairs but should concern myself with the salvation of my eternal soul. I see myself as trying to find a way I can make some money, so I can get out of here. Certainly, I don't intend to retire here. My thoughts are that this watercolor on birch bark is a postcard a local shop might pay a dollar for, and I can paint 30 an hour, minus costs. This looks like good money. There is a white-haired, unshaven, vomit- smelling dumpster man, sitting on the floor in the corner, who bursts out laughing. Later he takes me aside.

"You don't want to be here. You need the Salvation Army across town. They'll help you find work." Followed by a wink and a burp.

This turns out to be true. Friendly people with big smiles greet me. I take to them and the place right off. I snare rabbits in the woods, and we cook them up and share them. No one thinks that is 'nutso' as we share God's Bounty. I can handle the outlook here. Everyone helps wash dishes, clean up as we talk and laugh. It's like one big family.

"Who wants to be a janitor at a bakery?" someone on the phone yells. Local businesses call up when their people quit.

I answer up after a pause, "I think I'm qualified!" I have work a couple of days a week, and I like it. The work is mostly nights by myself, and I get to take out the day-old bread. Someone at 'Sally's' gives me a ride to work each day, so we can load up the truck with day-old bread and deserts. However, this is not work I can save money at, so I start going to the job center. Looking for work is new to me, but I quickly size up the routine—doors open at 8:00 a.m., line forms at 7:30 a.m. The serious people pack a lunch. We get a number when we come through the door, and this determines our priority when jobs are called in during that day.

Flash Past briefly ends

From my cot at the Salvation Army, I think about the 'money,' the 'being a bum' comments, and the people here. The past flashes along as I remember when I got the job I needed.

Flash past continues…

Most of the jobs through the unemployment center are one-day type work. Some old lady needs her sidewalk shoveled, and 50 people scramble for the job. This can be discouraging, but I get to know many of the people who show up regularly. While flirting with the gals at the front desk, I exchange lunch and gossip. After a week, they all know me and are rooting for me to find good work. I had been a ski lift operator, shoveled snow, and was tired of these short-term jobs. One day, I look at the bulletin board.

"Hey, what's this about veterans' preference? That's me, Vietnam Vet; does that get me a job?" I say while doing my Groucho Marx eyebrow bit. The secretary laughs,

"Be serious, Miles!" but adds, "It does mean the civil service jobs listed have vet preference."

"Hmm." I study the board closer. "Janitor/maintenance man. Steam line utility door work." That fits in with my Navy training, so I mention this. The secretary is thrilled for me and sends me out to Eielson Air Force Base. I have to hitchhike the twenty miles to the base. When I get there, the receptionist says,

"Oh-Gee, they shouldn't have sent you; we're looking for previous experience with our facilities." I use my lost puppy dog expression until she says, "But, since you came all the way out here..." The result is that I get the job, and it turns out to be primo work—full time, good pay, long term, lots of bennies, and seasonal.

"So I can go trap at the end of the season." Living on the Air force base helps me save money. I get a lunch pass and a movie pass, so I can live and be entertained cheaply. I'm really sacking the money away.

The Salvation Army keeps my kayak for me but finally sells it (they give me nothing for it). I had nowhere to keep it. The work at the base develops into a routine, with lots of listening to the radio, drinking sodas, and a dive underground a couple of times a day. There is a small crew of us that travels around in a truck, or we sit in the truck, watching women go by. Making comments about them seems to be part of every job all over the world. Most of the guys like the big busty blondes with lots of makeup, sprayed hair, high heels, and mini-skirts. These women seem 'plastic' to me.

"So, what do you like, Miles? Show us a knockout!" I point out a cute thing across the street. She has no makeup, long loose dark hair, jeans, narrow hips, and little tits.

"There's one I'd jump!" The guys think she's homely and kid me, but I tell them, "Someone has to take care of the rest of the women you guys turn down!" It seems the world always spins the other way for me than it does for most folks, and I never do seem to like what others do, but I fit in okay, I guess.

I'm liked at work. I'm a hard worker, honest, reliable, and knowledgeable. The peak of the season is going by. We've got the main steam leak problems that came up over the past winter solved now, so the boss can afford to cut back on workers. I ask if it's okay for me to get let go early. I've made enough money. That's not a problem, and I'm told I have work next summer if I want it, just 'get in touch.' I have saved $2,000. From talking to people, I have learned what to buy and what to keep an eye out for at garage sales for my supplies[3].

There are signs around town that other people have the same dream I have. Now that I'm not working and have some money, I can look around for the first time. There are stores that sell traps, tents, stoves, guns, and other bush-type goods.

"Just came in from the creeks; get the scales out, missy!" A prospector is in front of me at the bank. I strain to look over his shoulder as he dumps a leather pouch of gold onto a scale on the countertop. He's young but looks old, happy though, I decide. He wears dirty, smelly clothes, yes, like he's in from a winter in a hole digging dirt with gold in it.

My conscience again, *What a cool place this is, a real prospector!* While walking around looking for last-minute supplies, I notice a poster advertising round trips to Hawaii for $200.

Less than a trip to the lower 48 states! I've heard a lot of people here have a property in Hawaii. This topic interests me because I was born there, and it sort of makes a connection, completes a circle, enforces the idea this is home.

There are tropical fruits for sale in better shape and of more variety than I was used to seeing down south, and I conclude it comes in on all those Hawaii flights. It's possible to walk the length of Fairbanks in an hour, so I decide it is just the right size place to find anything I might need by walking. I'm hungry, and I recall there is a pizza place in town, as well as a couple of places that sell burgers or chicken. There are fancier places too, but I do not consider them. Most any wilderness tool is for sale somewhere in town, or I can at least order it. There is a place to buy bulk food in 100-pound bags at a special price where all the homesteader types shop.

In the evening, there is a good place for entertainment. The Howling Dog Saloon is just out of town. There is sawdust on the floor, live fiddle music, and a crowd of foot-stomping cut loose people. This is not just a put on for tourists, I see. This is how people live, just like out of a movie set, only its real life. The first time there, I noticed a sign, "please check your guns in at the bar." I waited around to actually see someone check a gun in! There's a movie place if I want to go see a movie. The library is a historic log cabin with rocking chairs, planted flowers out front, and overlooks the river in a quiet section of town. Fairbanks has a sense of space.

Most buildings are single-story and very spread out compared to cities I was used to. There are a few two-story buildings, a couple of three-story buildings, but one would be hard-pressed to spot anything taller. Certainly, I can look up and see the sky. There are no highways, no cloverleaf, and no rush hour traffic. The roads are all two-lane, and a lot are unpaved. This is the second largest town in a state bigger than Texas and is the hub people come to from a thousand square miles. This is the biggest city a lot of these people have ever seen in their lives. Fairbanks is a small enough place that clerks in stores remember most locals, and greet them by name, and exchange personal words.

"Remember that saw I got? Well, I need a spare plug for it, and a spare chain" is a typical way business is done here. I'm struck by the fact you do not need a receipt, a serial number, or proof of purchase.

I'm also struck by the fact people are out walking around late at night, including women and children. Some might not like to go walking down 'two' street late at night, but mostly because they do not like to be asked for money. There is some crime but not a lot of the violent type. I can hitchhike and expect to get a ride. When you are in trouble, people tend to stop and help. Maybe not everyone, but enough for this to be normal.

A lot of people wouldn't like Fairbanks. There is little class here. There is no opera, no concerts, and no place to really dress up. There is seldom a need or a place to wear a suit and tie. A lot of working women in town wear pants and drive beat-up trucks.

This is a place I can expect to wear jeans, a lumberjack shirt, a fur hat, a knife at my side, outdoor boots, and not stand out, even at a wedding. This means a lot to me. I can't count how many times I tried to "dress the part" and been laughed at, considered a nut, wearing my coonskin cap to school, or whatever. People do not seem so concerned about what you wear here. Often, the guy covered in mud is a prospector, or trapper, coming in for supplies, ready to spend a thousand dollars in a store. The guy who owns the bank may show up somewhere in coveralls to shop after just feeding his horses and didn't feel like changing. I'd lived in places where you wouldn't be allowed in an eating place without a suit, and I'd had to wear a suit and tie to school, so this is all new to me. I take it in as I walk around. I'd felt so guilty and horrible much of my life, being told I dress funny, just to get attention. How immature, what a problem! Now I am so relieved to not stand out! I'm wearing the uniform of my people, among my people, for the first time in my life!

A bumper sticker goes by on a truck, "I will give up my gun when it is pried from my cold dead fingers," and it reminds me I see a lot of "radical" type stickers. The guy in this truck is wearing a bear tooth around his neck. There are a lot of anti-government types, freedom people, pro-hunting, and independent thinkers, able and wanting to take care of themselves. This is a state where pot is legal, not that we have more users, just that it's up front. A lot of Alaskans want to secede from the United States. There is a strong division between "before and after." They mean the flood in sixty-seven, I think.

Flash past ends

My reverie from the past is broken, as the present screams at me.

"Hey, Miles! Hear you are headed to the wilderness soon, good luck!"

I've made a few friends here at the Salvation Army, so it is nice to be asked about my trip. I am not quick to remember names and do not remember this guy to answer back, but it is nice to be thought about. *Yea, this is the guy I think stole my camera.* I get up from the Salvation Army cot and decide to write a few letters before flying out with Piper. My job ended, and I figure I'll just come back here for a few days since I spent my money on the basic supplies I need for the wilderness. Back in the community room at Sally's, I write letters that need to be taken care of before I head out into the toolies.

I start a letter to my father but do not know what to say. After a long pause, I continue writing

Dear Dad

Sorry, it has been so long since I wrote.

Yup, I'm ok. Looks like I'll have my chance to get out in the wilderness. I know you expected me to come visit after being deported, and I appreciate the invitation, but you know me, places to go, things to do, and really, I need to get on with my life, move in the direction of my goals. Hope you are well. Take care. **Sunshine, Miles.**

In my original plans, I had intended to do a more gradual transition from city life to wilderness life. There would have been a taste of village life. I would have picked up skills, tried the life out on a small scale. I might have even settled for village life, happy to get out in the wilds on short trips. Because of the Canada deal, this plan has changed. There is no use dwelling on it. I have no intention of crawling back to the nest in defeat. There is little use in telling my father about all the new things going on. He would not understand. The kayak deal, loss of everything I own, it would only live up to what he expected. I cannot do it and should just give up, come home, and be a normal person. With my father being Dean of a college, I could go to college free. Yes, I already said that. Because I also am told that often. I'm a rebellious teenager breaking a parent's heart, getting what I deserve.

I fill out one of my water colored envelopes with the address. The painted scene is Canada geese against a gorgeous sunset with the address 'Dr. Miles Martin,' which I always write with pride. I add, 'Plattsburgh NY.' I picture Lake Champlain, the house on the lake, and Dad's sailboat at the dock. But that is his life. This is the world he made for himself. My desire is to make it on my own, not in the name of my father. There is a desire to be my own person, not ever hear, "Well, of course, you do well. It is all handed to you on a silver platter." The privilege of the upper-middle-class could be handed to me. I'm not against any of that, only that I have my own destiny, not a chip off the old block, and I could talk on and on, but that sums it up.

Surely, I cannot head out into the wilderness without writing to my best friend and love.

Dearest Maggie
How is school going? How's "What's his name" and yes, you are right, I can't keep them all straight.
:)
Your grades are good, you say? What will it mean when you are married, have children, and live in that nice home with the white picket fence...
...and maybe I'll be able to send you a wolf hide to hang up or something. Try not to be depressed. Things will work out. You're a good person, just hang in there! Oh! Did you ever submit the 700-page letter I wrote you to the book of world records like you suggested? Ha! As for me, yea, the Canada bit was a bitch all right. I should have seen it coming. No one really liked me much anyway. I was the outsider, trying to change things. I got the ice rink opened, put in free work at the library, and tried to get the kids off the street. I was trying to be a mover and shaker. It was a lumberjack

community, rough- tough, and dirt poor. I come along, 20 years old, buy my own home cash, educated (by their standards). I was set up by the whole community and lied to. This is what bothers me, but whatever. They had promised me working for the library for $2 an hour was not 'working without a permit'- because no Canadian wanted the job, and they were shutting the library down. You know me, and how I love libraries. Heck, we met in one remember! Ha! Anyhow that's all I wanted to do, keep the library going to help the community I hoped to call my home as soon as I got my papers. I'm sure my being there had a downside. I wasn't perfect. I'm sure if they told the story, their version would show I deserved what I got. That is what makes you special, I can be who I am, and you forgive me for being eccentric! It might be a while before you hear from me again. If I don't survive, know I gave it my best shot! Take care, be good! **Sunshine, Miles.**

I write about twenty pages of gossip and the usual stuff I write Maggie about.

Her letter barely fits in one of my painted business envelopes. Flowers, a blue sky, with a bright sun, are the theme. Soft, gentle, far away colors all wash together dreamily behind the address of My Maggie. There is no one else I wish to write, so send my two letters off.

The day has finally arrived to fly out, and I will be faced with a new reality.

There will be no more pretending or playing a role in a movie or a book. There will be no women around to swoon over my acting or women being disgusted by an insecure dramatic macho guy. There will be no more collecting odd bits of wilderness lore to frivolously paste in my album. Indeed, the album, my survival manual that I spent a lifetime putting together, is now in a Canada dump. No more daydreaming that the camping trip is in the middle of the wilderness, and I'm Daniel Boone. Once I am dropped off in the true wilderness, it will be real. I will be climbing out of the simulator, leaving boot camp, setting aside my poetry, discovering who I am, what I am made of. I'm going to be…

FLYING.

Flying in the small floatplane with Piper Wright. We are headed for the Yukon River, and he's grinning at me.

"Never been in a small plane before?"

I'm looking out one window, then the other, gawking at the vast wilderness with no roads below. If I had a tail, I'd wag it.

"What's the name of this lake below?" I ask.

Piper tips the plane, and I fall against the window. As the plane engine maxes out, Piper matter of factly looks at the mile-long lake below us, replying, "No name.

Most of the lakes below have no name; whole mountain ranges have no name here."

This is when I notice the entire map I look at in my lap is marked "unsurveyed." Other maps are marked "aerial surveyed 1952."

It has never been ground checked. Nothing on this whole map has been ground checked. This is like the Amazon. There might be whole civilizations below us that no one has met or seen. The plane lurches, drops, skips a beat. My heart is left on the ceiling. Piper calmly adjusts something.

"Willy-wam" is all he says.

I smile and nod like I know what that means. *Piper seems so much more at ease in the plane than he does on the ground,* I'm thinking. He's part Athabascan Indian from the village of Minto but doesn't look very Indian. Average height, stocky build.

"Yukon ahead." Piper interrupts my thoughts and points out the river on the horizon. It is half a mile wide where we are going to land. "About a thousand miles long," he adds, as the plane loses speed and wobbles at tree level. "The largest village has 800 people. Most villages have a hundred or so. No road crosses the river. We'll be thirty miles from the only boat landing where a dirt road ends." We bounce a few times on the silty water, and 'splosh' a hundred feet before the engine slows. With water spraying, and trees flapping from the prop wash, we turn into a river eddy at his fish camp. Not that I know what an 'eddy' is, but it sounds good.

There is no time to get poetic or take in the beautiful scenery. Like in the Jack London story I read, where he writes how people are too busy living to write it down or consider it romantic. My city legs tremble on the river silt. Right away, Piper gets me in his sixteen-foot riverboat and starts the twenty horse outboard. He wants to check the King salmon net he'd set the day before.

"This is the topline" Piper grabs the top of the net as he gets ready to check it. "The topline has the small football-looking floats on it, spaced a couple of feet apart. One end of the eighty-foot net is tied to the shore. The other end has been played out in the eddy with the boat drifting, and an anchor is holding the leadline down."

I assume from observation that an eddy is a place in the river along the shore where the current forms a whirlpool and creates slack water. Looking at the net, I ask if the leadline is this bottom part.

He grabs hold of it and continues, after nodding, yes. "This is a hollow rope about an inch in diameter filled with slugs of lead to make it heavy and holds this side of the net down. Remember not to twist the leadline over the topline when you set it or check it." As Piper pulls the net hand over hand into the aluminum boat, I see the mesh has squares about five inches big, made of string, and extends about twelve feet deep when set. A fishnet looks a lot like a volleyball net. Twenty feet are pulled into the boat before there is a Salmon. This one is a medium size at thirty pounds. Piper is talking fast. I'm straining to remember everything he says. Something about expecting several thousand fish in the next few weeks—we'd caught several in just an hour.

He shows me how to get the fish out of the net and how to reset the net. We move the net to a new spot, so I get to see how to set it if I have to move it by myself. I even need lessons in how to start and stop the outboard engine. I'd never seen one up close before. Very little of anything I'm experiencing was in any of my mountain man books or on Walt Disney. School teaches nothing about this. Piper shows me how to get the camp ready. There is a plywood platform to set the tent on and a board table to clean fish on.

"You cut the Salmon like this." Piper cuts the Salmon in half with one clean swipe, making it look so easy. "Then you make a cut like so, to get the backbone out, go to the other side and get the rib bones. Don't forget this row of bones and the fins."

"What do I do with all the guts and bones?"

"Just toss em in the river." This is new to me, tossing garbage in a river. There is a creek nearby to get water to drink and rinse the fish in. Piper explains, "This is the brine barrel. You put about this much brown sugar and salt in." Piper dumps about five pounds into the fifty-five-gallon drum. The fish are rinsed in this. "These are the poles to hang them on." Piper shows me some sticks about four feet long. He sets them on a small rack near the cutting table. "Let's go to the smokehouse, and I'll show you what to do there." We walk the fifty feet through the red rose bushes, and pink fireweed flowers up to a galvanized tin shed about twenty by twenty feet. This is just sheet metal nailed to spruce poles. Inside there is a fifty-five-gallon drum turned into a simple stove. Piper goes over and closes its door. "Use only poplar or alder wood, never use birch. Willow is ok but not the best. Spruce is too hot." He shows me what the wood looks like. All of it grows within a stone toss of camp.

Piper sums the instructions up.

"Well, that about covers everything. Better get going, things to get done today yet." Piper walks over to the floatplane and climbs up on its floats. He trips getting in, and once again, I think how the plane seems more like his real body. He's more graceful in the air than on land. I help him untie. "Grab this line and hold the nose out to the current till I get the engine warmed up. I'll wave when you can turn loose." He hands me the rope. No good-byes, or asking me if I got all the right things, and no treating me like a child. Piper must have known I was nervous, but he doesn't make a thing about it. "See you in about a week; I hope you have a pile of strips for me!" Piper grins as he waves his goodbye, letting me know I can release the rope.

Handling Fish on the Yukon.

CHAPTER TWO

INTO THE WILD, GUNS, BEARS, MOOSE

I'm in a bad mood and frustrated. The fishnet has to be moved for the first time because the water level is changing, as Piper had warned me about. I got the net in the boat but don't understand what to do next. The 'topline—leadline' stuff sounded so simple when Piper explained it. The rain is pouring down, Mosquitoes are out, and the net is in a tangled mess in the bottom of the boat.

My conscience speaks to me. *What if I can't figure it out or can't get the net in the water catching Salmon?* I express my frustration to my conscience since there is no one to talk to. It seems impossible to feed the net out of the boat and keep the leadline on the bottom! *Maybe if we just start setting it, straighten it out as it goes in the water, a solution might present itself and be self-evident.* I'm afraid to do it this way because I think I have to concentrate on the engine, proper angle heading into the river current eddy, and maintaining the right place in the water. One-step at a time, I handle these problems. Problems from how to fix food, to how to make camp, to how to do this job, all are solved.

From my Diary:
    August 10, 1972. I have 57 Salmon to strip today. Days and days of rain. Will I ever get dry?"

With pen and diary in hand, I just sit and stare, tired and overwhelmed by all this. But yes, happy too. This new life is healthy and filled with opportunity. This is a lifestyle where you reap the rewards from your own work. Life is hard, but the rewards are great.

Conscience—*Can you imagine what these fifty-seven fish would be worth in New York? About a year's wages! We are rich beyond our wildest dreams!* Time has been lost track of. Days blend with weeks. Often I hear sounds that I think are familiar, like people talking, cars, trucks, things I'm used to. Now I hear the thump of a canoe paddle on a boat. Darn cabin fever again. I try to go back to reading, which I've been doing to relax. "splash, drip, splash."

A pause. "Is anyone home?"

I frown. My conscience frowns. *Maybe this isn't cabin fever, but real.* I've stumbled out of the tent before, so sure it was some real human sound, only to find out it wasn't. Now I'm sure this is the same thing, and I will laugh at myself.

Two real canoeists greet me. The rain is just ending. The never-ending sun is out. It's midnight. The river is dappled in mist and rainbow.

"What brings you two out in the rain?" I ask. The reply is a shuffling of feet and awkward silence. I can spot green folks easy enough. I interrupt the silence. "Well, set by the fire and have some coffee!" This is the Alaskan way to say hi. We ramble on about this and that, weather and such before, "Question and answer time." After being deported from Canada, I don't especially care if I ever see anyone again and am not very trusting.

One finally speaks up, "Started off from Whitehorse a month ago, floating the Yukon, hope to make it to the ocean."

Tourists! I think to myself. There is a vast unbridgeable gap between those who are passing through and those who are staying. It never occurs to me that these two had probably spent more days in the wilderness than I have, even had more interesting experiences. I saw the difference as "intent." This is my home, where I will spend the rest of my life. These are bubbly-grinning-clean-shaven-pink-faced tourist heads sticking out of brand new LL bean shirts.

My conscious comes back to hear them,

"We made camp up there a ways." He's pointing upriver, explaining, "Had a bear come around during the night, bit through the tent and into a can right next to my friend's head!" The friend is shaking his head in confirmation as my attention turns to him.

"We made a fire and tea but couldn't sleep. Bear kept coming around, so I tossed a cup of tea in his face."

I'm thinking to myself, Anti-guns, anti-hunting- trapping.

The other guy speaks up again. "We decided we should leave! The bear ran off woofing! We didn't want to hurt him, and we realize we are intruders in his world." It occurs to me; this guy sounds like a queer. This alone is not a big deal, but something about the package these two guys are, rubs me wrong, and I find myself wondering, *Why am I so angry at them. Are they simply an intrusion on my private world here?*

Without listening to them, I stare out across the water, as in a trance, staring inward. There is a double rainbow over a sandbar, and gnarled driftwood reaches to the sky in worship. The smell of wet wood and silt mingles with wood smoke and the sound of a crackling fire. Far off across the river, spruce trees are like teeth on a saw, even and spiked on the horizon. The way the light reflects off the sand, the spruce trees, the gurgling water made the conversation stop. To these tourists, this is picture-perfect. To me, this is one continuous movie. To me, this is life. This is my religion, my family, relatives, friends, and children. *This is what I live for, and in a hundred years, this is what I will die for.*

Under the double rainbow, a bald eagle sitting on a driftwood stick turns its head as a robin's song wrinkles the silence. We pay no special attention. Each of us is wrapped in our own thoughts. After what seems a half-hour of silence, I wonder what day it is and am about to ask, when I think I see a moose standing in the water.

"Up yonder, you see it?"

"Naw!" they both say at once. "Just a tree."

However, I see it move, so I run for my boat. This could be meat for the winter. I pause long enough to ask,

"Want to come along?" They look at each other, then back at me in disgust.

My conscience—*These two are among the meek, who will inherit the earth when people like me are done with it. These two are among the ones people like me will have to protect and feed in hard times. There is a time for beauty and a time to eat, and I will spill blood under this double rainbow so I can stay alive this winter. I can't eat the rainbow!*

As I take off in the boat, I know I must dismiss these two and their intent to try and make me feel guilty. This is about the moose and me. This is a ritual that is thousands, millions, of years old. The hunter and the hunted. Music. A dance, needing only a partner. *Will I be worthy of this partner?* I am inexperienced, have little knowledge of hunting, of moose. In the back of my mind, I know I am cocky and arrogant. I'm like a wolf pup, setting out to drag a moose to its den by the hind leg. The moose may have a few tricks up its sleeve.

The moose sees me and is trying to make up its mind what I'm about. By instinct, I play the game. Moving slowly, I try to speak to the moose with body language and thoughts. Bow to your partner and do-se-do.

Minding my own business, see? Just another boater, nothing to worry about. My mind is working a mile a minute. How fast can he move? When will the critical time to move be? A twenty-two magnum rifle is at my side. This is usually thought of as no more than a rabbit gun. I don't know that, and the word 'magnum' means 'big,' just like the guy at the store told me. I'm confident this will do the job, provided I can get in close, my shots are true, and my mind takes over the mind of the moose. The moose must have the mindset of 'defense.' not program itself for 'attack.' Quit thinking and speculating, move, move, move! My conscience says to me.

When I move in close, the moose shakes his head, and I know he suspects he's the object of my attention. There is a feeling I cannot explain, only described as "feeling his mind search and locking with my mind." Just as our minds lock, there is a "rush," and before I can grasp what has happened, the bull charges. He stops short, shakes his big rack in anger, then frustration, for I did not turn and run. My mind is racing in overdrive and seems to be even leaving the present and overlapping the future. This would only be by a second, and I can't explain it, but somehow I know what to do and what he will do. Even as we stare at each other, I am thinking, *After a lifetime of frustration, I am in my element. I know what to do. I know how to fight for my food. In town, I'm at a loss as to how to take care of myself. I'm a constant victim, unable or unwilling to fight for my life. Something very 'animal' is coming over me.*

This is not a situation where I can simply shoot the moose from a distance. The moose is in the water, and I'm concerned that if he is killed in the water, he will sink, drift away, or just be too hard to pull out of the water. Someone had given me the advice to never kill a moose in the water for these reasons. The twenty-two magnum has me a little nervous. This animal is so much bigger than I ever imagined! It now seems clear to me I'm underpowered, so I'm more conscious about a close, good shot. The changed strategy is to get him backed up out of the water first. The moose has plans of his own. He stands glowering at me, unwilling to back up and give ground. An animal smell of wet fur fills the air. I study, figure, and learn. I slowly move in, slowly back up, watch his reaction, see how fast he can move, circle as a wolf does, looking for a weakness.

Why did I choose a twenty-two as my weapon? There is a realization that I come from a world where 'guns' are taboo. I once had to go to counseling just for showing too much interest and asking too many questions about guns and weapons in general. No one I ever knew who could be considered 'sane' would wish to discuss how to place a death shot or how a bullet behaves as it hits. There is a morbid fear of the very words 'gun' and 'bullet.' I must overcome this upbringing. Perhaps my own fear slows me. Now this lack of understanding can be my enemy. Ancient things come into my head,

You have charged, and it failed. My medicine is stronger than yours! Sing your death song!" The bull has his own song about an irritating cub.

Every other animal I ever encountered in my life was terrified of me. There were rabbits, squirrels, ducks, once even a deer. The bull is impatient, snorts, raises the hairs of his neck up, and shakes his head. This is so unnerving I almost break my concentration and pump fear into my blood. He must be seven feet tall and weigh 1,500 pounds. The bull spins and makes a rush for the shore. This is a move we both know he has to make, where he has a fighting advantage. I was prepared, so I gun the engine to cut him off. *What if I end up shooting a moving target from behind!?* Or *what if he gets ashore and I'm chasing, and he turns and charges while I'm stuck in shallow water, unable to move the boat!* Shooting him on shore doesn't seem the best plan anymore. Plans change as fast as I think of them.

My trying to cut him off angers him. He turns and charges. The water is shallow here, so he is able to build up some speed as he comes to battle the boat. There is no time to shift the engine in reverse to get away. *Very clever,* I think. *A false fear that is a ruse for an attack.* The rifle is knocked into the bilge where I cannot reach it as the boat rocks from the impact of the bull's full charge. *This is it! The test! Am I a coward arrogant idiot punk kid with a low Jesus factor? Or a warrior, capable of survival.* This isn't just about getting meat; it is about "fear." If I back down and run now, I will never stop running. I will forever be filled with doubt, probably have to give up this lifestyle. *If it is my time to die, I will die right here and now, as a warrior!*

With an animal yell, I give the engine full throttle. The boat leaps forward and rams the moose head-on. This is something the moose will understand. "Wham!" We make contact. I have hit a brick wall. The engine is at full throttle, yet the moose holds the boat back. He can't keep it up, loses his footing, and gets pushed into deeper water. There is a short-lived concern for what he might be able to do in the deep water, but my gut feeling is that he is almost helpless. This is partly based on the fact that it is the last place he wants to be! Spinning in circles in the current, I can steer him wherever I wish, "so relax." I make him swim upstream to wear him out. I don't want him getting to shore with enough strength to fight or run. No more playing warrior or making this a battle. This encounter could already have got me killed, so it is time to do what I must. Maybe I'm just a little scared.

The boat moves him over toward camp. *How will I move all this meat? Maybe if he is near camp, he will be easier to deal with.* I'm not even sure I know how to go about skinning him out, and I'll feel better near the camp where I can look over all the tools, get bags, and think over what I need. When the bull climbs out of the water near the camp, I see his full size for the first time. He fills my whole field of vision like a mountain. From only five feet away, I watch him slowly climb up the bank with labored breath. The boat is quickly run ashore. I jump out with the rifle. I'm reluctant to fire from a rocking boat. If he does turn to charge, I do not want to be in the confined spaces of this small craft. Perhaps I'm just afraid to make that final move, to actually kill him. Walt Disney never showed this part, so I'm clueless.

Before the moose regains his strength, I dash up to him, place the rifle close behind his elbow, where I know his heart is. This I know from my experience and studies as an artist. The twenty-two only makes a "pop," muffled by the fur. The bull looks momentarily stunned, gets glassy-eyed, exhales a wheeze, and passes from this world on to the next. For all my bravo, I'm taken back by the enormity of the deed and am left trembling. Needless to say, it is a very memorable experience for me, but the feeling that dominates is, *I did it!* Even more important is the feeling God didn't let me die, so he must want me to live and favors me. I have been given a sign. He doesn't hate me. I've considered God hates me for any number of reasons. I left society, hurt my relatives, am interested in guns, and wear socks that don't match. God, however, doesn't seem to be punishing me. *It is, in fact, possible for ten million people to be wrong! It is possible to take a life and not be struck down by lightning.* If the moose got away wounded and in pain due to my ignorance, or if the moose had got the better of me, I might have given up on my plans.

When I cut the moose open, I'm immediately drenched in blood. This is not in little splatters, but as a garden hose sprays. Blood covers my face, goes up my nose, and in my hair.

This is not 'Tom Sawyer.' Did my heroes ever go through this?

Death is a grizzly matter. Wrapping both arms around the guts, I lean back. It takes all my strength to even get the insides to budge. The stomach is thirty gallons, liver another five gallons, and there's all the other 'stuff' in there. Stuff polite people do not talk about.

I'd forgotten about my two visitors, but remember them when they walk up behind me, and with a grin, I say,

"Look at all this meat!" As I step forward to greet them, my shoes go splish-splash from the blood in them. One of my guests throws up, while the other is so filled with anger he's about to punch me. A look on my blood-drenched face has the punchy one stepping back. His nervous blinking shows fear, but my action is defensive, not aggressive, so I smile, *no problem,* and say, "So do you want to help butcher, or what?" My unconscious says, *If you do not want to help, you can get out of my face, but you are welcome to stay if you want to learn something or want some meat for your trip.*

"We'll be back at camp," is the answer.

The moose is too big to roll over without help, but when I peel the hide back and see how the parts separate, I think I can manage the butchering. The peeled back hide makes a clean place to set the quarters as I take them off at the joints. While coming back to camp with the first 200 pound steaming quarter on my shoulder, I see my guests packing to leave. The one asks if they can have some meat to take with them. My silent conscience comments,

And it will be people like me, feeding people like them. It's like the chicken little story of, 'who wants to harvest the wheat?' Who wants to eat the bread? Why give a lecture, or make a comment. What's the use? I give them a generous portion of meat and wish them a good trip.

"You guys have a good trip, and be careful of those bears now!" My parting last shot and memory of them is as they go off in the canoe, furtively whispering and looking back at me in fear. I know they are afraid of me, but I feel sad that they do not understand. It is me who has the most to fear from them. They represent the power of the majority, the voters, and the law. It is me who is in danger of being strung up from the nearest tree, not them. The uneasy feeling is shrugged off. Maybe I'm feeling paranoid.[1]

Hmmm, I think to myself, Claw marks on the back of the moose. I hadn't noticed before. Grizzly. Must be a big one for the claw marks to be up on the top of the seven-foot back. Maybe it was a grizzly that chased him into the water?

Exhausted from the emotional and physical events of this day, I go to bed early, after washing the blood off in the river. In the morning, I'm not sure how to deal with all this meat and see that there are already flies laying eggs. The sun is beating down, and I think, *Darn, I should have covered the meat and put it in the smokehouse!* The lessons of this lifestyle come hard, and I feel so stupid. This cannot overwhelm me, however, so I dwell on the good side. This meat will keep me alive in the winter, and I killed my first moose. As I drag the meat to the smokehouse, I remember the skinning job and realize all the work to do yet. I have a lot more respect for the Athabascan who lived here thousands of years off the land, doing this with bows and arrows, followed by a flint knife.

I'M STUFFING my mouth with fresh moose. I wipe a greasy paw across my face as I belch. I speak to my conscience.

"This meat sure tastes good. There isn't the wild gamy taste I expected. It's not tough, and I do not taste the chemicals used in town meat!" I sure enjoy all this meat, which in town would cost more than I could afford!

My guests are gone, and I never did find out what day it is, or even what week.

I'm not that excited about seeing people and realize I'm not going out of my way to visit the fish camps along the river. *There is one,* I think vaguely, *about five miles upstream,* and think, *"somewhere downstream too.* There is no effort on my part to make contact, flag boaters down, or stop for tea. *I'm not paying attention to local custom, just not up to it.* I have thoughts of Canada and other events in my life. One day I get a visitor who introduces himself.

"Norm Fid, and this is my family. We have the fish camp a few miles downstream from here at Caribou Creek." This is a white man, a little older than me, with a native wife. They seem to know this lifestyle well. We exchange small talk till his little girl goes,

"Yuck, you eat dog Salmon!?"

Conversation stops in embarrassment.

Norm speaks up in my defense, "I remember the old days when dog salmon was all we had. Everyone ate whatever they could."

Apparently, 'Dog Salmon' is named so because it is what people feed their dogs and is not considered edible for people. This is the first I know of it. I suppose I am eating it because the good King Salmon belongs to Piper, and I am making strips, working for him. My mind drifts.

> **Past Flash**: I'm fifteen. This is the first day of my first real job. One of my father's students has a ranch in Montana. I live in New York. The ranch needs a hired hand, so I take the greyhound bus cross-country to Montana. I'm settling into the bunkhouse when the five-year-old son of the owner comes around to 'check me out.'
> He asks, "So whatcha prefer? Farm-all, or John Deer!?"
> I apologetically reply, "Sorry, I don't smoke." I have no idea he is talking about tractors, not brands of cigarettes. He looks at me as if I'm about the dumbest guy in the world. It is hard to explain to a five-year-old who has never left the ranch how dumb he'd look in my world, standing in his Stetson hat, making like he has a chaw of tobakee in his cud. **Past Flash ends**

The past gets unfocussed in a mist, as the present and the reality of 'now' dawns on me like a bright sun out of the dark.

Piper is getting the best of what is being put up. He'd told me not to put up the dogs. "There's no oil in this fish." I do not have a dog team, but I sort of hate to just throw away these dog salmon when they get caught along with the Kings. The other fisherman must be throwing the dog salmon away. I'm strongly against waste. If you kill it, you eat it, period. Oh well. Fish is fish anyway, pretty much. I never was a real big fish eater, but I don't plan to be fussy in my new lifestyle. All my heroes ate anything that didn't eat them. I'm determined to be a mountain man or die trying.

Norm gives me some whitefish from his boat, and I give him some moose meat. I assume by this that whitefish is a preferred fish.

Norm explains it, "Whitefish are not as plentiful, and are mostly found in the clear creeks off the main river, and have no commercial use, but we like to put out small nets to get this clear-water fish, as a change from a salmon diet." I sure knew what he meant about a straight Salmon diet getting pretty old. Like that guy in the movie 'Forest Gump,' that talks nonstop about all the ways to fix shrimp. The moose is the change I need, but I'm polite about the whitefish, and maybe I can put some up in the smokehouse for the winter. This whole conversation is new to me, in that I had never given much thought to how to fix food, except as interesting survival notes in my diary.

When young, my mother simply put it on the plate. The military was the same. There's fish, meat, chicken, salad, and such, but I never considered all the details. Maybe I'm just too busy to give a lot of thought to meal planning. I simply mindlessly 'eat. It's similar to gassing a car. I then hurry up and get on with important things.

Norm is talking on, telling me a little history of the area. "The Indians at the camp on the other side of the river and down a ways wonder if you are here because you are wanted by the law. They think 'Miles Martin' is a made-up name. I'm telling you, so you know what's going on. Piper isn't that well-liked around here." This puts me a little on the defense, for it was Piper who believed in me when no one else did. Norm is still talking as I am thinking, *"and is considered a white Indian by the rest. He has a plane and runs a big-money business. Yet he flies out here every year to stake out one of the best fishing eddies, claiming a subsistence lifestyle. Now he's brought in a green, white boy, so he can keep his claim on the fishing spot."*

Norm is going on. "A few years ago, an Indian kid was suspected of going around checking other people's fishnets. Piper was missing a lot of fish. One day while Piper was around, the kid mysteriously disappears. Most people here think Piper killed him. Now here you are, working for Piper, not talking to anyone, hiding when people boat by, and it doesn't look good."

I appreciate Norm being open and honest with me and realize he is trying to be friends. All this is so deep and overwhelming. Way out here in the middle of nowhere, you'd think a person could be left alone. You'd think that people could mind their own business. I'd been given the impression outdoor and country people were kind, less stressed, helped each other, and are generous. Once again, this isn't exactly "Walt Disney!" This reminds me of "Back home" about 200 years ago. Indian wars, bushwhacking, and killing over hunting rights. If true, this would mean Piper is just using me, even putting me in danger. How can I expect to call this area "home" if the locals think I'm wanted by the law and think I'm out to steal their fishing spot with Piper?

My response to Norm is vague and noncommittal.

Unheard Conscience, Am I hurting anyone? Can't I just be left alone? I'm not asking anything from anyone!

I reply out loud, "Thanks, Norm."

"So Miles, I just wanted to stop by and introduce myself, and hope you feel free to stop by to visit. You'd be welcome at our camp." On that positive note, Norm gets his family into the boat and takes off for Caribou Creek and his own fish camp. I never go visit. It's not my boat or gas, and I want to be left alone. I'm on a vision quest. I'm on a walk-about. I wish to return a man, so I can hold my head up among others and be worthy of being seen and spoken to. I was raised on the concept that children should be seen and not heard. Yet at what point does a child turn to a man or be allowed to be heard? My first job was slave labor. In the military, we were called 'maggots' and understood to be so much shot stuffed down the cannon of war, with no rights whatever. In Canada, I had lost all I owned with no recourse, treated like a nothing and a nobody. I'm twenty years old. I want to be alone so that I can be more than a slave, a maggot, or a bleating sheep. Maybe I want to sort out where I am at, how I got here, what I want to do with my life without being controlled or manipulated.

Returning from one of his trips picking up fish strips, Piper brings me a puppy.

Guess he thinks I need companionship.

"Thanks, Piper," I politely respond.

"These strips look great, Miles! There is more than I thought there would be. This looks like a good King run this year."

I've learned that Salmon live in the ocean. They come up the freshwater rivers to spawn in the shallow creeks, sometimes thousands of miles upstream. They do not eat the whole trip, so the further upstream they go, the less firm the meat, and the less valuable. Here on the Yukon, the fish has a lot of oil, is worth more, makes the best strips, and is why people value a fishing spot close to the source. The salmon fry lives in freshwater for a couple of years, then work their way down to the ocean. It is seven to ten years they come back to where they were born, for the sole purpose of spawning. Then they die.

"So Miles, here's more of your supplies."

There seems little point in bringing up the conversation with Norm.

THE PUP IS OK, I guess. He's a little white thing with a few black spots and a waggly tail. There should be more feeling on the subject. I'm having a hard enough time taking care of my life without the responsibility of a dog to take care of. I didn't ask for a dog and don't want one. The pup needs to be chained up.

"Got no collar or chain pup. Do you think you can behave yourself?" The pets I had as a child ran free. *How can you care about an animal and put it on a chain?* Sometimes we play, but I have little time. Mostly the pup gets into trouble. This costs me a lot of time and loss. He is forever getting in the smokehouse, filching salmon strips, then going on his back wanting forgiveness, then going back to the smokehouse for more fish. I don't name him yet. I just call him "Pup."

I awaken one morning to the sound of fish poles falling in the smokehouse.

"That's it, you mutt!" The sound stops as I holler. These fish are what my life may depend on this winter, and they taste awful covered in sand. *What will Piper think if I can't take care of his portion of the fish?* From the sounds of poles falling, I guess there are hundreds of salmon strips in the sand now. Pre-dawn this time of year is about 2:00 am. Half asleep, or maybe fairly awake now, I go dashing up the path to the smokehouse in my underwear. I'm ready to thrash that pup soundly. Under the poplar trees and through the thorny rose bushes, I fly. I catch a view of the side of the smokehouse, wondering if I will find the pup there or if he has run off. The sound of more poles falling enrages me to where I have murder in my heart as I enter the tin building.

The light is dim in here, but I hear chewing, so head to that corner. Seeing red, foot drawn back, I'm ready to kick the dog. As I round the corner of the smoke stove, I start to yell,

"You damn—," but "dog" sticks in my throat as I kick a bear in the butt! We both say, "shit!" in surprise at the same time. The bear jumps straight up, and in midair, spins around, and lands on all fours facing me. His eyes are wide open in astonishment, as are mine. Both our mouths hang open in disbelief at what has just happened. It is obvious this bear has never been kicked before, and cannot comprehend how such a thing has come to pass. The bear's expression tells me, *I can't believe this!*

I know without a shadow of a doubt that my life is on the line when his expression goes on to ask, "Was this an accident, or did you do this on purpose?"

He's waiting for me to either wet my pants or follow up and smash him to the ground. Since he doesn't know my intention yet, his own reaction is in check.

Probably he knows about things like porcupines that look inoffensive but are animals not to be messed with. He's never seen a person before. It is rare for an animal to attack another without the means to back it up. Even though there is nothing in the wilderness that would jump a bear, even so, there is hesitation on his part. Should he be angry and attack, or be afraid and run? My feelings of complete anger at the dog turn to an instant apology, but I know if I show this, the bear will jump me. Seeing the question in his eyes shows me what to do. I bluff him by leaning forward and growling. I think the bear is impressed because he blinks fast. This gives me confidence. I lean forward more, and with as deep a voice as I can muster... "grrrr." The bear 'woofs' and runs off. The "damn dog" stuck in my throat turns to a sigh of relief.

The mosquitoes have had a field day on our naked body, is my anticlimactic thought. Alaska mosquitoes live as a dark cloud and are legendary the world over.

Though it wasn't completely the pup's fault, I feel if I didn't have the pup, I'd know any animal in the smokehouse would be something hostile. The pup may learn, but I do not want to die over this pup. My mind turns to the bear and the fact I ran to the smokehouse without a gun. The trouble I could have got into sinks in. The fact that I'm not used to dealing with bears, but better learn how sinks in. At least I own a pistol. The new 357 magnum has just come out on the market.

The very next day, another bear shows up, but not the same one. This one is not as big and acts unconcerned with me. The bear I ran off would at least be a little unsure of himself if he came back. I know ahead of time, I'm dealing with a bear. From the tent, I see him across the clearing by the smokehouse. He tries to tear down the wall, but is having trouble, then discovers the door and walks on in.

Before there are more crashing poles, and before every salmon I'm to eat this winter is covered in sand and garbage, and before I have to hand over crappy strips to Piper, my boss, I'm going to deal with this bear!

The 357 magnum Blackhawk is in my hand, but I decide the 'across the clearing' shot is beyond my ability.

This looks like close encounters of the third kind. I say aloud, "In a few moments, one of us will be dragging the other out by the hind feet, Clint Eastwood style." The 'clickety-click' of the cylinder spinning reminds me of Clint Eastwood since I have little real experience to offer as a memory for gunplay. My plan is to run across the clearing as fast as I can till the bear spots me. Then hope I've come close enough before he runs away to get a decent shot in.

Like the taking of Bunker Hill, I sprint full tilt pell mell, come hell or high water toward the enemy. I feel a silent *"Charge!"* of adrenaline as I crash through the rose brambles scattering delicate pink flowers.

The bear walks out, sees me, and calmly sits down to watch. My charge wavers, falters, winds down to a stop. This is like, well, when a knight goes through the ritual of battle, puts the armor on, climbs on his trusty steed, solemnly pulls his visor down, takes up his lance, charges off into the dusky dusk, and finds his opponent without any armor, sitting on a stump, laughing his head off at how ridicules you look. Maybe the lack of concern of the bear and his not reacting as expected has me afraid and un-nerves me. I'm twenty feet away when I stop. One bear-leap away, and point-blank for shooting.

This isn't a game. I am not your entertainment! You are trying to take my food, and it is time to pay! With trembling hands, I raise the pistol. The pistol comes back down. *Time out!* I forgot to pull the hammer back. "Click." The hammer is back. Up the gun goes again. The bear gives me the same concern he might show a fly. Certainly, he doesn't treat me like I'm the king of the forest, nor does he even treat me like he is the king of the forest. I'd show him! "Boom!" I expect to see the bear fall into two halves. I'm not prepared for the violent roar that almost takes my eardrums out. This is the awesome piece of weaponry I'd heard advertised. The biggest handgun made, that is banned on the police force, will stop a car and put a bullet all the way through an engine block![2] As the smoke clears, yes, I expect to see the gruesome sight of blood up in the treetops and fur quivering on the ground. Peering through the smoke of battle, I see…the bear is still sitting.

Through my sweat of fear, I see him give a bored yawn, still watching curiously. Apparently, I have missed. Perhaps I closed my eyes as I squeezed the trigger. Truly, I'd have a 50\50 chance of a hit by not looking at all. The target looks that big. My mind takes me past the realm of "amazing!" and on into the power of terror. I'm beyond "speechless," as I keep trying to pull the trigger, to get off a second shot, forgetting to pull the hammer back first.

My mind is in "backup system #Two," which comes along in our lives sometimes when we royally screw up, and another part of our brain says, *Well, you sure got us in a pickle; you just better let me take over.* This is the old brain talking. The hypothalamus that is thousands of years old. Guns are very new. This backup system knows simple stuff like "charge," "run," or maybe "scream," or "pee." There is no memory of complicated words like "bear." Maybe the first part, "ba, ba, ba," is in the memory file. I'm about to throw the gun at the bear. I no longer know what the gun is. The bear gets bored and simply ambles off.

Man, oh man, is all I can think over and over, *Man oh man.* I'd never have got a second shot off if the bear had been aggressive.

PIPER FLIES IN. "Miles, this is probably my last trip picking up Salmon. The run looks about done, and it looks like you are catching mostly dogs now. Do you want to come to town for one last chance to get supplies and socialize? You did a good job on the strips, and I don't mind another trip. I need to come back to pack up the camp."

"Piper, you said I'd have a place here."

"You can use that cabin just downstream, and it's ok to trap around here. No one else claims it."

Now that this is settled, I give a hearty, "Sure, I'd like to get into town one more time, great!"

Fairbanks

We arrive in Fairbanks just as the Tanana Valley State Fair starts. I have some fish strips with me. I can trade them for goods in town, even at the stores. Someone had come by with a floatplane and bought fish eggs while I was at the camp. Piper had no use for them, and I had been throwing them out. Some sort of caviar is made from them, and they have quite a value, so I have a little cash to get things, though not a lot. The fair seems like a good place to go to trade or sell my fish, and maybe pick up some food. I hear there is dry fruit and maybe some tools.

The atmosphere at the fair reminds me of fur rendezvous from the 1800s, or maybe that is just on my mind. Everyone is happy and in a celebrating mood—crude booths made of rough lumber dot a grassy field with footpaths around them. I spot lots of tents and beat up old trucks. There are no permanent buildings and no cement. Looking around, I see people selling on boards set up on logs, and one Indian gal is selling beads from a blanket on the grass. Customers are hunkered down on haunches, dressed in leather, wearing sheath knives, feathers, and trade beads. Some play a game of chance on a knoll. Music blares. I hear simple fiddle-bluegrass, jug band tunes. There is a sense of no one being in a hurry. It wouldn't surprise me to see knife throwing contests or frontiersmen lined up with rifles shooting at turkeys. As I think such thoughts, I see a trapper go by with an armload of furs and notice someone else trading homemade pottery for a fox skin.[3]

Other people are in from the wilderness for the fair. Village Indians walk around shy, not liking crowds, not knowing how to deal with the con artists, but at the same time, intrigued by White man's babbles. *This is a scene right out of the mountain man books I read!* As evening approaches, I run into a bunch of zonked-out hippies. There seems to be no special group I'm part of, relate to, or would be accepted by. The rednecks and straights find me to scruffy. The wilderness people find me too green (though I fancy myself a frontiersman by now). The hippies seem to be the only ones saying hi. These are tune in and drop out flower children. One faction is the 'let's go live in a commune' group. One longhaired freak greets me with,

"We're going to the Howling Dog. Ya wanna come along? Ya might get some chicken!"

I happily reply, "Yea. I could tangle with a bird right now. Maybe I'll pluck her right there on the dance floor!" I'm just playing a role, not feeling this way, but the group laughs, and one member tells me,

"Hey, you're all right, jump in!" Two rough running pickups backfiring blue smoke are loaded with 'Howling doggers.' Some are Bob Dylan types, hippie long hairs with guitars who fancy themselves as changing the world through music. At least they have a goal. Others I meet are just wacko. A very few want to live off the land and live this new word, 'subsistence.'

We arrive in Ester, at the edge of town, and all us hippie freaks pile out as a mass of revolution. The Howling Dog looks like an old-time saloon. The broken-down log cabin greets us with the familiar sign, 'Please check your guns in at the bar.' One of the guys checks a gun in, so I decide to check my knife in. We step onto a sawdust floor. Blaring sounds of live jug band music with an electric touch vibrates our bodies. Someone hollers,

"Git down!" Another answers up,

"Whoo!" This place reminds me the most of a bar-scene in a 'Star Wars' movie, where there is a row of God-awful-looking creatures from other planets laughing and smooching at the bar. In the movie, as here, there is an undercurrent of adventure and danger. In the movie, this is a place a man might contract for murder or make a deal on a spaceship. Indeed after my fish camp experience, I feel like I come from another planet.

"This looks like a watering hole for animals!" I say to the girl next to me, by way of greeting. She opens her eyes wide and answers,

"Far out!" She's short like me, light build, and has long dark loose hair. Her brown eyes are sparkling clear and alert, so she hasn't been drinking and isn't on drugs. No makeup or jewelry adorns her, but she's well kept. These things are taken in with my glance of approval, and she must see things in me she likes because her eyes meet my happy brown eyes that reflect the mountains and do not look away.

After a few dances and some chit-chat she whispers in my ear, "I want to dance you under the table." We had been talking about how we both like to dance so much and tend to be 'marathon dancers.'

"I become the music," as I told her.

"Dance me under the table, huh?" As we sit side by side at a crowded table, my hand slips between the chair to her back, where no one can see, and this hand gives a quick, playful tug on her blouse as if to get it out of her pants. Before she can react, my hand leaves, and my face reveals nothing. I do say, however, "Nancy, you and all your friends taking turns, one after the other, couldn't dance me under the table." I'd never met anyone I couldn't keep up with. I'd never met any two people who could keep up with me on the dance floor. I'm so sure, in fact, I find the challenge amusing.

The band plays some slow music, and Nancy and I hold each other. I'm not much for slow dancing usually. I'm not much on touching or being touched. On the dance floor, I see it as a form of 'being teased.' It's like a rule, no slow dancing. My future wife is the only one I will ever slow dance with. Even so, I feel comfortable with this woman. I know she's just 'playing dumb' when she makes her eyes go wide in surprise, as she does. We all have to put on an act, a front in public, but this woman seems to know it, be aware of it, admit it, and is willing enough to be open and honest. If anyone takes the time, cares to get to know her, she'd be direct. She isn't going to bullshit me.

Playing a role we both know is cheap talk, I say, "I bet I can dance you under the table, and if you can't take it and drop down on all fours, I may not be responsible for my actions!"

"Oh my!" She answers once again while she spreads her jean-clad legs and rubs against me, and I lick the sweat off her neck, real slow. We work ourselves into quite a lather out there on the dance floor, dancing every dance in our marathon way. I'm thinking I know this woman. I'd seen her around. I know people she knows and have heard good things about her. She has a job and is stable. She doesn't run around. She doesn't have a boyfriend, isn't an airhead, fruitcake, doesn't drink or drug, isn't a lesbian, and these things alone put her in 'less than one percent of the population' category, or so it seems when I'm in this mood.

When the band is on its next break, I talk to her about my wilderness plans.

"And in a few days, I'll be back out, maybe all winter without seeing anyone. I'm mostly in town to get supplies."

She tells me she wants to be a schoolteacher, "Well, sorta, kinda, maybe!"

To which I answer, "They might make you wear a dress, conform, and all that."

She punches me, wrinkles up her nose, and pouts, saying, "I know. That's what I mean!" (About the 'maybe' part). We seem to understand each other as she squeezes my hand.

When the band starts up again, she doesn't seem in the mood for dancing.

"So you're off to the wilderness in a few days, following your destiny, and maybe will not be back for a long time, so I suppose you'd like to get laid before you go?" She looks at me with warm frank eyes.

I smile and reply, "Do you think it will rain tomorrow? The weatherman says it might! Do you remember when it rained last week? Wasn't it a doozy?"

She rolls her eyes up and continues strumming her fingers on the table, waiting for an answer. She doesn't fall for a subject change. I like to socialize and dance, and it is important to know I could be desired, but the reality is, I am on a path that involves 'being alone.' My path has a price to pay. It wouldn't be fair to any women, or myself, to 'get involved' without a lot understood between us. Though the drive to mate is a strong instinct, I do not believe in one-night stands, at least not on some pretense. I have to believe there is at least a chance for some future in it. I like to make things clear, give the woman a chance to back out, and not seduce her. Maybe I let her know my needs through flirting, but it is always her move and her choice.

"So Miles, you can't talk about it or what! Then let me make things more clear, I'm taking you home with me, and probably we should leave now. It's going to be a long night!"

She gets my 'anything to oblige a lady in distress' look.

"Miles, has anyone ever told you that you are impossible!" she says with a hand squeeze as we head for the door. I sheepishly remember to pick up my knife, to which she responds by sighing, 'men!' I like her a whole lot because she smiles when she says that. I can tell she'd be like Helga when Hagar the Horrible takes off in his Viking ship to conquer the world. She might well say, "Where have you been!" but there she'd be with dinner on the table, and the duck and the dog in the one-room cabin with a simple pole table, as the only furniture. I'd almost sell my soul for that. Maybe I would cry my heart out, that life is not that simple.

Morning

In the morning, I have a lot to ponder while looking around Nancy's cabin. This is a small place on the edge of town near the university where she studies. She bought a one-room log cabin with electricity but no running water. She keeps it neat and clean, with flowers in a vase and nice curtains. On a stand by a washbasin, I see a five-gallon plastic jug the water is kept in. Nancy told me she gets water at the Laundromat, where there is a deep sink and money timer on the faucet, set up for people like her. A woodstove is the main source of heat, with oil as back up for when she's gone. A single propane light with globe and mantle hangs from the ceiling as her main light. She cooks on propane too. The cabin was purchased outright for a few thousand dollars.

She tells me, "To get out from underpaying rent!"

This whole 'picture' interests me, so I make a mental note of it. I want to see how various basic problems are dealt with, like lighting, water, heat. It is good to see the choices, discuss costs and problems.

This brings my mind to Nancy. Why couldn't we just have a one-night stand like we joked about! Why do I have to care, get wrapped up in 'feelings.' Geez, we even cried. Cried over ourselves, life, the road we are each on, and why. There is so much we agree on. It is so easy to talk to each other. How easy it would be to be sidetracked from my plans and simply settle in here, in an atmosphere of warmth and acceptance.

What drives me? Why must I move on?

She's angry, hurt that I'm deserting her soon.

"Miles, I'll take care of you!"

"I know Nancy, but that is a little like a 'mother-child' relationship, and don't you want a man who can take care of you, as you take care of him? I have no occupation and am not settled." I have trouble putting feelings in words. The heart is not something to reason with.

"Miles, when you talk about the wilderness, I can see the mountains reflected in your eyes. You really light up! I guess I should not try to stop you from this quest you are on. When you pick up the sword and try to be the 'Man of steel,' be careful, you do not become hard and brittle and break. Everyone needs Love in their life to quiet and soothe the troubled heart."

I feel relief at her, letting me go without much of a fuss, then guilty for the first feeling. She sees the two changes flash across my face, so she sighs. I'd as soon change the subject.

Nancy drops me off at the fairgrounds on her way to work.

"Yes, I have your address and phone number, and when I get back, I'll let you know how things went."

Maybe if things work out in the wilderness and I get a place built and all that, there will be a way for us to get together, or I'll be ready for town.

I hear her, "I'll be here for you, Miles." She gives me a soft hug, turns to go, but comes back for a longer squeeze. "Where does the actor, the real you begin and end?"

I smile, kiss her, turn, and run…toward my appointment with destiny!

A longhaired hippie freak greets me. "Hey! What's coming down, man?!"

I answer with a peace symbol by way of greeting, and he responds, "Bogus!"

I know what he means because we have had previous conversations about how very little in this modern world seems real. What's-his-name wants to go scalp hunting, but I don't want to.

Don't listen to this guy. If we are going to stick a shiv in big brother's back, we want a partner more savvy than this airhead.

I do not tell him my private thoughts and answer, "This is no time for a raid, Man, winter's coming, and like, it's time to put up buffler for hard times!" He sees the wisdom of my thinking as I change the subject. "I'll treat you to the chuck wagon. I need you and your horse for a few hours. Mine got shot."

"No problem, brother got nothing doing right now! Glad to help out a fellow scout," says the hippie freak.

We jump in his truck and go out for pizza, then go to some garage sales to look for a window and door latch. These are the only two things that are store-bought going into the cabin project ahead of me. We get lucky, so now we can go back to the fair and relax. The rest of the 'wagon train' greets us. We meet up with a bunch of long hairs talking about life 100 years ago, and living the good life, so we talk that talk, thinking we walk that walk, wanting to tune in, drop out, and form like a commune or something. We all agree a nuclear bomb blast is imminent, and when it happens, only a few who live far off in the wilderness will survive. "Any scalps?" we are eagerly asked. From our looks, they know we didn't, so faces fall in boredom.

It's getting dark now, and I'm thinking about where I'm going to unwad my bedroll. The problem is solved when I hear 'the scout' stop a booth owner he knows to ask if all of us can spend the night in her booth.

"Yes, I guess you warriors can crash here, but I'm not going to be here, so you gotta be cool."

Everyone else said, "Far out!"

I say, "Bogus!" *Oops*. All heads turn to me because of my social indiscretion.

The scout stands up for me. "He's a little weird, but he's ok." If the scout didn't stand up for me, they might think I'm a nark or something.

We march off single file for the tent, *The five stooges*. No one but the booth owners are supposed to be on the grounds now. The fair gate closes. The leader of the pack gives a speech, as the loudspeaker tells everyone to leave.

"You heard her. We gotta be cool. That means no raids!" There are some grumbles, but we all settle down in the dirt to get some shut-eye.

"Can I use yer jacket for a pilla?" There is a sound in the dark of a jacket being crumpled.

Someone else from the darkness, "Put yer shoes back on fer Christ sakes, your feet stink up the whole tent!"

I lay awake thinking for a while on how all this is so new and different. Sleeping on the ground and being stuck in the past with these guys is fun, I decide, *Huckleberry Finn! No, Charles Dickens. Anyhow, this sure beats paying $50 dollars a night, which is a week's wages for a room in town!*

As I lay awake, I hear the scout get up and sneak out of the tent.

Oh-oh, he's going on a raid. Well, whatever, none of my concern. It isn't my place to wake up the leader and make a report. I'm not really one of them yet. Nor is it my place to holler, "Hey, where you think you're going!" Considering this guy stood up for me. I drift off to sleep. It's his life, and he has the right to live it as he chooses. He can reap life's rewards, or be punished, which is the choice we all make.

We all snap awake as one. As one, we all reach for our blades, guns, and various implements of destruction. One pulls a weapon from an ankle sheath. One weapon appears from under a shirt. All come out with one sound of 'swish.' The missing scout dives into the tent growling,

"It's in the fan. Pretend you're asleep!" followed immediately by "s--t," "*$#@," "d--n!" from the pack. I didn't say "bogus!" this time. The scout dives under a blanket.

The reason follows right behind him with the words, "I saw him go in here!"

Flashlights shine in on us. The light beam darts finger-like on each bedroll in turn. We all, of course, pretend to be asleep, with dreamy words like, "Hey, what's going on?" I almost burst out laughing when one of us has the gall to yell, "Someone call the police!"

The light plays on all our faces until it gets to mine.

A woman's voice barks, "That's him! That's the one!" We are all marched off to the main office, with a special eye kept on me. I have no idea what the scout might have done but guess I'm about to find out.

In disgust, I note that the scout is over six feet tall, black, and has an afro haircut that must be three feet wide. You could hardly find two other people as far apart on the physical spectrum than him and me. If I could be mistaken for him, anyone could be mistaken for anyone else.

So much for eyewitnesses!

Sure, I know the score. I'm 'one of them' and not 'one of us.' These Security people and cops do not care who they get, so long as it's 'one of them.' The facts come out. Some leather jackets were stolen.

A cop meanly pokes me in the side. "Do you want to go to jail for a while?"

So much for innocent until proven guilty. I just stare and look dumb, taking my cue from the rest.

Cop, "People like you should be hung on the spot!"

How long ago was it, the subject of our being lynched came up?

"This city needs to be cleaned up. Should we take you out back and work you over, or would you like to confess!"

Now it's 'beat a confession out of us time.' Burn the witches, gas the Jews, hang the commies and hippies. Does anything ever really change?[4]

The policeman waits for my answer. I've only replied in my head as I silently stare at him.

We all anticipate the arrival of the guy who owns the stolen jackets. If the policeman had been at all friendly and asked, "What seems to be the problem here?" I probably would have told it like it was. This talk of being beaten, the obvious 'hate,' gives me the sense he doesn't want to know the truth! What he wants is to beat someone up. He wants to get rid of his personal anger on someone. He doesn't care about the 'truth.' Can I prove my side of the story? What about this supposed witness! Will my return flight back to the wilderness be interrupted, even 'not happen?' Not happen because I have to go to court, a trial, hang around town until this is resolved? Not happen because I have my teeth kicked in and ribs broken by the police? Would any of these 'street people' stand up for me? All these questions go through my mind as we wait. What can I say to this policeman anyway? I may as well wait to see if charges will be made. Maybe it will all come to nothing. If I get 'beaten up' can I still go out to the wilderness? What a joke; to survive the bears and cabin fever, only to be torn apart by my own kind!

And people think it is the wilderness that is not safe!

Like this cop, I see things coming unglued. The very fabric of our culture coming unraveled. He feels it too. Revolution in the wind. Was it since the '60s? Kennedy's death? The march of the 'flower children' taking over the old guard? *God help us when the zonked out generation of the 60s are running the country.* Even though I do not want to be taken out back and worked over, how can I really hate this guy? There's a fly in the soup. Neither of us knows how it got there or who is responsible. He blames me, but I do not have a target to point the finger at. Maybe him. The wilderness seems like a very nice, safe place to be right now.

"Here comes the owner," the guy next to me mumbles under his breath.

We all pretend we don't notice. No one gets a good look at him as he is taken into a back room for a conference with 'those in charge.' More time passes as I just wonder about the world and think in my head, *Viet Nam. I volunteered during that era to join the navy. My country needed me. I was there only a short time, watched a seventeen-year-old shot, and killed. He went off the deep end, ran for the fence, and tried to climb it, screaming all the way. A war about what? Democracy? A war over oil and drugs. The protesting flower children. In the beginning, harmless enough. Perhaps not contributing much to society. Many on welfare. Some starting up communes, mostly peaceful, people looking for answers, a better way, a chance to get back to nature in these troubled times of fast change. Society beat them, put them in jail, and ultimately, the flower children became angry. Easy enough to understand.*

"Pst.... here they come" The door opens, and the cop comes out looking disgusted *(hmm)*.

He tells us, "The guy doesn't want to press charges. We think there is something fishy about this shipment of jackets like there was no duty paid, and they may even have been stolen. We don't have time to get into it, so you are all free to go." He walks away without looking at any of us. I feel sympathy for him and his job, for he senses as I do. *The system is falling apart. It doesn't work. Big time thieves pay people off, small-time thieves get away, and society gets disgusted and afraid.*

There's a pile of leather jackets, and all the dudes are picking out the ones they want as a reward for keeping quiet.

"So why you frowning, Miles? It was another successful raid, man! Pick out your booty! You should have first choice since you took most of the heat and almost got burned at the stake."

Another speaks up. "Yea, man, it's like, musical chairs! Nobody knows where the goods of society will stop! Everyone's stealing, Man!" So I pick out a jacket, why the hell not; but I'm depressed about it. Someone somewhere was ripped off royally, but who, where, when, or why? I'm sad, angry, confused, and then remember, *The cop had said maybe there was a whole shipload maybe, of stolen jackets, worth what? Millions? But there is no time to check it out? But there is time to nail me? Upstanding members of society will be overlooked? A polite wink? No wonder these 'Dudes' are pissed off at the world! Maybe they are only part of the 'karma' of those who manipulate the system, putting a crimp in their style, where they feel it, in the best way they know how and indeed, we are living in one big free-for-all.*

The fringe leather jacket I pick out fits, and everyone is quiet as I put it on, with great ceremony. The one who stole them steps forward and sticks a hawk feather in the top buttonhole, and steps back silently. It would be unmanly to say thanks, but I'm moved by his gesture. We, after all, escaped torture together. Briefly, I picture myself in the gutter with caved-in ribs, broken teeth, and am pretty sure every one of these guys has 'been there,' for their fear is very real. The common story is written in their faces.

Somewhere on the fairgrounds, a Janis Joplin tape plays bawdy blues, asking God for a Mercedes Benz, as the feather, badge of courage, flaps in the breeze. Squaring my shoulders, I picture a pirate flag waving in the background, *divvy up the booty time.* The weed is passed around, but I do not partake in the group's customary ritual. There is a smile on my face as I watch how they have to talk while inhaling and repeat the sacred words, "Good stuff, man!" Said while inhaling.

Someone shouts the group slogan, "Rape, Riot, pillage, and plunder!" We all give the reply and nod in agreement. The gal who owns the booth comes along, and

I say I have to get going. She's heard how I'm really going off to the wilderness. Others are mostly just talking. A couple of them have 'sort of real plans' for 'later.' I do not remember anyone's name. Just a bunch of people I meet. I needed a ride to get supplies and a place to spend the night. They helped me out, and I play along with where they are coming from without really understanding. I take in new experiences. I am young, and the world is filled with endless possibilities and choices.

The booth gal has asked me a question. Everyone snickers because I'm 'off in my own world.' It seems I do not need drugs to be 'spacey' haha.

"So Miles, aren't you afraid to go out in the wilderness alone?"

A watercolor I did of the booth gal in my sketchbook.

CHAPTER THREE

BUILD CABIN, LEARN TRAPPING, MARTEN, WOLVES, WOLVERINE

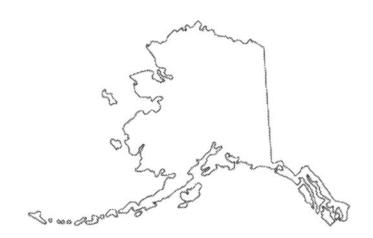

While I had been gone from the wilderness fish camp on the Yukon River, a bear got in the smokehouse and destroyed most of my fish and meat. There is no safe place here to store anything against bears. I had no knowledge, tools, or material to build something big enough in a short time that will protect my goods.

I thought we chased the bear off and taught him a lesson!?

"I guess not," I answer myself.

As I look around at the devastation of several hundred pounds of food, my conscience speaks up…

Peace and harmony; living with God's creatures…Gentle Ben…

"Shut up, you (blankity blank)," A contrite conscience answers.

Well, at least we've been practicing with the pistol, as indeed we have. Lots of cans and tree stumps have been shot up since the first 'gun shooting at the bear' incident. Squirrels and jays become moving targets as I stop them from raiding the fish. The pistol is becoming an extension of myself, and certainly, I do not ever expect to freeze up and not know what to do. The bear will be back for sure since there is still more food here, and he is used to the easy meals.

The bear problem is put on the back burner as I get my mind on building a cabin before winter and being moved out of the fish camp.

From my Diary:

Aug. 25th—Got all my things moved to the cabin downriver that Piper said I could use. The window is out, and door doesn't shut, but it is rainproof. The fish strips and moose meat smell too much to move in with me, and I do not think this cabin is bear proof so do not want the bear getting in during the night looking for the food—and finding me.

Over my shoulder is my ax, and in my head, great visions of my first cabin.
Do you like this spot? I don't. Let's go back to that pond we saw a mile upriver! Picking out a spot to build is a fun project. Piper has told me I can use the boat, telling me how to put it up for winter, and he left a chainsaw and other gear. The world seems a very big place, and I can build about anywhere my heart desires.[1]

The book I had on cabin building has long since got wet and rotten during 'tent life.' Most of it I had memorized anyway or thought I had. Cabin building is pretty straightforward anyway. Lay one log down, then the next. There are no tools to do any land leveling, not even a shovel.

The spot I choose is by an acre size pond, just out of sight of the Yukon River. There is a small stream, a stone's throw away, for fresh water. The Yukon water has a lot of glacier silt in it. A lot of sedge grass surrounds the pond, along with willows. Tall spruce trees block the wind and provide cabin logs. There is moss, cranberries, and permafrost where I will build. One option when building is not to disturb the surface of the permafrost but to build a short-term shelter right on the insulation of moss. Since I have few tools and am in a hurry, this seems like the way to deal with this spot.

It takes a whole day to cut my first tree down. Obviously, it is the saws fault. It takes another whole day to section and move the first log. This is so much work I decide not to take the time to peel the logs. It is the wrong time to peel anyway. The sap is not running, and special tools are needed to do the job right. Already, I do not expect this to be 'home,' just a trapper cabin that I can leave behind one day.

Dearest Maggie Aug. 30th
    I know it might be a long time before you ever get this, but I feel like keeping up my writing to you regularly since it has been a habit the past 5-7 years! I've started on the cabin, which is a very exciting time for me since I have dreamed about building in the wilderness a lot of years now. I need to get in shape. This seems like hard work. There are lots of berries out. There will be a time I can gather cranberries and blueberries for winter. The raspberries have come and gone, and I never found time to gather any. Rats!
    I'm sure I told you about Nancy? (Since I tell you everything). I think of her a lot these days. As you know, it had 'been a while.' Four years? Somewhere in there. Shall I tell you how many months, weeks, days, and hours? Ha ha. Maybe she will still be around when I get back from this time out here. She did tell me how cute I am, and you know how much I hate that! Cute! Yuck! This reminds me of teddy bears. Is this how I wish to be seen? (Humph). Maybe I will be mauled by a bear and get to wear a

patch over one eye, and surely then I wouldn't be cute anymore! I'm sure she meant well, meant it as a compliment. Anyhow, hope you are well. Are you married yet? Pregnant? (Whichever comes first, hmmm) Ha ha, I'm proud of you for doing so well in school, sticking it out, and making something of yourself. You notice my attitude changing? (You said in your last letter) Yes, it is hard to explain- for certainly it is another planet than your life – the life I also knew, and was raised in. Instead of finding answers, I seem to be finding even more questions! Ha! I do love the lifestyle itself, and see potential here as soon as I figure it out. Yes, life would be simpler if I just accepted my place in life and the class I was born in and settled down to some normal job. You seem to be able to accept life as it was handed you with few questions. In some ways, I envy that, but still would not trade places with anyone. Well hopefully Life will reward you. **Bye for now!**

As I'm sitting and thinking of something to add to the letter, there is a rustling in the brush outside the tent. This is a new spot for the tent, near the cabin building. I'm listening more closely to the natural sounds, trying to identify them. The bear is on my mind. While I'm sitting here, I write a poem.

> **I listen for the bear - End of Aug. Early '70s**
> From my tent
> I hear the pat, pat, pat,
> of an old lynx cat.
> I hear the humming bugs,
> and swishing of the grass,
> and the talking river eddies.
> I listen to the sounds.
> There's a click, click, click,
> from I don't know what.
> Then, waba, waba, waba,
> from something or other.
> I listen…
> for the bear.

The sound I've been listening to changes, and now I'm pretty sure it is the bear rooting around, coming closer. My 357 pistol is farther away than the rifle, so I grab up the twenty-two-magnum rifle, which I've learned to keep handy. As I fold back the tent flap, the bear hears me, and stands up on hind legs, takes a step toward me, and growls.

Without even thinking, the rifle comes up, the safety comes off, and the trigger is pulled. "Pop!" Before the gunshot fades, there is a faint "slap" of the bullet hitting flesh from fifty feet. The bear twists away and tries to run but falls down. A quick second shot to the temple drops him like a rock.

This is more like it! The skinning goes faster than the 'moose job.' The bear weighs only 3-400 pounds. This fresher meat will be welcome to replace what the bear destroyed and what I goofed up on with preservation mistakes.

There is a curiosity to know exactly where the bullets hit and what they did. As I skin, I explore the meat damage and bullet path. The first bullet caught him in the front paw as he raised it in front of himself while rearing up. The forty-grain pea-size lead traveled along the arm bone, went through the shoulder, glanced off the joint, angled down, and went through the lung, traveling through three feet of flesh.

Huh. There is not so much meat damage, but a lot of penetration. Must remember this. The second shot barely went through the skull and only made a tiny hole, no blood or visible damage.

Cabin logs.

We have no measuring tape. I sigh.

"So go get a piece of string. We'll use that."

Good idea. Me and I are having a conversation. The first long log I had cut for the cabin is re-cut until it is a length I can lift. About twelve feet? I have no way of knowing exactly, but it doesn't matter since this is all I can lift anyway. A knot is made in the string at this length so I can keep all the logs the same unknown length.

Piper left me his chainsaw. For the first few days or so, I try it. My diary explains the subject of 'the saw' best.[2]

Diary—Sept. 3rd: I tried the chainsaw again. Back to the house. Had to sharpen it. Back to the tree. Pull pull pull. Cough, cough, cough. It runs. Touch the tree. Sputter. Check the saw. It needs oil. Go get oil. Back to the saw, Fiddle fiddle fiddle. Pull pull pull. Clean the plug. Tote the gas, carry the saw, smell the gas, hear the noise, who needs it!!

My feelings go back and forth between elation and frustration. My diary is full of entries about spruce pitch in my hair, wood chips down my shirt, bugs up my pants, nervous about winter coming, and days getting shorter. I feel myself getting stronger by the day. One diary entry says I think I can lift twenty more pounds than the day before. In two weeks of work, I can lift double the weight I could the first day. One day my shirt feels tight, and just for the heck of it, I flex my muscles, and it rips my shirt.

The threads are just rotten!

"No way, check it out, can't you feel it too? Doesn't it feel good to lift something heavy?"

I take a day off to go hunting for grouse, pick berries, and maybe look for an animal sign and a place to trap!

> **Dearest Maggie**—I went hunting today. I know how you feel about hunting, but surely, there is nothing that tastes better than ruffed grouse stuffed with wild cranberries, cooked over a slow open fire of alder smoke. I got about 5 gallons of cranberries and 10 grouse. Life cannot get much better.
>
> That bear that charged me-- sure took care of him! I shot him just in time. Nah, I wasn't scared. You know me, not much scares me! (But women! Ha!). **Sunshine Miles**

No, no, you bitch! Fall the right way! The stupid tree wants to fall on the cabin. It slowly spins, trying its hardest to reach the cabin. It strains and huffs, makes up its mind, and with a mighty sigh and heave, falls…missing the cabin by inches. The hillside is crisscrossed with trees hung up, half down, partly down, almost down. Only half the trees come right down.

This notching thing we read about isn't so simple, is all my conscience has to say, as the last one just misses the cabin.

No tree is going to get the better of me! Every day I practice trying to control, or at least 'guess' where the tree will fall. I'm getting about a round up every two days until there is some new foul up (which is about every day! Ha!). Sometimes I don't get the notch in the right place, then I have to adjust everything, or there is an unseen 'wow' in the log, and it looks kitty-wampuss (so it needs 'womping' on).

How do we get the saw between the logs to cut the window hole in? The latest problem of the day. "Guess we have to take a round of logs off." Groan.

Hey! We could put the window in the roof. A skylight. Why not!

☺ :)

"Come on, pup! Let's go get some roof poles! Get in the boat!" The pup runs with his tail between his legs, and I feel sad. All I do is yell at him, so he doesn't even know when it's time to do something fun. The boat is not mine. I'm low on gas and do not understand the engine, so do not venture far. It is nice to get away for an hour, be out in the open on the river, in the breeze, the sun, "and no bugs pup!" We don't find any poles for the roof, only big trees grow along the water.

We go for a walk up the creek near the cabin since we are in a mood to do something different. We only go a few hundred yards, run out of big trees, and are out in open permanently frozen tundra. Along the edge are all the small trees we could use in a lifetime. Rather than starting to gather trees for the roof, we take it easy and walk around some more. The weather is a perfect fall day. The colors of red and yellow wave in a warm breeze. The smell of berries, spruce, and wet moss waft in the air.

Did you hear something? "Peep, cluck, peep, cluck." A whirring of wings that I know are grouse. Five, six. *No, I heard seven!* The pup gives chase as the birds all go to the tops of pole spruce trees and freeze. *So not ruffed grouse, but spruce grouse.* I'm learning the difference, just by their habits. I get all seven birds with the twenty-two and all in the head (about the size of a quarter). I think there are two more a little farther off and search for them, but with no real determination. I wasn't sure how I'd even carry these back. I tie them to my belt, freeing my hands as I walk along with the pup.

In the distance, I hear singing! However, it's not possible. There hadn't been any sound of a boat, and no one is around. It's been 'weeks' now since I've heard a human sound.

Maybe it isn't singing. We walk that direction anyway, just to check it out. The singing gets louder, then fades, then comes back, and I'm unsure now of the direction. *Sounds like a woman singing by the creek, happy and at ease, like she's getting water or washing clothes.*

"Just the sounds of the creek, pup!" The pup wags his tail, doesn't seem to hear what I hear. So maybe this is only a hallucination. I laugh, shake my head, and we wander on to the cabin site.

Fall is passing. The first snow comes, then melts. The weather warms again, but in the air is a sense of winter on its way. The cabin is almost done. The geese and ducks fly over every day, and many land in the pond out front. Every day I shoot a duck on the pond as a new batch flies in. I'm eating well. Piper's boat is put up for winter. He'd told me how to do it and warned me the water comes way up in spring. He pointed a way up there 100 feet in the woods when talking about 'high water,' but surely, he was exaggerating, just to make sure I got it up far enough. I'm not eating much of the rotten hard 'dog salmon,' not when I have the choice of all this fresh stuff.

"Honk honk, hoooonk." A Canada goose spreads its wings, shoves out the landing gears, flaps down, throttle back…teeter, teeter, teeter. Elevation drops as I watch. Stall speed. Feeling for the runway…blam, blam… swOOOooosh. The goose comes to a halt at the end of its runway. I watch the goose turn to the wind before folding his wings. He hasn't seen me yet. Just as I'm getting ready to shoot, a sweet feminine voice over my shoulder asks,

Will this be our dinner? I do not pay attention to the voice, it could be my conscience, my imagination, but I'm not going to miss this shot over it. Like Zen, I have to 'tune in' on the target.

"Steady steady, we have a target contact," pause, "we have a lock." I fire just as the sight swings over the target. The bullet travels over 100 yards through a shimmering mirage. The bullet is a trifle low but skips off the water and clips a wing. The goose heads for shore, dashes off into the willows, with me running in hot pursuit. Fresh blood and tracks in a skiff of snow show me a direction, and I beat up the brush, thinking he will hide like a duck does. My time is wasted until I catch sight of him sneaking off across the open sandbar for the river. With new determination, I take off as fast as I can run, to cut him off at the river.

We both reach the river at the same time. With a mad leap, I dive for the goose, grab him just as we both go over the edge and into the river. A pile of feathers, sand, and buckskin rolls into the water. My feet can reach the bottom, and I'm able to get ashore hanging on to the goose. With a quick twist, I wring his neck.

"Yip yip yoooo! Making meat!" I holler to the river. *Must be fifteen pounds of meat here!* I dance around, thinking I'm really something. Best of all, there's no one around to tell me I'm not! No one telling me how stupid and foolish it was to risk my life diving into the freezing Yukon after a goose and how cruel it was to wound the goose and then enjoy chasing it. I get tired of explaining and defending. What a joy it is to simply live.

I'm bringing my trophy up the path from the river to the cabin when I spot a cache of mushrooms on the low branch of a spruce tree. I know this is the winter stash of a squirrel.

Animals know what is good to eat and what poison is. I know I read that somewhere. You study animals and see what they do. It's in all the survival books and in all the Disney movies. There will be a certain satisfaction in taking something from the squirrels who chatter at me as if I'm an intruder, as they run off with string, food, and try to make winter nests of my clothes. This will be both a way to liven up the taste of this goose and show those squirrels who is boss.

"Hey, pup!" I call him over and give him the goose guts as I stuff the bird with cooked rice and mushrooms. This turkey-size bird gets slow-cooked over an open fire, and I'm mighty hungry by the time I deem it 'ready to eat.' While spitting out spruce needles (from the cranberries), I laugh about the squirrel's mushrooms. "Ha, ha! Hey, come here, pup!" The pup comes over to be petted. I wipe my greasy fingers in his fur, pretending it's all about petting him. Then let him lick my fingers. As he leaves, I find a clean spot of his tail to get the last 'dog spit' off. "Pup! Your baby tail is getting fuzzy; you will need a big dog name soon!"

With a full belly, I yawn, lie back in the grass, and fall asleep, thinking how nice it is to be able to eat and sleep whenever I wish.

"Argh!" I awaken from a fitful sleep with a fire in my belly. It's a moment before I realize where I am, but I know soon enough that the mushrooms were bad. When I'm done retching, I still cannot focus, my mind wanders, cold, snow coming down, and high fever. *My cabin isn't done yet, and it's snowing!* Is all I can think. I might be found frozen here in the spring, and the only comment, "stupid hippie," and "killed by squirrels, ha!" I can't get up, throw up again, and just lay in the newly fallen snow in a delirium.

Without knowing how much time has passed, I awaken with the hungry pup next to me. When my mind clears up, I feel lucky, once again, that this didn't cost me too dearly. In one of my reference books, I find one kind of mushroom a squirrel can eat, but people cannot. It has some long Latin name I can't pronounce that rhymes with "Silly-side-on" *The 'silly' mushroom.* The red cap one with the white spots. A squirrel chatters and laughs once again as I come out of the cabin door. I do not call him 'stupid.' I just glower at him.

Now that there is serious snow on the ground and it is colder, I'm more intent on getting the cabin done. The poles are all cut, peeled, and mostly up. I think I need to peel them because the roof gets a lot of moisture, and the poles might rot with the bark on. There is just that bothersome window and how it goes in, and the finish work. Once the poles are up and the window in, I lay some Visqueen plastic sheet down. There is log chinking moss leftover that I collect in bags. This is the first layer that goes on the roof; I decide to shovel the pile of husked pinecone shells the squirrels discard. These piles get many feet deep and seem easily portable and loose, and probably warm. The roof ends up two feet thick, of various 'things' that I hope will trap the heat. It took about a month, but the cabin is finally finished. The floor is only dirt. The logs are unpeeled and are chinked with moss. A pole bed with spruce branches and blankets, and a tin stove, with a five-gallon can as the 'stove roof jack' describes the interior furnishings. It seems to be warm. Certainly warmer than the tent!

Now that the cabin is done, I'm more relaxed. There is now time to try things I'd only read about. Making my own leather is on my mind, so I can make my own clothes and leather-goods. As a child, I tried to save 'road kills' and other sources of hides. These had mostly been squirrels and rabbits. None of the early tanning efforts worked, and I never had any adult help. A 'soup' made of tea was tried, but the tea may not have been strong enough, or the hides were already rotten. Now I have moose hide, and bear hide, and I do not want to throw these away. They are soaking as experiments in various buckets of solutions. One is in a lye solution; another hide square has been rubbed with liver and brains. There is the battery acid solution, bark water, pee, and one piece is being smoke tanned.

I had always been intrigued by the idea of people making their own soap, so I have the bear fat and lye to cook together. From my books, I learn to identify 'Labrador Tea' from a picture.

It grows all around me! This smells good, drying in the cabin by the stove, which I now light each evening to get the chill out of the cabin. Some of the tanning concoctions smell pretty ripe. The leathers start coming out of solutions and need to be 'worked.' Each method of tanning makes a different type of leather. It is interesting to see the differences. Some leather would make good harness type goods. Other leather is lighter in color, not as tough, but softer, for clothing. Some methods seem good for thin hides, other methods for thick. I keep notes on all my experiments for future reference.

There is still one part of the cabin I need to improve. The door. There is a blanket over the entryway now, but I have no plywood, and the poles do not stay together well. Finally, I figure out how to cross brace the poles. "Where are the hinges, pup!?" I ask because I have the feeling the pup has run off with them. I never find the hinges I'm sure I bought. I end up having to make leather strap hinges for the door. Moose hide 'babiche' holds the poles together, and the pup wants to chew on the door. He'd already run off with some hides I was tanning. There is a chair seat I made of leather, knife sheath, belt.

"Pup! Stop chewing on the chair!" As the door gets used, the moss between its poles works loose. Every few days, I have to re-stuff the door. The pole door is warmer than just a blanket and a little more bear-proof, or at least 'bear-resistant.' In the zero degree temperatures of early October, the cabin seems nice and snug. I'm well pleased with myself. 😊 :) (!)

The puppy is becoming more of a problem instead of less.

"That's my wallet, pup! Bring it back!" There goes what little money I have, my ID, and important papers, all scattered through the woods. *Either this dog 'hasn't got it' or it is me, who hasn't got it as a dog trainer.* I should have bought a collar and chain, maybe, but if I have to keep a dog on a chain, I don't want one.

"Well, that does it, pup. I'm locking you in the cabin while I go hunting this time!" The pup only wants to tree squirrels and runs around barking and scaring everything. Once something chased him back, and the pup ran through the woods toward me, bringing whatever it was right at me. I never identified what the animal was, just big and dark, but not a bear.

A fox? Wolf? Otter? Wolverine? I do not know. It just flashed by fast. Perhaps if I keep 'pup' in the cabin while I'm hunting, things can work out. Sometimes it's nice to have the pup around.

When I get over a mile from the cabin on this hunt, I get more curious about the lay of the land for future trapping areas.

"What's that?" There is a crashing in the woods coming toward me. My rifle comes up. It is only the pup. To get out of the cabin, he had to do something drastic, like chew his way out the door or dig a hole under the bottom log. There is no way to contain or control this pup, I see. The pup greets me with,

"I got loose! Aren't you proud of me? And I found you, it was hard, but now we can be together!!" The situation with this pup is 'dangerous,' the way he runs off with necessities. It is no use taking it out on the pup; it's not his fault he's the way he is. It may even be my fault because I don't have time for him, but 'fault' doesn't cut it if the result is non-survival.

When I get home, there is a hole under the logs. Everything is frozen from the cold air getting in. Some things were not meant to be frozen, like canned jars of food. My shoes are chewed to smithereens. I address the wagging puppy,

What will I wear in the cabin now? All I have is my winter boots! Maybe I can make a pair of sandals.

The temperature steadily comes down, and at the same time, I lose daylight. There is a problem keeping the snow off the skylight glass, but it is not serious. There is no weather report, no radio, no watch, and no clock. There is no time. *Remember, if you can't see it, it's not there.*

Diary—Oct. 15th: Music of the creek, music of the wind, music all around me! Who needs a radio! The walking room inside the cabin is 3 feet by 5 feet. The rest of the room is taken up with winter supplies and tools. There is enough room to turn around to get dressed, room to eat, sleep, and read. *Who needs more room than that?* Most things are done outdoors, which is really 'my home.'

One of my diary entries speaks of feeling sorry for 'ordinary' people, who have to go to work, sit behind a desk, and have a boss. No freedom. No time.

Diary—Oct. 20: Cabin hard to keep warm. The logs are drying, shrinking, and the moss is falling out. Restuffing is hard because the moss is frozen under the snow now, and 'things' are stacked up against all the walls. But the world takes on a 'virgin white' with the winter's snow; so beautiful with the black spruce. So 'clean' looking. I've seen snow before, but never so white, and realize I've always seen 'city snow,' yellow, gray, from car exhaust and pollution. The pup took off out the door and never came back. That was a few days ago. Some animal got him, or he got lost. For all his trouble, I miss the pup.

The first signs of 'cabin fever' come to me. My mind starts to play games. Thoughts I have no control over come to me. Many have to do with my childhood. Flashbacks from the past.

My diary gets filled with "nonsense" that has little meaning. Sometimes 'thoughts' that are what? Almost rhythmic poetry, but mostly hallucinations and disconnected words I later do not understand.

Diary—Oct. 30th. Life is the shadow that runs across the snow and disappears in the sunset.

The cabin door gives me a little trouble. The split poles twist every time I open and close the door. There is no real cure for this except a new door. The moss that wants to fall out from between the poles can no longer be replaced with new frozen moss. I discover that if I throw the dishwater on the door when it is cold, the water wets the moss and freezes it in place. More than this, the water itself tends to fill the tiny cracks with ice. Just one more solution to a problem that requires thought.

My trapping is not something I wish to think about, and I do not put much in the diary about it for a while. I thought I'd be out here knocking fur down right and left. The 'civilized world' had taught me that nature is 'delicate.' Everything is in a precarious balance, and we must take care not to disturb it overly much, least it does not recover. Care must be taken to hunt and trap wisely because so much is endangered. Restraint is called for.

It looks like wildlife can take care of itself just fine! My conscience says to me, cheerfully one day. I'm convinced I could spend twenty-four hours a day, and a whole lifetime at it, and never put a dent in the wildlife population. Trapping just isn't that easy. Snowshoeing is not easy. When I had seen the mountains off in the distance, I longed for winter, when I could snowshoe out to them. The reality is, I'll be lucky if I can make it through more than one valley. That is not even halfway to the mountains. *Nothing can stop me but me!* "Oh, shut up!" Sometimes my conscience is a bit much.

It is time to venture out and be trappers! Go forth, young man! Yes, it is time to stop being so cautious and head out a little further and do some serious exploring. *Let's get the map and compass!* We set out with the map. We think we know where we are, so there is no use using the compass yet. It is all pretty straightforward, after all. You find the sun, you look at the river, and you remember where you went! *What could be easier! Hey, look! A hole! Maybe it is a bear den!* I come over and look. We cannot decide if it is really a bear den or if it is just an upturned tree, but it is cool anyway. There are tracks, funny shaped trees, berries, creeks, and it is so fun and exciting! *"Do you know where we are?"*

Of course! The sun is on our left, well, sort of. It was anyway. That doesn't matter so much because the river is behind us, even though we haven't seen it in a while.

Then what is this up ahead? A creek? There is water up ahead, and sure enough, it is the Yukon! I was sure it was behind us! I am wondering how this is possible. Oh! I bet it is just a bend in the river! It is behind us, too, I bet! That's got to be it! Of course, that had to be it! How silly to get panicky. I know where I am!

Let's use the compass anyway, though just so it doesn't happen again! We do not need snowshoes because the snow is only a few inches deep. It is easy walking.

"Ok, so how do we use the compass?"

The 'N' points north, silly! How dumb can you get!?

"But we do not know where we are in relation to North!" The significance of this does not sink in until I think about it. I hold up a finger to point the way, as my mouth is open to speak and I look around confused, unable to point the way.

Well, then we just find a landmark on the map that matches something we see on the ground, and we know where we are! We are down low and cannot see anything. There does not seem to be a river bend that would make sense in this area where we could be. We could follow our tracks back, but are reluctant to see exactly the same country again. *Why not see something different?* It's not as if we are lost or in an emergency or anything! Well, at least we know we are on the river. We can just follow the river back! We start walking back, not knowing how far we have to go, but, "Oh well."

Hey! There are footprints up ahead! I thought we were the only ones out here! The hairs stand up on my neck. Someone else is out here sneaking around! Who are they? I bend down to inspect the tracks, to see if I can tell anything about the intruder. In the snow, the tracks look fresh. *Made today, I'd say!* This is most curious. We know of no cabin nearby, smelled no smoke, heard no saw. This is downright spooky! After an inspection and a pause, I sheepishly say, "They are our own tracks," *We have met the enemy, and it is us!* This seems impossible. I wonder where we were yesterday, thinking maybe it was from another day, but there is no way we were ever here. When looking at the river closer, I have to say, *We are going in the wrong direction on the river!* We had been so sure of our direction we did not even bother to check the direction of the current. I thought it was impossible to get that mixed up. I had spent a lot of time camping and walking in the woods! But always, there had been a trail, someone who knew the way, or it had been country I knew well.

This experience is very sobering. We are lucky we have seen our tracks in the snow. Suppose it had been summer? We are lucky the river is around. What if we had been in the hills?

We kept our eye on the sun, but the sun moves! We kept our position in relation to the river in mind, but the river is not straight!

ALL THE BOOKS tell me the sets I'm making to catch fur should work. All I have is drawings to go by. The main animal that should be here, I read, is the 'marten.' This is a lot like the Russian Sable, and since Alaska is only fifty miles from Russia, it could be the same animal. I think I recognize the tracks from the pictures but have no sense of 'size.' Something is wrong with what I understand, but I do not know what. The animals are just not stepping in my traps. Hours are spent going over books and going out to try some new idea, with enthusiasm and optimism.

I've finally figured it out! But I have not! Once again, I go back to design the 'perfect set.'

I'm out on the trail trying the trap set out. I am explaining it to my conscience "If I tie this fish-bait to a piece of string, then hang the bait from a tree branch, so it hangs invitingly just out of reach, I can put the trap right under it. Right where the marten will have to stand to look up at it longingly!" This is so ingenious and devious I almost feel sorry for the poor sucker.

The next day, bright and early, *more like dark, and early*, at 5:00 am, I eagerly go out to check the set. This is what it's all about. This is how I'm going to make my living, what I dreamed about all my life. A marten had visited. The bait is gone. The marten didn't bother going under the fish. He realized he couldn't quite reach it. He wasn't stupid, so he wasn't going to look longingly from underneath. He went up the tree, out on the branch, pulled the string up, ate the fish in the tree, climbed down, and laughed at me. Every day my diary is filled with a new idea, optimism, followed by failure.

Diary—Nov. 16: I'm running three lines, 10 miles each. All 25 traps are out now. Still haven't caught anything, and it's been a month.

It is now time for 'plan z,' but I'm unsure what that plan is. A red ribbon is used to mark the spot where a trap goes in case the trail blows in. I think I'm clever, with the red ribbon idea. I do not know everyone uses red surveyor tape to mark things in the woods. I learn to check for traps at the set with a stick or with my fingers curled up in the mitten after pinching my fingers enough times. Each day that I go out, I think this will be the day I catch my first fur.

Where is the darn trap? I find the chain under the snow and pull on it. No fur. Snowshoes are put back on, and it's off to the next set. Traps jingle in a canvas pack on my back that I made from an old tarp. Frozen fish for bait is in a separate compartment. Military green down-filled pants and parka keep me warm. My fox hat has the tail still on it. This is a hat I tanned and made from my first fox in Canada. Military surplus mukluks and mitts keep hands and feet warm. With the 'snowshoe shuffle,' I waddle down the trail. It's like walking like a duck.

Dig dig dig. Wish. Dig dig. Pause. Dig. But no fur. Hope. But no. Move on to the next set.

Here comes the hardy Mountain Man checking on his traps in the Alaska wilderness. But wait, what is wrong with this picture. Hark! Do I hear this Mountain man speaking of not catching his first fur yet?

"This is no time to get funny on me!" I'm crestfallen. Next set. Dig dig, *this is getting old*. Wish, dig. Snow flies. Tug pull. *A tuff of fur!* Dig pull dig. *Here she be! Our first fur!* Holding it up, so proud. But wait.

It's so little. I frown.

How come it's so little? This is what Mountain men lived and died for? We both look at the fur. It must be a marten. But it could be a sewer rat, *no, smaller than a sewer rat.* Not much bigger than a baseball, all curled up and frozen. *Where's all the excitement? The 'close encounters of the third kind?' Entries in the diary that speak of no time to skin all the furs? This really sucks. If you weren't so stupid and young, you'd think this was hard work!*

"What's this 'you' stuff, huh? What happened to 'We?' I notice you do that when something goes wrong. Anyway, what other kinds of job can a young, healthy smart guy find where he gets to work seven days a week, ten hours a day without a day off, no vacation, pension, security…?"

Don't forget, a whole month without pay!

"Oh yes, did I forget to add that?"

Yes, indeed! This is how I occupy my hours on the trail, talking to myself.

It keeps us sane! We both laugh. It's not so much the gold, as the looking for it!

"Sounds so noble when Robert Service writes it, doesn't it. Do you think he might have been full of doo-doo?" We look at the marten again as we snowshoe home. It takes a full day to skin it, from instructions in the book. I have to make a stretcher for it too, also from book drawings, by bending a willow stick. I'm beginning to think being a Mountain Man isn't all it's cracked up to be.

But does he give up!? "No!" "Did Joe meek give up after being mauled by the bear? Didn't he crawl 200 miles on his hands and knees to the fort? Can we do any less!?"

I know now why it took so long to catch my first fur. I had no idea how small he is. My sets were all wrong, having made them for a bigger animal! I have to file the triggers, make them have a lighter touch, and set them closer to the bait. After all the sets are drastically changed, I start catching marten regularly. One problem is solved, but it seems five more are always popping up. My equipment starts to fail me. When the temperature drops below zero, problems show up with the stove. It is made of thin tin, which can be all right, but this stove has the wood feed in the front. Most cheap stoves I had seen were with the feed from the top, and now I see why. The salesman had talked me into this one. When the stove gets hot, it warps. The door no longer fits the frame and leaks air. This means the fire can't be controlled. The fire roars hot, burns up the wood, and then goes out after about three hours maximum. With a top feed tin lid, the bad fit would not suck air across the flames. I never get more than three hours of sleep at a time the rest of the winter. Because the stove gets hot, the hinges to the door overheat and break. Baling wire fixes it, but the door doesn't line up even 'close' now. It surprises me that products can be made and sold that do not work, can't possibly work. No one who ever used a stove would design one like this.

Some idiot who doesn't ever have to use it designed it. This begins a general distrust of depending on products, believing salesman, believing what I read about products, or that 'the way it's done' is best. *Don't forget, depending on warranties!"*

At the same time my stove goes bonkers, the seams of my clothes rip out. Almost all my clothes have to be re-sewn. Anything made of 'plastic' shatters in the cold, like handles of tools and buckets. Fire starters sold to campers don't start; chemicals don't chemical. So many things turn out to be a 'joke,' sold with pictures of people going out in the wilderness with confidence, endorsed by rugged individuals. The reality is a bunch of hooey.

Someone needs to write the truth! What happened to pride in the American product! If I am to die out here, is it to be because products I depend on failed me? Will I be making a pile of all this crap and leaving a note behind for society to see?

"It wasn't the cold; it wasn't starvation. It wasn't bears. It was a hundred American products that failed me!"[3]

Another store-bought shirt seam gives out.

"Ho-ho! Fooled again! Those slippery con men!"

Where's my warranty card! I want my money back! My conscience says indignantly. We both think this is hilarious. We, of course, can't get in to say anything to anyone, so warranties become useless. In the middle of laughing, I'm feeding the stove again. Just as I load it, the legs fall off. We both pause and then burst out laughing. Like a three stooges skit, I shuffle off for the fix-it tools. Tra la la la I scuttle back. My conscience has been studying the job while I was gone, but I, the master, take over when I get back.

"Baling wire!" I demand with a hand out.

Baling wire! My conscience echoes, like a surgeon's assistant.

"Pliers!" Hand out again.

Pliers!

The legs are back on. *Masterful job, sir!* With a curt nod, I acknowledge the compliment and remove my surgical gloves. The crowd observing in the bleachers roars. I nod to the right, nod to the left.

Diary—Middle of December: The sunlight is so dim there is little color to see. Everything now is in black and white. The temperature drops, and I've seen minus 30 below in the cabin and 70 below outside. I'm not getting more than three hours of sleep at a time because of the stove. The quiet and great alone screams in my head. There is little to do now when I'm not trapping. The cheese whiz light is not enough to do any work by.

The 'light' referred to is a lantern I made from an empty 'cheese whiz' jar. There is a hole in the lid with a string down in the diesel fuel. This is very smoky and has about as much light as a candle. The skylight is given up on. Snow drifts across it faster than I can clear it off. Anyhow, there is very little light down in this valley now. My candles had given out. I hadn't realized how many hours of burning there would be, nor did I know how long a candle burns. I didn't know anything about 'lanterns' or assumed they put out about as much light as a candle.

"Hey, if Abe Lincoln could live by candlelight and get all that studying done, could I do any less? Wouldn't it be good enough for me?" Well, now I know why Abe needed glasses! *And was assassinated! Don't forget that!*

The first time I light the diesel fuel in the 'jar light,' I said, "Gee whizz! Light!" So it became my 'gee-whiz light.' *Or cheese whiz light*, just as the jar label said. 'Light' is not something the average town person dwells on. There is a switch; you flip it. There's light. If it goes out for more than an hour or so, a 'National Emergency' is declared. I spent a lot of time thinking about 'light.' Where it comes from, and various ways to get some of it.

Diary date entries are meaningless now. I've lost track of time, do not even know for sure within a month what day it is. The moon is supposed to get full once a month, but who thinks about it, or depends on it, or checks it out? Maybe this will be a way to know when a month goes by. I yawn lazily between chapters in my book (one of the Tarzan books by Boroughs). I have to lean closer to the light to read, with gee-whiz only inches away from the words.

Hey, what's that smell? I smell something burning, too, so sniff the air. Maybe some trash in the stove. There is a sound like bacon frying. *Hey, our hair is on fire again!*

There is a lot of slapping my head and laughter. This becomes a common entry in my diary:

"Hair caught on fire again!" The light is not very transportable. If moved, the wick wants to fall down into the jar.

When the wick falls in the jar, the light goes out. It means finding the wick in the bottom of the jar through the fuel. Usually, I have to empty the jar, first finding a container in the dark to put the fuel in. My fingers are wet from fuel, cold and numb, because the fuel is kept on the floor, and the floor is below freezing. With fingers that cannot feel, I have to find the wick and not drop it in the bark and dirt on the floor, or I will never find it until spring light. Once I have the wick, there is a tight fit getting it threaded through the hole in the lid. Often I have to put it in my mouth to get the wick to a 'point,' spitting the fuel out, sometimes several times, until it threads through. Finding the matches in the dark can be a project in itself. By the time it is all done, it is something I do not want to do again, so 'the condition of the light,' where, and 'how it is doing,' becomes a fairly major concern. Even so, now and then, I knock it over in the confined spaces, adding more diesel to the dirt on the floor.

Five gallons of rotten pee I'm tanning hides with falls over. How such a thing can happen involves a lot of understanding of how life is and could take a book to explain. I had to set the bucket on a box to get behind it to find something or other. Goods are stacked to the ceiling in cardboard boxes, on slanting pole shelves lashed with hide, uneven and rickety. I shrug my shoulders. There's a lot of things going on I doubt I can ever explain. Meanwhile, the place smells amazingly ripe. There's nothing to see. I simply accept being blind. I learn where everything is that I need by feel. 'Being involved in projects' is a joke. Try 'just staying alive.'

No, I do not consider it 'hell.' There is optimism for 'next year.' *Wait till I get a real lantern! More books to read! A watch!* They were all fairly simple, inexpensive things that I know will make life so much easier and are cheap to get. So I know all I have to do is 'sit tight,' survive this winter. There are a lot of positive things going on. The knife I created works. The soap I made, the leather I tanned and made things out of, all work. I learned how to trap and how to shoot. Most important of all, I know I've got what it takes. I know I am not afraid of any of this, nor is there anything I will not accept. Many of the books I read are about primitive life, and now I understand a lot more about it. I can see these people with new insight, and it is a very positive thing—to truly understand how life was 200 years ago. I feel like I am accomplishing the impossible! *So many people try what I am doing and die!*

THAT VOICE COMES BACK to me. The one I'd heard over my shoulder while shooting the first goose and the singing at the creek. I call her 'the squaw.' I do not think one way or the other if she is real, if I have gone insane, or if this is a ghost. This is not anything to make me afraid. She never scares me. Usually, I'm glad enough to have someone to talk to. Did I make her up? I do not care one way or other. I do what it takes to stay alive. If creating someone to talk to 'works,' I shrug my shoulders. I knew this life wasn't going to be easy.

We spend a lot of time telling 'light stories.' Me, my conscience, the squaw, and God. My diary, if it did not make sense earlier, is mostly the gibberish of insanity now. There is nothing to tell Maggie about. How would anyone understand any of this? Tell what? How God told the story behind, "Let there be light!?" How the squaw tried to clean the cabin but gave up in disgust and isn't talking to me now?

Diary—Winter: There is more light given off by the moon these days than by the sun. Switching over to 'moon-time.' When the moon comes out, so do the 'day' animals.

The squirrels start to chatter, and the ravens fly. When the moon goes down, and it is 'day,' the owl hoots and comes out. The wolf howls. This all seems so exciting.

This is like life on another planet! This is how I see it. A planet on which I'm the only person. The whole world is mine, for as far as I can see in any direction. There is nothing human to see, but things I put there. There is no footprint, no road. No planes fly over.

So I set up my own 'time,' which means getting up to trap by moonlight, going to sleep when people in town would be working. When moonlight gets dim, or goes behind clouds, or goes crescent on me, I stay in the trail by feel. I know where I am by stopping a lot and tuning in to all my senses. My hearing becomes acute. I cannot see the trap itself well enough to set it and keep getting my fingers pinched. A solution is figured out. A notch is filed on the flapper part of the trigger, similar to the way a mousetrap is designed. When the pan drops onto the notch, I know the trap is set and that it is 'hair-trigger.' This is the only way the number two double-spring victor will catch marten under the snow. The books say nothing about this. More and more, I put the books aside and rely on my own ability to figure things out. Mostly I'm trying to do things that haven't been written about. There are a lot of books on trapping, cabin building, and such, but not specifically on Alaska, or for thirty below zero and colder, or deep snow.

CLOSING my eyes sometimes helps my navigational ability in the raven dark. The only things I can't seem to locate 'blind' are branches across the trail that might be face level. So I 'duck waddle' along, waving my hands in front of my face. In my diary, I write, "Can't you just picture me!" a lot. Sometimes my diary is like a letter I write to someone else. I cannot write what is going on to Maggie, relatives, or any friends, because I know they just could not relate. Or they'd cry. My beard has gone untrimmed, body unwashed for weeks and months. My face is soot-streaked. The once-green-now-black torn snowsuit has had every seam in it re-sewn, mostly with mismatched threads. Some of the threads dangle down, red, yellow, blue. Patches of all colors and types of material are carelessly sewn on all over, but mostly the knees and seat. I chuckle at how I look. *I do not care what anyone would think because I'm 'being there!' Because 'I'm doing it' by God!* I assume all trappers are doing what I am, looking as I do, going out in the dark and cold being blind. I've never met another trapper, but I read what it was like in the 1800s, and it sounds a lot like this. So why shouldn't I feel like a time traveler?

In February, the temperature drops and stays dropped. The average I record is 'thirty below.' Common temperatures of minus forty below, fifty, sixty, and my thermometer can't register anything colder but disappears into the bulb, where I guess it is seventy below and colder. No one told me trappers sometimes stay indoors. I assumed when you are a trapper, by gosh, you trap! So I was not going to do any less.

If they can do it, so can I! I'm out there checking traps at seventy below zero. My nose freezes, my ears freeze, my feet, my hands. My concern is that they will turn black, fall off, or get infected. Having them all blister is 'just routine,' part of the lifestyle I chose. I assume this is also how we all will die. One day we freeze our feet and hands. We crawl till our eyes also freeze, and we fall over, saying, "Darn!" and grin. Some bear finds us frozen in the spring. I find this acceptable, honorable, and am not afraid, though I do dwell on death a lot and sometimes bring up the subject with God.

Diary—Winter: The northern lights are out again today as I check the trapline. Things are so pretty when it gets cold. Sound travels so well in the colder, dense air. My exhaled breath sounds like electrical static as it freezes going past my ears, leaving a trail of ice fog. I can just make out by the aurora red and green sheets of color waving all around me. I think I make out the North Star, which I've learned to use to help me know my direction.

My diary entry this day ends with a note in 'sort of' poetry form—

> The North Star guides me on
> My trail across a mountain.
> Below,
> The Yukon.

The next morning I get up eagerly, as I always do, thinking about the trapline, wondering if I have fur today. Always there is some special set I made that I wonder about.

Did it work? Was it visited? What new tracks will I see today!? There are wolf tracks and wolves howling.

"Maybe this will be the day I catch one!" There are Lynx all up and down my trail. Tracks of marten all over, mink, otter, wolverine, all of which I've seen signs of. Almost every day, I come home with either fur or a good story.

Today I'm on the line that takes me to the smokehouse. The trail goes through some trees, across a few creeks, over a mountain, back to the river, and then follows the river a ways to the smokehouse and summer fish camp. It has taken me a long time to get this line open because there is a windy stretch on the river with big drifts, and this is the longest line. There are two other lines, and I cover each one about once a week. I've discovered that checking any more often scares the game off the trail, and any less often, there is a risk of loss to other animals taking it or the set being buried by snow. Usually, if a set hasn't been visited in a week, it is either not functioning, or it is in a bad spot and needs to be moved. Today I hope to have caught a wolverine. There had been tracks at the smokehouse.

I'd read all the horror stories about wolverines. They run trappers off their trapline and are very vicious. I assume this is an exaggeration. There isn't an animal born that will run me out of anyplace if I want to be there, and that is not even a question. Never the less I'm intrigued by the reputation. The 'Golden Book of Animals' defines the wolverine as weighing about twenty-five pounds, having fur that will not frost, and capable of killing animals up to the size of a caribou (ten times the wolverine's weight). He's in the weasel family and is defined 'ferocious.' No other animal gets this description in the book, not even the grizzly bear. There is talk that the wolverine can run a grizzly off.

When there is enough light to see tracks well enough to define, which is about a two hour period of time each day now, I study a fresh set of wolverine tracks in front of me for a long time. I want to get information. What kind of animal, male or female? Why was it here? Was it nervous? Hunting? Just passing through?

Most important, "Do these tracks tell me anything about 'if he will be back?" Usually, there is nothing to tell, but I'm certain the information can be read if I practice. As I snowshoe this day toward the smokehouse and wolverine set, I review what I had seen on the last trip. When I came across the tracks, I memorized the size, the distance between tracks and studied this particular set of tracks to see if they could tell me anything. The animal had been moving along in a straight line and at a steady pace. Probably then, he knew where he was going and had been here before (so most likely would be back). No animal would venture out into this open place without even a pause to see if it is safe. An animal would check out what is surrounding the opening for something to eat, unless he had been here many times before, often enough to not pause here because it knew what was here and not here. There would be nothing to 'see' from where this animal stood, so I guess he had 'smelled' something. This thought is backed up by the fact he had stopped where I too stopped. This is important to remember, also remembering those small beady eyes from the pictures, which indicates that he goes a lot by smell, not sight.

Making a set for this animal involves his sense of smell, so there will be little use trying to catch his attention with visual things that dangle. When he got to the smokehouse, he did not slow down, so he is not made nervous by the metal or any human scent. This makes trapping him a lot easier. When the wolverine went into the smokehouse, one of the places he explored was the woodstove entrance. This looked like a good spot to catch him. A natural 'cubby set.' This is a standard way to catch an animal.

One of the 'top three basic sets.' A cubby is any hole, shelter, confined spot with a narrow entrance. In nature, the most common example would be a hollow tree, a rabbit hole, or a natural rock formation. This is a place you hope the animal will poke his nose in to investigate. Most animals like holes anyway, for food or shelter. They are curious about what might be in there. To encourage the animal to 'investigate,' scent and bait are used. The bait goes deep within the hole and is the food you want this animal to be interested in. The 'scent' is the lure that tells the animal there is food around, and is a marker that animals leave each other, sometimes on purpose, sometimes by mistake. Blood and other animal parts that have a strong odor can be more of a lure than a bait. This scent lure goes on a stick, side of a tree, or sometimes on something visual, like a piece of fur hanging. When placing the lure, I want to know what direction the wind goes and have some opinion or control over what direction the animal will come from. If I have an idea of what direction he will come from, I can make the cubby look appealing, like the entrance readily visible from his direction. It is better if the animal is so excited he does not stop to think.

It all starts with the scent, which has the animal thinking another animal has been here and marked this spot. A trapper wants his target to wonder 'why.' He will look around to see why some animal left its mark here. Animals mark places for reasons. They mark territories, mark where they got food, trail crossings, or a place where there's trouble. Animals do not just 'randomly' mark up the woods. Sometimes the scent I use is a strong odor, something that they like, or better, something they never had before, but is very attractive, like jam. This sounds very simple, but it is an art. Knowing where to put the trap is also important. Every animal has a different foot span. As his nose goes to the bait, you want his foot to be at the trap. (The bait does not go on the trap.) Some animals even step out with a left foot or a right foot, and this is 'useful' to know, so the trapper can favor one side. With a standard cubby, a trapper can narrow the entrance and set a trap between two small sticks, just the size of his foot. This works so well that it is used whenever possible, without getting too fancy, and is all explained in one word, 'cubby-set.'

So finding this stove as a natural cubby the animal has already been to is like a gift. The trapper smiles.

You're mine. In this case, there is nothing nearby to tie the trap down to. Sometimes a trapper can use a 'drag.' This is usually a toggle, or pole, tied to a long chain and fastened to the trap. This is set in the open, where there is nothing strong enough to tie to. When the animal gets caught, he runs for cover. The drag follows until it tangles in the brush as the animal passes through.

In this case, I was worried about the tendency for the snow to blow in here and get deep. Since this spot is so far away from my cabin, I know it may be over a week before I can get back, and if there is a drag and the wolverine goes far, I will not see where he went. About twenty feet away is one of the smokehouses upright supports, so decide to hook snares together to reach one of these solid poles to tie the trap onto. I set two traps to the same wire, a number four (for wolves) and a double spring two (pretty universal, marten, fox, otter, and will hold most anything if the foot will fit in it). A piece of rotten frozen fish goes in the back of the stove, some 'standard' lure is smeared on the entrance containing mostly beaver castor. All animals like it. Beaver castor smells strong in the cold and doesn't go away. Beaver musk is a main ingredient in the most expensive perfumes women wear.

So I had done all this on my previous trip out and am full of anticipation as I scramble up the river cut bank in front of the smokehouse. When I get to the top, I know right away that something serious has happened. The smokehouse tin siding is all down and gone. Looking past the upright support poles, I see nothing remains of the gear left in here. All I see is a pile of rubble, ten feet deep and twenty feet across. Nothing is larger than a pencil. This is what remains of forty feet of tin, a stove, ax, 100 feet of garden hose, fishing pole, table, chair…and somewhere buried in the mess is the creature that did this. With bulging eyes, I look for something bigger than a grizzly. Nothing moves. There is not a sound. I creep up, looking over my shoulder sometimes, a few steps, and pause to see what there is new to see. There is a piece of wire that I recognize as the snare wire I'd used to tie down the traps. This gives me something to pull on.

Do you see anything yet?

"No, you will see anything there is to see at the same time I do!" I answer my conscience. Underneath two feet of the rubble, I reach 'fur.' The wolverine is so small I'm amazed He could do this. His mouth is frozen full of chewed tin and wood chips.

He did all this with both his feet caught in traps!

This ends up even more awesome than the stories I'd heard! The number four trap is bent beyond fixing. This is a trap meant to catch and hold a 200-pound wolf. An image comes forth of the scene here while he was still alive. I'm impressed. The feeling would be no different if I were on Mars dealing with some alien creature in an unworldly hostile environment after being the only survivor of a spaceship crash. The frozen wolverine looks like nothing from the earth.

I'm having trouble skinning the wolverine by the gee whizz light. I can't tell my fingers from the flesh, the hide, or even the fur. I shift my position to try to get more light, but moving my mukluk clad feet slows me up in the clutter on the floor, where there is a foot of moss, bark, string, paper, and 'who-knows-what.' When I try to move the light so I can look, the draft at the floor blows it out. I yawn in the dark.

My fingers get cold again, so I shuffle over to the stove and put my hands on the stovepipe to warm them. Walking back to the chair, I think I kick up snow on the floor, but I'm not sure. There might be snow that never melts. I cannot see the floor until spring, but I'm not thinking about that as I work on skinning the wolverine. This work makes me thirsty, which reminds me of making tea and the ritual behind it.

The ritual starts before I even get up. I have to make the morning decision whether to get a fire going first or get dressed first. If I decide to get up and try to get a fire going before I get dressed, I risk not getting the fire going before my fingers get too numb to hold the match, with no way to warm them or get dressed. If I decide to get dressed first, I risk getting too cold to finish getting dressed or get the fire going. I have about 10 seconds after I get out of bed before I start to shiver uncontrollably. The temperature in the cabin is twenty below zero most mornings.

Before I make tea to warm up, I yell,

"Coffee break!" as I break off a piece of ice out of the pot on the stove. The coffee or tea cube goes in a tin cup and is thawed to make my hot drink. This is an important time because it means I got the fire going, and I'm still alive. The rest of the day always looks brighter.

As I skin the wolverine, I'm glad I cannot see. I suspect I'm botching the job. Thinking of what I cannot see has me thinking of the bed. Now I have to hammer the sheet and blanket with my fist to get it to fold or unfold.

Maybe they need cleaning? "Hm" As far as the condition of my clothes... At this pause, my conscience pipes up.

Do your whites look white? Your blues look blue? Do you use the detergent with the little green crystals? This cracks me up, and I burst out laughing. "Hey, do you know which pants we have on today, the jeans or the corduroy?" *Let's check!* I draw my knife out of its sheath and slide the knife across my pants to get enough dirt off to see.

Surprise, you lose, the jeans! Ha, ha, ha.

After a typical evening of discussion, the Squaw adds, "And I know I'm not insane either because I got the word direct from God!" After a significant pause, we all burst out laughing again because we know anyone with a direct line to God is nuts. A hoot owl interrupts the laughing. The wind blows. The snow swirls by the front door. The cheese-whiz flickers and almost goes out.

A voice over my shoulder, "What are you doing?"

I answer contritely, "Don't look over my shoulder like that. It's rude."

God backs up.

"But if you must know, I'm working on another mousetrap!"

We have all noticed the alarming rate at which the mice are multiplying. It had never occurred to me that 'mice' are worth considering as something to deal with, so I hadn't bought traps for them.

Did Tarzan have a mouse problem you ever heard about? Did Jim Bridger ever ask, "Anyone pack the mousetraps? No! Jim would have said, "With Griz and catamounts, you spect me to war-ee bout Mice??!"

The squaw is looking over my shoulder along with God.

"Will it work?" There have been a hundred other attempts that failed. There was the figure four deadfall made of toothpicks and a book. The mice ate the peanut butter off the pan of the number zero trap. (Boy! Were we mad about that, all that peanut butter going to waste. We're pretty low on peanut butter.) Solving the mouse problem has now become a matter of honor! Will it be the stupid mice who finally do me in? Not the bear, not the wolverine, not the cold…?

Nights are spent dreaming up new mousetrap plans. This is the latest in the series. "Ok, see this can tied to the board? This is the cubby. The lid is hinged. This string goes through the bottom of the can and hooks to the lid, so when the string is pulled, the lid shuts. The string goes up to this hook, over the roof rafter." (Everyone's eyes follow where I'm pointing). "And over to the bed. Peanut butter is the bait." There are groans at the mention of using precious peanut butter again.

I lay awake in bed, waiting. Waiting with the end of the string in my hand. Waiting in the dark for the mouse. Everyone has to keep quiet.

"I think I hear one coming," someone in the dark whispers (suspiciously like the squaw).

Shhh, be quiet. I slowly take up the slack in the string. This is every bit as intense as killing the bear. I'm tired of mice moving in under the blanket with me as I try to sleep, or making nests out of my books, or storing stolen rice in my boots that I have to dump back in the rice bag.

It takes some guessing to know when a good time to pull the string is. Finally, I decide the mouse is well in the can and busy eating. I give a yank on the string. The lid closes, and I hear the frantic efforts of the mouse trying to get out. When I run up to the can, the mouse is gone. I had yanked too hard and pulled the can off its foundation. None of us dare speak for a while. God has left. He only wants to let me know He's keeping an eye on me in case I need Him. I told him everything is just fine.

There is still a nagging concern for what time it is. What time of the month, what time of the year? As the food level goes down, it becomes increasingly important to know how long I have to ration food. I realize I use the same amount of flour every day, and the level in the 100-pound bag goes down at a steady rate,

Like sand in an hourglass! The bag is marked. Time is measured in 'flour bag levels.' The sugar is measured in terms of how fast the flour goes down, and peanut butter is marked by the spoonful. Each day I measure out one cup of rice, one spoon of peanut butter, and a half cup of flour. The rotten, maggoty, mouse turdy meat and fish doesn't get mentioned much. Now and then, 'someone' forgets to put the lid on the peanut butter. In the dark, it is hard to keep track of everything. The mice get in and leave turds on the surface. At first, we take the time to pick them out. This takes hours in the dark. After a while, we stir them in. *If you can't see them, they aren't there, right? Anyway, did you know flour has all kinds of 'stuff' in it? Plenty of ground-up turds and such.* So we don't worry about it. No one gets sick. But I dream a lot about light, and when I have light, I will be able to check the peanut butter. This will be a wonderful time to look forward to! More and more, I want to hurt the mice.

First wolverine

This isn't from the same planet I used to live on.

CHAPTER FOUR

THE DARK, THE COLD, WOLVES, FLEAS

"There's a lynx in the trail ahead of us."

Do you think he's in a trap?

"Don't know, we'll have to check the sign and decide. Just letting you know there are tracks in the trail." My conscience and I are checking the trapline by moonlight. The moon went behind clouds. We are in the pitch dark, and I follow the trail by the feel of it under my snowshoes. Bending down on my knees, I pull off a mitten and gently run a hand on the trail to feel for the tracks, reading it like Braille. We have done this many times.

Use a match. I get out a wooden match and, by its light, see where a lynx took a rabbit from one of my snares and headed on up the trail. The flickering light shows black dwarf spruce trees covered in snow, and through the fog of my breath, I barely make out the saucer size tracks of the lynx before shaking the light out. While waving my hands randomly in front of my face, we proceed on, with a shuffle, duck-walk, slide, up the trail. I can sense obstacles on the trail, and I sonar-ping large objects in front and to the side. Much as a blind person does with a cane.

Though trapping is not quite a routine yet, I catch fur regularly now and study every sign I can, trying to learn from it.

The lynx had a rabbit, think he'll stop at the next set?

"Maybe. Could be curious."

"We made sets for food and the sense of smell. I think the lynx will be in a visual mode and will pass it by." The next set ahead will tell the story. When we get to it, there is a frozen jay.

Rats!

The jay is called the 'camp robber' for a good reason. This bird had been taking the bait from this set and storing it in the trees. Finally, he was caught in the trap, long before the lynx came along. The bait was gone, and the frozen jay holds no interest for the lynx.

"How far is the next set? Do you think we have his interest in that distance? Because I think not. I think we lost him. How long an attention span do you think a lynx has?"

Longer than a marten, but shorter than a wolf. This is no news to me.

The tracks show the lynx is less and less interested. The tracks stay on the trail for shorter distances. I cannot see them, but know when they are there. The lynx leaves the trail to explore and wanders back, but less and less often until I no longer sense a return. I forget about the lynx after a while. The next set might have a marten in it, and this is on my mind. Hobble-wave, hobble-wave. We proceed down the creek bank and up the other side.

Suddenly I sense something off to the side of the trail and pull back just as a scream lets loose, and claws flash by.

The lynx! The number four trap seems to be holding him secure, but he has moved the drag from where I set the trap. From the sounds, I know the drag is caught in the willows on the creek bank. He must have been following the open trail dragging the trap. My hatchet comes out of its sheath as I boldly step forward in the dark to meet the lynx. As he leaps, I swing and catch him on the side of the head with the flat of the hatchet. The quiet peace of the milky way night is rudely interrupted by the cat's scream. When the echo fades, my adrenaline is still rushing through my veins, pounding in my ears. The lynx goes limp. All is a silent night. But not holy. My hands slowly, delicately, feel along the body I cannot see until I find the neck. With a swift pull, I snap the neck to make sure he is dead.

We'll have to carry him. It is too dark to skin him here. I do not bother to answer but tie the cat to my pack board. His thirty-five pounds of weight will be all right since I set a few traps and lightened the load on the way out. Hobble-wave, hobble. We head up the trail to the last set. My fur mittens wave in front with the tail of my fox hat gently swaying back and forth to the snowshoe shuffle. The warmth of the dead cat creeps through the pack board and feels good. The cats' feet softly slap at my ankles to the rhythm of my snowshoes.

The cold pink light of dawn washes over the trail as I approach the last set. There is nothing to see, but I think something is here, so I cut a stick from a nearby willow before approaching. There is still not enough light to see well by. My stick lashes out and connects with the head of a lynx. I never saw the cat, just sensed where he was. There had been no sound this time.

Two cats! Not bad! I vote we skin them both here, carry only the hides home! Sounds like a good idea, so once again, I do not say anything. There is light now to see enough to do a rough skin job. The paws will be done later, also the heads. My hands are kept warm by sticking them in the carcasses every now and then. Blood freezes to the steel knife, and I clean that off on the teeth of the lynx. Bending over, working in the trail on my knees is awkward and time-consuming in the surrealistic rose light.

Let's use the meat for bait at this end of the line. We can put the two carcasses in the crotch of this tree and set our last trap here to catch anything that tries to steal it. We can come back later to bring some meat back home for us to eat and use the rest as bait. This pile does seem like more weight than I wish to carry back, and the meat is all bloody right now and would be easier to deal with after it freezes. We put it in the tree with a trap under it.

On the snowshoe trip home, the 'day' begins and ends. The pink of sunrise turns to a brief color of red for half an hour, then fades into the purple of sunset. 'High noon' has come and gone. The temperature is dropping.

Do you notice that just before the temperature drops, the fur moves? It seems a truism when we catch the most fur, we can expect a big weather front to move in. Sometimes I know by the tracks that the weather will change. With no weather report, this becomes something to note.

Bloody, tired, cold, I snowshoe on toward the warmth of the cabin, ten miles away, as the temperature drops. I had worked up a sweat while skinning the lynx. The moisture in my snow pants is not good for trying to keep warm. I have to stamp my feet, slap my hands, and snowshoe faster to stay warm. On the way to the cabin, I start making up a song. I had thought out a few of the verses previously, but this trip out is the one time I get serious and write some of the lines down. They are recorded in my diary.

GOING WILD

**My Thirty Below and Dropping Song.
Winter of 72**
When I'm out trapping
I like to sing
cause the time is passing
that I'm freezing.
And if I miss a line,
or I'm out of time,
well it don't matter none
when I'm frozen.
And I can play cards
as I make up the lines,
"Let's cover the bets
with 5 more degrees!"
So I grab a card,
but it hits me hard,
cause I have to pass,
and then I lose!
Instead I start playing
a monopoly game.

I lose more degrees
and the temperature drops
but I smile all the same,
life is just a game!
On one of the chance cards
I get to park place
but I notice the trees
all look a disgrace
so I start singing
about their trimming.
And I can sing, "Oh well!"
I'm out on the trail
and it feels like hell,
but at thirty below
I develop a glow
cause then I can sing...
"Thirty Below and Dropping!"
That's one in particular
I yell loud and clear.
If I could sing louder,
I'd raise temperature!
So I sing the beginning,
"Oh it's thirty below and dropping!"
Oh well at thirty below
I once froze a toe,
but I grab a degree
and it warms me.
So I take more degrees
and warm up my face,
now it's thirty-five now it's thirty-five
but I'm still alive.
Now I sing to myself
how I like my scarf'...

What rhymes with that? Hmm, anyhow, we are home.

Still cold out? Tell me what the temperature is!"
"Still fifty below and dropping."
No use going trapping.
Seems like a breeze is coming,

which means a warming."
"Stop talking in poetry!"

:)

LATER IN THE WEEK, I take a chance and head out on the trapline. I am anxious to get out. I do not care that it is still cold. I am tired of the squaw, tired of nothing to do in the cramped, smelly cabin.

It will be good when we get to the lynx bait we left in the tree. Seems like every set has the bait missing to those stupid camp robber birds. "Yea, I wonder how many trappers have lost fur due to those birds getting the bait." There is a special sound of the snowshoes on the fifty below snow that is a squeaky crunch. I like this familiar sound. The Northern Lights are out and giving enough light to see by. When it is cold like this, I can hear the lights hissing. Tonight the lights are green with a lot of red in them, radiating out from one central spot, looking like a cross as big as the sky.

Looks like there's a large male marten on this pole set! I can see for myself but have given up making this comment to my conscience. I have not caught many marten on pole sets, so I look this over good. The pole set is the second most important set a trapper uses besides the cubby. A pole, similar to a tent pole, is cut. This could be anywhere from a couple of inches to a half a foot in diameter and from seven to fifteen feet long. This is leaned against a tree but preferably set in the crotch of a tree, so there is at least a foot of pole suspended in the air past the fork. The end of the pole should be about five feet off the ground, with the only access to the end of the pole being 'up the pole' where the bait is tied or nailed. Usually, something visual is tied with the bait, like a piece of aluminum foil, ribbon, or feather on a string. The lure is put at the base of the pole. Often the bait is rubbed up the pole to be sure the marten knows the path to take. Similar to a trail an animal would leave dragging food up the pole in order to hide it up a tree. A notch is made in the pole where the trap will be set. There are various ways to help hold the trap in place, but a small hole is provided in most small traps so they can be set over the head of a nail. The trap should be one to two feet from the bait. The trap chain is fastened to the end of the pole. It is not necessary to boil the traps to cover scent or hide the trap, not with marten anyway. (I had read before that everything has to be boiled). The more the area is messed up, the more the setting attracts marten.

The marten follows the scent trail up the pole and has his eyes and mind focused on the bait he sees up at the end of the pole and not on the trap. Sometimes he puts his foot in the trap upon approaching the bait. The jaws act as 'guides' for his foot going in the pan, which is the trigger. Other times the marten steps completely over the trap and starts trying to get the bait loose. While he is struggling and working, he is moving his feet around and steps in the trap. When the marten steps into the trap, he jumps. The trap chain pulls him short, and he is dangling from the pole and off the ground. With a foot caught, he cannot climb up the chain or get back up to the pole. Hanging from the chain keeps him away from the ground where mice and squirrels could tear off the fur to make a nest or eat the meat. This 'hanging' also keeps the fur out of the snowdrifts that can form, and the set will not be buried. The marten does not tangle himself in branches or get tree sap in his fur using this set. The marten dies quicker in the pole set because he cannot curl up or bury himself in the snow to keep warm. He freezes to death within hours.

But is it a cruel, inhumane, long-suffering way to die? That's what I want to know! I pause a moment to reflect on this as I stare at the pole set. Me is asking I, pretending to be a tourist, shocked by the inhumanity of it all.

As if addressing an audience, I reply into the microphone, so all may hear. "There are very few pleasant ways to die in the wilderness. Even natural ways tend to be mostly traumatic, violent, bloody, painful, terrifying, sometimes long, drawn-out, and common." *At the risk of sounding cruel, there must be fifty ways to leave your lover. Step out the back jack, making new plans, Dan.* Yes, like the 60's song. Speaking of fifty ways to be cruel, "Walt Disney," I sigh, "Is full of doo-doo. That's a terrible thing to find out about our childhood hero, huh?" With tears in their eyes, the shocked audience falls silent. I am not moved. For I understand. *This same group would do worse to me than I do to animals if given a chance.*

The drawback to the pole set is that the marten has to work a little harder to get at the bait, and sometimes he will not go up the pole. He has to be very hungry to go up the pole set. The cubby set will work if he is only curious.

Look over here. I look and see that we almost did not get this one. "Yea, tracks look like he did a lot of thinking, looking, hemming and hawing, before deciding to go up the pole." After snowshoeing a ways, *Is the pack too heavy? Want me to carry it?* "When it's heavy with furs, what do I care about the weight? We'll be up late skinning, maybe even have to take a day off again." "The end of the line up ahead. We need to get some of that lynx meat for bait. Sure seems a long way with the trail drifted in like this! Shall we sing our song to pass the time?

Thirty Below and Dropping!?

Slosh squeak, slosh, squeak. The snowshoes keep time to the song, as out there, in the middle of a thousand miles of whiteness, yours truly breaks a trail that winds through the trees, up the creeks, and over the mountain. *I'd love to see God's expression this morning as He rides his chariot hauling the sun, looks down, and sees our trail, until…"*

I interrupt myself, "Huh? What's this? Looks like tracks headed for the lynx meat! Didn't we set a trap there? Do you remember doing that? Do you remember me saying we should and you saying we shouldn't?"

Well, I sort of remember it was me who suggested the trap and you who was too tired. And if it hadn't been for me…"

"The lynx meat is gone! What happened? Looks like the trap was buried in the snow and did not go off!" A wolf had come by after the storm, maybe only minutes ahead of us. If I had gone out a day earlier, a few hours earlier.

If we had unburied the trap and reset it. The tracks are as big as moose tracks and sinking as deep in the snow. This is awesome, like a phantom. My breath is taken away. Looking closer, I see he stepped exactly in the middle of the pan, but there had been too much snow on the pan for the trap to have gone off. *But at least we know we set it in the right spot!* "Imagine an animal that could eat two lynx carcasses in one sitting!" *A couple of weeks' worth of food for the two of us!*

The trap is re-set, but there is no bait to use, only lure and not wolf lure, so I am not optimistic. Many snares are set for wolves, now that I know they are around and leaving tracks in my trail. There is, once again, only a picture and description to go by for setting wolf traps. There are drawings in my books showing how to make my own snares. Snares seem simple enough when looking at the drawing and description. Just wire with a slipknot in it. When checking out trapping supplies in town, I had looked into the price of snares and was appalled at the high price. At the dump, I had found a bed frame with braided wire as its mattress support. This is what I use for my snares, along with a bent washer with a notch and hole in it, just like in the drawing of, 'how to save money and do it yourself!'

I love books that have sections like that in them.

These homemade snares are set out randomly along the trail wherever it passes close by two trees, a natural intersection, or under a fallen tree.

Fox and traps. Traps stored outside the cabin to cut down on human scent.

The wolf pack is hanging around in my area. It is hard for me to know just how many, but I think there are at least seven. In a single day, three snares catch wolves. *Only one problem. Ya gonna talk about the teeny problem?*

"Hmm."

The fact you tried to save a couple of dollars by doing it all yourself instead of buying real snares!

"Sigh."

"The wolves got caught, but the lock did not work well enough, and the wire was not the right kind and did not kink on the lock. The wolves stopped struggling, slipped a paw under the wire, and worked it loose. Every one of them did the same thing!

Pobody's Nerfect? (?) However, I do not wish to listen to my conscience because I know that if anyone heard the truth, the people who know me would laugh and say, "That sounds like Miles, doesn't it! Har har, always trying to re-invent the wheel! Pinching pennies and losing dollars! He's always good for a laugh, huh?"

😀 :)

Well, the main thing is, there was nobody to tell me I'm an idiot, right? So? No problem. We have the rest of the winter. We learn. We change. We do it better next time. This trapping business is not as easy as it sounds. The wolves are still around. We are smarter than wolves. "Anyway, no wolf is going to out-smart me! I refuse to be discouraged! What about you!?"

Hey, I'm with you!

"Ok, that's better; we'll dwell on the positive!"

Hours and hours and days and days are devoted to drilling holes in washers with no drill. Washers are bent with no pliers, no vice, and no light. They become handcrafted works of art before they are done.

Am I one stubborn son of a bitch?

"You are one stubborn son of a bitch! Even God is flabbergasted!?"

Yes, God is impressed. We both grin. ("Did you hear God chuckle in the background?"). I forget the dark, forget the cold, forget the hunger, and forget the mice. Forget the fleas. *You dropped a finished washer on the floor.*

"Forget looking for it, too much dirt on the floor, not enough light, just hand me another one." My hand calmly goes out.

But we spent hours on this one! My hand remains calmly out, with infinite patience. With a sigh, my conscience hands me another washer. We start all over again by the light of the gee-whiz.

Diary:

Here in the wilderness, there are Kings and the King's super. There is not much in between. I feel like a monarch of a thousand miles. I climb onto the mountains and look down upon my domain. Yet, under God, I feel humbled by this. I feel so alive. I snowshoe every day and need less rest. The trees I cut and drag back are larger, drug further, so I know I am stronger. I feel like I will live forever!

About the time Christmas should be here, I sort of wish to know what month it is. I wake up one day and look out the door at a perfect winter day. The spruce have ice crystals that the moon shines through, making them look like chandeliers, and scattered diamonds are tossed across the treetops. Spruce grouse and rabbits left trails in fresh snow, leaving a crisscrossed lacework in the moonlight. A rabbit hears me and runs. Birch branches, laden with snow, are disturbed, springing up, throwing arcs of snow through the moonbeams. It is a scene so beautiful, some would never see its equal in all their lifetime.

Shall we open the special box, sir? My conscience is pretending to be the butler today, and the 'box' referred to is the single box of cake mix we purchased in the 'damaged section' for twenty-five cents. The idea was to save it for a special occasion. Every now and then, we get it out and sniff the edges, then put it away again.

Since we are not sure when Christmas is, and this seems to be a special day, and it could be Christmas.

"Yes, let's celebrate!" We had all the words and colors on the box memorized.

Chewy Fudge, get it all. Add egg and oil. Less fat. Preheat oven to 350. "Yes, yes, just fix it, please!" I wave my hand in dismissal as the butler tends to the cooking. He will cook it in the woodstove. It was discovered we could put green logs on top of hot coals, then put a bread pan on the logs because there is no flame.

350 coming up, sir!

"350 it is then. Let's do it!" We are both drooling. The mix is ready. We have no egg, but who cares? We are learning how meaningless instructions are.

Cool completely before cutting, Sir.

"Yea, right. You can wait. If there is any cool cake left, you can have it."

🙂 :)

We wolf down the whole thing in one sitting and do not care that we have burned lips.

Aren't you glad your mother isn't here to tell you to eat slowly and share?

"Did you wash your hands first?"

While you were washing your hands, I ate an extra piece."

"Yea? Well, while you were out back taking a leak, I ate an extra piece!"

And if you put your finger down your throat, you could give my stolen piece back!

"And if we waited, I could give you your stolen piece out the other end!"

Yes, Merry Christmas to you too!

" Gosh, that sure was a good cake. Maybe the best twenty-five cents I ever spent in my life, and the best Christmas!"

KEEPING the trails open is a constant battle, and I push myself to the limit about every trip out. The trip to the old smokehouse always seems the hardest, with its stretch of windblown river. The smokehouse has a lingering fish smell that attracts animals. There is a set I had made outside the smokehouse, knowing that some animals will not wish to come in, even though the wolverine had. This is the set I am checking. Surely, some animal will have been attracted to the mess the wolverine left when he had been caught here. The wind has blown the trap in, and I cannot find it. This discourages me because I do not have very many traps, and they cost a lot. These big ones are about fifty dollars each. The harder I look, the more it seems to me, the trap is just not there, and that means something was caught and drug it away. Yet I had chained it to a big log, which was ten feet long and a hundred pounds. So, of course, nothing could have moved it. My conscience is not as sure.

A gust of wind grabs at my hand, which is getting cold. I curl the ends of my fingers in the fur mitts to warm them while I hunch over, studying the signs in the snow. Short willow trees barely stick out of the snow, and the dead, dry, shriveled leaves wave tauntingly in the wind, laughing at us. There is a moonscape quality to the way the granular snow makes horseshoe shapes around each little stick in the snow. The roller coaster slant of drifts is not on a flat, dull plane but follows the parabolic curve of the universe. Through the stargate is Einstein's time-space continuum. I think I see an outline of a wolf track. The tracks of the wolf seem large and surreal in this scene. A track seen in Van Gogh's Starry Night. If I got a wolf, then it might be alive yet, here somewhere, maybe in the nearby bushes, or behind that next drift five feet away. I feel I should walk carefully around here.

There is no trail to follow, just a few single tracks I cannot read. I start to make wider circles on the chance I can cut across a sign. About 100 feet away, I pick up the first evidence in a clump of bushes. The branches are chewed off as if the trap drag had caught, and the wolf had to chew himself free. I have spent over an hour here looking, and it is getting gray dark, with just enough light to see a trench going over the riverbank that could have been made by the trap log. The wolf may have realized how the drag works and headed for the open instead of the brush.

Are you scared?

"Of course not! Are you?"

We are mighty trappers stalking the tooth-ed monsters of the wild. Dragon-slayers, protecting the world from evil.

"Oh, shut up! Has anyone told you that you are just a bit much sometimes!?(?)" I have hurt my conscience's feelings as we both creepy- crawly slowly to the river bank, all big-eyed and gulping, peering into every shadow. The witchy fingers of the willows on the bank waving "oooo," "OOOO" in the wind, reminding me of what will happen if the wolf is still alive.

I cannot see over the bank, so I am cautious in case the wolf is just over its lip. With anticipation, perhaps even with a lump of fear in my throat, I slide over the bank.

Something happened here. I cannot make it out at first. The ground everywhere is trampled, and there is blood. Frozen blood, everywhere. After taking it all in, my eyes focus on the center of this cleared area. Here in my trap is the leg of a wolf. The leg is attached to the neck, and the neck has the head of the wolf on it. The rest of the body is missing. The mouth is frozen open, exposing all the teeth. The tongue has been ripped out, but the eyes are frozen amber crystals of terror. Following the gaze of the frozen eyes, I look up over my head. Blood had been slung or had spurted, ten feet up into the brush hanging over the bank. The wolf had been caught and might have got away, but the pack turned on him, tore him apart while he was alive, and eaten him. This was not exactly 'Gentle Ben,' or 'the social wolf that mates for life' that somehow has human-like morals. More than just the blood scene is scary here. The very cloth of everything I had learned about the wilds from civilization now has a thread loose, and if I dare to pull at it, the whole beautiful tapestry will be turned into a pile of kinky fiber. [1]

"I have this often repeated crazy thought that I no longer live on the same planet I did a year ago. Have I mentioned that before?" As if in answer, the granular snow blowing across the open ice makes a snake-hissing sound, "ssssssss," as the dead trees laughingly, "heeeeee," in the wind. Looking up at the sound, I see the globs and splatters of frozen blood that surrounds me.

'Fear' is not quite the right word. The issue might be a lack of comprehension of how wolves could do this to others of their kind.

I thought only people were insane and psychopathic, not animals.

"Well, you thought wrong. Come on, let us reset this trap. The pack may come back here to eat up the tidbits." The wind moans, "Bewarrrrre," and follows behind, ahead, beside us as we snowshoe toward the warm, safe cabin.

Don't worry; that is just the devil talking, not God. I think my conscience is a little afraid, asking questions concerning killing anything out here. Is this some warning or something to give us the shivers and make us give up?

After a long pause, I respond, "I consider that the 'devil,' and 'God' are one and the same. That the devil is God when God is angry, or more, that we pass judgment when we call things either 'good' or 'bad.' There is no good and bad, only events. It is for us to ponder the event and try to understand what its purpose is in the big picture. Evil may just be some event that we do not understand, whose meaning eludes us for a while until we have more knowledge. Maybe events must simply be filed away and remembered. It is MAN who needs a sense of good and evil, not God. Just a thought."

We have friends, you know, who would not let us in their home if we spoke like this. They would be afraid of us.

"Well, we will not tell them what we consider then, will we? We wouldn't wish to hurt anyone's feelings or cause anyone to feel nervous about the great unknown."

Our thoughts ramble and speculate as we snowshoe along, eating up the miles, trying to make sense of a world we are not prepared to meet.

I have a question for you. If we are confronted with evil, and we hold a cross out in front of us, does the cross protect us, or does our belief in the cross protect us?

I think on that one for a while.

"Squeak, squawk, squeak," go the snowshoe bindings hour after hour as I curl and uncurl my fingers in the mittens to keep warm.

"The cross is not necessary. With a strong enough faith, in theory, a person need not hold out the cross. The cross is merely the symbol, and without someone holding it and believing, it has no powers unto itself. Because God would not desert someone just because, for some reason, he did not have a cross with him." Taking this thought further, it is the belief that matters, and the cross is just a symbol of that belief. The cross itself has no powers. So if one believes, one merely accepts life as given, hopefully with appreciation. We ponder the wisdom in what we do not understand, but without fear, for God knows what is best.

So let me get this straight, we will not give up trapping just because things are really creepy here. We do not believe in the Devil; we do not believe in omens. And if God does not like it, He can stuff it.

"Well," I grin, "I do not see lightning bolts striking us dead, do you?"

There is so much going on, so much is new, different, strange, overwhelming, that it is natural to wonder about 'God,' about religious beliefs, about where to get strength, where to turn. The subject of 'God' becomes a common topic to ponder as I think aloud, with no one to talk to. Talking to my conscience, talking to God, seems natural.

On the way home, I come across fresh marten tracks, made since I was here this morning. I try to understand the animal, try to 'be the animal.'

Here is where the marten first sees our trail. See how he paused there a few feet off the trail?

"Yea, and he waits and thinks a little about what to do. Probably knows it's a fresh trail, nose in the air, sniffing, and cautious. Here he takes a few more steps forward, slow, see by the tracks?"

"Then the marten gets bold when he knows we are gone. He comes to the trail, turns around a few times, looking first up the trail, then down the trail."

Uh-huh, then decides to mark the trail with urine, right in the middle. What would that mean?

"Well, he is not afraid, must have decided to let us know who owns these woods, makes sure we would see it."

Then does not run off but slowly walks off. Must be feeling pretty proud of himself.

"Most important to us, it means he will be back to see what we thought of his message!"

Shall we answer him with a trap?

"Wait, after I'm done pissing on his mark. Do you think he'll be impressed? Look how much higher I can pee up the tree than he can! I myself am impressed!" We follow a ways and realize there is a set up ahead.

Think he went for the set? Want to place a bet?

I have to think about the tracks and 'be the animal.' "My guess is that he will go for the set. He does not like these strange tracks, does not know what they are, is shy and nervous, but bold too, and wants answers, wants to be cocky, wants to show us who is boss. My guess is he will go right to the trap and take the bait, just out of orneriness, Just to mess with us."

"Yea? Well, the proof is in the pudding. We shall see what he did."

Sure as heck, when the marten gets to the set, he walks right to it, no hesitation, right up the pole for the bait, just as I guessed. He is still here, very much alive, all beady-eyed and growling. I stop to study him. I even smile and talk to him.

"So. You thought you were king of the forest, did you? Well, I do not blame you. It is a very nice forest." I stroke my beard and look all-around at the wonderful world we both claim. In answer, the marten growls deeper and makes a lunge for me, but I am not in the least surprised or concerned. I know the length of the chain and have stopped short of it. I only smile.

"Your fur might buy me some beans and rice. I really appreciate your giving yourself to me." I am just resting up here, just rambling to another creature, since I do not get to talk much. Am I a little reluctant to kill him? Well, not that so much. Maybe just wondering about the best method, from a technical standpoint, so there is the least amount of blood, and the least chance of getting bit, and the most efficient, and least waste of time. My mind wanders as I watch the marten growling at me. 'Marten' and my name, 'Martin.' Is this significant? What would a shrink say? There is a 'flashback memory.' A conversation with my father—Knock out nifty of the past.

Past Flash. "Son, why do you want to hunt and kill these animals and know about guns? Why not hunt with a camera?" Dad speaks to me in the same voice my conscience does. I am absolutely and totally disgusted and in shock. My father had once wanted to single-handedly sail around the world. In preparation, he and I had sailed from England with just a compass and sextant 'for practice.'

No one talks back to my Dad, but I thought, "Dad, maybe you should get a toy boat and play with it in the bathtub! All these books you read about ocean survivors and explorers are about people who ate sea turtles, seagulls, and polar bear fur to stay alive when they had to!" But no—he thought you could be picky about what you eat and never have to defend yourself. Dad and his wife do not believe in hunting, in guns, in trapping, and will not wear fur. I do not even want to consider what people like this are called. I try to understand, but this is just too much. How can there be so little understanding! I would think someone who wanted to sail around the world would understand about the challenge, about adventure. About seeing what you are made of. The feel of muscles bulging, about being a warrior, and proving your manhood. About life and death. **Past Flash ends.**

I shake my head to clear these thoughts. The marten faces me defiantly. I smile and talk to him. In the middle of rambling with a soothing voice, my hand flashes out and grabs him before he realizes I have moved.

"Faked you out, huh?" I say kindly. As my fingers find his heart and I give a hard squeeze that stops it, I keep rambling. "Yes, life can be such a bitch, can't it? One minute you are walking along without a care in the world, king of the world, and then all of a sudden you are in hot soup." This is the last message this creature will ever know, as his lights go out, with my smiling face dimming forever in his mind. This is something I ponder over and over, the workings of nature, the why, the how, the when. Those that live, those that do not, wondering if there is any point to it all.

These thoughts come with a laugh, not sadness or concern because I cannot let it get to me.

God—"A nice big fat male I see, are you pleased? You look a little glum, peaked around the gills." I smile. God always wants to check me out, test me.

"No, I'm fine. Yes, a nice fat male." I pick him up higher, turn the marten around to look at it. The first marten I had caught had been small, and the fur had been frozen wet. It had not been a good example of what to expect. I decide marten are such pretty animals, such silky soft fuzzy fur. They are like a little cat, maybe skinnier, smaller in the face. The fur is reddish-brown. There is a white underneath, often a bright orange spot at the throat. The back is darkest, a slow color change toward the belly. Little furry feet with claws for climbing, just like cat feet. A very big one might stretch two feet to the base of the tail and weigh a couple of pounds.

A marten hide dried- ready to be sold. The most important fur to catch for an Alaska trapper.

God— Does all the blood and death bother you?" I know God is just testing me again and wants to know if I feel guilty and will give up. I believe God wants to know how much effort to put into me. If I do not have what it takes, God will not bother with me, as it would be of little use. God gave us freedom of choice, so he wants to know what I choose.

I reply, "I can handle the blood. I know that Life feeds on life. I know some things have to die so that other things can live. Even plants kill each other in the fight for light. I'm not about to freak out on you, don't worry." God looks at me close to make sure. I think God is pleased by what He sees. After all, would God choose to visit me if God did not like me? I have every intention of doing what it takes to live this life and have God proud of me. Sometimes we have to do things for reasons that are outside ourselves in order to be healthy.

Out on snowshoes, the same trail, a hundred times run now, just routine, mind spinning in neutral, I'm eating up the hours. The constant sound of squeaking snowshoes and wind is all I ever hear. My head needs scratching. I had caught my hair on fire again. I sigh. I'm full of excitement, though. The thrill never really leaves, of fur waiting in traps, bait stolen, tracks in the snow, stories to read.

I'm out on the river trail, and the trail feels 'funny' underneath me like I'm walking in a big slurpy of wet ice cream. But of course, this is not possible since there is three feet of ice, and the temperature is well below freezing, like thirty below zero.

So many strange things going on out here.

I keep on snowshoeing, must be getting tired, having a hallucination or something. The further I walk, the more I feel like I am sinking. The truth of what I have been taught is greater than the truth of reality. It is impossible for water to exist at thirty below zero, and since it is not possible, then it cannot be. If it cannot be, well, obviously, I'm not feeling it, and this is not happening[2]. Finally, I cannot ignore the feeling and have to look down to see what in the heck is wrong with the trail. There is water boiling up around my snowshoes!

This is impossible!

I try to go ahead, but I am stuck. I try to reach my snowshoes to get them off so I can walk, but I cannot reach the binding underwater. When I pick one snowshoe up, the water and slush immediately freeze. I put that foot down and try to lift the other. That one freezes, too. Now I have two ice balls for feet! My hatchet is pulled from my belt. I try to bust the ice off one snowshoe while balancing on the other foot. It takes too long, and I almost fall headfirst into the water. I try to knock the ice off underwater, but the hatchet is now coated in an ice ball. There is no way to get the ice off the hatchet.

What was that you were saying the other day about thinking you are the king of the world, and all of a sudden, you are in a world of doo-doo?

Suddenly I have an image of myself frozen into a block, out here on the ice, and when the ice floats downriver in spring, having everyone in the next village seeing me as a statue, majestically floating by.

Some Native would comment, "Some dumb-greenhorn trapper got hisself in a bind, huh? Better call in somebody, I guess. These white pilgrims sure are entertaining, aren't they?"

My feet are getting wet now, getting cold as I stand here thinking, going over all my options, wondering what to do. I cannot feel my feet now. I cannot move my feet now. They are blocks of ice now. My only means of getting the ice off is my hatchet, which is a popsicle now. What can I bang my hatchet on? I try to bang it on my side, but no use. I can get the tip of a snowshoe up enough to expose it, to bang the hatchet on it. This gets some ice off the hatchet, but not fast enough to help, and even then, I had tried earlier to get the ice off and think now that this will not work. There is no way to get the snowshoes off underwater or under all this slush that I cannot see into.

This is crazy! Surely there is something we can do!

I think the water is deeper ahead of us than behind us, and anyway, ahead of us is the unknown, behind us, we know what we are dealing with, so no matter what we do, I think the wise thing is to go backwards.

How can we go backwards?

Looking around, there is only snow, with nothing sticking up. The river is a mile wide here. Nothing but white, as far as we can see in every direction. There is no change in the landscape. I see no ledge of ice, no hummock to grab on to. There is nothing to snag a rope on, no way to pull us back up, just nothing. No James Bond type gizmo tool to help us.

What if we just fell backward, use our weight going back to lift our feet up, roll over, and crawl?

"Yea, but if the feet do not come up, we might break our legs instead. We might not reach dry snow, but end up face down in the water! Instead of just our feet being wet, we could get our whole body wet! What if we got our whole body wet and still could not move? Well, we'd have a very short time to move out of the water. The temperature is thirty below zero. We have miles to go to get to the cabin. There is very little to burn nearby to have a fire to keep warm. It would be risky."

But surely we cannot just stand here as our feet freeze.

With a mighty heave, I throw myself backward. My feet come up out of the slush, but not fast enough for me to turn around and land face-first. My hands out behind me hit first, go into the water, but not very deep, and instantly my hands come up, as I roll over and stretch myself lengthwise out on the snow to distribute my weight on its thin crust. We do not break through, so I am able to crawl back up the trail we were just on. It does not take so long to go ten feet or so. This is far enough to be on a firmer trail crust. Once there, I roll in the deep fluffy snow just off the trail to let the moisture on my clothes get soaked up in the snow, using the snow like a sponge. I had read once this is a good thing to do if you're wet in cold country. My mittens do not seem wet now. The snow has taken the moisture away and instantly frozen it all before the water soaks in.

I can now bang my hatchet on the trail enough to get some ice off it. The snowshoes can barely be moved, and I cannot stand up because of the three-foot diameter snowballs under my feet. I use the frozen snowballs to get the ice off the hatchet until I expose the wood of the right snowshoe. It is good to get the hatchet free of ice. Now I can use the hatchet freely to knock the snowball apart. Once I can get at the bindings, I get the snowshoes off and in front of me so I can more seriously hammer at the ice.

SHOULD WE BUILD A FIRE? Or should we just try to get back to the cabin?

I consider this question. To build a fire would take an hour. I am uncertain that even an open fire at thirty below would warm us enough to ever feel comfortable, or to where we were gaining strength, not losing even more. I consider the strength it takes to walk to where there is wood while breaking trail all the way. There is the time needed to find birch bark to get a fire burning. The dark is coming fast. We are not so cold, not so wet. My feet are cold, but not frostbit yet. All the survival books, of course, say to build a fire. 'Build a fire,' as if this is the only answer, and surely one will be safe if one only builds a fire. I have built fires and not been impressed. I feel more tired after getting a fire going than if I just walked! When I stand around a fire, I get colder than if I just walk! (At colder temperatures anyway).

The work of hammering on the snowshoes has warmed us up. My hands are warm, mittens not wet, just a little ice crusty on the outside. The snowshoes are a little heavy, so going will be awkward, but if I pace myself, I think this will be the best choice, to just press on, stay warm by snowshoeing, and not spend hours with a fire and trying to dry out, and then having to be out in the weather even more hours before we get home. There is no food with us.

No, let's press on. I vote we press on.

So we press on home. It is a long, cold, hard trip back to the cabin. I cannot feel my feet or my fingers by the time we get in the door. I fall in front of the stove and cannot get up. I just roll next to the fire that is going out and hope I feel some warmth from it and get enough rest before the cabin freezes us. Who knows what would have happened if we made the other choice, to stay out and try to get a fire going. I think it was the right decision to head for the cabin. I think any mistake here could have cost me my life.

One of the first wolves I caught got away but had been in a trap and left toes behind. Over the weeks, I noticed the 'three toe' marks in the trail so I could identify a particular wolf now. In my diary, I start calling him 'Three toes.'

Diary:
Three toes at it again, turns over one of my traps, and pees on it. Maybe next time, I'll try boiling and waxing traps, covering them with wax paper as I have read about. Three toes now taking game from my traps. Seems to run alone.

The boil and wax paper thing does not work, but I am always optimistic that 'tomorrow,' the latest plan shall work! For reasons I do not understand, the weather warms up. (There is no sun, and it is not the time of year to expect warm air to move in from anyplace). The warmth is not for very long, but it is a break in the frigid cold and allows me to change my routine a little. There is less time spent cutting firewood. I have been happier not using the chainsaw, and all the firewood is cut with a bow-saw. There is a hillside full of dead wood right behind me, so I never have to go more than a hundred feet for wood, and coming downhill with the load is not hard. The sawhorse I use to cut the logs into stove length was lashed together with some of the leather I tanned. Mostly I burn poplar wood, which is not as good as spruce for Btu's, but burns fast and hot and is easiest for me to get. Books rarely say 'Burn what you can to stay alive!' but say 'Select birch, and age it, by cutting the year before, preferably on a south-facing slope.' Reading this becomes funny. It is not as funny when people die trying to follow the instructions.

Future flash
It's 2013.
"Speaking of following instructions, Miles, I had two guys drive into the river in the past week. Come to think of it, four people drove across the airport runway this season so far. We had to finally put up a roadblock and a sign. One driver drove through the gate in his quest to follow the instructions on the GPS."

"Yes, these GPS devices are nice for navigation when they work. Now complete idiots are capable of getting places they do not belong and get themselves in trouble because the equipment fails, and these people do not know any other way to navigate."

"Well, apparently directions to get someplace were put in a computer wrong. So the wrong instructions are given to get there. Instructions like 'Keep driving straight till you see,' and people blindly do what the instructions tell them and drive right into the river or across the airport runway. What are they thinking, Miles??"

"I do understand why. How often do we hear, "You can't do that!" Instructions, rules say you cannot. How often do I stop people in their thoughts and ask, "Can not? Of course, I can. Here watch me!" I pause at the confusion on their face and say, "Don't you mean, not suggested?" Are these instructions set in concrete that one must die before disobeying? Even if the instruction is 'obviously' wrong? Certainly, you can go through a red light. It's just not usually a good idea. Or there may be a consequence you do not like. But there is, in fact, a choice. So what I see going on is people becoming conditioned to believe there is no choice. The law is the law; the rule is all there is. Instructions are written for a reason and must be followed at all costs. Death is preferable to disobeying the order."

"I hear ya, Miles. I get your drift. People are not taught to think, to reason, to make decisions on their own. We are taught to obey. Yet from what I see, it is common for the rule to originate from one person or an entity with a hidden agenda that has little to do with the public's welfare beyond fleecing us. So I guess you are right. I mean, a driver is reading a computerized map and believes it. Believes it to the extent it is more real than what is seen outside the windshield. There can't be a river there because it is not on the GPS map. Following the instructions and the computer map is more real and more likely to be correct than what is seen through the windshield. Who am I to have an opinion, how can the GPS be wrong, and me, right?"

"I wonder as well if there is no world of nature for many modern people. Just the world of the computer screen. In my view, it is a beginning place to ask what reality is? Or truth. Or fact. One and one is not always two. Possibly reality and truth are relative agreed-upon terms. Other facts can be just as valid if believed and agreed upon."

"Now you are getting a little weird on me, Miles!"

"Well. Whatever works, right?" When we are alone, the world can become a very different place when we become free to think.

Future flash ends

The stove is burning out of control again, so I have the door open and am sitting just inside with tea in hand, taking a break, looking up at the stars and dim northern lights. I can see the whole Milky Way and try to pick out constellations.

Isn't that Orion? The red star, the one in his belt?

I'm not so sure, though.

Hey, I'm getting cold. Let's shut the door some."

"I shut it last time. It's your turn!" One of us shuts the door a little, and we sit and watch through the crack in the door. We have no window that works, so being able to see out is a novelty.

Isn't that the sound of a moose walking I hear?

I listen and think it must be a moose, slowly walking.

Quick, get the gun!

I rush to the nail the 357 pistol hangs from and get back to my stump chair. We sit very still because it sounds like he is coming up the path right to the cabin. I think if I am still enough, maybe the moose will not know we are here, and I can get a shot at him. No. We do not want to talk about the moose last summer that should have fed us for a whole year.

For some reason, I can no longer see the stars or northern lights. There must be a cloud in the way, but this seems strange and such bad luck. I was in hopes the background of stars would give me something to silhouette the moose against for a shot up close.

The sound of the moose walking has changed. I think he smells us or sees us now. I hear heavy breathing and sense he is right nearby, but straining eyes cannot see anything. I hold the pistol up in front of me, not moving. My arm is getting sore, but all I hear is his heavy breathing. Finally, I hear the walking start again, and the sound goes on by the cabin. I see the stars again.

In the morning, I want to know where the moose was, so look for tracks. The tracks stop right in front of the door. The moose had been five feet away. The reason I could not see the stars, I conclude, is that he was blocking the whole doorway. If I had closed my eyes and just pointed and shot anywhere out the door, I would have got him! I did not really need a moose that badly anyway. I already got one but had handled the meat poorly, full of maggots and rock hard. There is plenty of bear in the same condition, and if the shot on this moose had been easy, it would have been nice to have fresh, good quality meat that would stay fresh and frozen all winter. We eat dried maggots and sand with our meat. But, "Oh well!"

Not long after, I look out the door with my tea in hand and see a moose on whip cream snow. I hadn't seen it at first. Fresh snow is falling gently. The flakes are exceptionally large, maybe dime size, and sticking to the trees, making everything so pretty, sparkly, and white. The beauty of this postcard picture would be spoiled by my footprints, and I just wish to enjoy the undisturbed scene for a moment before I step out into it to gather morning snow to melt. The light will only last an hour or so anyway. My eyes stop at the outline of a moose that I hadn't seen before. He is standing up, sound asleep on his feet! Snow has been falling on his back and is several inches deep.

I wish we had a camera now, wouldn't this make a great postcard picture? Indeed it would. Plenty of time to focus and get the right shot as he stands there asleep. I briefly think back to my nice camera, among the things I lost when the kayak went over. But no, I forgot, the camera had been stolen.

I take another look at the moose every half hour or so. I think of shooting him. *Should we?* How badly do we need the meat? Wouldn't it be great to throw out all this maggoty meat?" No. We will not kill the moose. We decided we killed a moose already. We should not waste the meat, even though we messed it up. Most people would not feed what we are eating to their dogs, and indeed, most dogs would turn up their noses at it. I did get the rifle out, though, the twenty-two magnum. The shot would be under 100 yards. I sighted in on him just to see how hard the shot would be…

The temptation is too great to turn down. I want to try the shot.

You're drooling!

"Ya, well, I'm hungry! Couldn't you go for some fresh steak about now?" Maybe, but wouldn't it be better to just wake him up? Wouldn't it be fun to see his expression? If you like, put one right over his head, so he could feel the wind and know how close it was! I bet some wolf has been chasing him all night, and he's exhausted, and that is why he is asleep on his feet. This isn't normal, is it? We shouldn't kill him. We already killed a moose for this year, and if we are too stupid to figure out how to take care of it, we do not deserve another moose.

I haven't decided what to do yet, as I sight in and just see if I can even make the shot. A well placed twenty-two right in the temple. I bet he'd drop like a rock and never even wake up. In the shooters Zen trance, I savor the moment when the hunter, the gun, the trajectory, the target are 'one,' and nothing else exists in the world. I slowly take up the slack in the trigger. The twenty-two goes off, 'pop!'

The moose drops like a rock. I laugh. It is so funny.

Did you see that?

"He didn't know what happened!".

I had opted to just wake him up. The bullet just missed him, and he woke up so startled he fell down.

He's looking around, doesn't know what he heard, isn't sure what he felt, never been shot at before, doesn't know about guns, never saw a human before. You can read it on his face, looking around scowling. Doesn't know if he should run or fight.

I step out the door, so he can see me. I laugh; raise my rifle over my head.

"Greetings, and good morning, Moose!" I shout. (Only in my head, I didn't really shout).

Yes! Greetings from the human race! The most vicious, deadly animal to ever inhabit the planet!

The moose snorts, turns, and runs through the brush.

From the frying pan, into the fire, first the wolves, now us! Do you think he learned any lesson?

"I don't know, but I'd guess next time he smells a cabin, smoke, hears a gun, or sees a human, he will run for his life!"

As well he should if he hopes to live to be a ripe old age!

"Well, let's start our day; it looks like good weather." Out in the wood lot are the tracks of Three Toes. Maybe this is why the moose was asleep on his feet. It is interesting that the wolf would come so close to the cabin, within 50 feet. I rather enjoy seeing his tracks, even though I also wouldn't mind catching him. The dry wood is getting thin. I have to burn more of the green wood. The stove does not like green wood. Loading the stove becomes an art. I have to know if the outdoor temperature is likely to go either up or down. Then I have to judge the liveliness of the coals, to know if they will take green wood or just how much dry to put on. If I put green wood on coals that cannot take it, the whole fire goes out. If this happens, I have to unload the stove and start a new fire from scratch, which might take an hour. If I put too much dry wood on, I cook myself out of the cabin and then need more wood in only a couple of hours. I end up getting so frustrated with the stove it becomes an item in the diary and subject of poetry.

Master of the Stove Dec.
I just had to feed
my stove some more wood.
I have to do this,
as otherwise
I get this curse.
My cabin gets cold,
unless it's contented.
The degree of cold
is related
to how well-fed
my stove is, I've found.
How hungry the stove is,
is related, it seems,

to attention it gets.
Like if I leave;
when I get back, I have
to stuff my stove.
Even before I eat.
I have to feed 'it'!
I even tried
a strangle hold.
I cut off the air,
to try and smother.
It hissed and smoked.
And bit my hand.
We used to get along,
with it heating,
and doing the cooking,
while I was out trapping.
About mid-winter,
it quit doing its share.
At first it got picky
about wood quality.
My stove would feel fine,
with poplar or pine.
But now it's a bitch,
and will only eat birch!
It often conks out,
halfway through the night.
I devote about half
my time to that stove,
and it still won't behave!
The draft-hole eyes
just fix their stares,
which always say,
"I'm ready for logs!"
If I ignore this
the metal pings
and the temperature drops.
My hungry stove
must be alive.
I have decided
I will be devoted

to having it mastered.
"My stove will be conquered!"

If there is any change in the environment, the stove situation changes. The wood type, temperature, time I get up or go to bed all affect how to load the stove. It is amazing how much the stove runs my life. Surely, this was never covered in 'Walt Disney.' It was never covered in any mountain man book I ever read. I consider that all these sources are 'full of doo-doo.' I question that anyone could have written any of the mountain man books I read, saying what they do if the writer's life had ever depended on the woodstove or campfire. Who shall I ever believe? The story 'Waking up the Moose' become a poem.

Our whole life is a poem!

> Thinking of Robert Service and his Alaska poems—
> I had been there sitting,
> with my coffee drinking.
> I was sitting on
> the favorite log of mine
> inside the cabin...

The poem goes on for five pages telling the story. Except. I do not drink coffee; I drink 'tea,' but 'coffee,' sounded better in a poem. I wrote poems about 'Three Toes' and poems about the weather, trapping, my clothes, and food. In fact, my original idea is to write a book, all in poetry! I am inspired by "Hiawatha" by Longfellow. It is one of the few books I brought along to read. I have read it 100 times and have it memorized. Only mine would be 500 pages. This has a lot to do with storing all my feelings and events through poetry, for my 'someday best seller poetry book.'

Hey, what we can't do in class and quality, we can make up for in volume! Right!
☺ :)

WITH THE MIDWINTER DARKNESS, I seem to get out trapping less, and I am inside dealing with the stupid stove, the mice, the question of what time it is *as in 'what month.'* Three Toes comes around and laughs at me, howling. Everything seems to be going wrong, or slowly, or like I can't get ahead. There is leather still in its tanning solutions. I have no sense of time to know how long I have left it in its solution. Instructions must be useless anyway because the solution is cold, and the times suggested in books have to do with normal temperatures, with no adjustments for, "If you're in a freezing cabin while you're doing this, try doubling the time." There are no such suggestions. Likewise, no cookbook gives suggestions like, "If you are in a remote cabin melting snow for water, maybe you can forget the 'rinse many times' part, just eat it, it will taste fine!" No instructions say, "And if you can't see it because of your weak Gee-Whiz light, try feeling it." The table of contents of instruction books never says, "In the back, you will find the 'feely-touchy' instructions."

"Feely touchy?" The squaw chimes in seductively. I glower at her.

This 'time' thing seems pretty important because I want to know how much longer winter is, so I can ration things, and somehow it keeps people 'sane,' knowing the time.

"People who do not know what day it is 'lose it' really fast." Wits of wisdom from the squaw.

Comments from the peanut gallery.

My conscience chimes in. We are all staring in the sky, trying to find the moon, trying to remember about the moon.

Moon means 'month,' right? Didn't I learn that somewhere, like in school? Were you paying attention that day?

"Who me? I was trying to get you to listen; you were busy throwing spitballs at the girl two rows over."

"It didn't seem relevant at the time. Anyway, I'm pretty sure 'month' comes from 'Moon,' and there are pictures on some calendars that show the moon phases. But I do not think the moon is full, exactly the first of every month." "Another thing too, is like, the moon has phases, like a 'quarter' moon, but does it quarter to the right, or the left, and will a 'last quarter' be different than a 'first quarter'?" This would be really helpful to know if I am at the end of a month, or the beginning of a month, when I see a moon phase. I seldom see the moon twice in a week, so I do not know if it is getting bigger or smaller. We go through this every couple of weeks, this same conversation, has varying opinions.

Squaw says, "When we cannot see the moon, is it still phasing?"

Does a tree that falls in the forest that no one knows about still make a noise?

"Like if the moon is below the horizon, or comes out in the day instead of at night, does it faithfully phase? Can we assume it can be counted on like clockwork, like the sun?"

The Squaw has a good point. Surely, I am puzzled. Does the moonrise and set like the sun, at the same time every day? Can we predict where to find it in the sky each day, so we know where to even look? Do we know how many days in a row it is below the horizon? Is it weeks? Days? Only hours?

"Well, the moon circles earth, right? And the earth circles the sun, right? The chances of the moon showing itself on the same schedule as the sun then seems remote since they do not both circle us, nor we circle them. We have to concentrate and imagine the moon circling the earth, the earth circling the sun, and the relationship between all three." While they are deep in concentration, I look over at the squaw in the starlight. She is not what you'd call 'pretty,' but she would make someone a good wife, maybe. She is kind, honest, devoted, and easy to get along with. She has no temper, easy-going, laughs easily, is not bullheaded, and has no bad personality traits. She is...oh...'primitive' looking, a Mongolian look. Dark complexion, round face, with slightly slanted smiling eyes. Her hair is jet black, long, dirty. Her clothes are plain but neat, 'peasant' looking. Her hands show a woman who works a lot. She isn't someone to look at with 'lust,' but someone who is easy to love because of the wonderful personality. In the starlight, I want to hold her hand, give her a loving hug.

She is explaining the moon. "Wait, we are looking at the wrong things here. It doesn't matter, the earth going around the sun. What matters is the distance of the earth to the sun, and the distance of the earth to the moon, and as the earth spins, the sun is further away, so moves slower, as we look at it from one point on earth."

We all try to picture what the squaw describes as we search the horizon for the moon.

Ok, if the sun is a big ball, and I have it on a string, and I have it spinning around me..."

The squaw and my conscience are trying to picture this as she goes on. "Then I have a smaller ball that is the moon, closer in, tied to another string, spinning it around me faster. How would all this look if you were a flea on my head?" We all laugh. This sounds like the punch line of a joke. We can all picture an experiment, a scene in a movie, some idiot in the wilderness trying to figure out how to tell time, out alone by himself, spinning in circles with string and balls at different speeds, pretending he is the earth, the balls are the sun and moon, and he is talking about it to people who are not there. Any observer would surely think he is 'mad.'

So once again, we forget about it. We cannot find the moon, do not know the time or month. I am not about to make an idiot of myself spinning around with balls and twine, asking the squaw what this would look like if you were a flea! At the mention of 'fleas,' we all go stiff, shudder, and start to scratch. We have picked up fleas from the furs.

Walt Disney never talked about fleas. You ever notice that? We are developing quite an attitude about 'Walt Disney.' "Who would ever think fleas were worth consideration? Do you suppose Jim Bridger had fleas and worried about them? Do you suppose Kit Carson ever asked his squaw? "By the way, did you remember the flea powder? No? Holy bee-Jesus woman, we gotter turn back!" What did the Indians do? What do animals do?" As we scratch ourselves, we do not care what anyone else does. This is not 'fun.'

"Thirty Below and Dropping! That's one, in particular, I yell loud and clear…" We are out on the trapline again, singing our favorite song.

If I could sing louder, I'd raise temperature!

My pal sings the harmony. We both laugh. Suddenly I stop in the trail. I slowly tilt my hat to one side and smile. We have done this many times, and so I need say nothing. We snowshoe a little bit, stop again, and I tilt my hat the other way and smile again.

Do you think the fleas are tired yet?

"No, let's make them run some more!" I tilt my fur hat the other way. We picture the fleas, all warm and snugly on my head, under the warm hat. The hat tilts. This side of my head starts to get cold. It is a long trip for a flea to the other side of my head. They may even have to pack a lunch. They start the long trek across my head to the warm side. About the time they get to the warm side and are about to sit down for lunch, I tilt my hat again. Pant, pant, pant, we keep the fleas marching all day long back and forth across my head. There is a perverse pleasure in giving them a workout.

My hat comes off. I throw it on the ground and stomp on it.

"I can't stand it, those stupid fleas! I will get rid of them once and for all!" My conscience is flabbergasted and a little afraid. We can't survive unless we keep our act together.

Look! Look at this news clipping from the future! I look over as my conscience reads, *'Mad Trapper Killed by Fleas. Last Entry in Diary Reads, 'Damn Fleas.'* There is a picture of myself to go with the article, really gruesome.

"Ok, OK, I get your point!" I sigh. When we get home, I have a bright idea.

A bucket of kerosene is gotten out. The cabin is slightly warmer, so I think I can survive taking my shirt off. *I bet the fleas hate kerosene. It's poison. (Haha)* . This will teach them a thing or two, show them who is boss, who runs my world! The squaw, of course, thinks it's a great idea. She is really into cleanliness. This is a woman's job to keep men on the right track.

"Without women, men would be complete bums!" she says as she gets the kerosene ready, and we all look forward to the screams of dying fleas.

"Are you ready? One two three!" And on the 'three,' I hold my breath and dunk my head under five gallons of fuel. I remember to keep my eyes closed, thinking 'fuel and eyes' would not like each other. When I come up for air, the squaw is ready with a towel. I sop up the main fuel running down my body but leave my hair wet so it will kill the fleas. It does not take long for my head to feel the effects of the fuel and start to feel like it is on fire. But I hate the fleas more than the pain and manfully bear it. The time comes when I have to rinse the kerosene out.

"Your hair is falling out, dear!" She is rubbing my head in the rinse water. Hair is falling out. To get the fuel out of my head, someone gets the bright idea to use tide to cut the oil.

"It works on clothes!"

It sure cuts the grease on hides good too! Great idea!

We laugh at what a scene this would make in a movie or skit for a commercial of some kind. God runs the camera so the rest of us can be in it.

"Camera! Lights! Action!" It is time to pour the tide and scrub. As I scream and yell and cuss, God thinks it's funny as heck as he rolls the camera. "Great acting, Miles!"

"I'm not acting, you idiot!"

God says the equivalent of "Rats" followed by, "Oh gee, I'm sorry, there wasn't enough light. Can we open the door and do that scene again?"

The sun can be seen now, so I know time is passing. I take a special trip sometimes to go up the hill so I can watch the sun for a while. There is no heat to it yet, but there is a sense of 'winter's back being broken.' Psychologically, I know I have gone through the worse half of winter, and the big colds should be shorter in duration. I can spend more time on the trapline. Three toes is still living off my bait, following my trails, and getting harder and harder to catch as he learns each new trick I try. He learns my behavior faster than I learn his, so who is smarter? Even so, and 'What-ever!' I am learning about 'wolves.'

I am able to sew up the holes in my clothes now that I can see and am able to keep my equipment in better shape. One special day comes along after a batch of cloudy days. A day when the sun seemed to be especially bright. I write a poem about it that rambles on for many pages.

The Day the Sun Rose, February or so, maybe off a month or two.
You have to be without it
to really catch my thought,
of winter's back broke by light.
A few words can't describe that.
For the first time in three months
I could actually see my face.
I mean I jumped outdoors,
with mirror in my hands.
What I saw I couldn't recognize.
A beard many inches longer,
and more to the length of my hair;
all black from the soot that was there,

and the eyes with the yellow stare.
Lack of light made my skin whiter.
My clothes were stiff rags,
and actually shined from the grease,
yet it is the look of my face
with yellow eyes I remember best.
I didn't just like that light;
it's more that I needed it,
and for the first time I blinked,
and yawned, stretched my arms out---
Hibernation's over!

For the first time, I can see more than in black and white. I can see colors! For the first time in several months, I can take my clothes off without worrying about freezing to death.

Squaw, "Isn't it nice to get clean?" I'm not about to go so far as to claim soap, and I have any friendship, but I am willing to go so far as to admit that even a mad trapper has limits.

I feel ten pounds lighter!

"Well, it is not just an expression this time. I bet it is the truth. You are ten pounds lighter! Ha-ha!"

Very funny yourself.

"Yea, no comments from the peanut gallery." We were all glad to get clean.

Trapping gets good again. Fur wants to move around in the new light and warmth. Maybe fur was looking around for new areas, or so it seemed. For some animals, this time of year is the time to start thinking about finding a mate, getting restless, wanting to move, check out the damsels in the next valley. Every day I have something in the traps. Life feels grand.

Today is a nice, warm, sunny, calm day. I am feeling strong and have my rifle with me in case I see game. Maybe I will see a grouse or a rabbit. Now and then, I see small game and have a variety of fare on the table. About anything is better than the maggoty old bear and last year's moose. I expect fur in the traps, as usual, and have an early start. I see moose tracks, but I've seen them sometimes on and off all winter. These look 'fresh,' though, and I have my rifle and feel good. The tracks beckon to me, and it is too hard to resist.

Let's follow them and see if they lead us to fresh moose meat!

I pause to scratch my balding still flea-infested head while I decide on this.

We turn and go off my trail to follow the moose trail. Who knows? Maybe they will lead to some new country I haven't seen yet, or to food on the table. I just want to do something different, I think. In the earlier darkness, I had been so worried about getting lost. The travel by feel of the trail was not a situation for exploring. Now that I can 'see,' I can leave my trail.

Woof woof!

"Yes, if I was a dog, I'd wag my tail." Like two puppies, we bound off after fresh tracks. The squaw never comes with us. She always stays in the cabin. My conscience is always with me and knows everything, but the squaw seems separate from us, and we can keep secrets. She does not know what is going on unless we tell her.

It does not take long before we hear rustling in the alders ahead. We both stop and grin.

The moose knows we follow today, and he is not so far away ahead of us!

We come to a clearing, not very big, maybe half an acre of grass. Across the clearing in the alders on the other side is the moose staring at us, about to run. Up comes the rifle, and I get a shot off. The moose turns to run. In a hurry, I try to chamber another round in this lever-action rifle with a tube magazine. Something goes wrong, and the next bullet jams. Something else in the rifle goes wrong, but I do not know what. My attention is on the moose getting away. I cannot get off another shot.

This is disgusting! We have only fired a few shots through this all year, it is brand new, and this is the one time we really need and depend on it, and it lets us down? What a piece of crap! I demand a refund! I'm putting Mr. Remington on my crap list!

I do not even bother to answer; my mind is trying to figure out the moose up ahead. The moose veers off in the direction of the cabin.

Let's follow. Maybe he is wounded, and we can stop at the cabin to pick up the pistol, maybe pick up a blood trail, let the moose stop to rest, and go into shock.

"Sounds like a plan to me!"

We work our way back to the trapline trail and backtrack to the cabin as fast as we can. The squaw wants to know what is going on, but this is man stuff, and we do not have time to explain.

"Where's my pistol!? After a moose, need the pistol!" Without a word, she hands me my pistol. On the way out, we forget to grab extra ammo, but time is most important. Six shots should be enough. The broken rifle is left behind.

Bye. We dash out the door with no further ado. The Squaw can hear all about it when it's over!

Fresh tracks on the pond! Over here! I come dashing over. Sometimes my conscience can leave my body in times of emergency, help out, and do separate chores than I do, not 'work' but gather information. Sure enough, fresh tracks, but no blood.

Is it even the same moose?

After looking at the tracks, we agree it is.

Right by the cabin too! If that rifle had worked, we could have got him right here on the pond by the cabin, now look!

We are not even sure it is worth going after this moose. We see no blood, he knows we are after him, and he has such a head start.

Oh well, why not? We haven't got anything better to do today. It's too late now to go out to the trapline.

This is true, and maybe we will get lucky, and anyhow, maybe we will learn something about 'moose,' how far they travel when pressed, how strong they are, what their tactics are, and such. These kinds of questions about animals have intrigued me all my life.

We start on the trail. We do not go far, maybe a quarter-mile, when the moose charges off through the brush ahead of us in a panic. Snow flies, and it is like the rampage of an elephant. I almost have to laugh. Now for sure, he knows he is being dogged. For sure, he will not stop. I almost give up. I notice the day is warm, and I am getting hot. I have to take my coat off. I know the moose must be hot too, *But he can't take his coat off!*

There is a chance that if we keep on him, keep him panicked, never resting, keep his heart going fast, and we ourselves concentrate on keeping cool, make a lot of noise, but not expend energy, maybe we can get lucky and wear him out.

Worth a try.

We agree we will see what happens.

Remember, too, we have snowshoes to stay on top of the snow, and the moose has to plow through, and this will be harder!

With all this in mind, we make a lot of noise and conserve energy. Before long, we come to a spot where the moose leaves a trail of droppings as he runs. This seems encouraging, leading us to believe he is panicked, and this is to our advantage. We do not want him to 'think' and thereby outsmart us.

Notice how he stays away from the brushy country? Stays in the good travel, the more open country?

I notice this and am glad. There is some amazingly thick country around, and if the moose goes into the thickets, we will not be able to follow. We see, too, he is not running a straight line. If he ran in a straight line, over the hill and dale and gone, we wouldn't follow because we would be too far to carry the meat back. The trail winds around in circles.

Did he go your way? This trail looks like we just covered it, looks like a loop-de-loop to me, and off at a new angle here.

Once again, we straighten it out, and it does not take us very long.

Very clever of the moose, isn't it? I can see how the tactic could be effective. The trail and scent is all crisscrossed and all so 'fresh' they all look the same. It would take a wolf more than just seeing and smelling to figure it out. This takes serious thinking and outguessing. The moose sees after a while that we are not slowed up as much as he hoped by this, and his tactic is not buying the time he hoped for. In another panic change of strategy, he decides to head for the river. I can understand how this would be good in the summertime, but not a good choice of places to go in winter. If we were wolves, this would be his fatal error. This tactic of the moose has me believing he is pretty panicked now and not thinking straight. This encourages me. The river would be good for us if we have an open shot, even if it is a long one; we have a chance of a hit.

We speed up our pace, press the moose harder, and catch up to him before he gets to the river. There is a rumble of willows up ahead, and I get the pistol up in time to get a couple of shots off. "Boom! Boom!" I see the bull rear and turn and am sure I have hit him. We run up to the spot, but there is no blood!

Maybe the thick bushes here are deflecting the bullets?

The target seemed so big; it is hard to imagine missing. I've hit grouse further than this! I am discouraged; it had taken a while to catch up to him. Who knows if we will get so lucky again!

Well, he's trying for the river; let's see if we can get him in the open!

This is true; we might have a shot just ahead here, so we cannot give up so soon! It looks too, like the plan of keeping him panicked, us calm and cool, is working, and the deep snow is hard on the moose while we, on snowshoes, are having a better time.

Press on Mac Duff, and Damn to he who calls 'hold'!

Sometimes my conscience comes up with these witty things from books we read to inspire me. I have no idea what my conscience is talking about, but it sounds nice. We are going to give this our best, By Gosh!

We have a trapline trail not far from here that goes straight for the river, and if this is where we are going, we can make faster progress on the trail!

We cut over to the trail and get to the river, and the moose is out there, way ahead of us.

Hurry, get the pistol out. Why isn't it handy! He's getting away! I get off shots, but the distance is over 200 yards, and now I'm out of bullets, well, one left. I don't think I hit him. I saw him hunch over once, but maybe out of fear or the deep snow. It is worth going over to look anyway.

The moose has climbed the bank again, at least on the same side of the river, and by the time I get there, he is long gone. No sign of any blood. The chase has gone on for several hours now. I'm about to call it quits.

He is headed back toward the cabin again, may as well follow, since it's on the way.

Yea, may as well. I hate to give up anyway. There is little enthusiasm, though, but we make noise as we did before, so the moose is always tense and never fully resting. I feel glad we left the coat and hat behind so we could travel cooler. Even so, sweat pours down me. The moose goes through some hills, and this tires me. It is hard to know what effect it has on the moose. The direction is only 'sort of' toward the cabin, but then it seems to me the moose has limits. There seems to be a range, and when he gets close to the outer edge, panic takes over, and he wants to loop back to familiar territory. If this is true, this might be the moose that hangs around certain sections of the trapline I know about, and the trail will help us.

Yes, let's go over to our trail and take a chance; this is where he will go!

We take the trail but do not really save much time or distance. Mr. Moose does not go quite where we expected. We pick up the pace when we get close to the cabin because it looks like he will go by it a second time! Bad luck for us. The tracks go right in front of the door.

How nice it would have been if we could have caught up to him right here! Right on our doorstep, so easy to deal with here!

We both groan. Again. I almost give up right here. It is getting dark now, six hours of fast snowshoeing, and we should call it quits!

Let's just go a little further. He might be at the pond.

Before the sun sets, we have a little time, so we may as well give it our best shot. It will not be so far to come back home if we stay at it for another half hour or so. When we get to the pond, the moose is there! I see him in the distance and speed up. I want to get close enough to use the last bullet. *We can either push him hard enough to charge and then use the last bullet when he's right on us, or we can get as close as we can and shoot!*

Not over a hundred yards from the cabin, in the willows on the pond, the moose decides to make a stand. He turns and stares at us for the showdown. We snowshoe upon him fast. He has a lowered head shaking and wants to fight. We stop only 60 feet or so away, but he is in the thicket, and I cannot get closer. I have to make the shot from here. One bullet left.

Better get in closer! So I get into the thick brush as the bull takes a step toward me to fight. I'm so tired I can barely hold up the pistol. My heart is pounding so hard in my chest; I have to wrap my hands around myself to hold it in. I cringe in pain and can hardly focus my eyes. I have to wait to recover before I can hold the pistol steady enough to shoot. The bull, too, seems tired and ready to just stand and rest rather than fight. I do not want him to rest enough to be able to turn and run again, so I must keep the pressure up, even get him to charge.

Cram the last shot down his throat when he is on top of us!

"If he falls on us, we will surely die. I will shoot when he is about ten feet, step to the side, and let him go by, fatally wounded!"

Finally, I feel recovered enough to do battle. I raise the pistol to shoot and step closer to the bull to see if he will step in for a sure hit in a vital place. The bull shakes his head and steps forward to meet me. When he shakes his head, willows shake snow loose 12 feet over my head. He looks as big as a mountain. The hammer is back, and I am just ready to pull the trigger, with the pistol twenty feet from his heart, when the bull seems to hunch over. I hear a sound like water rushing through a garden hose, in the rhythm of a heartbeat.

"Hush...woosh...hush." I see the fur on his back, vibrating melted snowballs to the beat of that heart. I can make out every hair. I am close enough that if he falls forward, he will fall on me.

"Shh-a shhh." The sound of the blood rushing, the wheezing of a faltered breath. Then I see big brown eyes go back out of focus in his head, twitching to the heartbeat. Like a mountain, he comes down in a ton of hot, snowy flesh. There is a last exhale, long and drawn out, "shhhhhhh," reminding me of the sound of a leaking air hose. There is then a soft wheeze, "fffffffff," followed by gurgling deep within. A far away toilet flushing. Then he shudders, and all is still. I never fired the bullet. The moose died of a heart attack right here in front of me. I have run him down and killed him, on his own terms, by his own rules, on his turf, in the ancient way, of heart, against heart.

Winter Moose kill. I run a moose down on snowshoes until its heart gives out.

CHAPTER FIVE

SPRING ICE BREAK UP, MORE BEARS, EAGLE, WALK OUT

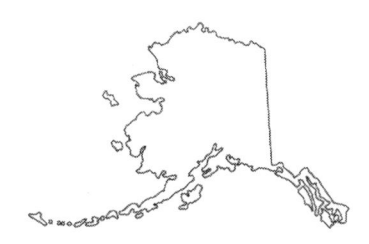

I still do not know what month it is, but I know it is spring. The weather is warm. The sun is out. A real bath can be taken. I can see things on the floor.

Hey! Here's that fork we dropped last October. Now we don't have to eat with the hunting knife! Cool! More holes in the clothes are sewn up, there is optimism and good cheer in the air. Ok, here it is, the part in the survival book that shows how to make birch bark Eskimo sunshades! It says here that we have to be careful of something called 'snow-blindness,' so we better make a pair of these.

I answer my unconscious. "Yea, yea sure. You know how this instruction stuff has been going so far, though. Looks like material written by bozo's that never stepped out the door in their life. People full of imagination and wanting to make a dollar. This snow blind stuff must be about those ski people back east. The ones who go jogging to stay in shape and think they are woodsman because they bought a tent and went on a weenie roast once. People who have pink albino eyes. What do animals do? What did the mountain men do? I doubt it is anything worth discussing, but. Ok, we'll make a pair if you want."

From my Diary:
On My own
Sitting in my cabin
that I built myself;
on a chair of skin
made from moose calf.
My hat, belt, coat knife sheath;

GOING WILD

most of the clothes I have,
were made by my hand.
Caught my own fish.
Shot and jerked a bear.
Put up cranberry mash,
and some caviar.
I dripped my own lye,
rendered my own fat,
made my own soap;
and I wash everything in that.
I tanned up leather
a dozen different ways.
With some I left on hair,
if I thought it looked nice.
Cooking up moose meat,
as I sip my tea;
that keep me nice and warm,
made in two foot lengths,
and yes, I cut a lot of them.
Made myself a knife
from a hunk of steel,
caribou handle, with
a nicely balanced feel.
Get a weather forecast,
by watching four footers.
Getting self-sufficient;
Coming mighty close.

Black powder rife I built and inlaid with my metal scenes.

We make a pair of these glasses with slits in them to let only a little bit of light in.

While we are at it, try to tap the birch tree we got the bark off for sap. It is still too early in the spring, so nothing runs out. Since hibernation is over, there is less sleeping. There is more daylight and longer time periods for me to get things done. With the cabin warmer and all these nice conditions, I get interested in all kinds of projects I couldn't do much about earlier.

Maybe we should write a letter to someone soon?

"Yes, I suppose, but it gets me thinking too much about 'people' and the outside world, and the fact we do not know when any mail will get out. It might be weeks or months yet. It is better to just live in our world here and forget about that other planet, with people on it."

My unconscious has found the pile of maps in a box on the floor in the corner. I look over my shoulder and make a comment.

"Look at some of these places on the map. Here's raspberry Island, and another called 'Eek.' Wolverine Mountain, rivers like Koyukuk, Tanana, and lots of 'moose creeks.'" We have been looking over the maps since we really do not know much about Alaska yet. These are places we will ask questions about from people who might know. This place where I am is nice enough, but we just happened to end up here because of someone else. There might be places we'd like better, who knows? For sure, we want some changes!

Yea! Like mousetraps, and a real light, and more books to read! We both laugh. These are simple enough things to wish for. There is nothing we can't easily get. These few things would make all the difference in the quality of our life. Because of this, it is a lot easier to sit tight and handle the various hardships we have. There is the anticipation of better times ahead. Already we are doing the unexpected! People told me I could not do this, that I would die out here. No one could be dropped off in the wilderness knowing as little as I do, with no arrangements to be picked up or get supplies. No one could build a cabin in time for winter, with so little knowledge, and learn to trap, learn to keep warm, survive with no help from anyone. I would go crazy. I had stubbornly said, "We shall see!" They had told me I was only running away from my problems, being suicidal, and this would be no solution, that I should, instead, face my problems head-on! I refused to let these doubts mess with my mind. This is my home, and my only thoughts are how to get enough money for another season and where exactly I wish to be.

I think we should build another cabin! Maybe in that valley at the end of the trapline, and use this one as a line shack! Since we are familiar with this area, I am inclined to just come back here for now until I learn the basics better. There is plenty of time later to think of another place after asking a lot of questions in town and maybe doing some exploring by boat in the summer.

We need a boat!

This would be nice, but only if we get a good enough job to pay for one.

Wouldn't that be exciting!

We go back to studying the map and all the places that can be visited by water in Alaska. Thousands and thousands of miles of waterways, and only one road across the whole state. Hundreds of little Indian villages with populations under 200, whose only access to the 'outside world' being the river system. "Wow!" We can hardly wait now for winter to be over, the ice to go out.

But how are we getting out of here?

"We will walk. The new pipeline haul road is over to the east somewhere. When the time comes, we will just walk 'east' till we come to it!"

Trapline.

"This marten has a black stripe in the skin from the back. Didn't we read that means it has lost its prime? I guess it is time to pull all the traps. The fur now will have little value." My conscience gives no response. Most of the traps are up now anyway because we can't walk the long trap lines in the wet snow. One of my knees has been acting up from all the snowshoeing in the hard going country. The snowshoes not being in good shape, with poor bindings, also affects my knees.

We never did get Three Toes! Maybe next year, huh?

My conscience has finally had something to say. It is true. We never did get that wolf.

"Something has been getting the scraps of moose on the pond, but we do not know what. Should we set a trap to catch whatever it is? A lot of meat is getting damaged by poop and dirt from this animal!" This is indeed a most curious thing going on. This is a situation I wish to understand, a mystery to solve. There are no tracks I can see.

The snow is melting, so maybe the animal tracks are just melting away.

This may be true, but I wonder how so much meat could be missing, with no trail I see going to it. Most animals I know would leave a trail. The poop I do not recognize from the scat piles I've studied all winter.

Maybe some seasonal animal that only comes around in summer, or is not very common.

This is possible, but the bear is the only animal I can think of that would be 'seasonal,' and I doubt this is a bear. Surely, this is not bear scat!

Yes! Let's set a trap to find out what it is!

"A number two victor double long spring?"

"Yea, that sounds good. I think the animal would be about that size. Surely we wouldn't need the number three!"

Should it be a pole set or a cubby?

I have to think about this since we do not know what we are after, but the cubby will catch more types of animals since it is on the ground. We build the cubby. I hope this is right, something about the size of a lynx. Everything is still a learning process. The cubby is looked over before we leave. The entrance to the cubby can be easily seen from the moose meat. We made a snowshoe path, well trampled down, that is easy to walk in and highly visible. Some of the best meat is put inside as bait. The trap is tied to a four-inch diameter spruce tree with baling wire. The trap itself is set just in the entrance of the little cubby house, set on a spruce bow so it will not freeze to the ground. The springs are off to the side, jaws set as guides for the feet to step over, and direct the foot to the pan trigger. We walk away, confident we will find out what this creature is.

I write my first letter in a long time.

Dearest Maggie—It has been a while since I last wrote, and a lot has happened. Mostly I am happy in this new wilderness life. There is a lot to learn. I have some furs to sell, so I guess I am a real trapper now! I would send you one, they are really pretty furs, but think it would not fit in the world you live in! Ha! I think of you a lot and hope life is going well for you? I'm sure you passed all your classes, but wonder what classes are next and if you know what you want to be yet. Have you turned any frogs into a prince? Are you married, and do you have several children yet? It feels like such a long time to me, that all this could have happened. You would like the northern lights here. The melted snow is nice to drink too, and taste so good compared to city chemical water.

I am trying to sort out my life while I am here. Doing a lot of thinking. I will tell you more about Canada sometime and then maybe you would understand more why I would as soon not live around people. I suppose the Vietnam War didn't help either. Even though I was not over there, the Navy experience taught me a lot about people. I cannot think of anything else I could be doing that would excite me as much! So it is 'excitement' that I look for in life? Maybe 'challenge' too? I also think this is what I am 'good at' and I believe people tend to gravitate (or elevate) toward what they are good at! If I had to, I could get a regular job, live a regular life, wear a suit and tie, carry a briefcase. In such a life, I'd be bored, feel unchallenged. I think it is almost a sin, to not be doing what you are good at, almost an obligation, to live your life to your fullest potential. Almost a religious obligation. God made us as we are, and that fact should not be denied, for it is a slap in the face -- to be displeased with what God created. Maybe I'm just talking crap huh? Ha ha. Well, time will tell I guess. **Sunshine Miles**

Dear Dad—Christmas came and went and I couldn't get in touch or hear from you. I hope you are ok. Yup, I survived the winter ok…

GOING WILD

Dear Nancy—Are you still around? You still go dancing at the Howling Dog every Saturday night? Will I see you there when I go? Do you miss me, think of me? Yes, I had an ok winter. Some things were hard. Some things were exciting. I know it is home though 'for better or worse.' It would not have worked out if you had come along. I couldn't ask anyone to go through what I've been through. Things might get better, now that I know more what is going on. I think next year will go well, and if you are still around and all. Well we could see if you would like to join me then. You are a good woman and I know I could find no better if I searched the world over! Anyhow, hope all is well with you, and hope you keep in touch! **Sunshine, Miles**

I get to some long-overdue letter writing, but in some ways, it is not good. It is now easy to be lonely, to think about people, and getting back, and getting impatient. Spring is here, but it may be a while yet before the walkout can be done. At one time, I had been infatuated with Maggie. In the big picture, she might be more like a best friend or sister than a mate. I am certain Maggie would not like much about this lifestyle I have chosen. Maggie represents what could have been if I had followed in my father's footsteps. Nancy is not someone I am infatuated with, but from a practical standpoint would possibly be a good match for me.

Hey! Check this out, look here, the village of Venetie, way far off, on the Chandler River.

I forget the letters and town now, as we look over the maps more, and a circle goes around this village, as a place to check out.

Can you still see? Don't burn your hair again on the gee-whiz light! Maybe we better put the light out and go to bed?

In the morning, the ravens set up the usual morning squawk. They keep a sentinel out in a tree on the pond. When smoke comes out of the chimney in the morning, the raven sentinel lets out a holler and flies off. It looks like 'day shift' lands on the tree and sits there and keeps track of where I am all day. The night raven goes over to eat at the moose gut pile. The day raven will follow me all day on the trapline. When we come back toward the cabin, say, within half a mile, he flies on ahead to tell the rest I'm coming. There is no way to not have the ravens know where I am or what I'm doing. It is interesting to watch them work together like this. I gave up trying to shoot them to keep them away or stopping them from feeding on the moose. The raven problem has me thinking of one of my projects, the twenty-two rifle with the broken firing pin.

Without tools, it is hard to take the rifle apart. I see what I need, though, and realize a nail could be made to work if I flatten it, put a hole in it, and file it just so. The morning fire is what I need as my heat, so set the nail in on the hot coals. Before the sun comes up, I have a new firing pin.

Is the hole too big in the end? That sewing needle on the white-hot metal made too big a hole, I think!

"Well, I did the best I could; we'll just have to see! My concern is the right temper, now that I cooked this steel. The pin has to have exactly the right hardness, with no stress in the metal. The end that contacts the bullet must be hard, while the rest needs to gradually get softer to handle the sudden blow and absorb the shock without breaking." The new pin fits in.

Just a few adjustments with my jeweler's file. I will try it out on the way to the pond while checking out the trap we set.

Hey, walking without snowshoes feels funny, doesn't it? Ha ha.

"It feels like we still have them on!" We are walking down the trail without snowshoes, and it is the first time we have walked outside the cabin without them in many months.

So, do you have any more guesses about what that was getting the moose meat? Maybe a wolverine?

"No, I'm completely stumped; I have absolutely no idea. There is nothing I know of that fits the facts." "Let's try the twenty-two on the stump over there, the one with the fungus." "Pop!" We walk along the path toward the stump and the set. *Looks like I hit the fungus, and the firing pin works, great huh!*

I interrupt myself after seeing the cubby set in the distance "Something is in the trap, come on, hurry up, let's see what it is!!"

Diary:

Today, I got a Golden Eagle in the trap by the moose meat. I have no idea what he was doing here in the wintertime. He was only caught by one claw. The wingspread was about 8 feet, and he stood over three feet tall. The claws open and would encompass my whole head if he could get near me.

What do we do about this Eagle in the trap? Should we try to let it go?

It looks to me like nothing is wrong with the Eagle. The one caught claw looks fine, but letting him go is another matter. He is not a happy camper. As I study him, he follows me with those massive claws.

The one free foot opens and closes slowly, as if saying, "You just try to get within reach of these, and see what happens!"

"He's hissing at us too. Do you think his beak is as much of a danger as the claws? What would he attack with first? What would his preference be?"

We find out by moving in close, as a test, to see. The claws come out first. The head stays stationary. The message is more of fear and pain, not so much attack. I am not afraid of him. I want to convey to him that we wish to let him go.

Let's try coming in slow and from underneath, in a non-aggressive manner.

This does not work. The wings are spread out, and the feathers fluffed up in the stance I see on the back of a quarter.

We used a double spring trap, too, which means to get the jaws open, we have to get it over our knee!

"Well, now we know why we didn't see any tracks! The scat should have told us it was a bird! Where was my head! It had to be a bird! In a million years, I'd never think 'Eagle' in the winter! As a scavenger!"

I read somewhere that people who deal with Eagles cover their eyes to calm them. In films about it, a burlap bag is put over the body, and it calms them.

"Being put in a bag wouldn't calm me! I think this is true because it was on Walt Disney. Let's go up to the cabin and see what we have!" I find a burlap bag and some heavy gloves. The Golden Eagle has not changed his position much. I approach with the things I brought and set them on the ground in front of him.

The bag goes over his head with no problem, but he does not want his feet covered. I am concerned enough about those claws, though, that I want them covered. It is hard without lifting him off the ground to get the bag under, and he is so big that the bag will not cover him anyway.

We have an extra bag; let's just put it in his claws and let him tangle his claws in it." When I hand the bag to the eagle, he immediately grabs it and bunches it up with enough force to tear the bag up. I'm convinced if he got those claws on my face, my face would lift off. Now that I'm up close, I notice the claws are longer than my fingers. The feathers in the wing are as long as my arm. When I go to pick him up, his weight is significant, enough I have to get a better purchase, and would guess forty pounds.

"The claws seem well tangled and occupied with tearing up the bag; let's get him on our knee and get the trap off." The Eagle does seem a lot calmer in the bag, and I get him on my knee but am reluctant to let go long enough to grab both trap springs.

Better do it before he gets restless; he's feeling pretty heavy too.

I have to get his face within reach of mine to work the springs, but he seems calm, and the beak did not seem to be the primary choice of weapons, even though the beak looks formidable. When the trap jaws open, the Eagle falls to the ground. There is a struggle as the eagle realizes he is free, except for the bags. The one bag over the head, I get off quickly before stepping away.

With a lot of struggling, the Golden Eagle gets his claws free of the burlap bag in his claws. There is a pause, and he runs through the snow to a little clearing in front of the lake. He takes to the air. It is awesome to see those golden feathers against a backdrop of bright white snow. The 'woosh woosh' of powerful wings puts a soundtrack to the vision. A look to the right, the left, and he is over the tops of the willows, then over the spruce, and off to his world, from whence he came. Graceful master of the air. I forgot to breathe, and my mouth is hanging open.

It's a good way to end the trapping season, don't you think?

"Yea, well, it is sort of a minor thing, all in all, nothing to brag about. Do you think we should save it?"

Looks kind of small, even though it is our first one, maybe we should just write a poem about it?

There is a long pause as I think. "I'm going to write a long poem, a trapping song, about getting my first mouse?" (?) Hmmm. Holding him by a hind leg, we both study our most formidable foe, then toss him in the stove and choose to forget this story.

Anyhow, it's not a 'mouse' you know, it is a 'vole.' There are no mice around here.

As if I really care what it's called. It's a little furry monster!

I HEAR HONKING! I hear honking! I hear Honking! The Geese are here!

"Hush up so I can listen!" Three honkers go right over the cabin but keep on going. "They come from the planet earth. The first sign from 'outside' to indicate we are on the same planet!"

Well, there was the Eagle!

"Yes, but we are not sure where he came from. Maybe he lived here nearby all winter. He was unfamiliar to us. We know all about Geese. We have seen them before. All fat now on Iowa corn." This is the time I call in my diary, 'the time of mud.' It is a time I cannot travel. There is not enough snow to snowshoe, but not enough open ground to walk far. It is a time all my leftover food outdoors thaws, and I eat the last of the cranberries. The new fresh shoots coming up through the snow look inviting. We try eating the ones I would guess are not poisonous. There are only a few plants to be careful of. I eat willow shoots, young grass, young spruce needles. Some 'last year roots' are dug up out of the frozen mud by the river. I crave fresh things, and my body feels better for it. I notice all animals feel as I do, and crave fresh greenery and scramble for the new shoots, just as I do. This is something I share with the animals, but not with people, and in a strange way, I feel more kinship to the animals than the people.

There is a restlessness about spring being here. I am used to outdoor activities, and I've been cooped up during this 'mud' time. I hear birds, hear geese, feel the warmth of the sun, and I wish to go somewhere. The riverbank thaws first. A long brown line forms around the mile bend in the Yukon River. It beckons to me.

GOING WILD

Let's pack for an overnight trip and walk as far as we can along the river, just to see what's there!

This sounds like a great idea! We pack food, the sleeping bag, and the twenty-two. "Don't forget the snow goggles we made!"

😀 :)

Yes, it would be good to try them out, too, while we are out on our trip.

It is not long before we are seeing new ground that we haven't seen in a long time. The riverbank has a slope to it, and this is hard on my knees, which have been giving me trouble.

Scurvy! I am so excited about getting out that I handle the hard walking with enthusiasm. At first, there are only small things to see that are 'stories,' to learn from.

I think a fox got a grouse here this winter. Looks like there was a snowdrift against this bluff, and the grouse was under the snow sleeping when the fox came along. It looks like the grouse was taking off and almost got away.

By studying the surroundings, the way the feathers lay, the scuffle, and other factors, we can tell what happened here.

Over here, mink tracks, a hole in the ice.

I bend over to inspect the hole.

A rabbit caught by a lynx!

"The wolf pack circled this tree!"

A wolverine followed the wolf pack! This is how it went the whole beach long.

Let's try the Eskimo sunshades. They look so cool!

We see no real reason to wear them, but try them on just to be able to say we did. "How did the Eskimo survive with these on? I can't hardly see!!" It is true; the slits cut down on the light coming to our eyes but are very restrictive of our vision. It would be easy to trip and fall. How could anyone hunt wearing anything like this?! My eyes feel a little sore, and think it could be sun glare, but nothing serious. Just a little headache and sandpaper feel. Nothing a night's sleep will not cure.

Should we build a bridge here to cross the creek?

The small creeks are running water now.

Wait! There is a log upstream where we can cross. As we walk up, I catch the movement of a small duck as it glides under some brush near the log. The twenty-two dispatches the duck, so now we have fresh dinner. "This looks like a good place to make our night camp, up here on the cut bank in this dry grass. We can build our fire lower at the creek mud." The little creek here has banks on either side that provide good shelter. As the fire gets going, and we wait for the red coals to cook the duck, we walk further up the creek. The snow blocks it off in just a short distance. "So it would still be early to try and walk out to the haul road. There is a lot of snow yet."

Wait, what's that under the brush here? I bend over and pick leaves off. It is a duffel bag, full of gear, and it looks like someone put it here. I don't think it was washed ashore, not way up this creek.

It's all sealed up, what do you think is in it?

Bending over, we pick it up. I bet it's not bank robbery money!

"No, I doubt it, looks like something a moose hunter would leave and forgot to come back to pick up." From the layer of leaves and decay level of the canvas, I would guess it to be three years since it was left here.

No one's coming back; let's see what's in it!

In the bag is old paper I cannot make out, some worn-out batteries, and a flashlight. Nothing interesting. I keep the flashlight, but this is just something different, some story to read.

The duck tastes great. *I think it's a pintail.* We were able to stuff the duck with some of the rice we brought and some old last year, Eskimo potato plants I dig up. "Burp" We lay back in the dry grass as the heat of the fire below swirls up. The sky is gray, no clouds, no northern lights, but the dampness brings out the nice smells of sedge grass and moss. A wolf starts to howl across the river. We drift off to sleep with a smile and without a care in the world. All is well.

"Tell me if the fish comes back while I get the fire going!" There is skim ice on the creek. There was a fish under the ice that swam away when we got a drink. I had dreamed about the puppy. The puppy would have liked to go on this walk. I have to shake my head to clear it. I sigh as I get a fire going and set a pot on to make a drink from some Hudson Bay tea I find growing up on the bank. The fish returns.

"Get the twenty-two. I think we can get him with the gun!" There is a refraction looking in the water, but I do not know what direction it is; the light waves bend, so the fish will not be where it appears to be.

"I think the rays bend 'down' so I will aim 'high' and see if it works. The bullet, too, should angle down when it hits the water." The fish is only a few inches below the surface and is about a foot long pike. "Pop!" We have to wait for the mud to clear that was stirred up on the bottom of the creek from the blast. A pike slowly rolls over and floats up under the ice. I break open the thin ice with the hatchet and pull up the fish. *The fish has no bullet mark!*

This is very curious. We examine the fish as we clean it. The air bladder is damaged. "The bullet hitting the water drastically changes the pressures around the fish and puts it into shock."

The fish is cooked over the alder wood coals. *Piper taught me that alder is the best wood to smoke and cook fish with.* The crisp frozen ground is easy to walk on as we head back toward the cabin, still chewing smoked fish. The creeks are running more water on the way home, and some present challenges in crossing. At one of the creeks, I stop to get a drink. My face goes in the water to suck up the liquid.

GOING WILD

The water helps my eyes feel better too. The night's sleep hasn't completely cured my sore eyes and headache. It is not so bad that I want to wear the Eskimo glasses.

Viewed out of focus at the bottom of the sandy gurgling creek, I spot a gold nugget. My fingers find it, and I pull it out. The water-worn nugget is the size of the first joint of my little finger. Not knowing much about prospecting, I look around for more nuggets but don't find any. I look a little upstream and poke a little in the sand below.

"This is part of the Rampart mining area of long ago. This area was covered pretty well, I expect, right off the main river. This must just be a stray nugget." After a few minutes of looking, I press on home.

The sun is out strong today, and I am walking back out in the open, looking out across the vast white ice on the river. The sun weighs down on me, and I have to pull the fur of my hat over my eyes when I face the river. "We should keep our eyes on the mud, I think." This seems to help. We try the Eskimo glasses for a while again, but it is too hard to walk when we cannot see 'down.'

When I get home, I see things have changed. A lot of snow has melted. The pond has floating ice.

A bear has been by the moose meat! This moose has been the object of great interest from wildlife since I shot it. There has been no way to protect my meat, like in a container of some kind. Now it is all thawed out. There is little left that is edible for me. What is left has been turned into jerky. The gut pile is still there attracting animals, though. There are the ravens, jays, the eagle, and now the bear. My eyes have got so sore I am dizzy, so decide to go to bed early.

In the morning, I almost scream. Any light at all hurts them terribly, so I cannot even step out the door. Everything looks pink. I do not even want to get out of bed. I cannot believe the sun would do this to me.

What do animals do? How can something so natural be hostile? Animals don't have sunglasses!"

With a groan, we stay in bed all day with a cold rag over our eyes. Without knowing anything about 'snow blindness,' it is hard to know how long this will last. We are in bed two days before we feel like going out.

Let's see what the bear has been up to at the gut pile!

Upon inspection, I see the bear has moved the gut pile and tried to bury it.

He thinks we consider it important and wants to steal it from us, mark it as 'his.'

I slowly smile at all this 'attitude' from the bear. "Shall we perform an experiment and see what the bear does? Let's move the pile somewhere else, bury it and piss on it, and show the bear who we think it belongs to."

🙂 :)

"Honk honk, hooonk...splash!" We hear the goose come in and land on the pond. With a grin, the rifle is fetched off its nail. In a crouched run, I make my way to the favorite spot to shoot from. This scene is repeated most mornings now, and I'm eating well. The spring ducks and geese are full of yellow fat and have such a nice grain-fed taste.

Yea, so different from the mud and wet grass-stringy taste in the fall. "Let's go over to the gut pile again, see if the bear has been back since we are at the pond here."

Ho-ho! The bear has moved the pile, and I think he is one mad bear!

I bend down and try to read the sign. "Some of the guts are missing, but he has moved the rest even further, buried them even deeper, clawed up the area, left marks as high up on a tree as he can reach." We both grin. This time we move the pile further yet, bury even deeper in the snow and leaves, and (?) Looking up in a tree nearby, I ask, "Shall we?" With a laugh, we get the nail on the end of the pole out. The one used in the summer to get fish out of the boat. This reaches way up the tree where we leave 'claw' marks higher up than the bear can reach.

So what's your call, will he be afraid, or angry. Will he leave it alone or come looking for us. Will he acknowledge our claim, or call our bluff, or what.

I stroke my chin. I put together all I know about my dealings with bears. "He isn't going to give it up."

The gold nugget looks cool. I toy with it as I sit in the cabin. In a way, it is like a good luck thing. Something that holds memories from that nice walk.

Let's keep it, but how, oh wait, let's keep it with the twenty-two we had with us! We can inlay the nugget into the gunstock.

"Sort of has the shape of a wolf head. Remember the wolf howling? Maybe I can shape it just a little more, so it brings out the wolf outline, and I will inlay it in the stock of the gun." This project takes a few hours. The day is done.

"Yup, he didn't give it up!" The bear is furious now. He knows someone is messing with him. We had made a good part of the pile disappear. He knows the pile is smaller now. "I'm tired of reburying this; let's do something else. How about putting it on the pond ice, where we can watch him out the door. I want to see how he moves, figure out what he's thinking."

He he he, ha ha.

All winter long, I had been throwing water on the door to seal up the cracks and hold the moss in. I had not been paying attention, but the ice built up to a foot thick. This was a good place to throw the dishwater. The heat in the cabin melted the cracks back out, but each day the cracks were resealed. I had been doing this in the dark, indeed doing everything in the dark. Now that spring is here, the dishwater will no longer freeze on the door, so I give up this habit. Finally, the existing ice starts to melt off the door. In the spring light, I see spaghetti sticking out of the ice on the door. Then a dishrag shows up, the prongs of a fork. All sorts of things are pulled off the door that had been tossed at the door in the dishwater and froze there. Now I have quite a pile of cool, and not so cool, 'stuff' at the front of the door.

The snow melts fast, and we get ducks of many kinds on the pond every morning.

"Which one do we want for breakfast today? That one bufflehead is too small, maybe. The mallard looks good, but maybe too big, and has a mate already. There are plenty of pintails, and there is one male by himself in the corner by the edge. If we get him, it is an easier walk over there." Pop! We get the pintail, and the other ducks do not even fly. They are in love and stupid.

Let this be a lesson to us about love!

"You mean like, 'He who lets balls get big, makes good target'?"

"Speaking of Big Balls, let's go down to the gut pile and see if the bear's been there." I wasn't sure I saw them from the cabin door. The guts are undisturbed, so we are disappointed. We walk around with the 357 magnum pistol because we do not know what the bear is thinking, and he might get mad enough to come for us.

Makes good target, isn't that what you just said?

"Balls and targets? Yea, but we are prepared anyway."

The bear, I see the bear at the pond! I hurry to the door to see.

Two bears, do you see! Indeed, there are two bears coming out into the clearing. One is a little smaller, more timid. The big one is a male. A male wouldn't likely have another male with it like this, so the smaller must be a female. The male is strutting and showing no caution. The male has been here before, but the female hasn't. By his manner and hers, it looks like I can figure it out.

The male is saying, "Come on, honey, I told you I'd take you out to dinner. Don't be shy. Check it out, free guts for the taking. All mine and I set them aside, just for you, so come on, give me a little kiss." The male is headed for where he 'knows' he left 'his' gut stash, and he's trying to snuggle up to her, but she wants to see the food first.

"First we eat, then maybe we'll see if you get a kiss."

I can't wait to see his face when he sees the guts are gone. I hold my breath because I know this is going to be a good story. The bear confidently walks up to where he knows the guts are, to impress the lady. He pauses, unsure of himself. "Darn, I'm sure I left them here; what am I going to do? I promised her a dinner date. I don't want her to think I'm some low down cur who can't provide dinner when promised!" In a panic, he looks around, digs around as she gets impatient. "Don't worry, dear, dinner, coming right up!"

With her saying, "Are you sure about this? It doesn't look too safe around here. Are you sure some bigger animal hasn't run off with it?"

He freezes at the thought, "Not in front of the lady, I will not take this insult, where is that meal?" He looks around further, trying to figure where I put it this time, so he can clear the question of his bear-hood.

"Oh, over here dear, no problem, been moved over here to the pond, come along, follow me, the path is this way!" He leads her confidently down our path -- leading to the guts on the pond ice.

She follows reluctantly, looking around with fear. Nagging him all along with, "Are you sure? This better be worth it; sounds like some cock and bull story to me."

When he gets to the edge of the ice, it is the first time he realizes the cunning of my deception. The guts are just out of reach on the floating ice, and the meal will have to be fetched very delicately, seeing how the ice flow is balanced and could tip the meal into the water.

I wondered if he would be clever enough to realize the problem when he saw it! Now we know! Yes, now we know he understands geometry, math, and weight; what will happen to the guts if he isn't careful. He studies this a while, looks at his options, a very thinking animal, very far from the 'stimulus-response' stuff I was told about animals. He also has a very definite relationship with this other bear. I may have the details wrong, but something very complicated goes on between them. She is submissive, staying back, allowing him to figure it out. She appears to leave it up to him. There is no question in my mind that she is nervous; he is confident. That he is the boss, and she is waiting to be fed.

He lies down on his belly and stretches an arm out to reach for the gut pile. He is very slow and careful. I'm convinced it is because he understands the situation of the ice and weight of the guts, and the fact he could easily lose it. He stretches and stretches but can't quite reach. He stops and gets another purchase on the bank, so he can put more of his weight out over the cold water. He doesn't want to fall in. Lying flat and stretched, he still cannot quite do it, so he turns his head to the side to increase the reach by an inch but is frustrated because now he can't see. This is so hilarious, with her, impatient for her food, and him, thinking this was going to be easy, that I burst out laughing!

"Har har, haha!"

The bear almost has hold of the guts. The ice is tipping. The guts are sliding into his paws when I burst out laughing. He 'lost it.' His concentration breaks, as he wants to see what the heck all the commotion is. The female is absolutely in a panic and turns to run. This panics the male even worse. He wants to calm the female, get her to stay.

"Really honey, I just about got it; just be patient!"

She acts as if she said, "Are you insane, you big stupid brute? This is not the 'easy free meal' you promised. There is some creature up there laughing at us. This is all very dangerous, and there you are making a fool of yourself!"

"But, but..." and he loses his balance and falls in the water. If I had a camera, the picture would be worth a million dollars. He comes straight up out of the water with bulging eyes from the shock of the cold. There go the guts, slipping into the drink, while he can't decide if he wants to save the guts, himself, or his relationship with the female. The whole story is written in the image before me. His expression, the tipping guts, the female in the background running off in disgust. He manages to drag himself out of the water. Rolling in the grass, he gets most of the water off and gets some warmth back. He looks at the guts in the cold water, now sinking,

"But wait, some is floating!" He looks up the trail the female took as if saying, "Do I want the food, or the woman, hmm. Should I get the food and bring her back; try to appease her, or just go run after her and apologize." From the cabin door, I watch him look up the path, back at the food, back up the path, like he is trying to make up his mind. He decides to forget the food and slowly, dejectedly, ambles off up the trail to go find the female. Just as he gets to the woods, he stops, turns around, and glares up at the cabin. "It is all your doing, and I'll get even with you!"

Ho-ho! The bear is angry! I think we better watch out! I grin, thinking it is funny. There will be a close encounter in the next few days. Everywhere I go, I am armed, often with the hammer already back. I look forward to the encounter

A RUMBLING

A rumbling like thunder gets my attention down at the Yukon River. I do not know what this is. At first, I think it might be the bear and reach instinctively for the revolver. With a frown, I realize this sound has to do with the river and the ice. Every day I go down to look at the changes in the ice, the landscape. There is a packed trail now, to the riverbank and back. This 'thunder' seems to be the pressure of the water lifting the ice from underneath. There is a definite bulge in the ice. The middle of the ice is five feet higher than the edges. *There is a lot of flex to ice! I didn't know it could bend this much without breaking!* There are cracks in the ice, but not from the pressure, just the natural cracks from the original fall freeze. Water squirts out these cracks to relieve pressure. Sometimes it is a geyser that shoots up in the air twenty feet and dies down. Other times it is vapor coming up, much like the actions of the prelude to a volcano. There is the rumble, the smoke, the earthquakes, every now and then things shifting, and a sense of power building up.

There is no snow on the ice now. I can walk anywhere, just like walking on a city sidewalk. Water is on the edges in places, and the ice looks spongy and weak. This is spotty, but I have enough respect to stay off. There are now sunken trees sticking up where the sandbars are and ice hummocks showing. These had been buried in snowdrifts all winter, showing only an all-white flat-looking landscape for five months. It is nice to have different scenery! I am still not used to the new light and new warmth in it. I marvel at the sun and the colors its light brings. There is an appreciation for this because I have done without it. We appreciate things more, it seems, when something we take for granted is gone for a while.

Let's say hi to the sun! I smile and get the rifle. *We will have to aim high. The sun is a very long way off!"* I remember to aim high at the rising sun. I fire. There is a waiting time where we just stand there. It will take a while for the bullet to travel all this distance. When we think the bullet has lost a lot of velocity and has started to drop trajectory drastically, we stand up, wave at the sun. "Hello! And greetings! It is us! On the Yukon, wishing you a good journey. We missed you and are glad you are back!" We smile and watch for a while. We do not know if the sun heard or not. It is enough that we heard. We understand the sun cannot have time for us. It is fun to think the sun saw the little message coming and smiled. This is a very silly thing, but I understand primitive peoples so much better. I feel and understand the need to 'relate' in some way to the environment. This becomes a yearly thing to 'greet the sun.' It has no effect on the world in the least, but it simply pleases me, and this is enough. *Anyhow, maybe God is hooking up the horses and chariot, getting ready to haul the sun across the sky, and sees our message, looks down, and sees us laughing, waving, and appreciating the sun.*

THE SOUND of the echo of the shot bounces around off the mountains. I picture the country the bullet travels over as it rushes toward the sun. The wonderful 'drip drip' sound of water can be heard coming off the snow in the trees. There is the long-forgotten but familiar sound of water gurgling and talking in the creek. There is no way to explain feelings that have no correlation on any level that can be communicated to anyone who has never 'been there.' *Almost every year, I take photographs of 'the first water' that I think at the time is so chock full of beauty and meaning. Later I look at these and wonder why I took them! It is only water.* So here I stand, holding back tears of emotion, over 'water' over 'the sun.' My diary is filled with pages and pages of the beauty of water and the sun.

A water geyser shoots up, and the rising sun behind it turns it into rainbows. The ice rumbles, settles, and goes quiet again. We walk back to the cabin, not because it is all over, but reluctantly because there are chores to do. *We need to think more seriously about our walkout and preparing for the trip.* "I don't remember. Did Piper tell us the Road went all the way to the Yukon? Did he say if it is open in the winter? We should accept the possibility that maybe it isn't all the way to the river or not open." It is too early to dwell on this.

The bear hide from last fall is done being tanned and softened. It is the largest single hide I have that is tanned. The moose had been tanned in small pieces because it is thicker. I have folded supplies up in the bear hide as a bundle before, so I think this will work as a 'pack.' I see how it likes to fold, and then I make a frame to accommodate the folds and provide a way to secure it. The hide is laid out flat on the ground, fur side down. It is natural to set supplies in the largest area, the middle, and in the bear's back. When folding, it seems natural to grab the arms and legs and pull them up and around the supplies. The head and hind end are pulled up next. I make the frame of poplar sticks, lashed with moose rawhide. Tanned moose hide is used for the adjustable straps. When I look at it, with arms and claws still attached, wrapped around the goods, with the head as the 'flap,' it looks like the bear is alive. His arms are around the goods, protecting them. The head rests on his crossed arms, scowling. The ears stick up on the top of the pack, and the button to secure it goes through the nose. It is a very impressive looking pack.

We should hang around, at least till the ice goes out, so we can see that. We do not know what month this is, and it might be good to know that it is at least 'spring.' The ice going out is a good marker of time to go by.

"This whole time period is best covered in a 'several page' poem I wrote months later. When I try to re-write it into a dialog, it seems some of the original feelings I have are 'lost in the translation.' I enclose the whole poem, intact, not for the quality of the writing, but for the intensity of being a twenty-two year old, after a middle-class upbringing, spending many months alone, and seeing the river ice go out for the first time.

Spring Break Up
The breakup of the ice
is just one of those things
I have to reflect on
before I can put it down.
To write about it seems
to do it an injustice.
But if I give statistics,
like some background first;
maybe you'll picture it.
If I talk in circles,
Perhaps you'll see its Circumference

Soon as the sun came clear,
marking the end of winter,
the snow began melting.
Though the air was freezing'
soon after, I heard thunder.

The sound would disappear,
and leave a mist in the air.
That was the ice shifting,
resettling, and leaving
a space for water vapor
to escape to colder air.
Because the ice was pressing,
this vapor came out hissing.
It was fair to look upon,
when seen against the sun,
as the hissing geysers
rainbowed in the breeze.
My trail would often be gone,
that I would make again.
I can remember once,
after just leaving a place,
and coming back to find,
that piece of ice had shifted.
Climbing all the ice levels
was tiring and dangerous.
I climbed ice hummocks
with ten feet to their heights.

Some had the look of sculpture,
were in the ice suspended.
It looked of awesome power,
with all the weight there.
The ice was often colored,
which made the sun look weird.
Sharp and jagged edges
through the snow would pierce
all along the river margin,
from horizon to horizon.
And now the images
within my mind race.
There was so much to see,
like prismed light would play
through paper thin ice sheets,
balanced on their edges.
Some defied gravity,

GOING WILD

it surely seemed to me.
I guess an air pocket,
or that boulder weight
would make some balanced ice
an, 'eye popper' I call it;
for surely it did that!

Here I am, lost in details,
and it's still a month previous
to that fantastic event
I was to tell you about!
A kaleidoscope of events,
and what a buildup it was!
Day by day the sun rose higher,
and stayed out a little longer,
causing a warm breeze at noon,
which made the buds all swollen.
Rocks came out like stubble hair,
and reached Diamond Willow shore.
Soon the colors reflected,
where water on ice collected,
which, after eight months of gray days,
well it just about brought tears.
Soon those puddles gathered,
ever so slowly trickled.
Like sheets of the daily paper,
each new day had different news,
and like the ripple of a page,
the gurgle brought a new age.
I feel everything awaits
the great breakup of the ice.

The first rain comes
and life crawls out of the ooze;
Just like in the beginning,
with the sound of flies buzzing.
Yet still the ice is motionless,
and each day I check on this.

The river is getting swollen,

as I hear muffled water run,
and each day, with shielded eyes,
I go and check the ice.
The light is so strong from the sun,
it's like a weight coming down.
Maybe you see how it is,
every day, checking, for weeks,
mainly huddled in my cabin,
against rain or glare of the sun.
I'd try and re-read one of my books;
one I'd read only fifteen times.
Nervous about my trip planned,
when 'city' would be visited.
A river opening meant people coming.
It's hard to describe the dread,
mixed with something you wanted.
And, like something ordinary,
just like any other day,
I went for my daily walk,
and to have my daily look.
Birds and ducks were on the way,
so my eyes went to the sky.
But I had a funny feeling,
from a far off sound, like a hiss,
a snake crawling through dry grass.
Then the ice started parting,
and I saw it all beginning!

The very instant it started,
and it was such good luck I had,
to watch the first ice crumble.
But to describe what I heard,
without your hearing, is hard.
It really sounds like nothing else,
nor nothing matches it for looks,
and nothing seems appropriate,
that would even come close to it.
But I'll try to catch impressions,
and some of my reactions.

GOING WILD

I'd run from one bend to the next,
and back again to the first,
as if I were missing something.
As to what happened first and last,
why I could never recall that.
Water rose. That's what happened!
Beyond anything imagined,
like whole trees disappeared in it,
without a roar, nice and quiet.
I think I had the water timed,
and a foot a minute it gained.
I actually watched the water rise,
till it was a mile across,
and I saw not only that,
but icebergs rising thirty feet!
Rising up like dinosaurs'
complete with sound effects.
But what was so impressive,
was how quiet it could move,
as I expected loud crashes,
where you'd have to cover your ears.
How slow, quiet, sure, it drove;
Yet fantastically alive.
I remember one iceberg,
that left a trail around a bend,
coming out of the water,
it slowly crawled along the shore.
The trail was deep, ten feet wide,
trees and rocks were neatly plowed.

Whole stories were there to show,
like the history of 'upriver,'
all ended up going by here.
What the moose, rabbit, wolves do,
and how why and where they go.
A section would meet a jam,
and disappear under them,
swallowed up under the depths,
thirty feet by an acre of ice.
You never knew where or when

such a piece would rise again.
A tree would often get caught,
and break with a rifle shot,
and that was the loudest sound
that would fade across the wind.
And there was a wind at that,
from the cold ice in the heat.
What an odd sensation that was,
like a chill at the root hairs,
when the spine gets a shiver
in the presence of power.
Feeling of freezing in your tracks,
and a view that would hypnotize.
So many sounds were unique,
Like ice moving on sand would make,
noise like a chewed celery stalk,
though constant and ever present,
with the sound of bowling pins hit.
That's when ice would hit and break,
though nothing sounds quite alike.
Ice moving through tons of slush,
made a kind of quiet hush,
and mixed with the rest of it,
you couldn't quite make it out,
but it builds like a mounting rush,
very deep, and not a roar or crash.

There's a sensation of moving,
but more like it's you who's going,
and I have to stop and say "wait!"
"It's the ice, not me going out!"

A section of cliff is dropping;
a quarter acre piece of land,
trees and all, sank in the mud.
But what was so surprising;
I never heard a thing!
Let me pause for a minute,
on the effect of just that;
having the earth drop away,

GOING WILD

unnoticed, and so close to me.
That land was part of a habit,
as one of my trails crossed it.
A place where I always paused,
because the cliffs view was so good,
and a landmark I looked for,
when far out on the river.

Now only tops of pines waved,
from the cliff that disappeared.
Yet how can I explain this,
being just one of the events,
like a frame in a movie,
just a spot in the show they say.
Yet each one so overwhelms,
you see the whole thing in flashes.
The ice is so powerful,
that sometimes the whole river will,
be forced to change its old course;
a river whose width is a mile.
Forty feet deep, moving like hell.
Anticipation gets to me,
predicting the reality.
Saying to myself, "Oh boy"
"things are really going to fly,"
When I'd see one of the small ones
heading for a wedge of big ones.
I'd rub my hands - shake with glee,
and that's how it went all day.

Three days I sat and watched,
and all that time excited,
just shaking my head in wonder,
as each event would uncover.
So many things to record,
I'd be three days straight if I talked.
I guess there's so much moving,
and so little that's left standing.
If I don't pay attention,
it seems I get, snuck up on.

A hunk would slowly part the trees,
with just the faintest little hiss.

The earth in front would slowly turn,
first pushed up, but then turned in.
It seemed the winter got scoured,
and all of its trash removed;
like the shore got cleaned completely,
jagged edges taken away.
Piled up ice is what remained,
That, with the water raised.
It was thirty feet deeper,
then it had been all winter,
and it was fast with whirlpools,
at the mouths of all the creeks.
A hundred more feet of shore,
in water, compared to summer.
Each year this happens,
which is hard to believe I guess;
a, 'once in a lifetime event,'
you could say, was just, 'old hat.'
Well I may see it many times,
but the first time always
remains.

GOING WILD

Black powder shotgun with two geese. I built the shotgun. Note the 'goose' patch box on the stock. The wing opens as the box lid.

From a letter—

Dear Miles
  The poetry is not so great but for sure it is filled with your feelings about the life you live and it is nice to read of it and know you are well. It's certainly long! 😀 :)
  Love Maggie

So how many poems do we have now? Enough to write the book? I answer myself, "Yes, probably, but I'm not sure. You know poetry is not a big seller. No one wants to read poems. People want blood, guts, and violence. Even if we write bloody poetry, it is a tough row to hoe."

The Squaw pipes in, "But what if Long Fellow thought that and gave up? Hiawatha is pretty popular now, but I bet his friends told him nothing about savages is of any interest to the public, and anyhow God would not want you to quit. If God gave you the ability to write, there must be a reason."

On another subject, "Well, the ice has finally gone out, let's hurry up and get this last goose cleaned and cooked, get the cabin closed up, and get out of here in the next day or two!" "I'm with you on that! I suppose we could wait here, and a boat would come by in the next couple of weeks, and we could get a ride to someplace.

Who can say where anyone would be going. Some village probably, and we'd have to fly out. We have no money to pay for that. Even if someone would be headed for Fairbanks, it is a lot to ask of anyone to take us on such a long journey we cannot pay for. It would be like being rescued! We are fine; we should take care of ourselves. We could walk all the way to Fairbanks if we have to, it wouldn't be but 100 miles or so."

Maybe ten days of walking, no different than ten days on the trapline, right? There is no question that we will go to Fairbanks. We need to work, earn money to come back, and sell our furs at the best price. The idea of ending up in an Indian village doesn't sound appealing, considering how the Indians here feel about us. I do not understand them and feel nervous. I could make a social blunder, say the wrong thing, and end up missing. *It would not be good to show up needing favors anyway!*

We could take Piper's boat and motor and run to the Yukon Bridge, but there is little gas, we do not know how far the bridge is, and then what? How would we return the boat? It is not ours to use anyway! Do we really wish to float downstream to Rampart and show up there with no gas, no money, looking as we do? Again, it would look like we need a rescue. To truly complete this journey we are on and prove to ourselves we are true trappers and wilderness material, we have to make it back on our own, without a rescue! *It's the rules of the WalkAbout! You know, the ritual the teens go through among Australian bushman to get a man's name and qualify to have a wife. American Indians call it a Vision Quest. Having to be rescued is not a good thing!* None of this is ever really discussed or thought out. There is just one acceptable way. We are walking out. We also know from past experience that early spring is the most critical time to find work in town before the tourists come! In only a few weeks, job hunting will be impossible. We also might get there in time to get the firefighting job back.

So hurry up with that goose! I scratch my head to make the fleas scurry. My knife is dull today, but I am in a hurry, so do not bother to sharpen it. The knife is too dull to cut the Goose wing bone. In haste, I set the goose on a wood block with the wing out and held in one hand. A mighty swing brings the hunting knife down. The knife is slippery and not secure, so it slips as I swing. The knife hits my finger instead of the wing bone. If my finger had been solidly on the stump, the swing would have cut it off clean. The finger was surrounded by feathers, so I only half cut my finger off.

Talk about lucky! You still look a little pale! It is rather funny when you think about it that you can look with such nonchalance at blood, so long as it's someone else's, but as soon as it's yours, you fall apart! "Yes, I do notice this," and see the dry (Or wet, in this case) humor in it. "Gee, I still feel faint. I almost passed out!"

Well, let's get it cleaned up, look at it, and evaluate what to do now about our trip plans. No bone was broken, and the bleeding is under control. I will have to keep it clean and not use it a lot, but there seems little reason to hold up the trip. It will heal or not, without regard to the trip.

I think we should leave the rifle behind, just take the pistol. The rifle will not be good to have around town. The pack has my food. There is the last of the dry rice, which is moldy, full of moss and mouse turds, but enough for a couple of weeks. I have the goose meat, and hopefully, there will be some game to add to the rice along the way, but I could survive without it. I have some moose and bear jerky. I have some tea and sugar and a mess kit. My pack weighs about forty pounds. The furs must go, but they will not fit in the pack. They do not weigh much but are bulky. I have the two lynx, a wolverine, and a couple of dozen marten. This adds maybe another ten pounds to my load, which is strapped to the pack in a plastic bag. I have a few fears of meeting bears coming out of hibernation or irritated moose with young calves, but I have my pistol. The map has been studied as much as it can be.

We will not walk a straight line, but walk upstream to Caribou Creek, then up this creek, or its valley. We have learned to use a compass a little, but there is some admitted lack of understanding of it. Rather than risk getting lost, it is better to stick to a single valley, which should eventually lead to the Haul Road[1] now being built. If the road does not come this far yet, we shall walk to the village of Livengood, where there will be a road to follow.

I review all this in my conscience as I close the door for the last time and tie it shut. The day is calm and warm. The sun is just coming up. The ice is still running in the Yukon, but all the really spectacular events seem over. There are still ducks flying over that land on the pond every day. The snow is mostly gone along the river, but in the woods, there are still clumps. I hope to simply avoid any drifts that I find. I will not bring snowshoes. I had expected to have trouble with the bear, but he may be busy with the female. I will be gone by the time he thinks to come back to settle things.

There are some dry last year high bush cranberries available at the higher elevation that I have not seen since fall. We stop briefly to pick and eat a few, but we keep in mind we are on the move and have little time to waste on old berries. Grouse like to eat these berries, so I keep an eye out for them. The country is open up here and easy to walk. The trees grow tall, with few lower branches. There are not many spruce trees, just tall birch, and some poplar. It is easy to avoid snow clumps. This is the trail over to Caribou Creek that game takes. This trail is shorter than following the riverbank. The river is so swollen that there is no bank to walk, and it is dangerous by the river now, at least for walking any distances along an unknown bank. The riverbank tends to collect thick brush anyway.

It is a good idea to be walking here, I think we made the right decision" There are things to be nervous about, so it is nice to think we made the right choice, to build up the confidence. Even though I am young and cocky, I am at least aware of it (vaguely) and am not 'stupid,' and know I had better take this seriously. I am at least healthy. I know how to pace myself, and know my physical limits, and am realistic about what kind of mileage I can expect to cover. This is now my home, and I feel at ease. The trees and ground smell good after a cold winter of no smells, except the bad ones in the cabin. It is nice to be living out in the open.

At the end of the first day, I feel good about what I accomplished. I have got to Caribou creek and have headed up its valley. I do not feel especially tired. No more than I do at the end of a trapping day. There are creeks that require some negotiating. Sometimes I have to find a log to set across as a bridge. There are snow piles to go around, and everything is wet. My feet are wet, but I am used to this. My evening fire dries me out. I get water from a nearby spring, cook rice and the goose. I have not met any wild animals or seen tracks, so I'm not as worried about this. My city upbringing is hard to leave behind. Civilization sees the wilderness as a hostile environment.

The view of the mountains is beautiful, even though I am still at a relatively low elevation. The lovely yellow-green buds are showing in the trees. The songbirds are everywhere, as well as the honking of geese, the cooing of cranes, the trumpeting of swans. As I drift off to sleep, I have a content smile and feel warm and comfortable. I could have a month of days like this. I have a good night's sleep and keep warm. This has me feeling relieved because I didn't know how I would sleep in the cold and wet! The cabin got cold a lot, though, because of the stove that didn't work. I do not feel at all weaker from the previous day's work. In fact, I feel better! Leftover rice and goose are eaten for breakfast, and I have enough to feel stuffed. The boots are dry, my snowsuit and mitts are dry, and I am anxious to start another day.

Every day is going much the same. There are a few challenges, but nothing that wears me out worries me. I just take it as it comes. There are the creeks to cross that can be a bugger. The tundra is the most tiring traveling, with the water between the tussocks and all the up and down work I have to do. I am surprised my knees are holding up. *I think eating spring greenery is clearing up scurvy.* I know in the dead of winter, I was worried about my knees. There are some snowy sections in the high country that I cannot go around, and I must wade through waist-deep snow in places, but never more than a few hundred feet. After such exertion, I stop to rest and stop sweating. I take my time to cool off. My meals are keeping me healthy enough, and I do not feel weak from hunger. I do not know how far I am traveling, and this is my only real concern. This easy travel is ok, but not if I am only going a few miles a day! I hope I am covering the ten miles a day I had planned on.

Let's see that map again. Do you think we are seeing this mountain? It looks like the right one, but we had been wrong before. Mountains that looked the way they should are supposed to lead to other recognizable features further on. So many of the mountains look alike, and it takes practice to get a sense of distance and sense of what the map looks like in relation to the real elevation features.

Future Flash[2]

The year is 2005. I am out surveying with my boss Seymour, who I have worked with off and on for twenty years. We have surveyed over 300 remote homesteads. Reading maps, knowing where we are, is our job. Not everyone can do it. I notice my buddy Seymour is among the best there is at surveying. He turns angles, computes distance, spins, draws lines on paper, and never has once in all these years had me cut a wrong line, or have we had to return to redo a job. However, he is a little nervous and disoriented till he is on a monument to begin surveying from.

That is where I come in. I can take in the physical work, look down at a map and translate that into 'where we are.' This sounds easy. There are only three elements. The compass, map, and physical world. How complicated can that be? I have found not everyone, even not many, can do this! I have met many trappers, old-timers, woodsmen who never mastered the ability to read a map or use a compass. I'm amazed. It has taken many years to master. I felt bad much of my life, believing map reading is easy, and I am just inept.

I spent a lifetime looking for a human sign, old trails, old cabins. There can be a mark on a tree an ax made almost 100 years ago, and I can tell the difference between that and all naturally made marks. I can spot trees cut with a stone ax from before the days of the white man. This can tell me of an ancient way nomadic subsistence natives crossed a mountain, where the lake I am looking for is, or where game can be found. This ability helped us find old survey trails we need to do our job. There are things I am not good at. I am even the village idiot. I'm odd, damaged. Strange. Not 'one of us,' a savage. But here, in the wilderness, I am gifted at what I do.

Future flash ends

Anyhow, all I know for sure is that this valley will cross the new road if the road exists. If it does not, then at some point, we will have to choose a new direction. This would be the most critical part of the whole trip. I have no other real worries than this.

"Another grouse ahead! Looks like a Spruce, not a Willow Grouse. See the tree he landed in?" It is on our way up the valley. I get the 357 pistol out and make sure the lighter thirty-eight loads are in. I miss on the first shot. *Let me take the next shot. I'm a better shot!* The next shot guts him, leaving the breast meat intact. "We have meat to go with the rice now! Can life get any better?!"

At the end of the third day, I start to get a little nervous. According to the map and the distance I think I am making, the road should be coming up soon. I have seen no sign yet. I sleep all right, but not as well as before. I am a little dejected on the fourth day and get a slower start. I have stayed off the actual creek bottom. The creek is just a lot of work to cross and re-cross in its many bends. The lower elevation is the tundra, the hardest walking. The brush is down low too. I had tended toward the foothills along the edge of the valley on the east side, but what if I had left the valley all together? It is amazing how difficult it is to trust a stupid needle in a bubble of water over what you 'know' to be true. This is something a book never says. The books make it sound so easy. There is a question then, as to if I have stayed in the same valley, which is five miles across and has some rolling hills in it. It is hard to forget the sun, and stay to the needle, and trust it. One wrong reading, one wrong, mistaken mountain, especially back in the beginning, can be magnified, and a single degree error can multiply to a fifty-mile distance error, given several days of travel. I do not see anything in the terrain that I am absolutely certain is what is on the map. There is also a twenty-six-degree declination error between true North and compass North, and this has to be set correctly in the compass. All I have are "maybe" and "probably." My life depends on it. *There should be more certainty!* If I have to make a turn because the road is not there, a small early error could multiply off the chart, as anyone who knows geometry will see.

When the fourth day ends, and I am still not 100% certain of any landmark, still no road, or trail, or human sign. I am experiencing the true vastness of the Alaska wilderness. I am on another planet. I have not even heard an airplane in eight months. How different things are from the trip into the Yukon by plane, covering this country at such speeds, and getting out to the Yukon in an hour.

"Well, may as well make a camp here, been a long day." We had put in another long day. There is plenty of food, but not for all summer. I am feeling healthy, am not tired or cold. The finger is healing even though it throbs. I boil water each evening, adding medicinal poplar buds to soak the finger in. There is no more open cut showing blood. *Do you think we should have used stitches?* I am studying the cut after the evening soak. I try to flex the finger, but it will not bend yet. I keep it lashed in a splint. I think the tendon is cut but not severed. *There will be a scar, but it will heal.* I think it is better to keep it open, so it can be cleaned. If we stitched it, maybe we would have sealed in dirt. This might lead to an infection we would have no control over, internal blood poison. I'd rather be able to get in there and keep it free of dirt. Let it heal from the inside out.

We have to learn about every aspect of our life here. We have to be our own doctor even. *I wonder what a real doctor would suggest here?* Again, I am not certain the book would be right. The books figure we have clean water, antiseptic, sterile thread, and all this. When dealing with the factors involved here, it is not a simple call, I think. I cut bark from a young willow shoot and make tea to soak my finger in again. *Willow has the main ingredient that aspirin has in it. This might help the pain, keep any blood circulation problem in the area straightened out.* I'm sure there are other barks and herbs around, and some I even know, like coltsfoot for coughs, but there must be other uses, cross uses, and a lot more to learn about this. *The poplar buds and the willow bark will have to do.*

With a heavier heart, we go to bed this night. There is no sense of panic, or true grief, or sense of tragedy, just the sobering thought that we might be walking for a few weeks. I'm fairly certain that if I at least go east, I will run into something connected to Fairbanks. My guess is that its tentacles of roads will reach out to be quite an octopus in every direction. It would be impossible to miss some artery. At worse, if I got too far North, I would hit the Tanana River, *and all river systems lead to civilization.* I'm confident I could walk another 200 miles in a month and think I could survive this long on game. I do not have enough bullets or other supplies to last any longer. *We could always set snares at night as we sleep, with our shoelaces, for the rabbits, and make deadfalls!* This is still a rather gloomy thought, just from the standpoint of needing to get work for the summer, if we ever hope to get out for next winter. We decide before drifting off to sleep that if we do not come to a road by the end of the next day, we will head straight east. We do not want to pass Fairbanks to the north. In the morning, there is a grouse in camp that I shoot for breakfast. While packing up camp and preparing for another day of walking, I look up at the hills ahead. This is the direction I think we should be going. The sun is just coming up. *Do you hear that funny sound in the distance?* I have no idea what the sound is. There have been so many strange things to hear, see, learn about that very little would surprise me. I keep an open mind. If a mastodon were to walk in front of me, I would say, "Uh-huh, Mastodon." And go back to chewing on my grouse. My mind is absolutely numb and fried on all the input. *So what do you think it is?* A far off rumbling, but not thunder, and it is coming toward us, *Probably from across the hills ahead.* As we watch, I see movement in the tops of the trees. I cannot make it out, but am sure it can be no animal or anything I know. I remember how the eagle had been such a wonder. How the sounds of the river breaking up had been so 'out of this world.' For all I knew, it could be a space ship.

That's what it looks like- a space ship!

"Yeah, right, we meet aliens out here, give me a break! Some hidden city of green men!" I didn't say it with conviction, however, for out here, anything is possible. Surely, it looks like a silver ship floating in the trees. We watch it in fascination for quite a while, coming toward us in the treetops. *Of all the ways for a Frontiersman to meet death, we meet ours in the hands of Martians!* Pause, and a frown *Wait! It's a truck!* "So it is! I'll be darn!" We conclude that the road is only 200 feet ahead of us. That, if we had walked another 200 feet last night, we could have camped on the road. *It is exactly in the direction we are walking!* " Of course! I knew that! I was going to tell you the road was just ahead, has to be, but figured you couldn't handle it."

Yeah! Right! We argue back and forth all the way up the hill to the road. "This must have been the first truck of the day passing by. If any had come last night, we would have heard them." We do not know how often trucks come by. It might only be once a day. We have to be prepared to wait a while. *It might even be once a week!* This is possible because this is a new road, and there is nothing on it all the way until the North Slope at the ocean. This is winter just ending. Probably there was not much going on this winter! How could they keep the road plowed? The road would be in bad shape yet until summer comes. There might be only an occasional truck passing with emergency type stuff every month.

The main thing is, the road comes this far north, and even if we have to walk it, there is a direction to go! We scramble up the road bank and see it is a two-lane dirt road, freshly built. There is a sign with a mile marker, and it says "49" on it. We do not know what the sign means but think it has to be more than forty-nine miles out of Fairbanks, but maybe this is out of Livengood.

Only a few day's walk! "No, we are not going to have to walk. Look at the ruts in the road. It looks like there is at least a truck a day coming by." We sit down a while to just rest, think, and wonder about the road. An hour passes. We get up to start our day's walk toward civilization.

We have walked another hour or so when we hear a big truck coming. *From the right direction too!* As the big pipeline truck comes toward us, we calmly put our thumb out to hitchhike. The truck slowly comes to a halt. The door opens. We toss the bear pack in and climb in after it. The driver checks to see we got the door shut good and starts down the road. The driver asks, "So where you coming from?"

My conscience answers, "Oh, we just come from the Yukon River, we been walking five days. We haven't seen anyone in maybe eight months! The driver keeps looking at us. I wonder why. I figure he'd have some kind of comment.

The driver asks again, "So where you from?"

Only then do I realize I haven't spoken. My conscience had answered in my head. I try to make words to answer the driver, but only a funny sound comes out of my mouth. *I have forgotten how to talk.*

A very long time of awkward silence follows before it is broken, and the first words I have spoken since last September are, "What time is it?" The words come out all mealy mouth and garbled.

The driver looks at his watch. "6:00 am."

6:00 am, cool. But what day, of what week, in what month! How come you didn't ask the month?

The driver speaks again, "I picked you up because there was a wolf watching you from the ledge over your head. I was afraid he was following you!" I am filled with warmth, as the driver is filled with doom.

The wolf followed us! It must be Three Toes! I bet it was he that howled at night, the single wolf. He is used to us being in his world. He wondered where we were going.

He is used to feeding off us, the trapline bait we throw away. I have no illusion the wolf is actually fond of us or likes us, but he may be aware that something in his world is changing and is curious. I'm certain the wolf is 'aware' of me and always has been. I know this driver is getting upset because I am not acting normally.

I try very hard to say something. I mumble, "I knew that wolf." This does not seem to come across as sanity. The driver looks at me closer, and I think he decides I'm dangerous. Maybe hopped up on drugs. He's now worried I might roll him. He is sorry he picked us up. I catch him glancing at my pack, the bear hide. He catches the furs sticking out of the torn plastic bag. He wonders if I went crazy. His nose wrinkles up, and I guess we smell. I haven't cut my hair all winter, am wearing clothes that I sort of washed in the pond once but are now smelly rags. If they were to be truly washed, they would fall apart. I still have fleas and hope he doesn't see me scratching myself.

"So, are you going all the way to Fairbanks?"

I wait for an answer but hear none and wonder who spoke and why there is a lull in the conversation. *Is it our turn to talk, or his? Who spoke last?*

The driver says, "I'm going to Fairbanks and assume that is where you are headed?"

I am able to mumble a "Yes," but it sounds funny, and my lips and tongue feel strained saying the word. They are not used to speech. I suspect, from past memories, I am the only one who can hear my unconscious. *So I can't be part of a civilized conversation; only you can.*

The driver goes right by Livengood and keeps on going to Fairbanks. When we get there, he pulls into the pipe yard on the outskirts of town. This is good enough for me. I have no definite plan as to where to go. I have no money and must sell my furs to get some. I walk out through the gate, out to the road, going into the downtown area. There are cars zooming, horns tooting, and awful smells. I cover my ears from the loud noise. I gag at the smells. My head wants to explode.

Photo Section

The village of Rampart- population twenty--the next village upstream 50 miles or more from where I built my first cabin and was rescued by helicopter in the next book.

Houseboat in winter. I pull ashore when winter comes. Often not knowing where I was. I have everything I need with me to live a year. I know 'some village' will be downstream somewhere. I'd head to whatever village it might be in spring. Manley, Tanana, Galena, Ruby, are all villages that remember me stopping. I'd have a winter's worth of furs to sell and a mouthful of stories to tell.

MILES MARTIN

Houseboat- getting ready for winter. I lived on this houseboat for five years as my only home. I'd have to work a month in summer in town, but the rest of the summer was spent fishing, writing, traveling the rivers. The boat comes out of the water for winter. A frame covered with a tarp is put out front to give me more room in the boat. A woodstove keeps me warm.

Man cannot live by the sword alone. I have always loved birds. Above- a birdhouse I made with colorful flowers. A swallow has a nest at the flower center.

GOING WILD

In winter, it is amazing the chickadee survives sixty below zero. I feed them, and many a time, one has landed on me and eaten out of my hand. I doubt I could survive without their beauty.

Bear damaged cabin. A grizzly can enter a cabin any way it chooses, tearing a wall out, lifting a roof off. It can get very exciting when you are in that cabin at the time.

Field of Arnica flowers. Much prettier in color, of course. Miles and miles of yellow flowers planted by God, unseen by any human but myself. A place to lie down and take an afternoon nap. Life is good.

Kantishna River- homestead marked taken from a floatplane.

There was less activity back in the early '70s, and it used to take three days by dog sled to get here from the village of Nenana. In 2002, the only access was 120 miles by the river or forty-five miles by the winter snowmachine trail. The river is about 300 miles long, and maybe 100 people travel the river or have a claim to any of it. Perhaps five people can call anything on or near the river 'home.' Except for the river, nothing in the picture has a name. In the whole area for 100 miles, 90% of the mountains and lakes are unnamed. One might call it 'Lots of room.'

CHAPTER SIX

ALASKALAND, RAILROAD JOB, FIRST RIVER BOAT, HARD TIME,

It is early in the day, and the first thing I wish to accomplish is to get my furs sold. I have to have money to do about everything else on my list.

Let's find the other trappers who are coming into town like us to sell furs, and then we will know where to go to sell them! This sounds like a great idea, so everywhere I go, I look for guys dressed with furs over their shoulders, like us. I wonder where the fur rendezvous is. *Maybe it is on the outskirts of town somewhere. That would be most likely.* Everything will probably be all right, as soon as I find other people like me. I assume they, too, have trouble talking and look and smell funny. *It's in all the books I read, and now I, too, am a legend.*

My bear pack is on as I go to cross the street. Cars screech and people scream. One car goes up on the sidewalk. The only word I hear above all the loud sounds are, 'bear!' There is a realization I'm the cause of all this mess, and somehow, I will be held responsible. These people do not sound like happy people. They sound like frightened people. I have enough sense to know that if large numbers of people are unhappy and scared, that there is going to be 'trouble.' I start to run. The harder and faster I run, the more people are freaking out. Drivers stare in open mouth shock at my backpack and at my dress. Finally, I take the pack off and carry it to avoid the crowds forming. Now I am concerned that someone called the police.

In great fear, I walk the back roads, wondering what to do and where to go. If the police get hold of me, I think bad things will happen. I remember the last experience at fair time. I know I cannot prove who I am, nor do I have any money. Most likely, there is some law I broke against wearing bearskins or carrying fur in public or causing a disturbance. I think it against the law to be broke and have no ID. I doubt very much the police will be my friends and help me. I have read all the trapper and mountain man books and know trappers bring furs out in the spring to sell them at rendezvous. *So, where are these trappers?*

In my wanderings, I see a shop that reads, "Tanning Salon."

Ah, huh! Here we are, 'Tanning.' They gotta buy furs if they do the tanning!

"Good thinking!" Confidently, we march up the steps to sell our furs. There is a big picture window at the top of the steps, so I look in to see if there are other people like me in there selling.

Maybe we can spot some furs hanging or something. I see a bunch of women sitting in chairs with space helmets on. All heads turn as one. My image fills the picture window. They all scream at once. In a mad panic of things falling, all the women head for the back door to escape. They cannot know I have not spent time around women and have no idea what they go through or where they go to get their hair looking like it does. Thus, they look as scary to me as I do to them! I'm on the run again. I don't think I have ever been so afraid in my life. I know exactly how a wild animal trapped in the city would feel.

Before crossing a parking lot, I stop to look both ways, not for cars, but to see if there is a bear on the other side of the clearing. This is an unconscious, natural habit. I catch myself and have to chuckle. In the middle of the parking lot, a horn honks. Instinctively, I reach for where I always keep my pistol. In one sweeping motion, I crouch, reach for it, and face the strange sound. As I spin, my conscience counts off hundredths of a second for me:

.00 start the clock - The crouch and spin starts, hand reaches for gun.

.05 seconds-- Into the swing, hand reaches for the pistol grip that's supposed to be in my belt as I follow through the spin crouch, hand pushing away shirt to clear the draw of the gun. Just as in a Clint Eastwood movie like 'Hang 'em High.'

.10 seconds - Start to comprehend I do not have the gun, there is not a bear, and I am not in the wilderness. The spin follows through and focuses on target.

.50 seconds - Spin in a crouch focused on target, recognize target as non-hostile, hand starts to come up in a wave of apology, smile starts to form on lips.

1.00 seconds and the clock stops - The driver recognizes the gesture of 'reaching for a gun' and throws his hands up in terror, coming to a screeching halt.

Gun drawn - ready to shoot' starting the countdown into the next second. I am surprised at how fast the first instant was. As fast as the blink of an eye. That's all the time I'd need to get the drop on a bear. Quite a change in a year. I vaguely wonder why anyone would lean on their horn in anger and not expect to get shot. *The man expected me to be afraid!* Because I am a kind, forgiving person, I did not clean his clock as he deserves.

A crowd is forming. The pack circles. I am still not sure I can talk yet, so I know I need to settle down. *The last time we were in trouble*…but do not let my unconscious complete the thought.

"Let's head over to the Salvation Army. They know how to handle whacked out people." The feelings and thoughts I have at this time are best recorded in a poem.

Wild Man in the City May 73
keeping mellow mellows,
and try and save the nerves,
nerving all the shallows,
shallow shallow ripples,
gurgle gurgle streams,
gurgle shallow smiles.
visual visual images,
attack attack my minds.
Icy icy, ice sores
really realities?
Optical illusions?
Tell me tell me please.
Did I imagine this,
gentle gentle breeze?
May I close my eyes,
closing up the maze,
amazing in the ways,
swaying to the songs,
singing in the mountains,
mounting in my thoughts,
spilling cross the tops,
crossing deep deep spots.
Talking in the depths,
of millions of peoples,
trying to make sense,
staring in the darkness.
From the city limits,
stagger to the creeks,
people people strangers,
cannot keep this pace.
All in all it goes,
spinning spinning wheels.
Wheeling wheeling spins,

spinning all the minds,
minding all the spins,
words and words words,
making little sense,
melting at the fuse,
shorting all the circuits,
falling to my knees,
hands upon my ears.
A talking talking noise,
repeating on the tapes,
coming from my lips,
racing in my eyes.
Keeping keeping distance
keeping a straight face.
Many wavy hands,
weave between the words,
leaving many gaps,
gasping at the weaves,
light within the holes,
holding up the sentence,
sensing all the holds.
Living in the boonies,
finding finding selves.
Shelving all the finds.

THIS POEM IS ACTUALLY about ten pages long, but I guess this much of it covers the feeling well enough.

I went through what might be considered a 'nervous breakdown' in medical terms, but I toughed it out. I had to. *Hey, why is it a breakdown? It might be a breakup!* A good thing to take advantage of, part of survival! To be 'caught' would mean jail or the nuthouse. Civilization is not my friend. Learning how to talk again took a while. Getting to the point of 'simple conversation' did not seem as hard as doing complicated communication. *A level, I confess, I may have never reached in my life,* except through my art. Mostly "No, I am not ashamed. What I have accomplished kills most people." Just because I survived does not mean I do not have damage and scars.

"Sure I remember you, Miles, sorry to hear the wilderness life didn't work out, but the Salvation Army is always open for you."

"Thanks," is all I can say. I didn't say how I'm headed back out to the wilds as soon as I can get supplies. He thinks I am defeated and does not know I have not even begun yet. I point to my furs and shuffle my feet.

The Salvation guy nods and says, "Trappers come in throughout the winter, Miles, don't you know that? All the fur buyers are gone by now. The trapping season is over. The prices will be really low now."

I only nod my head for a reply. I don't bother to ask too many questions out loud and look stupid, but If the trappers sell furs all through the winter-- how do they get in and out of the wilderness? The distance is far! It must be costly and time consuming just getting in and out. This does not make sense. Then there is no gathering of the trappers? There is no big celebration when they come out after trapping all winter? Aren't they ready to whoop it up? This sounds preposterous...that there is no fanfare, no horns, no girls, no extra police on duty. Are the books all lies? Have things changed that much?

I get a look from the Salvation Army guy that asks, "How can you be so stupid and still survive the Alaska winter alone?" The look also says he thinks I didn't make it in the least, I'm gone, off the deep end, and the wilderness got to me. In fact, he and I have both met those types who believe they did something and never did, never left their cot at Sally's. Yet claim to have left earth. I answer with what?

Being stupid is not easy! It takes work! I do not know who to talk to. I haven't even met a real trapper yet, and I've been here a year. So many people trying to tell me things are either 'bar flies' (who are flat out full of doo-doo) or 'civilized people' (who mean well but just don't know). Both groups are people from the bleachers, not out in the ring with the bull!

The next day I am out with my furs again because this is the only means I have of getting some quick money. I have to get flea powder, among other things.

"Why not just use the phone, Miles! Geez!"

I grumble about something or other. I just don't like phones. *How do you tell someone you can't talk?* The bear pack is left behind, and I've had a shower, so look a little more presentable today, so do not cause any traffic jams. I blend in. I feel like an animal, pretending I'm a person. *I understand animals better!* Animals and I have more in common! I study the crowd, walk the walk, and talk the talk. When people stop to look in the shop windows, I stop and pretend to look in the windows, too. But I really think, *What a bunch of crap, who'd buy this garbage? This is insane!* But I smile and nod along with everyone else. My survival depends on it. I'm nervous but unsure why.

A shop sign reads, "Fur Factory." I made a mistake about the 'Tanning Salon,' so I'm leery about this. I'm as skittish as the furry critters I trap. I see hides in the window. I walk in and see the owner behind a desk. I already know he is not a regular fur buyer. This is the guy who sells the finished product. I do not know who else to see. I'm sure he notices I have trouble talking and can tell he does not know what to make of me. This guy is well-dressed, clean-cut, and looks Mexican or from some other country. It is hard to imagine that we might be on the same wavelength.

I try to talk. "Um..." I pause, trying out the human sound. I press on. "I have marten." I hold them out. He looks them over. I know he is at least 'interested.'

He tells me, "That black one with white tips is pretty enough, but it can't be matched, so it's worth less than the rest." He looks them all over. "$12 each is all I can offer this time of year." Somewhere I heard marten are going for $35 each. The buying season is over. I do not know where to go. I can hardly talk. I'm glad to get anything at all. I am tired of carrying them. It is embarrassing to walk the streets and get stared at. I accept the money, but he only wants the marten, not the lynx or wolverine. I did not record the exact amount of money I got but think it would have been about $200 *for eight months of hard work*. I feel like I've been ripped off and that there is nothing I can do about it.[1] "Welcome back to town!"

Phone call. I hate phones.

"Hello? Is Nancy there?"

"Who is this?"

"This is Miles, she and I met last year, and I've been out in the wilderness all winter. She asked me to get in touch when I came out in the spring."

"Well, Miles, she's moved, and I don't know where she is. She met some guy. I think he was a drummer in the band that played at the Howling Dog."

"Well..." Click... "Hello? Hello?" I stare at the humming phone before setting it back in the receiver. *Damn phones anyway. How can people stand them?* "And women too!" *Yes, women too!* So much for Love.

Next call.

"Miles who?"

"Miles Martin. I worked last summer and was told to call back this spring if I wanted to work again. I thought maybe...

"Yes, well, there are mostly new people here this year. It's seasonal work. We're all booked up."

"Thanks anyway." Click. "Stupid phones. I can't stand them!"

Me neither. What happened to being friendly, kind? What's wrong with everyone?

There had been hopes of getting enough money for the furs to get a boat, maybe a few supplies, and getting back into the woods. This was optimistic, and I knew it, but here I am, right back where I was. Pretty much broke, looking for work, and facing another summer just like the last one. I had counted on at least having the same job back again. The pipeline is getting going full speed now. There are a lot of people here to make the big dollars. What is normally a month's wages are being offered as daily wages, or so the stories go. There are enough people blowing big money to lend at least a semblance of truth to the talk.

"Is that you, Man? Miles? How's it going! You get out to the wilderness? Hey, you hear about Bob and Sue? They were going out too, remember? They were around Rampart but didn't get a cabin up in time. Bob tried to walk into the village and froze his foot. They didn't have any money or any place to stay. They had to come back. Been bumming around Fairbanks all winter. Bob lost a couple of toes, and with no doctor, he lost his foot here in town."

I recognize this guy now as one of the group at the fair from the stolen jacket deal. *Oh, yea, the guy who did the stealing. I never did catch his name.*

"Sam, I'm Sam, glad you made it back OK. We was wondering if you died out there!"

It is nice to at least be remembered. Who else is remembering me? "Sam, everywhere I go, I get treated like shit. What's going on, man?"

"It's a cold, cruel world! There's them that conquer, and them that are conquered. Them that is the masters, and them that is the slave to Big Brother!" He speaks to me as if educating a child, telling the most basic thing that every street person knows the day they are born. Axioms, mathematical truths. A world where everyone looks out for themselves, and there is always an angle to things, a reason. *Use or be used.* This is not entirely true, for some of the Salvation Army people are genuinely kind.

Sam points out, "Yea, Miles? And who sold your boat and didn't give you a cut, huh? Who stole that camera you told me about, huh? Get real, Man. I don't know how you survive!" He shrewdly scratches his chin. "Hey Miles, you got a dollar, Man? My check hasn't come in yet, should be today."

I cannot believe this, trying to run a scam on me to get a measly dollar. Oh well, what the heck. I guess I got a dollar to share. I don't say a word, just get out a dollar. I notice he looks to see what kind of a money wad I have, and I consider I better watch my back. It wouldn't surprise me if he tried to roll me. I guess everyone else is pretty much the same. There are just different ways to do it, but it all ends up, 'people want your money.' Maybe someday I can live completely alone and not deal with all this. *But we are social animals. We enjoy the company of our own species sometimes, and so we have to put up with each other.* Sometimes it's better to risk being rolled than to be alone. Anyhow, Sam here doesn't know I'm on to him. I'm not going to let him know what cards I hold. He wouldn't likely do anything in public, and if we are ever alone and he tries to roll me, I decide I will kill him with my blade and dump him in the river.

With a smile on my face, I slap my buddy Sam on the back. The truth is, I'm confused. I was never treated disrespectfully while growing up. Logic tells me the world has not changed drastically since I was little. Logic tells me it is me who changed. I had no clue the world I am in now exists. There is a group of people the world takes advantage of, for who there is open season. It is ok to rip these people off, treat them like dirt, and there is not much recourse, nowhere to turn. I'm not sure why. Nor how to make things different in my life. *But for now?*

"Good to see ya, Sam! Wondered if I'd ever see any of the crowd again. What's going on for work? How come none of you have pipeline jobs?"

Sam angrily tells me, "Oh man, they is like, importing all the help. Hardly anyone local is going out. You can try the unemployment office, though, but forget da unions."

"Well, I got a pretty good job out of the office last year. May as well go there again." This sounds discouraging, though, if none of the crowd found work all winter.

"So Sam, where you staying? Where does the group hang out? I don't see any of you at Sally's."

"No, we don't go there. It's too crowded, and they only let you stay there a short time. We got a camp out in the woods behind Alaskaland. We all live in tents, now that the weather is warmed up. You should check it out!"

Well, it sounds like I can't stay at the Salvation Army for long, and they have been good to me to the extent I do not want to take advantage. *They are there for emergencies, not a way of life.*

It's not really a 'camp' as such. Everyone is just staying in tents scattered throughout the woods like a hobo jungle I see in the old movies. They dumpster dive and scrounge around for wood to burn, food to eat, steal, sell drugs, and such things. I am not very clear about all this. Everyone is so vague when I ask specific questions. Some of them end up at the unemployment office looking for work, but it seems to be a bad word, 'work.' Work is something to do when you're so down and out, you haven't eaten in a few days. It is just so 'cool,' living in the woods in town, hanging around a campfire dressed like mountain men. No one really trusts anyone else, so camps are scattered, and it is considered 'good manners' not to go looking around. Everyone is welcome around the communal fire, though.

I search around for a private, secret spot to make a camp. I find a tent at a second-hand store I learned about. Now at least I'm taking care of myself. Most everyone here is amazingly dull-witted. *Well, street smart, but...* Yea, I know what you mean. Like can barely repeat their own name correctly, have to stop and think about that. These people seem like insects, knowing when to jump when a shadow crosses their path. To them, I am duller than most of them and need looking after, with whatever kindness this group can muster.

And the Lure Spins On
King of the creeks, watches and waits,
quiet and silent, betrays no thoughts.
Behind the eyes, a mind lays,
not quiet or dormant, but hot.
Processing all that is passing,
(meaning anything moving.)
Trinkets and feathers and nice curves,
flashes some passes, plays on his nerves.
Instinct to strike is king in the pike,
(To hustle this little damsel.)
She holds the master switch it seems,
which bypasses everything else.
Twist for twist, turn for turn,
they dance in the light of the sun.
Armored and toothed is google eyed,
over sparkle and wiggles charms.
Eye to eye, and shine for shine,
the lure spins,
the pike follows.

THE UNEMPLOYMENT OFFICE hasn't changed much. I pack a lunch and get there by 7:30 to get a good number when the doors open at 8:00. The girls there have all changed, but it's the same type. It does not take long to get to know them after hanging out all day, chatting, and sharing lunch. The job situation does not look so great. Worse than last year. It is hard to look at all the women come and go, and see them on the street. They look so inviting with the way they dress. Being young and 'doing without' is not a fun situation to be in. During a lull at the unemployment office, while I sit and wait to see if there will be a job coming in today, I write a poem about my feelings on the subject.

Sam again.

"Anyhow, Sam, I've been looking at maps and want to know about some of these places. You ever want to see some different country?"

Sam nods, "Sure! Just no money for gas. I've wanted to go to the Yukon River out by Circle City. It got named because they thought it was on the exact Arctic Circle." I wouldn't mind going there either, just to see another section of the Yukon and see how it compares to where I was. This would also be the dropping off place if I want to go to some of the other villages upriver. This is the only road to the Yukon besides the new Haul Road, which is still private and not a public road. I want to see what kind of a boat landing it has, and what kind of a village it is.

"Well, what if I pay for the gas, Sam? We could go on a weekend and check it out! Should we pack some food and plan on a two-day trip? Wish I had my camera. You got a camera, Sam?"

He gives me a look like, 'get real!' This should be exciting and offers me my chance to see more of Alaska.

There had been no letters waiting for me after being gone eight months because I had no post office box. I couldn't afford one, and General Delivery only holds mail, I think thirty days. I had sent out all my winter letters this spring, and now the first reply reaches me from my Dear Maggie.

Dear Miles, Good to hear from you! I was worried about you. It sounds like you went through quite an ordeal. I don't think I could have survived. I'm too soft. I have a lot of respect for you for being able to do this, but I wonder why you would even want to! You're right; I don't think I would want a smelly hide in my apartment! Ha, ha, but I am curious what one looks like. I'd like the finished coat more! I wonder if the women who wear the coats understand the story behind it, though. I'm sorry Nancy found someone else. I don't like thinking of you up there so alone! I don't think I could be alone that long. I need someone around, someone to hold, and I need my sex! So what are your plans now? Will you come back home? It would be nice to see you. I graduated with top grades and have a job now—would you believe—in a library? Just temporary—a bank wants me to work for them but I like libraries! I have a nice apartment, am on my own, and really love it! Take care and keep warm. Know I worry about you! **Love Maggie.**

"The road looks pretty deserted Miles, the sign says the road is closed!"

Sam and I are in his beat-up oil-burning truck. I reply, "Well, I don't see any roadblock. There are tire tracks in the mud, so someone's coming through. Let's go as far as we can. If we come to a spot that is blocked by snow, or a gate or something, we can turn back then. Why give up before we even start? You got a full tank of gas?"

"You filled it up. Guess we are set."

We head out the muddy road that goes to Central and Circle. The map shows a hot springs there.

Sam is interested in the springs. "That'd be cool to jump in a hot springs, huh?"

We are excited. Sam, too, is interested in an adventure, and seeing the rest of the state beyond just the 'Fairbanks' area everyone knows so well. I know I didn't come here to see the city. If you want city life, you don't belong in Alaska.

"I still remember, Sam, when I first got here. I flew up. I didn't know anything about Alaska. I didn't even know where it was on the map. I go to the airport and ask for a ticket to Alaska, and the ticket agent asks, 'where to?' I didn't know the names of any places in Alaska so ask her to name some places!" Sam laughs at the image of that.

"What did she say, Miles?"

She says, "Almost everyone flies to Anchorage."

I told her, "That's not where I want to go then. I want to go where the fewest people go."

She tells me they only fly to one other place, Fairbanks.

"So I guess I'm going there!" I responded. "I didn't know where I was till I got here and looked at a map."

Sam laughs. He has his own interesting story about how he got here. "I notice Miles, that almost everyone here wanted to leave something behind and start over. I also notice almost every Alaskan has trouble with their family. I guess it makes sense. People who travel a thousand miles away from home to settle down are not exactly close to their family, or they wouldn't go."

I never thought of that. I feel a little better about letting my relatives down. There is more of a feeling that I am not the only one who let people down and is not understood.

"Yeah, Miles, my family pretty much disowned me. They do not know why I would want to come to such a cold place without any electricity and stuff."

We do a lot of talking, Sam and I. It is a long drive. I don't know the miles, but five hours later, we still haven't seen a cabin or another car.

"This has to be Central, Miles. Let's stop and check out the place."

There are only a few log cabins where we stop. A sign says this one log cabin is a bar, place to eat, or something like this. We are not sure. It looks like it is supposed to be a public place, but it could also be someone's home. We open the door and believe it is someone's home. There is a couch by a woodstove. There are three people sitting on stools, and they act like customers, so we come on in. They all turn to look at us because we are the first 'tourists' of the season. The first outsiders these people have seen since last September. We both ask for burgers, which is about all they are set up to serve.

The owner of the place starts talking to us as if we are family. "And that son of a bitch neighbor shot a wolf from a plane and scared the be-Jesus out of me and the boy. I should turn him in. That's not legal anyway, you know!"

Sam and I just look at each other. We don't even know this guy's name, never saw him before in our lives, and here he is spilling his personal problems on us. We think these people here must have cabin fever. This is my first introduction to 'village feuds.' This guy expects us to take sides, to 'care.' Sam and I could give a hoot about who is killing wolves from an airplane and what should be done about it. We came here for a burger. We find this situation very entertaining and humorous.

"Have you ever met the owner of a restaurant, Miles, who told you his personal and legal problems while you were trying to eat?" As we drive off, we think this is a very interesting place. "Next stop, Circle city, and the Yukon!" The dirt road winds and winds on forever. "We got to pull over Miles; the car is overheating."

We pull over, and Sam looks over the car while it cools. He puts more oil in it.

"You got an oil burner, huh?" Sam doesn't want to admit his truck is not in great shape. He's crazy fond of it. I'm sorry I said anything.

A few more miles down the road, the engine acts up, and we have to pull over again, but this time it will not restart. Sam fiddles with it, checking this and that but decides something is wrong with it. It is only now that we realize how far out in the boonies we are. Both of us, all our lives, have pretty much been within hollering distance of 'help.' I had my wilderness experience, but when you are in a truck, it is like there is always some sort of civilization around. Roads mean people. Sam and I hang around the truck for quite a few hours and eat the meal we packed.

"What am I gonna do about my car Miles, this is a long ways out? How could I get it towed?"

I feel a little guilty. My only concern is getting back. Sam has to get the truck back or come back here with parts later to fix it.

"Well, Sam, can you figure out what is wrong for sure, to know what parts you need and what tools? Then you can come back and fix it. Maybe even someone in Central would have the part and tools." We decide we should start walking toward Central. It is a lot further walking than driving. Dark is coming, and we have a long ways to go. We have not seen a car all day. We have no sleeping bag or warm clothes.

"Hey Miles, there's a cabin in the woods off the road through the trees here. Let's check it out." We wonder if anyone is here who might help us, but it seems obvious this cabin has been empty for a long time. "The door is unlocked Miles, come on in. Cabins are left open in the wilderness, in case of emergencies! Look, food and firewood and everything. We are going to have a nice warm night!"

Certainly, the thought of sleeping out in the weather without a sleeping bag or food is not appealing.

"We should cut some extra firewood to pay back whoever uses this place," I comment to Sam. There is no way to know if this is a public cabin on state lands, like a park cabin or a private place. There is no sign or indication we can make out.

We spend a nice warm night and open a couple of cans of beans for breakfast. The day looks a lot brighter after a good night's sleep and meal.

"Sam, let's wait at the cabin, listen for a car, and when we hear one, we can come up to the road and flag it down." This will be our plan. "It might be days or weeks before someone comes by!" The road is officially closed.

"Miles, look at all this cool stuff! We should take some of it!"

I'm thinking someone was nice enough to leave the lock off the door so people in trouble like us would have a place to come in out of the weather. It might even save someone's life, even ours. *We are going to pay back this person by ripping him off? I don't think so!* I feel bad enough we do not have money on us to leave, and not a decent way to repay. There is no saw to cut wood. I am more inclined to leave a thank you note with our names and address and try to pay the guy back. Send him something later, maybe. *Or pay it forward, help someone else, return the kindness.*

"Sam, what if it's the owner of this place that is the first one on the road through here. This is his stomping ground, not ours. There could be a lot of trouble if we got caught."

Sam reluctantly puts back the things he's making a pile of to steal. "Miles! I hear a truck coming, let's go!"

We get up to the road, and a truck comes and stops when we flag it down. We get a ride back to Fairbanks with little incident. Sam has to get a ride back again for his truck. I think he comes out with another friend, and they tow his truck all the way back to Fairbanks. I forget all the details, but he said it was quite a bitch. Mistakes and breakdowns in the wilderness get time-consuming and costly. There isn't much use, me going back out with Sam. He doesn't need any help working on the truck, and I don't drive or have a car or truck myself. I see what kind of problem they can be. I'd rather have a boat. They can at least float back to civilization.

I still have some of the $200 from the furs. Every now and then, I get a job for a few days. There was a cool job at a ski resort, working at the lift. Mostly it's one-day dishwashing and janitor type work. There is enough money, though, to buy food to eat and take care of 'basics.' I'm surprised that life like this is not very different from life in the wilderness. Trying to keep warm, no light, poor food. To me, it is worse than the wilds. *'No freedom.'*

My lynx and wolverine hides are hidden in the woods in plastic bags until I can find a buyer. These furs are worth more than the marten. I have maybe another $400 in fur if I can just find a buyer. Meanwhile, there is little money. Times are tough for all of us in the hobo camp.

Alaskaland is across the river from the hobo camp. I start to hang out there more. Alaskaland has a post office and places to eat. The log cabins are all historical and opened up as gift shops. The vendors are all dressed in old-time clothes for the tourists. There is a cute Choo, Choo Train that takes tourists around on tracks, as a guide tells wild stories. Everyone, of course, loves my stories. I dress the part. *I am the part*. Tourists love to stop me to take my picture. I make the rounds of the shops, and all the shop owners know me. I often bring in tourists to buy, so most do not mind my hanging around. I enjoy the shop owners a lot. We have a lot of serious talks about life, religion, selling, about the 'Alaska image,' and what it means, and how to sell and market it.[2] There is an ice-cream shop I enjoy hanging out at. The owners of the Diamond Willow wood shop seem to be especially nice people. I do not remember anyone's name, though. These are 'just people,' who come and go, like everyone else. This is like a little world unto itself, where everyone knows everyone else. I suppose if I was more 'with it' and wiser, I could end up with some kind of 'job' here. Most of the shops, though, are not making lots of money. They 'get by' and are all full of dreams. The ones who keep coming back are the ones who love it as a lifestyle. Really though, there was little money to hire a helper. I get my mail at the Alaska land post office.

> **Dear Miles**—I'm glad you made it out all right. I moved since you last wrote, but your letter was forwarded. My new address is at the end of the letter. I'm involved in some work I'm excited about. I have a chance to work with a new bunch of people and it will involve a lot of travel to other countries. We are forming a joint venture, and one of our first jobs will be in Russia. I do this on the side. I still have my full-time duties at the university. I have the chance here to teach courses more to my liking. I'd love to see you. If you want to come for a visit, I'd be happy to pay for the trip. **Love Dad**

The unemployment gal asks me, "Miles, have you ever thought of a pipeline job? Didn't you tell me you had pipe experience in the Navy?"

"I heard they bring their own people in. I wouldn't know where to go look for that kind of work anyway! You know how it is with me too, I'm not sure I approve of the pipeline going in! It kind of goes against what I stand for." *But the seed is planted.* "Anyhow, the pipeline is going in, and we can't stop it. Money is money, and we need work!" I have to write letters and get proof of my navy experience and education level, and such. When I do, I show up at the Pipefitters union.

"This looks good, Miles. You specialized in pipe lagging and steam heat?"

"Yes, this is what I enjoyed the most, but I was qualified at everything else."

The union rep looks up from my records in front of him. "It says here you were capable of doing anything in the trade competently. You worked with pipe, went to damage control school, firefighting school, mechanic school, and graduated in the top ten of your class."

"Yes, I enjoyed the work, just not the military, and did my job well."

After some thought, the rep tells me, "Ok, well, this is what we'll offer. You will need to go to our Pipefitter school to update you on the civilian application of your trade. It is six months long, and we'll send you and pay for it. After that, you will be considered a four-year apprentice because of your experience. You would only have two-three more years to be a journeyman. After the six-month school, you would have work through us up on the slope. I can't say what the pay would be. Some of my new guys pull in 180 grand a year."

"Sounds great, but would I have winters off?" The interviewer looks at me as if I have gone insane. "You see, I want to go trapping."

"Miles, you would turn down starting pay of $180,000 a year to go trapping?" *That's 1970's dollars.* I sighed a little and did have to think about this. *Am I insane? Will I sorely regret turning this offer down? Do I really want a union job? Working for someone else? Would it be exciting? Is this what I'm cut out to do? My purpose in Life? Is this the best I can do? Wouldn't this pretty much define the rest of my life? Do I really want to be a big part of the oil industry? Sell out what I love, for money? Do I want to be such a big part of the most destructive industry on the planet? Doesn't a person have to get their priorities straight?* Anyhow, I am willing to sell my soul for the summer and grab the big money for a season or a few seasons, but not make a career of it.

After a long pause, I answer, "I appreciate your offer, but I'm a trapper first, just looking for a way to grubstake myself." I stand up to leave, catching the horrified look on this guy's face. He thought he was offering me the deal of a lifetime. He expected me to get on my knees and thank him, promise undying loyalty to the union. He thinks I'm completely bonkers. We shake hands, and that is that. I stop at the post office on the way home.

Dearest Maggie—Got your letter the other day and am glad you are ok. If I can make enough money this summer I may come for a visit, but Alaska is my home now. I have a lot to do if I want to be ready for next winter. Once winter comes, I have to be settled in where I'm going to stay. I should build another cabin. The one I lived in last winter was small and had no floor. I don't think you need to worry so much about me now. I've been through the worst of things. I pretty much know what I'm doing now! I find it humorous, your concern for me in the cold wilderness. To me, it is the wilderness that is warm and safe. Town is cold, scary and unsafe! If I get in trouble, it will most likely be because of people! Yea, I thought of Nancy a lot and hoped she would still be around. I couldn't ask her to wait for me, and I can't blame her. It's my own fault, but even so, it would have been nice to have someone to come out to, and be received by. But 'that's life'! I still have bad thoughts over Canada, but guess I'll just have to get over it. It is hard to be among people after that. But maybe how I live, where I live, would have happened anyway. 'Canada' was just an extra 'push,' and maybe I needed that. Just trying to see the good side of what happened! Anyhow, I know that coming to Alaska, was like a duck discovering water. I'm meeting some new people, but it is slow. I still am bad about names. My mind is just somewhere else. My attitude about people? Yes I realize not everyone has these bad experiences and it must be me- something I'm doing – deserve- but am not sure why. Yes I know—none of these things happened when I was young to anyone I knew. I know you don't understand. I wouldn't have believed it either if it hadn't happened. No, I don't seem to be having much luck with human relationships do I! Ha! Hope all is well with you. Write when you can! **Sunshine, Miles**

When I get back to my tent in the woods, I realize my furs have been stolen. A good half a winter's wages gone. I am not especially surprised. This is just the human race being the human race. Why get angry? *Musical chair of all the goods, isn't that how Sam explained it?* We don't own what we work for. We only own what we can take and hang on to. It is not a set of laws I wish to learn to live by, and if society chooses to live like this? I will not be part of it.

At the unemployment office, the secretary is sympathetic. "But Miles! Why don't you tell the police!?"

I do not bother to tell her my feelings on this. *If the hobos in the jungle didn't do it, the next suspect is the police!* I store valuables on land that is not mine. I'd be charged with trespassing if nothing else. I have zero legal rights. I have no ID, no job, and no way to 'prove' the furs are mine. I'd be lucky if it wasn't me going to jail! They have a hatred for people at the bottom of the pecking order and look for any excuse to hurt us. I have a greater fear of the police than the criminals! At least the criminals I have a chance against! When a member of the law has it in for you, there is no escape, no way to fight back. No way to defend myself. They know I haven't got money for a lawyer. They beat us up with nightsticks and dump us out the back door every day, and who cares? Who even knows? *Look what they did to me in Canada! I lost everything I owned! The fair fiasco. I came within a hairsbreadth of being beaten up. Totally helpless to do anything about either situation.*

What is the use of saying any of this to someone who never missed a meal in her life or been without a place to sleep and store her belongings? Someone who has no idea what goes on in the world, because if she did, she would say, "I hope the police don't know anything about this!" I know such talk will get me nowhere. No one wants to hear it.

So I reply to her, "Oh! I never thought of that! Good idea!"
😊 :) ☠

"Oh Miles, you're impossible! But you know what? I may have some good news for you. There's a good job today, and you got in early, as usual, and it may pay off. You're the next one up."

While I wait for the job call, I write a letter.

THE JOB IS A RAILROAD JOB. A private rail company is putting in a line to haul oil pipe off some rail spur and into a storage yard. This is work that has lots of overtime hours and a deadline to meet. It is nice healthy outdoor work. This is non-union work, which I favor. My routine changes now. I live behind Alaska land and work on the opposite side of town. I have to get up at 5:00 am and do not get home until 7:00 pm. I work seven days a week. Maybe one day off a month. I suntan easily, and we work in the never-setting sun without shirts on, driving railroad spikes with a sledgehammer, hauling ties by hand, digging, swinging, lifting. I feel healthy, good. I'm as dark as a black man.

The boss says, "Ok, guys listen up! We got a new worker today, meet Jennie." No one wants to say much. There is an awkward silence. This is a new concept, women working with us. The beginning of some kind of 'feminine movement.' There was a hint of it in the navy, talk of allowing women on the ships. I'd been catching wind of it from the secretaries at the employment office. Secretaries and I go into conversations about 'equal rights.' I'd spoken openly and wondered why the talk so often got heated on the woman's side. This new Jennie is paired up with me, and so *'here we go again.'* She's all over me about women's rights. I'd hardly said a word! Good grief!

"Miles, Don't you believe in equal rights?"

"Sure, Jennie. I think when someone does equal work, they should get equal pay."

"Well, then, don't you think things should change, considering how unequal and unfair it has been since 'men' have been in charge? You didn't even let us vote until recently! Well, all that is going to end! You wait!"

"Wait for what, Jennie? Why are you directing anger at me? What did I do? Can't we just do our work and get along?"

Equal pay for a job well done and earned does not involve arguing on someone else's dime. I don't like 'trouble,' and frankly, I don't envy the boss none, being forced to hire people he doesn't choose, to meet some kind of 'quota.' Someone it is almost impossible to fire. The guys have trouble believing this woman will carry her weight. To do that, she has to drive railroad spikes with a sledgehammer ten hours a day. This woman weighs less than the rail tie she is expected to lift. If she is paid the same as us and doesn't drive as many spikes as the rest of us, then 'we,' the rest of the crew who only happen to be guys, have to make up for it, work harder to cover for her because basically, we are a worker short. We think she will end up with some cushy position for the same pay, staying in the truck all day, delivering doughnuts and coffee to the boss, something like this. Yet, if she can keep up with us, I know we would accept her as a fellow worker! 'Equal work, equal pay' sounds good to me, but I have to see it to believe it.

I'd feel the same if it was a 100-pound man with no muscles. I'd never tell her she couldn't do it. I'll let her prove herself, give her the same chance as a guy, but like a guy, if she can't do it, she should be out. To me, that is 'equal.' Likewise, 'equal' is I'm not going to open doors for her, just because she's a woman. I'm intriguingly curious by this new thinking going on. The boss has to put in a woman's toilet, I notice. The 'guys,' just go on the tracks.

I tell a fellow worker, "But you gotta be crazy if I'm gonna tell that to this woman!"

"Yo Mon, I know what ya mean, betta just make peace and pull a da load for her, I'm just a glad she ain't paired up wid me. Too dangerous!"

I don't understand what is going on. *Seems to me that 'equal' isn't defined as 'the same.' If I ask for an apple, I want an apple, not an orange.* Even if I think they are equal and like them both the same. Just so, if I ask for a woman, I don't want a man. *Next thing you know, we will not distinguish, and men will be marrying men, and women will be marrying women! Ha!*

"She might hold up and drive spikes all day long, but I'd bet a hundred dollars either someone's gonna get hurt because of her, or she'll end up with some kiss ass job here. So that's the size of it, I gotta woman today for a partner Sam."

"Cool, Man, did you get a squeeze yet?"

"Sam, are you crazy? She's one of these women that'd scream 'rape' if you told her that her hair looks nice today. She hates men, all men." The fire smoke is in my eyes, so I have to get up and change position. As I pass by, I check the rabbit stew. I'm hungry as heck. As I munch on a rabbit leg from the communal stew pot, I add. "And if I even looked at her crossways, she'd say, 'Men, that's all they think about is sex, and you're just the same, seeing women as sex objects!' so I wouldn't consider her if the two of us were the last people in the world. I talk to women like her, and I don't ever want to have sex again in my life.

"What a concept, Miles. You know, you're really weird. Me? I'd cop a feel. I'd hustle that bitch. That's what she really wants, you know. She knows she's full of shit. Don't let her get to you, man."

I laugh. "Yeah, well, whatever. I'm tired, see you tomorrow night."

ON THE JOB.

"Hey, Jennie! You heard what we are doing today yet?"

"I only know we are getting close to the road, and we are supposed to put the crossing in on Sunday when there is the least traffic, and we can run a detour. Looks like we need to get a lot done before Sunday."

"Hey, don't sound so gloomy, it'll be ok. Remember, lots of overtime!"

"Thanks for cheering me up, Miles. I came down on you a little heavy yesterday. I'm sorry. Just a lot of pressure. I'm trying to take care of a child by myself and work too. Things are pretty tight for me."

"I can understand that. No problem. Let's just get to work. We'll have to pace ourselves and work out a routine, so we can work efficiently. You can bring the spikes. I'll drive them. When it's time to move the ties, you have to be there holding your end. It's not too often. Usually, the ties are there already for us to use."

"Sounds good to me, Miles."

Another scorcher day, but we are all used to it. I take my shirt off and hope there isn't going to be a 'new rule' now because there is a woman around, that we can't do that anymore. It might be harder on her. I wonder vaguely how the people who hire her can ignore the fact she is a woman. She's doing well, though, and I feel better about having her as a partner. She's trying hard and holding up her end of the job.

I have my usual blade of grass in my mouth, trying to talk out to the side.

"Miles, why do you always suck on that grass! Every time I see you, you got a grass stalk in your mouth."

I answer her out of the side of my mouth after shifting the grass stem. "I'm orally fixated, Jennie."

"Huh? What's that? I wish you'd speak English Miles, you're weird."

"It means I was never breastfed, but never mind."

"We got a tie to pick up Miles. I don't know if I can do it."

"Well, do your best. It's an important part of the job. If it gets heavy, just let me know before you drop it, so I can let my end down too." We get through the day, and I cover for her, but we get less done than the other teams. I'm concerned that the boss will figure I'm lazy, and it might affect any chance of more work or result in a bad recommendation or less pay.

The boss takes me aside, and I'm ready for a chewing out.

"Miles, I appreciate your carrying the load for this new woman and not making trouble. I know it's not easy, but our contract says we have to do it this way."

"You're the boss. I'm the worker. However you want it done, I'll do my best." As long as the company is willing to be less productive by hiring this woman and doesn't blame me, it's fine.

GOING WILD

"So do we want to join the labor union, or what?" A union guy has come around to talk to us. There are signs up around town, boycotting, and picketers. The one issue that stands out is the boycott of one of the airlines because they hire non-union workers.

I tell the guys how I feel. "Nobody is going to tell me what airline to fly or not fly, and I do not support giving an airline a hard time just for hiring who they want, people like you and me, locals. Why should unions have a monopoly on work?" I tell them a lot more about how I feel, and we trade talk.

"Yea, but Miles, look how much more money we can make! It's easier to find work later, too, if you belong to a union!"

"Sure, and you got dues, and obligations, and one more bunch of people to listen to!"

Another worker says, "Well, the union rep told us, our boss is in trouble, and this would be a good time to unionize and negotiate for more money."

I turn to the group of workers at this meeting. "Look, guys, you do what you want, but I think the boss treats us pretty good and pays us fair. I don't pay people back by sticking it to them when they are down! It isn't about the money, it is about freedom, it is about rights, and it is about sticking up for each other and working together, without outsiders telling us what to do! It's about caring for our job and the people we work for!"

"Sure, sounds good, Miles, but do you think the boss gives a damn about you or any of us? He'd put the screws to us in a minute if he could!"

So we live by 'screw him before he screws us?'

We decide not to unionize, possibly because of me. The union people have it in for me now. I know it will be a cold day in hell before I'd ever get a union job. I wonder briefly why I end up in the middle of things so much and if I shouldn't just keep my mouth shut. There is an item in the news about a non-union trucker being murdered by teamsters. There is a battle over the Pepsi delivery guys and the coke delivery guys. Restaurants serve one or the other, but no one serves both. When I want a coke by God, I don't want to be served Pepsi. I do not know, or care, about all the details, but have heard it all has to do with 'unions.' The more I hear, the less I like them. They sound and act like Mobsters.

Later the union rep takes me aside, tries to change my attitude with threats. I try to be polite with my reasoning. The guy starts to shove me in a corner. I don't want to be part of any group that gets its way through intimidation, blackmail, threats, bribery, and violence[3]. I'm sad, and am sorry in a way, that I got involved and said anything. *Maybe we should keep our big mouth shut. Isn't this similar to what got us in so much trouble in Canada? We lost our home and everything we owned over this kind of stuff!*

Do you really want to get worked over out back and put in the hospital, even killed, over a stinking summer job?

"Hey Miles, come here."

It's the boss. Uh oh!

"Miles, I heard about your talk with the guys, and I appreciate it. You know we always look among the local hire workers for people we might want to keep on and make part of the permanent team. You are a hard worker and get along with the guys well. A real team player. I think you'd make a good supervisor. If you want to come with us to Seattle on the next job, you could work your way up into a good position with good pay."

I appreciate the offer, but I like this job only because it will be over soon. It is not something I want to do for the rest of my life. I stall and give some oblique answer. Society scares me. I think I'd rather just live away from society. I'd only get in trouble. I can't take on single-handed, the wrongs of the world! I'm not even sure it is the right thing to do! In society (I sigh), it is better to learn how to adjust and get along rather than be someone who makes waves!

"Huh? Yeah, we have another tie to lift, Jennie. Take it slow. And remember to tell me if you have to drop it." We each get an end of a railroad tie and get it up off the ground. They weigh over a hundred pounds. We take a couple of steps, and her end drops unexpectedly. I try to save it from falling on my leg. When it lands, my hand does not come away fast enough, and a finger catches under the tie as it slams on the track. The tie smangles my finger. The same finger that was cut by the 'goose wing cutting' incident.

The doctor puts it in a splint, saying the bone is cracked. I cannot work anymore. There will be a little workman's compensation, but I want my job, not some 'medical excuse,' to be out of work. I want a good finger, which I value more than money. The boss is sorry and gives me my last check, and a piddly bonus.

Now that I have a little money, I think I should have a bank account. I have never had one before, except when young and my parents got it for me. I'm shy about getting one, but decide I better go to the bank and look into it.

"No, I don't have a photo ID. I do not drive. I have a library card and a trapper's license. Do you want my money, or don't you."

The guy isn't very friendly. He's explaining to me that banks pay me a whopping three to four percent return when the bank 'borrows' my money.

Isn't that what banks are doing? Don't they spend your money once you deposit it, even gamble with it? Then, when it is my turn to borrow from the bank, I pay fifteen percent? Now I can understand a business doubling its money, and I can see having to pay twice as much to borrow as I get back when I lend, but five times the price? Am I missing something here? I have trouble understanding the long lines of people so 'eager' for the privilege of getting money in a bank. If I do not keep enough money in my account, there will be a low balance fee. If I want to withdraw money, there will be a fee. There will be a handling fee for any transaction. There will be a fee for keeping records and sending statements. I open an account, but I decide there has got to be another answer, and I'm going to find it. I don't need to kiss ass to banks because they think they have me by the short hairs. I don't understand a lot of this. Since everyone else just loves banks. *Proving it by using them, proving it by asking 'how much you got in the bank' to each other, as 'proof' of status.* Obviously, then, it must be me who is screwed up, not the rest of the world. Yet no one is able to explain to my satisfaction why banks are so wonderful for me. It seems to me, a bank sees a young kid come in, and they should see a lifelong customer here, someone they can do business with for a lot of years to come. Why not encourage them to come in, be friendly. Make it a pleasant experience. Be helpful. I'm treated as if the bank is doing me a favor by letting them borrow my money.

I'm also puzzled by the education I received in general, not just about the subject of banking. *I thought 'education' was meant to prepare us for real life.* Yet very little I learned in school seems relevant to real life. I had been upset that there is absolutely no education on basic map use, compass reading. There is zero education on anything having to do with animals or the outdoors. No track identification, no basic behavior knowledge. When I think about it, I realize not many people will ever go in the woods, so there is little use teaching us about it. What about things like, 'how to use a phone book,' how to open a bank account. How to find work. What a union is. Why we shouldn't steal. To me, these are very basic things we should be learning when young, not after we get out in the world! I feel more than confused. I feel sad and guilty for asking so many questions instead of just being happy and complacent. I think I just don't like being one of the sheep. Sometimes I wish I fit in better.

"Hello Bill, Hi Nora, how's business in sunny downtown Alaska Land today? Made your first million yet?" 😊 :)

"Hi Miles! How's that finger doing?"

"Well, it didn't really break, only crack, so I just need to rest it up some. I'm looking around for a boat and motor now. I'd like to get back to my home in the wilderness. Town is a nice break, but I miss home. Hey, this piece of willow looks nice! A lot of work went into it!"

"We enjoy finding willow, and it's relaxing taking the bark off. It's an ok season for us. You want to go get an ice cream? I need a break. Nora, can you watch the shop? We'll bring you your usual back."

"Hey, John! How's the leather business today? You sold that pistol holster I like yet?"

"Hi Miles, how's the finger?"

"Hello, Sue! How's the can-can cuties doing today? You girls working on a good skit? Should I come and be the critic?"

"Ha, ha, Hi Miles, how's the finger? Yup, always a new skit! We got a nice 'toss the leg up' one you should come see." 😊 :)

"Hi, Anne! I'll have my usual strawberry cone. You having a good day? You got enough to buy that car yet? I'll get Bill and Nora's ice cream too."

"How's your finger, Miles? Hey, you got any more of those strawberries you brought in a few days ago? That soda I made, with your strawberries mixed in, sure was good, thanks, we could sell them maybe!"

I fit in sometimes, for a while. I fit in until I say, or do, some 'off the wall' thing or make some off the wall comment. Till people figure out, I'm screwed up. It seems like people are always your friend when you're in a good mood when they want something, and everything is 'blue sky and fair weather.' Who wants to know you when you're in a bad mood, depressed, need someone? All of a sudden, everyone is 'busy.'[4]

Who wants to know 'the truth' about what you really think? About politics, religion, love, and such.

My conscience gives an example by asking, So Miles, what kind of government do you believe in?

I play along and reply, "Oh, I've thought a great deal about it and believe in 'Anarchy,' but since that is not realistic, I think any form of government 'works' as long as it is small. Democracy, communism, Dictatorship, Monarchy, it all works when everyone knows everyone else. None of them work when they get big. The bigger they get, the less they work. I think it is part of a natural check and balance system." That's a real crowd stopper—and that's only the beginning.

As we eat our ice cream, I think about Bill and Nora. He's not built big but somewhat wiry and athletically good looking. He enjoys dressing as a western sheriff. Every year he is the town sheriff for 'Golden Days,' the city celebration of our heritage. He was in Special Forces in Vietnam but never really talks about 'all the ways there are to kill people,' nor does he seem to have been overwhelmed by it. He told me briefly once, as a matter of fact, how he killed people with wire. He also told me it was the smaller guys who seemed to make it through the physical training. Not the big muscle guys.

He told me a story I forget all the details of, but something to do with having been married to a beautiful woman he loved. He had saved all his money in the war, been sending it home, to support a nice house he and his wife had. He looked forward to getting home after the war. When he got home, there was no money, and his wife had been living with another man of another race and class, both spending Bill's paycheck each month.

Nora, the present wife, is Canadian. She was a well-paid top model. She was in a car accident, lost her beauty, and her husband divorced her and took all the money.

"How Canada law works Miles, is there is an assumption the money is the man's because usually the man is the one working."

She couldn't work anymore, so she had to take a big step down socially. She is still very beautiful, but mostly there is an inner beauty that transcends the body. She met Bill, and they have been very in love and happy. An interesting story and good people to learn from. They both seem to have 'been around' 'been through the mill,' and so very accepting of people who are 'different.' Even though we do not have a lot in common, they seem to have big hearts. They are people who do not change things by being radical, loud, angry, lecturing. They change things by being a quiet example. Knowing them is very humbling.

"So Bill, doesn't it all get to you? All the crap going on?"

"Oh sure, Miles, but hey, life goes on. You have to find something you live for and rise above it."

I listen because he is one of the very few people I meet who I admire. I came to the same conclusion, put a different way. Maybe we are justified to complain, but so what. We have a reason to be unhappy, to not make anything of ourselves. How is that helpful? To rise above it, overcome adversity, and look at the silver lining of the cloud, not focus on the rain, is a path to survival, to success, to being happy.

I HEAR about a job possibility as a cook helper in a restaurant. The place is set up to look like the gold rush days and has a lot of trapper, dog mushing, snowshoe things on the walls. They seem to want that kind of 'atmosphere' around. This might be right up my alley. If it works out, I might get a job here where I have more contact with the tourists since I know from my Alaskaland experience that I am a real hit with the tourists. Maybe some job telling wilderness stories or selling some art on the side.

When I sign the contract, I notice the heading on the papers is from Las Vegas. I notice all the people in charge are city slickers who don't know much about Alaska and don't want to. I overhear them make rude comments. When I start my work of mopping the floor, a good-looking lady's man who works here comes up and starts talking to me. I don't understand what it's all about. This talk has nothing to do with my job or the job the restaurant has. I put it together later.

This place is running some prostitution thing here, and the guys are pimping. I never understood the exact setup, but assume they are appealing to the rich pipeline workers who come here to eat, and it's a way to skim some more of that big money off them. It's more than just 'prostitution' though and sounds like some elaborate way to actually roll the customer that everyone plays a part in. I'm supposed to be a lookout of some sort.

The physical building looks plush, expensive, fancy. Inside I see it is built very slipshod. I talk to a guy who says he was a carpenter constructing this building. He says a lot of corners were cut, and it's not up to code. I'm told a lot of places are going up fast in this 'boom' town, just to grab the quick money. I'm told once again, there is a lot of organized crime from outside places like Las Vegas, with shady things going on.

The things I see here remind me of this talk. This place is not in the least how it looks on the outside. These people are trying to capitalize on the 'image' of the rustic Alaska wilderness, with all the proper trappings. I picture the rich business owner saying, "Just give me some image that will make us money, you know, find some antiques, some gold pans, dog sleds, and crap like that." Someone must have said something about me to the boss, how I wouldn't fit in. I had to have what is going on explained to me, like what a prostitute is, in plain language. I never did get to the part about what a pimp does. The very next day, there has been some 'mistake' in the paperwork, some 'misunderstanding' and "We're really sorry to inconvenience you, but we have to let you go, blah, blah, blah."

I SPEND a lot of my time at Alaskaland, sitting in the sun reading. "Hey Sam, you ever go to the library? It's pretty neat! It's a little cabin on the river. I got some good books on the wilderness. There is a special Alaska section, and they have maps to look at. Seems like a good way to find out about things, without having to spend any money. It's a nice warm, quiet place to hang out."

Sam replies, "Well, I went a few times, but I don't have time. I don't read much. Maybe paperbacks I get from friends." About the library, he says, "There are a couple of pretty cute babes that work there. But I can't check them out!" 😀 :)

"Bogus Man, I can dig it!"

One of the guys around the hobo campfire chimes in. I didn't know he was listening. His head is nodding up and down. "Hey man, you got any dope?" He asks. I figure this is all he has on his mind, and he doesn't really want to contribute to the conversation.

I answer, "Sorry man, I spent all my money on food."

"What a drag, man, that's too bad!" He gives me a look, that he feels sorry for me, as I need to get my priorities straight. So many people are doing dope, I have to constantly apologize for not doing it. Once again, it's me who is the freak.

"Miles, didn't you say you was looking fer a boat? Check out the paper here. Guy's selling a twenty-four-foot wood boat with motor and trailer for $500."

GOING WILD

I look at the ad and copy the number down. There is a payphone across the river at Alaska land. Someone familiar looking is by the phone. I forget his name, but greet this guy, "Hey, it's the Leather Man. How's it going?"

"Miles, I heard you on the phone. You want to go check out that boat? Sounds like fun. I need to get away from here on a break. You need to stop at the bank first, in case you want it?"

"Nope, got the cash on me."

"Christ, Miles! You walk around with that kind of cash! You looking for trouble or what!"

"Well, I didn't like the bank. Four percent interest is crap and barely keeps up with inflation. I've discovered that cash talks and bullshit walks. I save more money by putting cash down and getting a deal than I ever would at this interest rate using checks or credit. Anyhow, who cares about my money as much as I do? So who is the most qualified to keep an eye on it? If something happens to it in my pocket, there's something I can do about it.

We have been walking out the back gate along the river to the parking lot as we talk. The Leather Man is listening. He's a university professor during the school year. In summer, he opens a leather shop and sells the work he does, sort of as a hobby, but hopes it will bring him some actual 'profit.' Mostly, this is just 'fun.' He's sensitive about his work though, so I always make sure I compliment it and ask how it's going. He's tall and starting to gray. He enjoys conversation that stimulates the mind and will debate about any subject.

While we drive over to the address I got from the phone, he answers, "That's an interesting outlook you have on life, Miles. I'm not sure I'd agree with it, but if it works for you, that's what matters. I guess I can see your point. I can't imagine a life without banks or credit, though. Your way seems very limiting to me." After some turns down some back roads, "This looks like the place here, Miles, there's a boat on a trailer in this yard." Before us is an old-time river rat that just doesn't get out anymore. We strike up a friendship, and he wants to see this boat in the hands of someone that loves the river life. He doesn't need the money, as much as just getting this out of the yard to make room and the thought that it will be used and appreciated. It was his baby for a lot of years.

"So tell me about the engine. Does it run?"

"She's the old reliable Merc. Eighteen Horse Hurricane. Not fast, but it moves a heavy load and will run all day. Good on gas."

"Well, I sure need a boat and motor, but I'm out of work now and trying to outfit myself to get back to the trapline for the winter. I'm going to have to do some work on the boat. I can give you $400 cash right now, and we'll leave with it."

"Well, I might get $500 if I wait and get the right person, it's worth that, but you got the cash, and I'm pretty busy. I hope you enjoy it as much as I have. Good luck to ya!"

The Leather Man and I hook her up and take her to the boat launch at the Alaskaland dock. I test it out on the Chena and am satisfied it runs. "Well, guess I'll just keep it parked here at the dock, put a tarp up on her and move in."

The Leather Man seems to want the trailer. "What you going to do with the trailer, Miles? I kind of need one like this. It's nice and big. You were saying you want to launch at the Yukon? What if I give you a ride there, in trade for the trailer?"

Well, I don't drive, have no use for the trailer. It would only be stolen, with no place to keep it, so this will work out good for me.

I still don't have a safe place to keep my supplies as I accumulate them. Some things get stored on the boat, but fishermen come down to the boat dock a lot, and it is an open boat. I have various hidden, buried stashes in the woods, but the furs had been stolen. I'm sure it was one of the guys in camp. Strangers do not wander around here, and anyone that comes through here, we know about. They know I'm getting ready to go sometime soon and must figure I'm accumulating supplies. The main protection I have is that few of these guys see any value in stockpiled food and trapping gear. They are looking for a quick turn over, easily sellable things a pawnshop would want. I don't really like hanging around these guys, but it sure saves a lot of money not having to pay rent. Here, I have a place to cook food and live off the land to some extent. Even with the thefts going on, these are pipeline days, with a month of lodging going for a hard month's wages. All those furs would have not even paid a month's rent. Prices on meals are just as bad. Everyone has the 'money' fever. Living here in the woods, I pick berries and tea. I catch fish, have rabbits in snares, and shoot grouse. Sometimes the guys are ok to be around. We go to the Howling dog, and it's good to get out dancing. We have good conversations sometimes. *Mostly, it's all I have.*

My life now is quite different from how I was raised, even from how it 'was' just over a year ago. My mind drifts back to a letter to Maggie:

Dearest Maggie—You asked me about Canada and I never really explained. It is on my mind now, so may as well tell you about it. It starts with raising the money while in the Navy. I want to see the bullfight in Spain. I want to see the ruins in Greece. Many things I do not see, because I take watches on the Navy ship for other people, so I can earn extra money. I want to amount to something. I have dreams for when I get out. I want to get information on living in Canada, but do not know how. Some of my letters are answered, but nothing that lets me know what I am to do. I think I have six more months' duty, and am waiting on papers from Canada, but suddenly the war ends, and I get discharged early. I have a year's wages saved up.

I decide to go to Canada and wait for my papers there. It is not technically what I am supposed to be doing. I should wait here in the U.S., but this would mean needing a place to stay, finding a temporary job, acquiring 'things.' I could have stayed with relatives, but I think, if I ever did that, I would never escape. They would talk me out of such nonsense as a life in the wilds of Canada. It would look bad to move in, and not contribute. The problem would stay the same, spending money with nothing coming in. Now would be the perfect time to move to where I want to settle down. I own nothing, and have no roots, but I have lots of money. If I have the money to live, and I'm not working, there is nothing that 'wrong' with being just a tourist in Canada as I wait for papers. Part of the whole Canada thing revolves around 'what are laws' why do we have them - what purpose do they serve? My own belief is that laws reflect the morals of the majority. If we were all moral we wouldn't need laws. I ask myself what the intent of the law is – and try to follow the legal intent if not the letter. To explain that - one of the few officers in the Navy I got along with told me I had a problem, and told me I believed in 'situation ethics' (whatever that is).

He asked me if I was traveling along a highway in flat country where I could see in every direction, and I came to an intersection, and there was a red light, would I go through the red light if I stopped first and saw no one was coming? I said without hesitation, "Of course!" I can't imagine anyone being silly enough to sit there at a red light with no one else around. The purpose of the light is to let people know who has the right of way when there is a question. The question doesn't exist if no one else is around. The officer sadly told me I was in for a lot of trouble – that if a cop saw me I'd be arrested for running a red light. I said, "that's absurd!"

With this in mind—I figure it hurts no one if I am a tourist in Canada, and if I have trouble getting residency papers, I might instead get work papers.

This way too, I can get the information I need better. I might make friends there, who could be a reference, which might help me get the papers to stay. Surely they would have no reason to not want me there! I'm a hard worker, honest, smart, young, stay out of trouble, and would be a good asset. I will do my art, photography, and trap. All honorable activities. I will live in some remote place, where it should not matter so much what people do, as long as they do not cause trouble. Anyhow, maybe I could go to visit, find a place, and then come back. I'm really itchy to settle down! After all these years, and having the money together finally, it is hard to contain myself. I want to check it out!

I end up in this little village 200 miles north of any city, called 'Beardmore.' I am only there a few days, trying to decide if I wish to take the bus further up the road to Moose Factory, on Hudson Bay, my initial destination. I am offered the chance to buy a house. I am only twenty years old, and bought my first house! I pay cash, and get it for about half price. I still have enough money to live a year, at these low prices here.

Everything is pretty much 'honky dory' right up until the police come, handcuff me, and cart me away. You think you are a king, and own the world, and 'bam,' you're up the creek with no paddle. Certainly, the memories are burned in my brain forever. The house, the boat, the camera equipment, everything that represented four years of doing without, and saving for my dream. Now all that is gone. Starting it all over, from scratch will take years and years to earn it all back, if ever. No one wants to hear 'what you once had, and lost.' We are judged for 'now.' No one wants to hear about 'what we will one day do.' The bars are filled with 'would have should have but didn't accomplish.' Out of the ashes, I will rise again! But I am no fool. I know I will compete with people who never had a major setback. I am at 'square one' and in my 20's now. I'm where most people are at seventeen. How mortifying! Even though there really isn't a lot of years there, tell that to a twenty year old! Those 'few years' of work are a quarter of my life! Every hardship I go through, in my mind, I didn't have to go through. How easy life would be, if I owned still, what was rightfully mine. I'd be a homeowner, with a pleasantly easy life, or at least have the proceeds from the sale of everything. It wasn't just one person who 'ripped me off,' it wasn't even, some uncaring government agency. It was a whole town. I'm willing to accept the blame that I went before I had papers, and maybe I deserved to be deported (but even that I do not really agree on, but suppose I did deserve this?) I don't think it was right to have lost everything, and if I could have afforded a lawyer, probably I could have won.

Everyone knew I was in a bind, couldn't afford a lawyer, and when I was down, they stomped on me. It would have taken only one person standing up for me, to go to court with me, or later, storing my things and asking to be paid. One person sending me my things, or selling them and keeping a percentage, but sending me part. But anyway, anyway, where do these thoughts lead? To happiness? I must go on. Rise above this. It takes time, much time. It is just 'hard.' I'm deeply hurt. I could have been a draft dodger and been accepted and 'everything' forgiven. So I want to know what the difference is between a draft dodger and myself, that the dodger goes free, but I do not? One of the locals in Canada had just run over a child in a stolen car when he was drunk. He was forgiven. Everyone understood. He never even went to court. Yet I am beat up with a baseball bat so to speak, for trying to keep the library open.

I have not told you everything – but that would take too long. Another chapter told and eventually you can piece it all together. Stuff no one wants to hear, not even you. The stuff nightmares are made of. Even so, I plan to survive. Anyhow, hope you are well! **Sunshine Miles**

I fold up the letter and mail it off. My thoughts come back to the present. People like the Leather Man, Bill, and some of the Alaskaland people are better quality people than I have known previously. But sort of 'out of my class.' They all have jobs, have homes. I'm not going to sponge off them, and that's how it would be. I couldn't contribute anything if I visited them. Everything they do cost money.

Going out to eat, even hanging out at the house. I'm trying to live a year on two months' wages. It's about impossible. Every dollar has to be accounted for and hurts when it's spent. I consider it 'splurging' to spend a dollar! I often trade berries I pick for my ice cream at the shop. Things will get better later on, but a person has to make sacrifices when they want something. The alternative is to end up in the rat race along with everyone else. Making just enough money to live on, and never having time to do what you want, and never getting ahead. Even with a 'good' job, you're under someone else's thumb. You can be fired, then what! You can so easily end up doing things you don't approve of because you can't afford to lose your job. I enjoy the things I'm doing, how I live when I'm alone. The problem here is a social one. A matter of the pecking order and social standing. Not having any 'rights.' Being a second-class citizen. In the wilds, I see myself as a 'King.' In civilization, I'm treated like a 'slave.' In the wilds, I have 'time.' I have 'freedom.' I am beholden to no one. I am healthy. I have no bills. I have no stress. Oh well!

The boat has to be worked on, but at least it floats and doesn't leak. It is an old-style longboat. The wood hull is twenty-four feet, handmade out of marine plywood. It's four feet wide at the bottom flat, five feet wide at the gunwale. The bow is narrow and well upswept in the classic line of boat beauty. The sanded hull is painted a robin egg blue. Only because I got a can of used paint at a garage sale. For the shelter, I stick a spruce pole in the bow and stern, run a rope between them, and drape a tarp over the rope. It keeps the rain out and becomes 'home.'

I have a **'Past-flash'**

My father and I have sailed his Yarmouth Key Punt from England, where he bought it, to Portugal. I'm seventeen. We had hoped to get it all the way to the U.S., but it proved to be a slow sailor, and time just runs out. Thirty days is all the leave I can get from the Navy. We had traveled without navigational equipment and been weeks at sea without seeing land. I remember one storm with forty-foot waves hitting our thirty-foot hull. The boat is our home. Because we couldn't get it to our country, the situation presents 'problems' for my father. He has to hire someone to watch it, and he cannot seem to depend on anyone, or else is unsure what is really going on. I'm unclear exactly. When I get out of the Navy, he asks me if I want to go live on the boat, treat it as my own. I can sail it to where ever I wish. This would help him out. He would want to use it a couple of times a year, maybe, for a week or so. I might have to sail it somewhere for him, but otherwise, it would be like my boat. How many twenty-year-olds would give one of their nuts for a chance like this? I could be a beach bum, or do my art, and travel around selling, exploring tropical islands. My head filled with possibilities. I have my own dreams.

I never wanted it said about me, "You got where did in life because of your father!" I did not want to be the chip off the old block. I wanted to be the block. I feel amazingly guilty for not jumping at the chance. It is very hard to say "No." Yet, here I am, living on a boat! When I look back over my life, I wonder how different I am, then how my father is. It would be nice if he could see that. Both involved in 'personal quests,' both 'goal-oriented.' Wasn't he only sixteen when he went to college? Like me, he took a completely different road than the one his own father was on.

My **'past flash'** ends, interrupted by Sam. "Hey Miles, you coming with us to the Howling Dog?"

The same sign has been at the Howling Dog for years, I think, about checking your guns in. I often like to just sit in a corner and watch everyone. Better than watching TV. Sometimes I even bring a book to read. If I see a 'situation,' like some woman who looks like she wants to dance and can't find a partner, or her boyfriend is busy with someone else, or she is too shy, I politely ask if she wants to dance. If I dance at all, though, I don't like to stop. I have never been able to dance just one dance. There are certain women who know me by now and come on the weekends. We recognize each other as people who like to dance. I never go out on a 'date' or invite any of them to come with me to dance or go out to dinner. I don't have the money. I may buy a dancing partner a drink. I only buy myself one soda, and it lasts all evening. Some of the women I dance with regularly, I do not even remember their names. I just recognize them as women who like to dance.

"Oh, hi Wendy. I didn't see you here earlier when I came in. You just get here?" I put the book down that I've been reading.

"Am I interrupting anything, Miles? You look deep in thought and all alone. I came over to see if you are in a dancing mood! Jim's off with the guys getting drunk." I see sadness in her this evening, not serious, but I can see she got dressed up to go dancing with her boyfriend, who didn't notice her.

"That's nice beadwork on your blouse. Did you do it yourself?" She brightens up.

"Why yes! I like the purple beads, and tried a different design, and wondered if it would look all right."

"Your hair looks nice this evening too. I'm a sucker for long hair anyway, but you did it up very nice. It makes you look good. Ok, let's go dance!" I march her off to the floor.

"You're really sweet, Miles. You know, someday some woman will be very lucky to have you. You always have the mountains reflected in your eyes."

When the evening is over, once again, I get a ride back as 'the 3rd one out, in a threesome.' It gets old. But there is no way in hell I can afford a car. I can't even afford a bicycle! Ha! Sometimes I hitchhike out, but late at night, it is hard to hitch-hike back. It's too far out of town to walk. A dancer hollers out in the parking lot,

"The fair starts soon! Going to be a good band playing!"

"Yea, I'll be there. I can get a lot of my supplies there."
"It's hard to believe it's August already! Where did the summer go?"

FAIR TIME.

At the Fair gate, I don't have the money to get in, so I show up way early and carry a box as if I'm delivering something inside the gate. The guards wave me in. As each day goes like this, the guards recognize me and just wave me on as a worker or delivery person. I vaguely recognize some of the booths and vendors, but not by name. Many people remember me, though, remember talking to me. I walk around and enjoy the hustle-bustle of setting up. Now and then, I help someone raise a tent or go fetch a meal because someone can't get away.[5]

There's a lady who buys and sells herbs and berries that I remember because I had asked prices she pays for the raw and how to get things to her. In the back of my mind is an idea that I could pick herbs in the woods to sell. She seems to do good business. I had traded her fish last year for locally made jam and honey. The dry fruit guy is around again, and I buy some dry fruit for the winter. I have little to trade this year, though. That had been a good experience for me last year, trading the fish for goods. Everyone is happy and full of excitement.

I like to look at the children's section. There is poetry, artwork, and the 4H section, where kids have raised a duck, or a goat, or some animal they exhibit and are proud of. I always have to go see the record size produce Alaska grows. The eighty-pound cabbage. The basketball turnips. Once again, I talk to 'the mushroom lady.' She comes from the university and knows all there is about mushrooms. She remembers me because of the story I told her about getting sick from the squirrel mushrooms. She had shown me what this mushroom looks like, fresh. I add a few more edible ones to my list.

She tells me, "There are only about four kinds to really remember, that you might find in any kind of quantity, and that taste good enough to bother with." She shows me the exhibit, and I try to remember what the four good ones look like.

Every evening, I dance in the field around an open fire along with all the other hippies. I have the boat to sleep on at night, and it is not a very long walk, down college road to Aurora, and left to the Chena River to Alaska land. I have a little bit of artwork, but not much. I have a few watercolors I did on birch bark. I do this at the library, using reference books, or on a picnic table at Alaska land. I get a dollar each, but mostly use them for trading with. The main thing I trade for is my daily food. I love the fresh corn on the cob. Young kids run the booth and maybe grew the corn. They think it is cool to trade. Most want a gift for their parents, who they talked into paying their way in, giving them money for rides and such. I'm not taking the art seriously, of course. It's only chump change. I mean, to make real money, like a couple thousand dollars, that would take a watercolor operation beyond my means.

"Hey Miles! How's the finger?"

I don't know who this is, but tell them it is fine, and the splint has been off for a long time now, and it's all healed. I hold up the finger and bend it, by way of 'proof.' The guy I sold my marten fur to is set up selling fur and asks me if I still have any lynx for sale. He might have a buyer. I tell him I sold them already—I don't want him feeling sorry for me because they were stolen. We make small talk, and I wander on. Summer is about over, and it is time for me to get back to my wilderness life.

"So you ready to go, Miles? Looks like quite a load for the boat. You think the boat can handle it?"

"Well, it's all downstream, so I can just idle down." The Leather Man and I are headed out today. I have managed to gather all my supplies faster than they are stolen. We just have to get gas. It's mid-August and time to get going. This is about the same time I went out to start on my cabin last year, so I know what is ahead of me. It has been a long summer, and everyone I know has sensed my restlessness. There is 200 pounds of flour, a hundred pounds of rice, dry fruit, and some luxuries, but not many. I got sixty pounds of honey in a five-gallon bucket. Of course, I have mousetraps, matches, lanterns, and, well, all the things I had on my list. I have a piece of plywood for a cabin door. I have a new stove that is better.

GOING WILD

The houseboat loaded with a ton of winter supplies with the runabout alongside.

CHAPTER SEVEN

YUKON RIVER, SECOND CABIN, THEFT, NEAR DEATH, RESCUE

I'm talking with Leather Man. "What are these tourists doing way out on the haul road pulled over on the shoulder like this? You think they are broke down?"

"Check it out Miles, looks like there is a bear at the car."

As we slow down and drive on by, the Leather Man and I hear an ecstatic female voice, "Isn't the bear cute!?" We take in the scene and figure it out as we go by. The tourists have seen a bear, pulled off the road, and have been tossing food at it until the bear has come up to the car. Now they are getting the bear to 'beg.' The bear is trying to get at the main source of food in the car. It is reaching its paws close to the window as food is tossed into its mouth. A young teen is putting popcorn in its mouth. This is such an incredible thing to see that we spend the rest of the trip talking about it from every angle, for six hours.

"Should we stop?" This is the first initial question.

"Why?" This is the second question we debate.

"So we can save their lives! That little girl in the passenger window is about to get her head lobbed off."

"No, if we chase the bear off, these people will be mad at us and will only wait until we are gone to entice it back. They look too stupid to me to believe us if we tell them they are in danger. Let them cull themselves from the gene pool."

"We could kill the bear?" My laughing reply is, "Could you picture it? We walk up with the 357 pistol and sidle up to the bear. Drop him across the hood of the car in an explosion of gore. We then tip our hats and politely thank them for baiting the bear for us." ☺ :) (?)

. . .

"They would wet their pants, wouldn't they? Maybe make some statement to the tourist department, or write a letter to the governor. I doubt very much they would thank us for saving their lives." They remind me of the beginning of that movie 'Deliverance,' when those guys were floating down the river end for end without a care in the world, with no idea what was ahead." "Speaking of heads! I wonder how fast a bear could unscrew a head off a little girl?"

"Yeah, and if that happened, and we told of it, we'd be arrested for negligence and refusing to lend assistance." We go on by. Not much else we can do.

"Tell me when I see you next year, if there was a thing in the paper about a family found slain by a bear."

The Leather Man answers, "They think they are in a zoo, huh? They will go home, if they are lucky, have their pictures, and tell all their envious friends about all the cute wildlife they saw. They, and all their friends, will be firm believers in turning Alaska into a park and taking away all our guns."

I nod in agreement, adding, "If they get mauled, the bears are the meanest creatures alive, and there will be public outrage. A vigilante group will come out here to find the culprit and kill every bear out here, to make sure this remains a 'safe place. There seems to be little conception in society at large of reality. The world seems in the extremes, huh? Bears should be petted and treated as children, or they should be exterminated because they have no morals."

On this subject, I add, "Yeah! Sometimes I pet them, and sometimes I kill them. Sometimes they are funny, and sometimes they are dangerous. We shouldn't be surprised by either experience and should know that the situation can go either way pretty fast." We exchange bear mauling stories we have heard, bear hunting seasons, limits, regulations, and bears.

"Bear-ly at the river! Look!" The Leather Man points. The Yukon is very inviting to me and looks about the same as it does thirty miles downriver where I'm headed. There is no slip to launch a boat here, just a mud bank cut with a bulldozer sitting off to the side. There is no bridge across the river yet, and it looks like the mud road has just been put in here this spring.

"No, there must have been an 'ice bridge' over the winter because the trucks were getting through."

I think I spot a hovercraft off to the side for getting the trucks across the river. "Well, whatever, let's figure out how to get this boat in the water. The bank doesn't look good here."

We look around. Not many people have launched boats here during the summer. There are some Indians sitting on the bank off the road. We see a little shack in the woods.

One of the Indians comes over to us with a scowl and is looking cocky, saying to us, "Hey, you can't put your boat in here. This is Indian country!" Finger in the chest poking us away. I'm about to be apologetic, calm this Indian down, bribe him, negotiate.

Before I can assume the proper position, the Leather Man comes unglued. He grabs the rifle off the rack inside the truck, jacks a bullet in the chamber, and yells at the top of his voice like a maniac, "You low life Indians want to get dumped in the river? I was born and raised here in Alaska, and this here is a public road. If any of you want to stop us from launching this boat, step forward!"

He said a few more things. I don't recall the exact words, but I do remember the Indian's expressions. They fall all over each other, running backwards to the woods. It is true; no road here is an Indian road. Indians have no roads. White man builds roads. Nor did Indians use fuel oil before the white man. So this whole issue about gas and oil is not Indian money or of Indian concern, beyond how they can get in on white man's action. Nor do I know any Indians involved in taxes paying for all this. It's ok to say it was Indian land and the white man took it and 'we owe,' but the respect gets lost when some Indians want the cake and eat it too.

We get the boat in the water without incident, but I'm very concerned with what has been done here. *I'm the one who has to live here, and it doesn't seem like such a good way to introduce myself.* While we launch the boat, we talk about it.

"Miles, I watch you and think you let people walk all over you. You're always trying to make things right with people—get along and all that. Sometimes that's the thing to do. But here? These people are shit-heads, and someone needs to tell them. What were you going to do, huh? Turn around and go back? Forget about this winter?"

I have to admit, I'm not sure I could have talked my way out of this one. I have to admit that he got the job done, quick like. I don't have a problem with his 'no bullshit' attitude; it's just not my style. I wouldn't bluff like that.

"What if they go get armed, sneak through the woods, and pick us off?"

"Because they are chicken-shits, that's why. If they were real men, they would be more considerate."

"But what if—"

"Miles! I'm getting real tired of this. You see any police around? You see a phone around? Any law in this country? Who is going to take care of you if you don't take care of yourself! There are five of them, and two of us. They don't like us, but they'll at least respect you if you stand up for yourself."

This might be true, all right. I just don't like violence. When it's with animals, that's different. It's food, it's my bread and butter, its defense. When it's 'people,' it all changes. People aren't animals, and they are my own kind. I don't recall ever in my life yelling at anyone or threatening anyone. Anyway, I have a lot to think about.

The boat is in the water, and it is time to pull the trailer out from under it. The Leather Man starts up his truck and puts it in gear. The wheels just spin in the mud right down to the axle in the gloop. I'm thinking in terms of shovels, logs, and such solutions.

"Miles, you see that dozer up there? I'll go start it up." As he walks up to the dozer, the operator of it comes out of the shack to tell the Leather Man a thing or two about borrowing his dozer. The operator is the burly fighting type. I've seen the look before. Nothing would please him more than to see a couple of town looking folk get themselves in trouble. He's laughing at the thought that someone has the audacity to start up his dozer. He looks forward to beating us to a pulp.

I see one of the Indians run up to the shack from behind, whisper to the driver, and point at us. I couldn't hear, but the operator scrambles back into the shack, slams the door, and closes the curtains. The Leather Man acted as if he didn't see a thing, calmly and assuredly, whistles on up the path to the dozer. He hot-wires it, starts it, warms it up, and "thuga, thuga" in a cloud of smoke, here comes the dozer. I can't believe I'm seeing this. I almost have to rub my eyes. I'm too flabbergasted to even comment. He backs her right up, sweet as you please, "thuga, thuga, click, click, shhhh, thuga thuga," and yanks that stuck puppy truck right on out of the mud, with no muss and no fuss.

Now, I ask myself, *"How long would I have had to talk, how much would it have cost me if I'd tried to explain the awful situation I found myself in, and 'ask' for help?"* I can guess! The Conan looking guy would be pleased as a hoot owl to listen and laugh. He wouldn't care if I had to walk all the way back to Fairbanks! He wouldn't care if it cost me the whole winter. If I fell face first in the mud, he'd step on my head and hold it under. If you asked him to use his dozer, he'd want $100 an hour. If you told him you could run it yourself, he'd ask what planet you came from. If you are lucky, he'll only flatten your nose. Mostly though, you're just better off taking care of yourself, and don't ever get in a bind, because when you do. (I make the finger across the throat sign, 'fffftttt.')

The Leather Man runs the dozer on up to its parking place and shuts it off. He calmly walks down to the truck. He never worked up a sweat, never got muddy. *And who would believe this is the mild-mannered university Leather Man?*

"Well, Miles, I'm outta here—want to get back by tonight. I wish you luck this winter. See you next year!"

It's possible I will not see anyone else until next June. I may boat out of here next spring as my only way out. I expect to see at least a few more people before winter.

Right now, I'm anxious to get out of here. The Indians and dozer operator are not exactly my friends. Then? Who is? The Leather Man is 'nice enough,' but I don't even remember his name, and he made the trip in trade for a trailer, and something different to do, not necessarily to be nice. Well, it's good to be on the river again, and there is a desire to put distance between the warpath Indians and me.

The riverboat is overloaded. As I pour the power to the Hurricane engine, the bow plows under the water. The boat wants to take on water and sink. I back off the throttle, just in time, before swamping. There are thirty gallons of water in the bilge's I have to bail out, and now a lot of my winter supplies are wet. I've been in the wilderness an hour, and I'm already finding trouble! *We just have to get back to 'bush time,' right?*

"Yea, we can't be in a hurry!" I yawn and smile. I will not get to the old cabin today, but there is always tomorrow! I have my tent with me, and the weather is nice. I'm headed downstream, so it's not like there should be a problem. I still don't know much about outboard motors, but I'll learn.[1]

AT THE CABIN.

My cabin looks a lot different in summer. A bear has ripped the door off and moved in. Everything is scattered. It takes a day to clean it up. There is no more dry fish or meat left, of course. No human has been here since I was. The one thing that survives the bear is my 'sourdough.' This is the wilderness person's way to get flour to rise. The older it gets, the better it is. I'm enjoying some sourdough pancakes. A camp robber jay flits by the open door, and without looking, I know what he's up to. Stealing.

I have with me a used twenty-two rifle bought at a pawnshop. It's not like last year's magnum, so I want to try it out. I hadn't liked the cost of shooting the magnum at ten cents a shot. The twenty-two short is only a penny. I'm still drying wet food and sorting goods in the yard. I don't need my belongings scattered by jays and pooped on. The twenty-two hardly gives a bang or even a 'pop,' just a 'fffttt.' The jay falls from his perch. I'm walking the path to pick him up when I spot a moose at the pond. I don't know when I'll see another moose. He has heard the shot and is looking up with a scowl. Seeing nothing dangerous, he bends his head to get more munchies from the muck in the pond. I have the 357 pistols and think this is my choice of weapons in this situation where I think I can get close. I still can't afford a high power rifle.

It's not hard to get up close. *Check the wind, stay downwind.* I only nod. When the moose makes noise, I move. When the moose stops and looks around, I stop and keep my mind off the moose. From thirty feet, the moose does not know I'm here, and this is close enough for the shot. I'm still not quite sure where the heart is in relation to the angle of this shot, but I fire and get a solid hit. The moose is in deep shock, slowly turns, and walks into thick brush. My second shot is deflected in the brush, and he is out of sight. *He never saw us, never heard the shot. He'll lie down if we don't follow.* Slowly I walk up to the cabin to get the knife sharpened and plastic bags. The moose has died on the creek, and I can get my boat right up to him. The moose is dead in the thick mud, which is a bugger to deal with, but I manage to do the butchering without getting mud in the meat.

I had seen an Indian fish camp on my float down. It is the one I never visited last year. I had no real reason not to, but mostly it wasn't my boat or gas to go running around, I didn't know how to run it well, I was busy, and I wanted to be alone. Nothing personal. *It might be good to go down to introduce myself and offer some fresh moose meat.* This is a lot of meat to deal with. I know from my experience last year that it will be hard to keep and to deal with. It is at its best fresh!

There are about five Indians around a campfire. Behind them is a big gray canvas tent. They all sit on pieces of driftwood that they will later put in the fire. None of them say anything or look at me as I pull my boat up. They aren't dressed in leather. There is no teepee. No feathers hang from their hair. There are no beadwork moccasins or bows and arrows. Actually, they sort of remind me the most—of people. I neither look down on them because they seem so primitive, nor do I look up to them as woodland gurus.

I calmly go about my business of tying up my boat. I get a piece of plastic out, heft a 200-pound hind leg out of the boat and set it down on the plastic.

"I thought you might like a change in diet from the fish, so I brought some fresh meat. I just got a moose, and it's more than one person can eat." I do not know what response I'll get. Maybe word has traveled downriver like wildfire about the crazy guy and the rifle that almost killed their brothers. For all I know, someone has a bead on me off in the woods. That's how life can be out here in this wilderness. There are a lot of stories told. But I'm calm. I want them to know I mean no ill will and want no problems. An elder in the group steps forward.

"We appreciate the meat. My boys will put some whitefish in your boat." He waves to the boys who go off to their boat. They had just checked the little net in the creek, just like Norm had told me everyone does around here. The elder's hand goes out, and he introduces himself. I'll never in a million years remember his name. I'm not trying to make friends or start a visitation thing back and forth. I've met enough people to last a lifetime. All I want is to be left alone. I'll help in an emergency, I'll mind my own business, and that's how I kind of want it.

"Tucky Mayo."

The hand comes out again. I didn't make eye contact the first time and mumbled. *An elder notices.* I introduce myself. "I was here last year. I got my own boat now and just came back."

"We know."

How could these people know? I had seen no one when I went by the camp and had gone a mile on the other side of the river. No boats have been by. I'm puzzled.

"We saw you go by and knew it was you." How could they have seen? How would they know it was me? It's a totally different boat!

"We knew it was you by the way you run the boat. Everyone has their own style."

What he is politely saying is, I run my boat like a stupid tourist white man, easy to recall.

"The barge's coming, Dad." Tucky gets binoculars off a nail on a tree at the riverbank and focuses upriver.

Nobody goes on this river without every camp up and down the river knowing about it. I can't see the barge yet.

Tucky is saying to his boys, "Must be headed to Galena. Running late. Not going to stop in Rampart. Worried about low water. Must be picking up a load of fuel somewhere. Hmm. Wonder where. The price of fuel will be lower in a few days. Better head on in and pick up a barrel or two." He's talking to his boys.

He's reading all that from watching a barge I can't even see yet? He has to be full of moose turds. Sometimes I 'read sign' and think I know what's going on, a little. Anyhow, it gives me the shivers thinking of people up and down the river sneaking around with binoculars and knowing everything that's going on. However, *these people seem nice, and I think I like the old man here.*

"You sure you're not wanted by the law? Name like Miles Martin sounds made up." He's still looking upriver through the binoculars.

He's as nervous of me as I am of him.

Understanding this, I try to talk in a way to put him at ease. I tell him a little about myself. I tell him of my childhood dreams, of my war experiences, and how I just want to be alone. He has a very penetrating, intelligent gaze.

He says to me, "I meet a lot of white men who have to leave and be alone. I never met any Indians like this. What do you think it means?" He wasn't asking a question, as much as giving me something to think about. " So Miles, how did last winter go for you? Did you meet God?" There is a chuckle in his smile.

I nod. "Yes." There is nothing to say. He understands. I tell him I walked out. He nods, deep in thought. I am talking a little about my times over the winter. The boys are quietly listening. It appears to me to be a custom to let the elder do the speaking until he says it is all right for them to join in. I see a few differences between the cultures, but nothing that is not understandable.

I'm telling a story, "So I hear this singing on the creek, and it is like a woman. I think she is washing clothes, and all winter, I talk to her." The expression on the boy's face is changing, but I am unclear why. I think I must have broken some taboo, a breach of proper protocol.

For the first time, one of the sons speaks. "You know nothing about this creek? No one has talked to you about it?"

I'm puzzled by the question and the reason for it. "No, why would I know anything about this creek? What's to know?" I look around at everyone.

"We call it the Singing Squaw Creek. A long time ago, an Indian woman lived with her White prospector husband on this creek. He went crazy, and she had to kill him or die herself. It is said, she was always sad about this. She lived here alone and missed her husband. She was always glad when people came by. The White prospectors would cut her wood, help her out. She finally died herself. It is said, though, that her spirit is still there. She used to like to wash clothes in the creek. Prospectors brought her clothes to wash in trade for food, supplies, and help."

I assumed it had been just my own conscience speaking to me. It must be so. Someone somewhere, maybe Piper, had told me something, maybe put some idea in my head or something. Maybe Norm told a story, and I just don't remember. I tell this to the Athabascan. They are still uneasy. Certainly, I'm not going to be superstitious. Anyway, what difference does it make to me? I don't care one way or the other.

It is time to go anyway. I just wanted to drop the meat off and introduce myself. They do not invite me to come back, and I do not invite them to come to visit. I know this would be the custom. I hope they understand why I avoid custom.

I answer Tucky, "The White man ways are so far away from the land it is easy for some of us to feel lost. Some of us need to find our way back. The Indian never left!" *It is not easy to leave your people.* I smile and thank them for the fish. I understand that in every culture, it is not polite to accept things for free. There is usually some exchange of some kind. These Natives wish to show me that they are not beholden and do not owe me. This was never my intention. I'm glad, anyway, that I made the trip over, and I hope they know a little more about me and are not afraid of me.

This is just a fish camp, so not lived in through the winter, *so these Natives will not be neighbors in the winter.* On the way back to my cabin five miles downriver, I have a lot to think about. There had been a time when I believed in all the aspects of being independent. It is common to hear from people on the subject, "Be yourself, please yourself, it doesn't matter what other people think! You must only know what you think! There is little use keeping up with the Jones family!" I believed this, lived by this. *Think outside the box.* Canada taught me something different. As I boat along, I go in the past with a...

> **Past flash**: I am in Canada. I am very proud that I have purchased my home. Life will be easy while I wait on my Canadian citizen papers so I can work. I decide I wish to be an artist, as well as a trapper. I can do some artwork now, as long as I do not sell it until I have my papers. I want everyone to know how to find my place. 'The home of the artist.' I decide to make a life-size sculpture of a wolf for my front yard as a symbol of my independence and artistic ability. The plan is to make it out of clay first, then cast it in cement from a plaster mold. I've already had experience doing this with a life-size human diver in high school. I know the oil clay I use will not support itself,

so I will have to use a wooden support inside it. The support has a pole all the way through it so I can set the sculpture between two sawhorses. This way, the clay weight is not on the legs of the wolf. I stay home and mind my own business as I work. I have just got out of the Navy. I was on a carrier, the 'Wasp,' with 5000 people on board, which slept eighty people to a room. I wish to be alone for a while to lose myself in my work and private thoughts. I do not visit much or concern myself with what other people think about me, themselves, or whatever. I wish to stay out of trouble, pay my bills, be polite, and get the beginnings of a lifetime business established.

The wolf is almost done. I have used about 300 pounds of clay, and the wolf is a realistic four feet tall. I think I'm really something. *This is just so cool! I bet people will come from miles around just to see this sculpture. Why, when I can finally hang out the shingle with prices on it, I will be a famous artist and known the world over. Not to mention rich.* Dare I dream this? No, I must be more humble. I will settle for just being famous in Canada. This is my first art piece in four years. Only the third one I have ever done. I can move on to bronze. *I'm young yet with a whole career ahead of me. Haven't I received recognition already? Didn't this piece come out good?*

One of the village people is hanging around by my fence, so I walk over to say 'hi' and introduce myself. I'm thinking he is going to tell me this is just the coolest sculpture he's ever seen.

He clears his throat and asks, "We were wondering why you like to string up dead dogs in your yard." He is very polite and being curious. I think this is hilarious! *These people think I'm stringing up dead dogs?* I explain that this is not real and that it is a sculpture. I am very flattered, though, that this is so realistic people think it is real! Wow! Cool! I never really take the thought to its conclusion. It doesn't matter what anyone thinks, only what is so. After I get deported, I wonder if what people think does matter!

My **'flash past'** ends.

I have to watch this place in the river where I have to cross the main channel and go in behind the island near the cabin. The talk with Tucky gives me insight into what happened in Canada. The people there must also have been a little afraid. If they truly thought I was stringing up dogs, what must have they been thinking of me? What sort of person tortures dogs in their yard? What others think is important, and it is not true that 'it does not matter.' When there is suspicion and doubt, there is trouble. If we are 'outside acceptable limits,' we are branded as a problem. The 'truth' isn't the only thing that matters. What people perceive as the truth is also important. *We cannot live in society and just do whatever we wish, even if we do not bother anyone.* It is beginning to look like we cannot even live outside society and do, be, whatever we wish. Society will find you and impose its rules. This is something I do not like to think about. I'm in the middle of the wilderness. It is almost impossible to live more remotely. Certainly, if I wish to be alone...

"Bam!" Whoops. Better pay more attention to my driving. *What is the bottom doing here? This is the middle of the river!* I scowl at the thought of a sandbar in the middle of the river. Who'd a thunk it? *But this is so exciting, look at this river we travel. I can't wait till next year when we can spend the summer out on the water!* But it will not be this year. There is much to do before winter. I'm determined to have a new cabin.

THE CABIN.

This is not exactly 'routine,' but things progress as they should. I cut the logs with the bow saw as I had done before. The logs are dragged to the site by hand, but I'm stronger this year and heft bigger logs. This cabin will be about 15 X 15. I figure out how to put a window in and have bought one at a second-hand store. Poles go down for the floor. *It will be so nice to have a real floor this winter!* I admit this winter will be so much nicer. Plywood goes up for the door with real hinges! The new stove goes in, and I think this will be so comfortable to be able to control my heat.

When berries are ripe, I pick them. There are still a few raspberries out. I have five gallons of cranberries. I pick about five gallons of edible mushrooms. There are grouse to eat and a few rabbits. I get the usual assortment of ducks of all colors. I have plenty of rice to eat with the meat and make a lot of thick stews with meat, rice, mushrooms, and dried spices. Sometimes I make bread to go along with it, but usually, I have the bread as 'breakfast' in the form of sourdough pancakes.

This new cabin site is five miles from my previous den, and is also on a pond, and has a creek for water. The trees overlap over the roof, so it can't be seen from the air. It takes about a month to finish the cabin, which is the same time it took to do the other one, but this is so much nicer. *We are learning!*

"Yea, this is nice, huh? This is not going to be our permanent home. It is just for this winter."

I had purchased an inexpensive 'survival net' at a sporting goods store, thinking I would like to do my own fishing in the creek the same as Norm does. I can check this without a boat. I get some grayling, whitefish, and a burbot. I have to look up 'burbot' in the book. It looks like it is related to a catfish. There are no scales, and it has a whisker under its chin. It is a bottom feeder. This is the kind of fish that had swallowed a salmon head while I was cleaning fish for Piper. It has no teeth.

I had talked to Piper on the phone and told him I'd be around again. He told me if I did some end of season fishing for him, he would bring me some supplies on his last trip out. He'd wrap up his camp and pick up fish I put up for him. This way, I could get some fish for myself too.

Piper's net on the Yukon is producing some salmon, but not a lot. The weather is crisp, and fall is here. The leaves are turning yellow, and the water is dropping. A boat from upriver comes in sight. I watch as I check the net. The boat pulls to shore at the empty cabin. This is the cabin I had put some things in last year that Piper has told me about. This year, too, I put things in there until it is time to move into my new cabin for winter. I have put a tarp over my supplies and left a note, leaving the cabin usable for any traveler who stops by. This cabin is never locked up.

I am a little concerned about the boat stopping, though, and feel I should go over to introduce myself and ask if my things are in the way. Because of various troubles, I wish to make sure these people are not upset. There had been the drunk last year who had told me how his great grandfather had trapped here, and he didn't like the idea of a white person trapping around here now. He was drunk, so I had dismissed this as something he'd forget. Norm had warned me of trouble and talk. There was the recent 'Indians at gunpoint' episode with the Leather Man. Hmm.

I had to finish checking the net, so it is a little while before I got over to the cabin. The visiting boat is still loaded, and the people are just getting ready to go.

I introduce myself. "So I plan to trap here this winter and just have a few things in the cabin. I hope they are not in the way?" A pretty, middle-aged Native woman is in front of me. She has a couple of children and a dog with her.

She replies sweetly, "I'm headed upriver. I just stopped here for lunch. I hope you have a good winter. No, your things here are not a problem."

We have been walking the path back down to the river. I never go into the cabin because she had met me on the path. She gets the children into the boat. Her things are all under a tarp and out of the weather. I admire her for running the river alone with her children. She gets the big engine started. *Electric start too!*

She waves good-bye, and with a sweeter smile, wishes me again to, "Have a good winter."

As long as I'm here, I go on up to the cabin. I want to make sure everything is still all right and as it was. *Maybe I should get some more oil for my gas.* When I go into the cabin, I see that almost all my things are gone! I look upriver, and the boat is moving fast and well up on step. There is no way I can catch up with my eighteen horses. She must have eighty horses hooked to her boat. I'm convinced she had been loading my things into her boat under the tarp as I checked the net. I had seen her going to and from the boat. Maybe she hadn't seen me. If she hadn't known who it belonged to, or there was a problem, she could have told me. She knew I would need these things to get through the winter and had smiled and wished me a good winter.

I make a mental note of the things I'm missing now. The good fuel for the lantern is gone, as well as some luxury foods and some extra traps. A new handsaw, new ax, oil for my boat gas, flea powder, containers so mice and animals can't get into things are all gone. Looking around, I notice the most important thing missing is the lantern. I decide I can survive without what is missing. I have before. There is no way for me to get back to town now. I could boat to the landing maybe, but not without the oil for the gas. If I got to the landing, I'd need a way to town from there. It is too late in the season to go to town and expect to come back. The water is dropping, and the first hard freeze will be here any day now. If I go to town, then what? I have no place to stay, no money, and no job. Out here, I have my food and supplies, a place to stay and work. When I come out in the spring, I will have my furs and some chance of a job in the summer. My situation is a 'Bummer,' but I'll get by. It certainly reinforces my thoughts about not being happy to see anyone.

"A five dollar lantern, big deal. But look what it cost us. Yet look what the loss will mean to us. Another winter of the gee-whiz light." It would be easier to understand if the gain for the thief was $1,000. Doing this to someone just to make a crummy five dollars is lame. I could go get supplies from Tucky, ask for help. I'm out here to take care of myself, not to get help, not to bother people. I have no more money to pay for anything. Piper will be here one more time, but there is no way to get a message to him to bring replacement things. Even so, I still don't have money. I'd be asking Piper to pay for it. I'd have to acknowledge I couldn't take care of myself. This is unacceptable. I realize I have a strong belief in paying your own way and not being a burden. If you can't cut the mustard, step aside and make room for someone who can. Neither do I believe in crying to someone else about 'my problems.' I don't expect someone to take care of things for me. Don't count on anyone else. This seems like the road to disappointment. If someone steps forward and offers help, this is nice. This is kindness, but this is no one's obligation or duty. *Well, I wouldn't mind if we never saw another human being for the rest of our lives.*

"Yes. Maybe World War III will come along while we are out here, the human race will be wiped out, and we will be the only ones left. Wouldn't that be nice?"

There is no one you would miss? I feel guilty about this thought.

"Well, maybe Maggie, but you know she wouldn't like to live like this. Maybe Dad, but it's not like we are really close."

Not our mother?

"Yeah, well, we don't know where she is." Our stepmother has her own life, her own world. She's with a new guy now and will never be part of our lives. There is no bond between us either. Maybe Eileen, our sister, but she's stuck at being five years old and doesn't leave there. I think she'd be better off dead."

Well, without people, we wouldn't survive anyway. We need rice, beans, flour, and such. It wouldn't matter who we got them from. If we come into society and the Russians have taken over, it would all be the same to us. They probably wouldn't be especially concerned with a hermit in the wilderness. Keep our mouth shut. Mind our own business. Come into town once a year. Get a few supplies and get back out here again. *If anyone comes around and tells us to have a nice winter, we can laugh in their face, and say 'Yeah! Right! What have you got behind your back! Huh! My lantern?'"*

Piper manages to land on floats with his plane to pick up the fish I have for him. We wrap up the camp together. He has a few groceries, mail, and words for me. Piper wishes me a good winter. He wonders maybe why I'm not very talkative, but I manage to at least be civil. I have to admit, Piper has been good to me and honest. I can't think badly of absolutely everyone! *Just 90% of the apples are rotten! Ha!*

As if to emphasize this feeling, I come across some 'end of the season boaters.' I heard them before I saw them while coming back from grouse hunting for dinner. They were down by the water, where I had a few things still left hidden on the brush. I hear them loading my things in a boat. I sneak on down to where I can see them. I'm only thirty feet away.

"You want these gas cans too, Ralph?"

"Sure, why not!"

I put the hammer back on the twenty-two magnum. This is the first and only thing they hear from me. They both freeze, knowing what that sound is. "You two can start putting my things back where you got them from," I calmly say. I consider killing them.

These guys are all full of apology. "We didn't know anyone owned this!"

Yeah, right, so who left it here then, tweety birds?

"Hey, where did you come from anyway. We never heard a thing. Where do you live?"

Like I'm really going to tell them? What kind of an idiot do they take me for?

I vaguely reply, "Oh, here and there. Back in the woods, all around."

They are dumbstruck. "Hey, I got a mine. I need someone like you to look after it over the winter!"

Tries to rob me and then offers me a job? Lucky I don't kill him right here.

"No thanks, I have other plans." They give me back my things. I think, overall, they are normal type guys, have families, and are well-liked. It is me who has strange ideas, not them. What if I hadn't come along! I'd be out even more supplies. I'm glad to see them leave and am glad I built my cabin well hidden.

So much for the myth that people in the wilderness are friendly to each other and help each other out.

Dear Maggie—Do you remember when I came over to your house in the rain and asked your mother if you could come out and play? She thought I was crazy! Ha, ha! You were behind her and said you'd be right out. She thought we were both crazy! We ran the back roads laughing in the rain, barefooted and soaking wet. Remember how the flowers looked in the park? We had it all to ourselves.

We went to that corner cafe and barely had enough money between us to get two sodas. Some man felt sorry for us and gave us money. Told us to go get some shoes. I find it curious how people can see the same situation and perceive it so very differently. What would 'the truth' be? I think of the lines in that Beatle song we liked. "That would be something, to dance in the falling rain." I would guess your mother still thinks I'm a bad influence on you. (Sigh)... Is your father well? Is he still teaching?

I'm in a 'dwelling on the past' mood today. Perhaps trying to figure out where (or when) I went wrong. Why I deserve the things happening to me, or if there is some purpose that will reveal itself later on that will make sense of 'all this.' Was I born this way? Can I put the blame on my parents? My upbringing? Society? The educational system? A past Karma? Why have I always been weird? Is it in my bloodline? I told you I traced my bloodline, and it seems to go back to Miles Standish off the Mayflower. Interestingly, he was a rather 'odd duck.' He was short like me. He was the only non-religious person out of the group, 'stood out' and was the military advisor. The one who wandered off in the wilderness to deal with the Indians. He didn't like the confines behind the ramparts. He had an interesting love life too. Some story or poem was done about him about a 'Priscilla' or some such name. He loved her, but he was gone a lot and so eventually, she went out on him and married someone else. He lost her. When I read about his personality, it reminds me of me. I know there were five generations of 'Miles's I can trace through in the New England area who are related to Boston Whalers. One stole a square-rigger with the crew and was never heard of again. Hmmm. Ha! Well, I was hanging out at the library a lot this summer reading about 'stuff.' The library is one place you can hang out and not be a vagrant. Every other place wants to collect money from you.

I used to spend my watches in the Navy writing to you. Well, guess I'll close for now. Hope you are OK! **Sunshine, Miles.**

I have a belief that we are all responsible for our lives and the events that happen to us in our life. Something can happen 'once' by accident, a 'fluke.' When something happens over and over, then we are 'the cause.' I just do not grasp what it is I'm doing wrong. I'm puzzled. It seems obvious that the things taken belong to me. It seems equally obvious that it is wrong to take things that belong to someone else. It seems straightforward, nothing complicated. Maybe someday I will figure it out. If I am a 'victim,' there must be some way in which I make myself one. Such thoughts are beyond the wisdom of my age, and I know it. *This is not a good way to be starting the winter. This is not the greatest way to see the last people we will have contact with for a long time.*

Diary: The creek froze today. I'm not sure what day it is, but early in October. The wristwatch I was going to use to tell the date with was among the things stolen.

My boat and motor have been pulled ashore. No one else is out here now (thank God). *There is nothing around but us animals.* The cabin door is open to let the heat out as I cook on the woodstove. As I flip a pancake, I catch movement outside through the lighted crack. I think it is a grouse and get the rifle off the wall. Fifty feet away, a marten freezes and stares at me. Before he can make up his mind what to do and overcome his panic, I get a drop on him and fire. The bullet hits him, but I do not know where. He is off running. It doesn't take me long to fetch my coat and gloves. The first skiff of snow is on the ground. It is easy to follow his tracks.

He likes to stay on the high ground, you notice that? I always try to learn about animals. I'm surprised he stays to the ground. I had assumed a marten would take to the trees. Within a mile, he does take to the trees, and I see him way up at the top. I shoot him down. This becomes my first diary 'fur entry' and begins the trapping season on a good note.

Because of the problem of not having a lot of dry wood last winter, I collect dry wood off the ground and drag it to the cabin, leaning it up so I can find it in the deep snow. This cabin takes more wood to heat because it is bigger. Even though I have a stove that works better, this is offset by more space to heat, so the problem is the same as last year. This is discouraging because I thought this winter would be so much better than last! *Oh well! We are young, and there is always next year!*

I'm anxious to trap, and the best trapping will be across the river, but I have to wait for that to freeze. I get to the island first, but the main river on the other side is still open. There are fresh Lynx tracks. *Where do animals go when we do not see tracks for weeks on end? Are they somewhere else? If so, why aren't there pockets of them somewhere else to find?* More questions about animals and how they live. *Three Toes! You see the tracks!* I bend over and inspect the tracks. They are indeed those of the three-toed wolf. *Think we'll get him this year?*

"He only has to make a mistake one time."

As the cold comes in again, I go through the same familiar routine as last year.

Diary—Mid November: First, I stir the coals to warm my hands so I can get dressed. I put three sweaters on, long underwear, wool pants, and wool socks, and then boot liners. Now I light the gee-whiz. My hands go back to the coals in the stove to re-warm them. Frozen food goes on the stovetop to catch the burst of heat when the stove takes off. I put kindling on the coals, dry wood on the kindling, and half-dry logs on the dry wood. A half-cup of boat gas goes on the kindling. Standing way back, I toss a match. The inside of the stove burst into flames, and a new day begins.

Shall we water the mushrooms today? I think about this and get the melted snow off the top of the stove. We lift the logs off the floor. In the moss down there under my floor are our growing mushrooms, but they no longer need water. They have frozen.

Rats! We had a great garden going, too! We are at least able to eat the frozen mushrooms cooked in our rice. There is one kind we especially like called 'fried chicken,' but we do not know the Latin name. There is a whole series of 'Boletus,' which are mushrooms without gills and are all spongy underneath. The mushroom lady at the fair told me that none of these in Alaska is poisonous. "But some may not taste good." There is one kind that I learned to recognize that is dried, and we have a lot of these. *I wonder if mushrooms in pancakes would make an interesting meal?* I think not. We do not try it. We do discover that leftover rice in the pancakes tastes good. We also learn we can take sourdough and powder milk and make something that tastes like cheese when it ferments. *I think we should write a recipe book!*

While out on the trail, my conscience and I talk, *Did you know this one trap has caught us ten marten just by itself?*

"Sure is better than last year, huh? Maybe this year we can actually make a profit." 😀 :)

"End of the line here. I don't think we went any further with traps."

We got a snare here somewhere. Must be blown in. We set a snare on a tree branch at the end of our trail before we turned around. *Over here! It is around the next bend. We have a live wolverine! Should we cut a branch to smack him with?* Usually, we find a branch to stun the animal before we move in on him. This spot is in the open, and the river cut bank is too high to get up to reach any branches. The wolverine has six feet of snare wire, is backed up with it, and growling at us. *He doesn't like being in the snare.*

"Would you? Hmm, why is he still alive? I don't understand! The wind started up three days ago, and the tracks in the trail were made before the wind. How could he live in a snare for three days? He shouldn't last three hours! This is impossible." As usual with wolverines, he tore up everything within reach. There is a hole in the snow down to the ground, and the tree and its root system are all chewed up. He'd fought the snare to where it is gnarly, kinked, and many of the separate wires are broken. For all his bravo and pluck, the wolverine can't be strong anymore. *So we'll fake him out and sideswipe him with the hatchet handle."*

I move within range of the wolverine's reach. To do this, I have to step down into the pit he has created by digging and throwing out the snow. I feel like a Gladiator climbing into the arena. The Wolverine steps forward boldly to fight. I make a fake move. He falls for it. I get a swipe in, but it is ineffective. The Wolverine doesn't fall for this move again. We move back and forth like the mongoose and the snake. He lunges, I dodge. I lunge, he dodges. I don't want to be bit, so I hope to hurry this up. I get over-involved, and then I do a double fake and get a good opening. Using the flat of the blade, I give a hefty swing with all my strength. The wolverine's head flies back. The body follows. Tumbling through the air like a rag doll, end for end, he is yanked rudely short by the end of the snare wire. When he lands, I expect to see lifeless fur. Instead, he lands on his feet. He wishes to lunge at me, but the side of his head is caved in. *That swipe with the hatchet would have killed a person. We used all our strength and got a solid hit.*

He swallows his teeth on that side to clear his mouth to bite me. The rush forward is unexpected, and he contacts my leg with a bite that will not let go. He has only the snowsuit, though, but I have to kill him and pry the dead wolverine's mouth open with the hatchet to get the jaws to release my leg. *When he makes up his mind to do something, he doesn't quit!* I have much admiration for the wolverine, and it is a lesson to learn from.

The loop around his neck has the diameter of a quarter, holding by one strand of wire. I think it possible he would have escaped in a short time. The flesh has been cut right down to the bone and windpipe. The wolverine has an amazing desire to live. I put him in the backpack and head for the cabin. It will be dark soon.

On the way home, the pack comes to life. It is all I can do to get the pack off as legs and feet work their way out of the pack. When I get the pack off, the wolverine head gets free and almost grabs me by my head. I have to kill him a second time. *Is he really dead this time?* I consider just leaving him here somewhere and picking up a frozen body later, and even then, taking precautions.

The wolverine is strapped to the outside of my pack. He's too bloody to go inside. I'm snowshoeing the trail back to the cabin on the Yukon. I hear a small plane coming. Instant panic overtakes me. I feel like a wild animal caught out in the open. I have the desire to be hidden in the woods. Before I can get off the river, the plane comes around the bend. The pilot spots me and veers over to get a better look. I must make a pretty site, dead wolverine on my back all covered with blood, out 'in the middle of nowhere' on snowshoes in the dead of winter. The pilot must be staring at me. I see the plane head for the mountain and barely gain enough altitude to go over it under full throttle. He hadn't been paying attention to where he was going.

A few days later, I am cutting firewood and cut something in a tree. I look at the cross-section of the tree. I had cut a round 50-caliber lead black powder ball in half. By counting the growth rings around the entry wound in the tree, I come up with eighty years ago. *Someone shot this into the tree with a black powder rifle. Was it a prospector? A hunter, a trapper? Had he been shooting at a moose and missed? Had he just been out target practicing on the tree?* By examining the tree, I can see that the shot came from the river. Someone had shot from a boat. In those days, it would have had to be a pole boat, a raft, or maybe a steamboat. *I wonder what hunting was like back in those days?*

"It would have been fun to have lived in those days, huh?"

Yes, but the real days to have lived in would have been 10,000 years ago. Imagine what it would have been like crossing from Siberia to this continent following the Woolly Mammoths. We have been reading 'The Land That Time Forgot.' Yes, it must have been days that God wept, considering what Man has done to this continent after we found it. Well, whatever. That can't be changed. There is a price for everything, and we can't go back, so no use getting stuck in time.

Some people I have met, and know, wish to go back to another time, not just for fun or for pretend. They go back, stay, and never return to the present. The dark times are coming again. The days of the gee whizz light are here, and we are sitting in the dark, silent serenity. The biggest job of the day is merely to stay alive and sane.

Sometimes though, it is good to be lost somewhere other than where you are, in another place or time, as part of a healing thing. Like being on snowshoes on the river and eating up the miles in a white snowscape that time has forgotten. It could as well be 10,000 years ago. The scene would have been the same. Handmade snowshoes, wearing furs, out in the snow hunting. The forever squeak of snowshoe bindings. Sometimes the sound is like a song or voices, mixed in the wind, which beckons me on. The sound, again, just like a voice calling to me. Ha! How odd it can be, but of course, it is only another hallucination. The wind and the snowshoe bindings. I stop to tighten the bindings.

The sound comes again. "Heyyy Youuu...overrrr hereeee" Ha! Just like a voice, and it can't be my snowshoes, but it can't be real either, because no one is around. If they were, I'd know about it. I do not even bother looking around.

"Hey, over here!" More distinct this time. I look across the river. Way off, I see a human and a dog team. When I get over there, the guy asks me how come every time he hollered, I looked down at my snowshoes! How is a man supposed to answer that? Huh? It would take a book to explain.

I just smile and don't answer as he introduces himself, "I'm Bill Henry. Are you OK? What are you doing out here?"

I tell him about trapping and all that. He tells me he runs his dogs out this way sometimes. Bill knows Piper when I mention the name. *Name dropping works even in the wilds.* Bill has his truck at the Yukon, where the road ends. *This would be the spot the Leather Man and I launched my boat.* He tells me he might come back this way and is there anything he can bring me.

"I had food stolen. Could you bring me some food? About anything will do. I could pay you with furs." He doesn't promise to return, and I don't tell him I'm in any kind of trouble. I don't want him to return just on account of me. My situation is only a great bother--but not life-threatening.

"Well, Miles, I better be on my way. I'd like to get back to the truck before dark!"

I'm taking all this in. The six dogs in harness, all lying there quietly minding. Bill, the 'leader' on the runners. He can put things in the sled (while I have to carry my goods on my back!) I note the fact that he expects to be at his truck by dark, and he will not even be tired. The dogs will do the work. He will cover the thirty miles in the time I cover five miles. They eat fish, which comes right from this river.

Bill takes off at a simple command to the dogs. They all get up and just trot away, without a sound, like a wolf pack. This reminds me that I'm really not alone on the planet. Bill had stayed in the cabin I had used to store things in, so this cabin must not be as 'deserted' as it had first appeared. It seems that the people who pass through here know about this cabin and stay here when they need a night's shelter. No one person owns it. Everyone owns it. This is a different concept than I was raised with. If I believe 'there is no free lunch,' then how are these people paying to stay here? Are there people who can pay and people who can't? Are there rules about it that need to be followed? Who takes care of the cabin? Everyone? Who built it, and why isn't it 'theirs' or their relatives? Are they all dead now? Things to ponder. [2]

I am not especially 'pleased' about meeting Bill. Just one more person that knows where I am. If it weren't for 'people,' everything would be fine. I at least know what day it is now. Bill told me the date. November 28th, a few days after Thanksgiving.

As the dark and cold of deep winter sets in, the fur stops moving. I catch less and less. It has nothing to do with my trapping ability. There are few tracks out, and I don't understand. It seems to me there are either animals around or not. How can they disappear, come back, and disappear again? This isn't logical. There is optimism that things will get better if I just sit tight and be patient.

The moose meat runs low. When on a high protein diet, it is amazing how much meat a person can consume.

Diary: Steaks, so big, they have to be folded four times to fit them in a twelve-inch frying pan.

I make a note of it in the diary because this would not be usual fare for 'poor' people in town. My diary goes on—

I feel sorry for town people who can't eat this good. Who can afford five-pound steaks? Every day no less! This adds to the sense I have of being 'rich' and 'well off,' so unlike how I feel in town. The problems I have are only minor.

Once again, as last year, I have trouble with the mice. I am not sure if the mousetraps were in a box that was 'stolen,' or if I lost them, or if they were missing from things stored and ransacked in the hobo jungle. It doesn't matter. What matters is that, once again, I have no mousetraps. Once again, mice move in and multiply. *At least we have flea powder! It sure is nice not to have fleas, huh! We thought that was stolen too, but it turned up!* My conscience is trying to cheer me and be optimistic as we eat a skimpy meal by the gee whizz light. I cook up marten carcasses and add them to the rice. It's meat. It tastes OK. There is moose meat left, but not enough to last the rest of the winter. I assume I will get game of some kind, like another moose. Last year I had plentiful game. This year should be pretty much the same. I'm just not seeing many tracks of anything at all. I haven't seen even a moose track since I got the one moose when I first got here. *It's the squirrel in the roof again. Do you think he knows we are here or cares?* I keep munching on a marten bone in the dark without saying anything more to my conscience. After a while, to break the silence, I bring up the subject again. *There goes the sound of the other one. Do you think they will find each other?* The one sound pauses while the other sound starts. The first sound stops, the second one answers, only closer. They tentatively work toward each other. They are living in my roof.

"It must be warm for them up there."

My conscience doesn't answer right off but expresses an opinion finally, *I think we should kill them.*

"Hmm." Is all I say. They are ruining the roof. Squirrels are eating holes in the plastic vapor barrier. They dig tunnels through the moss, gathering insulation to ball up wherever they please and make nests.

I'm not feeling well, but do not know why. Maybe just depression. Maybe I need more exercise. Maybe something in my diet. I don't even wonder why, really. I think about the woman who took my supplies.

I keep picturing that smile and the, "Have a nice winter!" I wonder if I should take the time next summer to boat on up to Steven's village, where she said she is from, take all her supplies, and tell her to have a nice winter. Maybe it would be doing her a favor and teach her an important lesson in life. *'Do to others as you would have them do to you.' 'What you sow, thus you shall reap.' 'Karma.' 'What you do, you shall get back tenfold.'* I could tell her this after I clean her out. "Next time you steal from someone, remember this lesson."

I could say, If someone takes your ax, that's attempted murder. I wonder if she sees it that way? My thoughts run deep and dark.

I check the trapline again—not one set of tracks on the whole line. The northern lights are out, but I don't care. I fool around tanning more leather, but with no real interest. I feel tired. I had hoped this winter would be so much better than last. Now I know it will not be, but anyhow. *Anyhow, what's that sound I hear? The deep rumbling like a big truck coming?* It's not possible for a big truck to be coming, so I dismiss this. Maybe it is some kind of plane. Some odd natural phenomenon. *I see lights! Down at the river!* We go down to the river. The sound is a bulldozer coming upriver on the Yukon ice. I am not interested in letting them know I am here, so I just watch from the trees. They go slow, maybe five miles an hour. There are several people yelling and fighting the drifts. In an hour, they are out of sight. I can only conclude they are headed for one of the mines by Rampart.[3] This is a very strange sight to see, and I wonder why they use this method to deliver a bulldozer. This seems very dangerous to me. The river ice couldn't be trusted for very many miles.

Like last winter, the temperature is often fifty below and colder, with sixty below not uncommon. Like last year—I go on 'moon time' and snowshoe in the dim moonlight a lot, duck walking with hands waving in front of me. I freeze my face, hands, and toes. I still haven't met another trapper. I still don't understand how trappers sell furs in the middle of the winter. I've been cooped up in the cabin with the gee-whiz light for a week of colder than sixty below zero, and I decide to get out and check the traps. "We should adjust the snowshoe straps before we get far and make sure our hands can come out of the mittens long enough to accomplish this task. I feel that if I cannot adjust my snowshoes because I can't bare my hands long enough, then going out on a long trip is too dangerous.

The air at sixty below zero is dense enough to feel. I have to dress like an astronaut in a spacesuit. My eyes have to blink fast to keep them from freezing, and I breathe slowly, so I do not freeze my lungs. Light seems compressed, and its waves are sluggish. The slow, cold, purple end of the spectrum is most visible. There is usually a fog of some kind. My breath hangs in the air around me as suspended ice crystals. There is a ribbon of cloud following the river. Nothing moves. Not a breath of air, not a living thing. Every few seconds, I gag on hostile, cold air.

My mittens come off, but my fingers are numb by the time they get to the snowshoes. I manage to tighten them, though, and get my mittens back on. I decide I'm going to give it my best shot. I'm going to go out the trail. *So let's get the pack loaded up and grab some bait.* I'm using jays and squirrels from the traps as bait with lure I made. Some sets get fish when I can spare it. I work up a sweat loading up, even though I have been moving slowly. I am too bundled up, maybe. I have to get at the zipper of my snowsuit, and it means taking my mitten off.

When my mitten comes off, my hand immediately balls up uncontrollably, and I watch the back of it bubble up. There is moisture on my hand that freezes. The freezing spreads through my hand. I cannot even open my fingers enough to get the mitten back on. I put my balled up hands between my knees and use my knees to squeeze the fingers open enough to get the mitten back on. *This is not good!* I manage to get the mitten on and go out on the trapline. I only hope there is no reason to have to take the mitten off.

We can't get this marten out of the trap without taking a mitten off. He's frozen in.

"Well, let's put the marten and the trap up in the tree and set a new trap. Then if it's warmer on the next trip out, get him out." The trap is nailed to the pole of the set, so it is not possible to just take the marten and the trap home. The marten is the only thing that has moved in a week. There are no new tracks anywhere. I memorize every set of tracks on the trapline. Tree branches turn as brittle as ice in this cold. All I have to do is tap them to break a fork in the branch for the marten to hang. Every few minutes, I have to run the thumb of my mitt in my eye and 'spin' to get rid of the frost in my eyelashes. Ice balls form on my lashes and bounce in my eyes like Christmas ornaments. Ice in my beard freezes my scarf to my face.

When I get home, I put my scarfed head against the stovepipe to thaw it out enough to undo the knot and get it off. This is not an unusual day. This is 'routine,' and so is standing on top of the stove with my arms around the pipe. Sixty below is cold, always was, and always will be.

We better lift the right foot; I smell steaming, stinky socks. The right foot comes up. I wiggle my numb toes.

"Ahhh." Before I put my indoor boots on, I shake them, as usual, to give any mice in them time to leave.

Diary—Sometime in January: The last of the dried apples are eaten. Rationing to a half-cup of rice, half-cup of flour, and a spoonful of peanut butter a day. No more moose or fish left.

"A fat moose would be nice about now." I only grunt. This is said about a hundred times a day. The flour and rice has got wet from the boat trip here and has put a crimp on the quality and salvageable amount. My belt is pulled in.

Diary—Sometime in January: Cooked up empty flour bags today and ate with peanut butter. There is still food left, but do not know how much longer there is to go. I decide to start eating what I can, now, so I have enough to stretch through the winter. I still hope I will get a moose or start catching more fur so I will have the carcasses to eat.

Diary: Cook up the wolverine, tastes awful, it must have spoiled up on the roof. That had to be the worse meal I ever ate in my life! Yuck!

Diary: Shot a Raven today. Tasted good.

Diary: After two years, I catch my first mouse in a tin can trap! Mice have taken over the cabin. Every day I search my shoes and behind boxes to find piles of rice the mice have collected. I dump the cup of collected rice back into the rice bag. The mice have been eating more than I allow myself on the 'ration program.' A mouse runs across my face and wakes me up one night. Many times, they move into the sleeping bag with me.

He's in the can. How do we get him out?! Last time we had one in the can, it jumped out!"

I do not want to take that chance, so I decide to toss the whole can into the stove. "See if he can escape from that!" At the last minute, I decide this is a little extreme. This will maybe ruin the can trap.

Let's just open the can over the stove and dump just the mouse in. I shake the can like a can of dice. The lid comes off, and using the same motion as tossing dice, the can is emptied into the woodstove full of burning logs. The mouse lands on a flaming log spins around, catches on fire, makes a mad leap to the top of the stove rim. In another leap, the flaming mouse leaves the stove and scurries under my pole floor.

The dry moss under the floor catches on fire wherever the mouse runs. The further the mouse gets, the longer the trail of fire under my floor.

"Get water, quick!"

There are places the mouse has gone that I cannot get to from the top because there are boxes in the way. It only takes seconds for major flames to start shooting up from under the floor.

We didn't have nails to hold the floor logs down. Pull the floor up, quick! With superhuman strength, I rip up the floor and throw snow into the fire. Finally, the fire is under control and out.

Who knows where the mouse is now. Who cares? *The mouse almost burned down our home!* This is the low point of my depression—that I cannot outsmart a mouse. The mice are winning. My diary is filled with hatred for mice, anger, and ranting and raving. This is mixed with blank spots where I just sit and stare for days on end. Sometimes I forget to eat. My anger for the woman who stole my supplies grows. I no longer remember just what she took, or may have taken, but the list grows, and everything becomes her fault.

ONE DAY I'm crawling around on all fours, intent on tracking a mouse down. I have a pair of scissors in my hand. All of a sudden, God shows up. There hadn't been a sound, or an announcement, or trumpets, or bright lights. Just 'God' sitting in my moose hide chair.

I scowl as God asks, "So Miles, do you know what day this is?"

I have no idea and couldn't care less.

"It's Christmas, Miles."

I still don't say anything. What's that got to do with me?

"Well, I just wondered if you wanted anything. I thought I'd check up on you and visit for a while. Most people want something from me, especially at Christmas, like I'm Santa."

There is nothing I can think of that I want that I cannot take care of myself. I'm having a heck of a time, but I'll manage. I just have to get through the rest of this winter and get into town for some more supplies. Nothing I cannot handle. I brighten up. "You could bring me a mousetrap!"

God nods sagely. He's thinking. "Oh yes." God looks around. Here I am on all fours with scissors in my hand. "I see how a mousetrap might be handy."

There is a long pause, so I wonder if I'm supposed to say anything. Maybe I'm expected to get down and pray, promise ever-lasting loyalty and devotion and all this. Nothing is free. God can keep His mousetrap if that's the price.

"So Miles, would you like me to deliver a message to anyone? Your relatives, friends, anyone like that?"

I sarcastically reply, "And what sort of message would be appropriate on this Christmas? What could possibly be said that would cover this situation? 'Everything is great. I'm eating flour bags and am only halfway through winter, have gone off the deep end, but don't worry about a thing!'"

"I could tell them you are thinking of them, and you send your wishes for a merry Christmas and happy New Year?"

I don't say anything. God sighs and leaves.

I get back on my hands and knees and pick up the scissors, angry at the interruption. "I might have had that mouse, too, if my concentration hadn't got broken!" I poke behind a box and find a brand new mousetrap caught between the logs.

Diary: I have no idea where that mousetrap came from. Certainly, I would have searched every box and known by now what I have and do not have after all this time. Maybe it fell out of a box and got stuck here where I had to look from exactly this angle to find it. It's almost as if God gave it to me. What a nice Christmas present!

STILL NO MOOSE TRACKS, still no furs in the traps, or even tracks, not even Three Toes. I am at least catching mice now. Dead mice go in a shoebox and are saved, "Just in case."

"In case of what, Miles?" God is looking over my shoulder, looking at what is in the box. "Do you really think you'd eat them?"

I pause so I can word my answer. "Yes. I remember the Wolverine. How he fought against all odds and would never call it quits." I ask, "Why are you here? Why do you bother? Don't you have better things to do? Aren't there people praying somewhere? Doesn't the squeaky wheel get the grease?"

God answers, "In all your life, the only thing I ever heard you ask for is a Mousetrap, and I had to pry it out of you."

I'm puzzled. "So?"

"Most people ask for a great deal more than that."

I'm still puzzled and don't see where this is leading. "What do other people have to do with me?" "From a selfish standpoint, I just don't want to be beholden to you. Nothing is free. I also feel there are many people in the world needier than I am. There are people not as strong as I am, who can't handle life as it's dished out to them." I also feel everything happens for a reason, even if I cannot understand the reason. I make the assumption it will all be understood in time. I assume there is a reason for things being as they are. Maybe I am being tested. Maybe I have done something wrong, and I am being punished. I don't know. I try to accept what is given, but it's not easy. When it is not easy, certainly I do not wish to blame God. I'm not looking for a bailout. I assume God knows what is best and will do His will, without my opinion or personal, selfish request. Neither am I interested in Jesus, God's son, being punished for my sins in my place. If I have done something wrong, even been born of the wrong species, let me accept my own punishment, not put it on someone else!

"Well, I just came for a chat," God says.

I scowl. "About what?"

God looks around. God doesn't have a face or a voice. Since this is how people perceive things, God gives me an image to focus on in my head.

I am sitting in the moose hide chair staring into the darkness of the forever winter night.

God starts to speak. "You know how you are angry about Canada, and the village woman, and the mice? They do not know you are angry. Your anger affects them not one whit. Your anger hurts you, not them." God pauses to let me digest this.

"Maybe," I reply. This is new to me and a very radical way of thinking.

God goes on with the next thought. "Someone who steals from you loses what? They have lost their good name. It is very hard to ever get that back. You are missing what? Material things. Something you can easily replace." This sounds good and rolls off the lips nicely, but meanwhile, what am I supposed to do?

I tell it to God as I see it. "I don't believe in turning the other cheek to those who slap the first one. I see how 'getting angry' gets us nowhere, but what about getting even? I have a problem with the 'vengeance is mine' bullshit from the Bible. "

I decide I can talk how I want and call a spade a spade. Why should I try to fool God? God knows everything! I didn't ask God to be here. If God doesn't like how I feel, God can leave. God is everywhere, all the time, not just some 'Sunday air' to put on. God is a way of life.

God makes no special comment but answers, "People are rewarded and punished right here on earth if you think about it. Sometimes it takes time, or you have to look and think about it. Like a thief, for example. How many do you know that have it made in life? How many ever truly amount to anything? How many have real friends who can be trusted? Sometimes they temporarily have big money, but doesn't it always seem to get spent with nothing to show for it?"

"That sounds fine, to point my finger at someone else, and judge them, but what about me? How many friends do I have? How well respected am I? I try to do the right thing, and look!"

"Well, you said yourself things take time to understand. Rome wasn't built in a day. Little plans take a little while. Those who never lost never risked. I could show you the future if you wish." I think about that. *Who wouldn't jump at the chance to know the future!* When I have the chance, I decide life would lose its excitement in knowing how it would be. If I believe in what I'm doing, then I simply follow the road and don't give up.

I do ask God, "What about getting even?"

God can see by my grin that there is no use talking to me about this. God only smiles and says, "Try it, and see."

I spend a lot of time digesting what God has said. I start getting flashbacks in the past and know God is showing me examples of life situations and where my feelings are coming from. Some things I 'know' but cannot remember and God tells me there is a reason I cannot remember, and not to worry about it. These are things God has taken care of. Things God thinks I cannot look at right now, for whatever reason. Maybe it is too painful. Maybe there is no good that will come of it. Maybe my energy simply needs to go somewhere else. In my diary, I call these past flashes, 're-runs.' Re-runs are like watching movies, only I can smell, and it is '3-D'. At first, they are 'educational' or 'traumatic' previously repressed experiences. After a while, these scenes become 'entertaining.' At first, these scenes were about people and have words. Later they are about my wilderness life, animals, trapping, and have no words, just 'feelings.'

All my life, I have lived in emotional cycles of up and down. Who knows if I am manic-depressive or bipolar or just an artist. I certainly never had the intention of being examined. It would be nice if we could commit suicide—sigh. *Ya bummer—but you know we can't.* Yes, I know, for we have had this conversation many times when the pain and the loneliness get to us.

I answer my conscience. We can't because we have to fulfill our destiny. We cannot let God down. God has given us a gift, and we have an assignment to put that gift to good use. I'm picturing the conversation if I call someone or make an appointment for help,

"Hello? Yes, we'd like help."

"We? You and who?"

"Me and I—this is me talking – would you like to talk to I now?"

Long pause. Conscience. *Yes, I see what you mean. There's a name for us, and it's schizoid. People get a lobotomy as a cure, and shock treatments, stuck with needles and put in a padded room and—*

"Ya like in 'One Flew Over the Cuckoo Nest.' Remember that movie?"

I liked 'Harold and Maud' better—you remember when the nut is seeing the shrink, and the shrink asks what he likes to do for fun?

"Yes, I do. He says, 'I like to go to funerals!' There is a long significant pause."

My conscience and I pretend we are in that situation on the couch being asked by the civilized guy in a white smock, pad, and pencil in hand, asking what we like to do.

My conscience plays the shrink, and I play myself answering, "I like to kill little fuzzy creatures—sell their fur—stick my finger in the bloody hole in the meat, find the bullet and examine it for clues on how I can do a better job. Oh, I'm very good at what I do—ever so good at it."

This sobers us both up. The truth would not set us free. Indeed the truth would get us tortured, quartered, and hung by our necks. A worse death would be a gift compared to what society would do—if they knew. All of this, of course, is where 'God' comes in when we think of life and death. I cannot let Him who created us be disappointed I was created. If we love God and we love the life and gifts given to us, then the proof of that is to live and honor our friend and savior no matter what gets in the way, what pain there is to bear, nor what imperfections we discover about ourselves. We must endure it. *Yes—for this too shall pass.* I smile because this is a joke to cheer me up. My conscience knows we have not read the Bible—yet somehow, we seem to come up with enough Bible quotes to get by. It is, well, not a joke, as much it is 'proof.'

Proof God is almighty, loves, and forgives us, for God, and God alone, knows why we never read the Bible and never pray or go to church—and He understands and forgives.

There is the Jesus story I think of. *Look what society did to Jesus...and He was perfect.* Sometimes I am ashamed to be a member of the human race. God forgives us. Even so—being 'sorry' doesn't cut it. The only thing that 'cuts it' is to learn from that, never forget the lesson, change and live your life accordingly—and prove that to God. Everything else is bullshit. This belief in God keeps us alive sometimes, and that too is the bottom line. Whatever it takes. For even this, 'Jesus' story has a flaw in my way of thinking. I have trouble looking up to Jesus. Anybody can give up and accept death. I sigh in sadness. I do not care for sadness.

I would much rather look up to Rob Roy or Clint Eastwood as Dirty Harry—pick up the sword and yell 'Charge!' Go down in a hail of blood and screams and glory, cussing and grinning. It's just hard to rally behind someone who just stands there being nailed up while being filled with forgiveness.

It's a good story for sheep. Accept your lot in life of being fleeced, then slaughtered. Put down your weapons and accept the violence, be a victim. It is a great way for those in power to instill in the masses an acceptance of the King. The meek shall inherit the earth! Yes, like that—inherit the earth after no one wants it. After it is ruined. How do I know King James did not accidentally on purpose misspeak God's words when the bible was translated?

Once again, I look at the wall to find the appropriate clipping I pasted there to remember. "How about this one— 'There is one thing and one thing only – to rise, to turn your face from the dark night and greet the white dawn.' You think this is appropriate for the occasion?" I smile. This is a quote from a book we read, 'The White Dawn,' supposedly written about a time before recorded history. This is a primitive Eskimo line that a caveman thought up. A reminder that even a million years ago, it was the same struggle, and somehow primitives survived, and so can we.

I look at another clipping. How about this one that is about the purpose of an artist written by L. Ron Hubbard, the founder of Scientology?

"I like that part about 'quiet revolution through beauty.' What do you think?" Yes, it is about trying to make a difference and changing things through art. No matter what is going on, there is beauty all around if we look for it.

Or this one about being stupid, 'When I want to know that, I'll look it up in a book!' Hmmm.

"Yes, written by Einstein—one of the most brilliant men in the history of mankind." Even Einstein forgets stuff he is supposed to know by heart. No, I do not feel like I did anything especially stupid today. "Hey, what about this one, on being short, and stuff short people have done. Naw- I'm not feeling bad about being short today, are you?"

No all that stuff about big things in small packages, dynamite, and all that, is not the medicine for today.

"So what is the issue today? I forget? The fact no one loves us?"

Not really – heck, I'm into a 'God loves me' mode. Actually? I think it is nothing but a chemical imbalance—nothing in the real world is getting us down—it's just chemicals in the body doing something to us. That's what I think.

Possibly, there is some counteracting chemical that would make it go away and neutralize the bad one. But who knows? *Prozac!* It is not as if it is over the counter stuff we can experiment with. Drugs scare me anyhow, and for sure, I am not going to be evaluated to see if I need it or not. *Lobotomy and all that.* We have to live with it. Anyhow, most drugs are about masking the problem, or more of a chemical lobotomy. Offering a stare of glazed eyes and dull smile. Oh! Here are the words on the wall that work!" "

Yes, We have been here before, and we will be here again,' written by us, a long time ago! I smile.

Yes. We have felt this way a zillion times and gotten over it to feel this way again. For every up, there is a down—for every ying, there is a yang. For every in, there is an out.

"Exactly! Instead of trying to deny this fact of nature, or try to stop, or alter it, we must learn to accept it."

Yea, kind of like the Jesus story!

"Very funny!" I frown a moment. "I still like Clint Eastwood!" We are getting into the new cycle. We bottomed out, are over the worse, and we both know we are on an upside now.

Wow! That bottom was a doozy! It must mean the next 'up' will be fantastic. We should get ready for it. I bet we do some great art or get a lot done, huh!

"Yea. Wow, we better be prepared to feel good then, huh? Look, the down was only a few hours long, isn't that great? We can reap the rewards of our down, on the corresponding flip side of the up!"

Diary: Life is a lot better, now that I have thinned the mice out some. Re-runs today are about my sister. Food is still on my mind, and there is no way to get around the fact that there is going to be a problem if we do not get a moose. I think we may not survive unless we get one.

Diary: Maybe February. I think it is time to come up with a 'plan B' in case I do not get a moose. I have enough food to possibly survive the rest of the winter, if I do nothing but conserve energy and cut myself to starvation rations. I wouldn't be able to trap or look for a moose. I could follow another plan and eat up what I have, gain some health back, and commit to a 'walkout' in winter. I could walk to the Haul Road thirty miles in about five days. I might be able to carry enough furs out, to get to town and sell them. Maybe there would be enough money from furs to buy supplies and come back here for the rest of the trapping season. I could then boat out as planned, in spring.

I spend several days hemming and hawing about what to do. The weather is 'OK,' so I decide I will eat up a good portion of the food to get some strength back and try to walk out. The furs will fetch more money in winter anyhow, I'm told. I assume all I need is some food in me to feel better.[4] Once I start this plan, there is no turning back because I will be eating the precious food I'd need to survive the rest of the season.

What happens next is best described in the article I wrote for Alaska Magazine, printed in July of 1977. The first page sums up how I have to be out here in the wilderness.

It continues with:

Finally, I decided to head out while I still had my strength, and the weather was good. I made only seven miles the first day but still felt I could make it in three or four days. The next day was windy and cold, and the weather didn't look like it would get any better. I didn't want to hole up for a day because my whole plan revolved around traveling fast and light.

I had tried to fortify myself with the food on hand. I was not satisfied with my health after several weeks of eating better, but I was in a situation where I did not have enough food to make it through the winter. In all this time, I had not seen any moose tracks. I packed dehydrated-type foods. There are some sugar and berries left, so I make a 'taffy' out of this, thinking it would be good 'energy' food, just like the survival packs the military has that they sell in all the sporting goods stores. I have some rice and old fish. I think I have enough to last me for a week if I ration myself. I have a few vitamins but think they will be of little use on such a short trip.

Then the temperature dropped to fifty below zero. I made only two or three miles as the snow was starting to drift. I was becoming a little concerned, but there was no point in going back to the cabin. I slept off and on that night. I'd always heard sugar gives 'get up and go' energy, lots of calories, and warmth. I knew it wasn't very healthy to do what I was doing, but still, weight for weight, it was the best choice of what I had.

There was no real choice to go back. There is no food back that way. My only hope is to press on. Making the five miles the first day is not impressive. I had made up to twenty miles snowshoeing on a good day. But at five miles a day, I could still make it within my time frame of food limits. Then I only make two-three miles the second day. I feel so much weaker instead of stronger, and the weather is getting worse. I feel I am in trouble, even at this early stage, but I do not want to let it get to me. I try to be optimistic.

I started the third day and was tired after a hundred yards. The snow was discouragingly deep. It was still fifty below, and I was very hungry. I worked in relays, breaking trail, and then returning to the pack. Toward evening, I was taking two or three steps, then resting five minutes before going on. I was frustrated at the end of the day to see my last camp behind me. I'd gone only a mile all day.

Then I began to perk up. My reserve tanks must have begun operating. I thought if I rested, I'd be OK. I couldn't sleep, though, and I was eating the last of my sugar. My toes and fingertips were freezing because my body's thermostat was worn out, I was breaking down. I was so tired I couldn't even build a fire. This was the first time on the trip I thought I might die.

The snowshoes I have are 'bear paw' for walking in thin snow or on an existing trail. I should have had 'trail-breaking' snowshoes. The kind I have, sink in the deep snow. When I take the pack off, I sink in the snow less, so I had to break trail and go back for my pack.

I saw wolves gather across the river as the sun set. They just sat and watched me. I knew they felt confident, exposing themselves like that. I also knew they wanted me to panic, but that knowledge made me fight harder for life. I was not afraid of them because I was reasonably sure they'd wait until I was dead to come to me. I was glad to see them in a way. All these months, I'd been trying to catch them, and all I had gotten was respect for them. All of us were in the hands of nature, sharing the same hunting grounds and waiting out the same storms. If they made a mistake, I'd kill them. If I made a mistake, they'd kill me. Three Toes was probably in this group. If I had to die, I wouldn't mind feeding Three Toes. At one point, I considered 'pretending' I was in worse shape than I was by lying in the snow but with my knife ready. When the wolves come in for me, I could kill one and have food. I decided I might be in worse shape than I realize. I also think I might waste a lot of time laying there and simply get colder and colder, without a fire and unable to move, or give away that I'm not dead. I also think the wolves might know by my body heat, or sense of smell, that I'm not dead, and, well, what if the wolves have the last laugh and are stronger than I am? Maybe too, I could not move fast enough, or after all the time it would take, they would run away. These things went around in my mind as I watch the wolves gather across the river.

I shivered, shivered, and vaguely wondered when I was going to die. Then the temperature rose to minus fifteen below. I feel now that the rise in temperature saved my life. I got the fire going and warmed up good. I also noticed my boots had given out in the back. I'd put maybe 500 miles on them over the past few months of trapping, and the snowshoe harness strap across the back had torn them.

I had about seven more miles to go. Yet, at my last rate, I'd take more than seven days! I was getting weaker all the time, too. There was one thing to do, admit I'm in trouble and ask for help. That's a hard thing for someone like me to do.

The boots are just one more example of equipment that doesn't hold up and gets me into trouble. Having to admit I had to get help is hard. 'If you can't cut it, step aside' is something I believe in. I believe in self-sufficiency, looking out for yourself, paying your way, and I don't want to have much to do with society. How can I now turn to that society and say, "Help me!" I'd be a hypocrite because I say I don't want anything to do with society! What would I be if I gave up? If I die, and all I had to do was swallow my pride and ask for help, I'd be an idiot. What a waste of a life. I'm not even certain help would, or could, be there. I haven't seen or heard a plane in a long time, and no one has been on the ground here.

I spent a full day stamping out a big triangle in the snow. I place a dark blanket at each of the three corners to signify distress. I stamped out "Help" just in case there was any question. My life depended on it being seen, so the word covered about a quarter-mile.

The back of my trapper's license showed some survival signals. There are lines of all kinds. I decide that 'lines' might blend in too much with the surrounding cracks in the snow. The writing tells me that 'three' of anything is a distress call. They suggest three fires or three gunshots. I know I cannot keep three fires going. The three points of a triangle seem appropriate for the conditions. This will be something 'geometric' that does not belong here and so will be known to be 'human.' The blankets would show up against the white, be 'three,' and not look like something someone would normally do. Building the triangle kept me warm by keeping me walking, so I am able to just keep stamping it bigger and bigger, accomplishing something as I also make my signal.

I lost track of time, but I think it was two days later when a Wien Air Alaska crew spotted my signal. All I saw was the jet trail in the distance. I was told later the passengers saw my signal and told the stewardess, who told the pilot. The jet circled, and I ran down the riverbank in time for me to wave at all the passengers staring out the windows. The pilot tipped the plane's wings, so I knew I'd been seen. It was sunset, and I was not sure I could last another night.

I'd run out of all my food. This is the first plane of any kind I have heard or seen in months. The plane comes by just as the sun is setting. If it had been a half an hour later, I would not have been seen. As the jet passes by me, it has to bank to fit between the mountains and cannot fly very slow, but I see it all in slow motion; hands like haloes around the faces against the lighted round windows. I think it looks like a spaceship full of aliens.

The previous night I had burned a hole in my sleeping bag when I rolled in the fire trying to keep warm.

About an hour later, an army helicopter came by and picked me up. I was happy to be with people again. After the physical examination at the nearby pipeline camp, I was told that I was in better shape than many people they see every day. My toes were frozen and will likely always be sensitive, but heck, I was very glad to have gotten off so easily.

I remembered all the people who had told me I'd never make it out if I went in the bush. I had said some boastful words, and now I had to hang my head and admit my friends were almost right. I was happy at how they treated me. They made me feel anyone can run into bad luck, and at least I can say I learned something.

The article ends followed by—

Editors note: The author, known to his friends as "Wild Miles," has not been discouraged by his brush with death. He's back in the bush and happy to be there, thank you.

I now reflect on how this event was for me…

When the jet had come by, I knew it couldn't land here. Night is coming, and I have no functional sleeping bag. The temperature is dropping again. The jet leaves. After a short time, I believe it didn't really happen; it was a hallucination. I tended the fire and went back to 'staying alive.' The helicopter is a big 'Chinook' that opens like a frog, and trucks can drive into it. They are coming from upriver. I hear the blades in the distance, "Wumpa wumpa wumpa," following my tracks in the snow. I'm proud that the tracks go in a straight line. I concentrated on that very hard. If I was to be found frozen, I wanted everyone to know I was headed in the right direction to the last, I never panicked. I hope I am found frozen facing the right way. This sounds easy until you have been there. It takes being angry and being determined. Sometimes I have to gather my strength for ten minutes just to take three more steps and rest another ten minutes. It is hard to not give up. It is hard to turn around and see your last camp after a day of hard work. My conscience leaves my body. I am not sure where it goes. The wind swirls the snow around me, so it is hard to remember what direction I am going. I promise I will not walk in circles. *We aren't crawling yet! When we start crawling, we've got to be good for at least a few more miles!* I thought to myself. But a few more miles is not enough. It is fine to fight until you drop. It is also smart to know your limits, and know what you can't do, and think of your other options. Any fool can die in the wilderness. The true stories are told by those who live, not those who die! How embarrassing! I fall face down in the snow. It is hard to get the strength to even turn my face so I can breathe, yet I must go on, and on, and on.

The helicopter can't land, won't shut the blades down. The fifty below suddenly goes to a hundred below wind chill with the rotors turning. The snow swirls everywhere. Hands reached out of the lighted snow.

"Over here, over here."

I finally make it to 'over here.' I have to hold my breath. Who can breathe 100 below wind? The first words I hear are, "My God, you smell like a forest fire!" Then, "Are you the only one here?" I guess they don't know and are wondering if there is some kind of major catastrophe going on out here involving a lot of people. They are all young kids, new to Alaska, and in the army.

I'm asked, "What are you doing out here all alone in this hell? Are you telling us you choose to be here?"

I reply, "As soon as I get supplies, I'll be back out!"

They think I'm insane. Someone has a box of the Colonel's fried chicken, and I'm offered a leg.

"How can you live without this?" a pimpled face asks me. I have to smile at people who do not comprehend a world beyond hot fried chicken every night. How sad.

I do not know it, but the five-mile pipeline camp will not let us land there. It is a restricted area. There is a big stink about it. They call me 'an emergency.' We land at the camp anyway. Everyone there knows there is some kind of medical emergency going on. I'm herded with great fanfare to the mess hall while someone fetches a doctor. It is mealtime in the mess hall. Everywhere I look, I catch faces out of the corner of my eyes, turning away.

The female cook puts some food down in the tray for me and bursts out crying, "You poor dear!" She leaves the room, still crying. Everyone is quiet.

We must look a mess, huh? The gee-whiz burned hair, the patched snowsuit, the black from the fire. I'm down to 118 pounds from a normal 150 pounds. The doctor mostly wants to hear the story from the guy's own mouth. I tell him what he wants to hear. He taps my knee, looks in my ears. The usual stuff. He's from the 'lower 48.' He doesn't know a thing about frostbite, malnutrition, cabin fever, mental deprivation, or any of this. I do not care. It is just a routine to go through. I just want to get back to my life.[5] All I need is some food and a couple of day's sleep.

The helicopter whisks me away again. We are headed for Eielson Air Force Base, where these guys are from. I almost fall asleep in the warm chopper. Everyone else complains about how cold and drafty it is.

We could tell some cold and drafty stories, huh? What a bunch of pussies. I dreamily smile as I drift in and out of sleep. When we land at the base, I wake up. It is now very dark. It is nighttime, maybe 10:00 pm. The guys tell me this 'rescue' is good practice for them, and they have to do 'mock' rescues and simulated war games. I'm concerned about what this cost the taxpayers and how I am going to pay this back.

"Rescues usually have to be paid for, yes. We'll let you know what it cost." Some guy with stars and stripes is behind a desk talking to me. I have paperwork to fill out. My name and address and phone number and all this. The only part I can really fill out is my name. What would I put for an address? A phone number?

"No, I have no message, phone, or address." Again, "No, I have no close friends or relatives. I'm not sure where any of them are. Is it a legal requirement to have friends and relatives?"

The paperwork is all filled out, and the guy behind the desk says, "Ok, you're free to go now."

I open my mouth to ask, *Go where? It's the middle of the night, this is a military base, and the town is twenty miles down the road.* I see this guy has dismissed the incident. His involvement is over, and he has other business to tend to. He doesn't want to be responsible for me or my life. His part is over. He rescued me.

I smile with appreciation, "Thank you very much for picking me up. I'd have died if you hadn't." I turn and walk out the door.

I'm not even sure of the way to the gate to get off the base. I was flown in here. A row of lights marks what I assume is the main road leading to a public highway, so I just follow it. The temperature is still thirty, maybe forty below zero, and I feel the cold. I am now wet from melted snow on my snowsuit. My toes were frozen during my ordeal, and in the warmth of civilization, they have thawed and hurt like heck. I can hardly walk. I am not someone who thinks anyone owes me anything. My life is my responsibility, and if I can't take care of myself, I should be culled. The excitement and high of having been rescued has worn off. The adrenaline is burned off, and I'm left falling asleep on my feet. I've been about three days without sleep. *It would be funny, wouldn't it, to step off into the fifty below the snow, go to sleep and die. Found here on the side of the road in the morning—dead. Headlines in the paper—* 'Trapper rescued by chopper found frozen just outside rescuers gate.'

Hey, I hope we find a ride to Fairbanks before we freeze, huh. There doesn't seem to be much traffic on such a cold night. The ice fog hugs the road, and in twenty minutes, there hasn't been one car. The first one to come by doesn't stop. *We must look like a bum!* I haven't had a chance to have a shower, wash up, or anything. My snowsuit is dark and may be hard to see in the ice fog.

The next car stops. "Get in, you going to Fairbanks?"

I'm not good at talking yet, though this transition to civilization seems better than the last time. Maybe because I'd been through it before, but also not quite the same amount of time has gone by.

I ask, "What Month is this? I suppose that's a stupid question. I've just been out on the Yukon River trapping since last September. I had some supplies stolen and was rescued. It's only been a few hours since I was on the river alone and freezing to death." I'm rambling on in the excitement and emotion of it all. The guy hasn't said much, but I catch him looking over at me, the same as the trucker had last year.

He finally speaks, "Could you remind me to pick up some milk when we get to town?"

That shuts me right up. Milk. The guy has milk on his mind. His grocery list. Doesn't want his routine interrupted. The rest of the ride is spent deep in thought.

"So, where do you want to get dropped off?"

"The Salvation Army, I guess." *Where else can I go?* I couldn't get my furs out. I don't even know what happened to my pack. I only had a few of the furs with me anyway. I decided to travel light and to get the furs when I came back. Now I'm in a pickle. *How am I going to pay to get back?* As we travel the highway in silence, my conscience is thinking a mile a minute.

I'm going to have to find a job. In the dead of winter? *Why do so many people think I'm crazy to want to go back to the wilds?* Why is life in town considered so much better? *Is life at the Salvation Army so wonderful?* The smell of vomit. People stealing from you, being treated like scum. Maybe getting a job, but jobs come and go, at everyone else's whim. I can get fired at any time for any reason, real or made up. *I'm in as much trouble here as in the wilderness! What's the difference?* If you don't have any money, you're a dead man. You could fall down on the street, and you may as well be in the wilderness. In the wilderness, I at least have a fighting chance. I can kill a moose and have food. In town, you can't find good food without money. *Food lines? Places like this?* Yeah, right! Standing in line half the day? Listening to everyone's bullshit story? Smelling booze-breath, looking into drugged-dead eyes. The depression is so overwhelming I may as well die in the wilderness with a smile and a joke in my heart! *At least in the wilderness, I can have a dream. There is hope.* All I need is a break; get into a good pocket of fur. Get a moose. Hang on to my supplies. These seem like realistic, attainable goals. What hope does a street person have? *Winning the lottery?* Discovering a rich relative has remembered them in a will? *Get real!* The reality is dying in the gutter, lying in your own piss. Freezing to death in some dumpster. The reality is lying on the sidewalk, as everyone steps around you in disgust. Is that any different than laying in the snow on the Yukon River? Will a single meal save the street person? Will a bag of rice? *No! Such a person needs a whole new life!* A whole new body! In the wilderness, there is hope. Nothing that can't be solved by a bag of rice and some more experience.[6]

"Here you are, Salvation army!"

"Hey, thanks for the ride. I really appreciate it. Don't forget the milk!" I smile.

"Oh, yeah! Thanks! My wife would've killed me if I forgot the milk!" I chuckle and wave him good-bye. The Salvation Army takes me in.

The next morning there are headlines across the paper. This is national news all over the country. The associated press carries it, *'Trapper Rescued by Chopper; Vows to return to the Bush.'* I don't see the article until I can afford a paper weeks from now.

The article goes on—

"An Alaska bush trapper rescued Thursday by an Air Force helicopter after he had stamped out a distress signal in the snow says he has every intention of returning to the wilderness. But 24-year-old Miles Martin says that when he heads back up the Yukon River, he'd prefer to go this time in a houseboat."

I pause from reading the article. I don't know where they got the information. I assume one of the helicopter people.

I settle into 'life at Sally's.' The people in charge are nice people and remember me, of course. My feet hurt. A couple of my toes turn black. If they don't make it, I'll cut them off with a hammer and knife. I don't have any money, so I just keep the toes clean as best I can. I'm interrupted washing dishes.

"Hey Miles, phone for you."

The phone gets handed to me. I'm puzzled. *Surely, this is a mistake. Who even knows me?* Who would know I was even here? "

This is Nora, from Alaskaland. It has been hard tracking you down! No one knows where you went! Bill was in the pipeline camp when you came in. What are you doing at the Salvation Army!?"

I laugh. "I'm washing dishes."

"Well, Miles, you can't stay there! You have to come and stay with us until you get your health back and get back on your feet. Did you know you were national news the other day?"

Bill and Nora pick me up and take me to their home. I start getting quality home-cooked meals and put some weight back on. The newspaper headlines bring us to the subject of my own writing and doing my own story.

I explain, "Yes, Bill, I like to write, keep a diary, and have written all my life. Goodness, I used to write hundreds of pages in a single letter to girlfriends in school! I think I feel comfortable enough with the written word, but that is not the same as being a writer where you have to know how to spell and know all the rules! I'd never get anything accepted by a publisher where competition is stiff. No one would take me seriously as a writer. Society treats me like an uneducated, low life trapper."

"Well, Miles, only some of what you say is true. Remember that many people who know how to write spent a lot of time behind the desk learning the rules and know them perfectly. Yet if you think about it, most of these folks would have nothing to say, as they have not experienced life. You are the one who lived the adventure. It is nice to hear it right from the horse's mouth, so to speak—in the raw. Other people can fix the grammar and spelling, but who can come up with the true story? I'd give that some thought, Miles. Even if what you wrote was not perfect English, it might be great material that would get accepted!"

I'm not convinced. We talk about this same subject off and on. The subject is changed.

I ask, "I'd like to call the pilot that was flying the jet and thank him for turning the jet around. Can I use the phone?"

The pilot wants to meet me, invites me to dinner. We get to chat.

The pilot starts off, "So it's great we can meet for lunch, Miles. You know, you are lucky in more ways than you realize. I do not understand it myself."

"Well, I sure want to thank you for turning around!" There is a pause I do not notice till the silence becomes loud.

The pilot hesitates before going on. "You know, I wasn't supposed to be the pilot that day. The regular guy got sick and couldn't make it. He probably wouldn't have turned around. I only did because I used to be a bush pilot, so I know a distress signal. It's against regulations for us to take a jet off schedule and turn around like that. We have passengers, a certain amount of fuel, and a flight plan. It takes a lot of permission and decisions to change a course. There could be another plane in the area, or maybe not enough fuel to go back. People on the plane expect a time plan, and appointments, and deadlines. The regular pilot wouldn't have put his butt in a sling over a 'maybe problem on the river.' There was a passenger on the plane watching the river, who saw your marks in the snow as the sun set across the river. The light was just right to pick up the depression in the snow. She told the stewardess, who came to tell me, and by then, we were almost at our destination over Purdue Bay on the Arctic Ocean. There was no time to get permission to turn around, it would be dark, and I wouldn't be able to check out the distress situation. Of course, there was no certainty there was even a problem at that point. I'm taking a big 707 off its flight plan over some unidentified marks in the snow. By the time I got back, less than half an hour later, we couldn't spot the signal anymore. I'm not even the normal relief for the regular pilot. A lot of different things that are unexplainable ended up with me doing the flying. It was almost as if I had to be the pilot, and after all this, it seems pretty spooky."

I didn't mention the fact that I felt my conscience leave my body. That's weird stuff, too. I don't believe in tarot cards, reading the stars, and that kind of thing. Sometimes things happen we cannot explain, that seem to go beyond the reaches of just plain luck or chance. It is easy to think of me talking to myself. Some sort of game, or insanity. It is a whole different story to think about leaving my body, and affecting events in two places at once, very far from each other. Having a spirit you talk to, live with, your best friend, God, or an Angel is certainly not anything I wish to talk about.

"Well, Miles," he puts his hand out to shake mine. "I think you are a special person, and the Gods favor you. I'm proud to have met you, and I think the world will be hearing about you. There is a reason I was sent to save you."

I am embarrassed a little. *People sometimes make such a big deal out of things*. I went out to trap, didn't know what I was doing, got overconfident, made some mistakes, had some fairly minor things stolen, which may or may not have been a major factor, and needed to be rescued. End of story. Everyone's life is a story if you think about it.

MILES MARTIN

I trapped from this cabin and lived here for several years. The wagon wheel is from the gold rush days about the 1920s. There was a note on the table when I first got there—from a barge company ending "Sorry I missed you," dated 1952. It looked like someone had just stepped out the day before.

CHAPTER EIGHT

FUR BUYER, ASSOCIATED PRESS, HOUSEBOAT PLANS, MAIL ORDER WOMEN

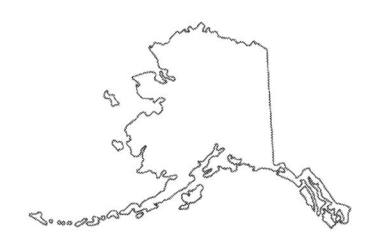

There is very little work in Fairbanks in the winter. I have no transportation other than walking. The Underhill's live out on 26th street. I walk down to First and Second Street a lot, where the main businesses are.

"Hey Sam, how's your winter going? Seems like whenever I'm in town, I run into you!"

"I'm getting by. Car's broke down and no work, though." He doesn't seem especially glad to see me. His voice sounds far off, eyes dull like he's on drugs.

I have a place to stay and have no real reason to hang around him. "Well, see you around, good seeing you again!" We both say "Ya" and give a short backward wave.

There are a few odd jobs that last two to three days out of the unemployment office. I shovel snow mostly. Bill Underhill is working for the pipeline. I'm not sure 'at what.' They pay him to go to school, I think, and he has an agreement to work for them after he is trained. They treat him well, he is loyal to the job, and I admire his ability to fit in.

"Nora? Are you two still going to open your shop at Alaskaland?"

"We enjoy doing it Miles, I guess we will. You got a call today, the number's by the phone, someone named Tucky?"

The name doesn't ring a bell, and I wonder what it's about.

"Yeah, Miles, Tucky here, from the fish camp on the Yukon. I picked your furs up for you. I heard about your problems. You can come on over and pick them up."

I remember Tucky now from the Native voice. He is the elder I chatted with on the Yukon.

I go over and see him. "Thanks, Tucky, for getting my furs out. How did you get in? What do I owe you? You want some of the fur?"

"I went in by snow machine. I saw your story in the paper and wondered if I could help. I needed to go out anyway and take some things to the camp. It was no big thing to swing on down to your camp. I don't want anything, just glad you got out all right. We natives call that 'starvation country,' you know. Sometimes there is game, and sometimes not. That's why we never lived there in our history."

"Thanks, Tucky. I can sure use the furs. I don't expect to live there anymore. I want to build a houseboat, I think, travel around, and see what Alaska has to offer. It sure seems like the Indian understands things about the land, about Nature, that the white people don't know. I wonder about scientific knowledge now. When you really live close to the land, white man's knowledge seems pretty lacking."

Tucky only chuckles, as if he knows this is only the beginning for me.

"Where can I sell my furs, Tucky?"

"That'd be Don Long." Tucky looks up the number in his address book. Tucky has kids around, but they do not say anything and seem well behaved and respectful. I am once again impressed by this Athabascan. *This would be a good man to have as a friend.* It's a rare person from any race who will help someone out so unselfishly and return furs to me, rather than just keep them. It is humbling to know someone like this and helps me not be upset with 'all Indians,' just because a few have a bad reputation.

FUR DEALERS.

"Hi Don, I'm here to see if we can do some fur business. Tucky Mayo sent me, says he knows you."

"Come on in, yes I know him, my wife is Native, comes from Rampart. I know about every Indian on the river." Don is white, medium height, stockily built, and always seems to have a plug of tobacco in his cheek. The way he talks makes a person smile. He paces his words differently, is expressive with his gestures, and pauses a lot as if he's thinking. Seems to say whatever is on his mind in a very honest but maybe not so tactful way. He's done a lot of fur business in his life.

"Used to be a professional Wolfer in Montana. There was a bounty on them back in those days."

After I loosen up a little, I get out my furs. The first thing Don says when he sees my marten, in almost a holler.

"Jesus Christ! What did you do! Put these on muskrat board?!" I'm puzzled by his reaction, and he sees I don't know what he's talking about. "They are almost as wide as they are long, Miles! We pay by the length. Look at these over here. This is how they are supposed to look!"

He takes me to the back room of his house. His wife says, 'Hi.' She's a tall, well-dressed native woman, very nice looking, with a good business head. I'm shown marten that don't look very much like mine. It is hard to believe it is the same animal. I, of course, have never met a trapper, talked to a fur buyer, seen 'real fur' that is well handled. All I have is my books. I tell Don I made my own stretchers (Proudly said).

Don looks at my fur and shakes his head, and I think I hear him mumble, "I'm sure!" under his breath. He knows I'm not going to be happy with what he offers. "Maybe I can re-stretch them," he mumbles to himself, so I can hear, followed by an audible sigh.

He looks at the tails. "Did ja split the tails? Of course not; how would you know about that?" He looks at the tails and snorts. Well, I don't want him to lose money on me, and if he tells me honestly what is wrong and that the value is low as a result, then I'm not angry. I just learn and do better next time. I admit I'm sort of a slow learner sometimes. It is easier to think the marten in my area are defunct. That I could use a few minor pointers, but I know what I'm doing. *I followed the book, didn't I?*

I hear Don mumble "Christ! Another educated Idiot," under his breath when I mention the word 'book.'

Don quits insulting my fur. He doesn't want to lose my business.

"Some guys got a forty-five dollar average earlier this winter, on the first auction in Seattle. I can give you…" He does some figures on the calculator and pauses, "…your average will be thirty dollars. You have a couple of really nice furs in here that might be worth fifty and some others that might go for only twenty." This offer is still almost three times what I got last year, so I'm happy enough. I learn that I have to pay attention to my 'average,' not what the buyer offers for the best fur.

Don explains it. "A lot of trappers will quote you the top dollar paid to them for the best fur, but do not tell you what they averaged!" Don is educating me on the business in general. I walk out with over a thousand dollars cash. This is the first time I see this aspect of my lifestyle. The feast and famine. *Sometimes big wads of money in my pocket, other times, flat broke.* This, to me, is really something. I'm counting out piles of bills on a kitchen table in someone's house. My conscience cheerfully adds, *And no paperwork, no receipt, did you notice that? Huh?* I'm hooked. 😊 :)

"How many odd jobs would it take to make a thousand dollars? At least two months??"

The odd jobs take care of a few basics I need. I've spent more time than I should with Bill and Nora. The weather warms up. I move back to the woods behind Alaskaland. I don't have to cut my toes off, so I'm glad enough about that. I'm sure the nice care I got with the Underhill's helped. There is no one else living back behind Alaskaland this year, so I have the woods to myself so far.

"Hey!"

My head snaps around to see who called. I'm just walking out of the woods onto the road. The usual blade of grass is hanging from my mouth, fur hat pulled down to shield my eyes. A guy in a car on the side of the road has hailed me.

My blade of grass shifts to the other side as I answer. "So what's up?"

A big strong farmer-type guy says, "Every morning I see you just walk out of the woods! You live back there?"

I'm not sure I want to let on where I live. I don't need my things stolen, and maybe it's not legal to live here in the woods.

Before I can answer, he adds, "I'm living in my car here, and I see you come out every morning. I wondered if it would be better to move into the woods."

My reply is, "No, lots of mosquitoes. Got a tent?"

We get to talking. His name's Will. He's my age, maybe twenty-four. His family moved here from Iowa. Sold the farm just before the bottom fell out of the market. They used the money to move here and are trying to get pipeline jobs. His father has a job, but Will hasn't got one yet. Money's tight. He has transportation but no money for gas to do anything. I have enough money for gas but no transportation. We drive around and check out job situations, go to garage sales, and become friends. Will's twice my size. His arms are as big around as my waist. He's easy-going, slow-talking, doesn't like crowds. Prefers wearing farmer coveralls with suspenders, his way of identifying with his tribe.

"I wouldn't mind living out in the wilderness, Miles. It's kind of why I came up here. Just want a pipeline job to get the money to do it."

Will is good at welding, working on cars, trucks, bulldozers, and just building mechanical things, but not really wanting to be a mechanic. The kind of jobs Will looks for are not the same kind as I look for, so we are not in competition over work. I like Will mostly because he is level headed, honest, not into drugs or being a street person. He's temporarily down on his luck but doesn't plan on making a career out of it. Will seems to accept my bad habits and takes them in stride. We both love the wilderness.

Alaskaland opens for the tourist season, and I still haven't got serious work. This is May, breakup of the ice, and it is tough for me, knowing boating season is starting. My boat should be safe up on the riverbank where I left it on the Yukon, but how do I get to it? Will has heard me speak of this problem. He says he'll take me out the Haul road. We could maybe get hold of a small boat and motor to go down and get mine with, then put the small boat in the big boat on the trailer to come back. Will wants to see the Yukon and see the country I lived in. We round up a small lake boat, an old motor, and a trailer we can borrow.

GOING WILD

"This is the place where I walked out, Will, mile sixty-four." We stop to get out and look around. I tell Will about the trip as I point down the valley I walked up. We get to the Yukon without incident, except the weather gets bad on us. The rain will not let up. We are trying to sleep in his truck to stay dry. I haven't got a problem. I can stretch out on the front seat and not even touch the doors. Will is pretty scrunched up in the back seat.

"So Miles, why do you think anarchy would work. The impression I get is that with no government whatever there would be chaos."

We have a lot of hours to pass and are talking about all sorts of things. I answer, "I agree, certainly at first anyway. In the beginning, when everything we know collapses, the things that we count on the most would fail. What would affect us the most, that takes the most organization, would be transportation and communication." We have been talking about a possible revolution, a war in which our country loses, or the collapse of society as we know it due to natural causes.

I'm rambling about what I think would happen. "The power would go off. This will freak out a majority of people who can't even comprehend life without electricity. A lot of people consider it a necessity, not a luxury. So right off the bat, a high percent of the population will start to wig out. As proof, just look at the news! A remote community loses power for even a day, and it becomes a national disaster. There would be backup generators at first and emergency radio and TV. There would be a semblance of civilization going on. Transportation would fail as soon as the power went out. The elaborate process of fuel refinement and the distribution of everything civilized would get costly.

Generators would get overtaxed and need repairing while everyone would be running around. Those who freak out first would try to see that they are taken care of, operating in panic mode. This means acquiring a generator, and if they don't have money, they will try to steal them. People will try to steal food and anything they want. Just look what happens when there is a temporary blackout. It's everyone for themselves. People will steal generators, then not know how to get them to work. They will try to take over power plants, not knowing how to run them. They will highjack trucks, and highways will not be safe. The level of inefficiency would increase ten-fold. It wouldn't be but a week. Truckers won't want to leave families while they go out on the road. Without delivery, the goods of the world will pile up. Those who are still sane will try to ration gas, conserve goods, and sit tight. But too many others will not believe in sitting tight. Security, the government, the police would begin to be ineffective. Too many people don't believe in doing the right thing unless they are forced to. It is the law and threat of punishment, not personal integrity, that holds it all together for the majority.

Once there is a lack of fear of getting caught, followed by the other fear of doing without, many will go on a rampage. The stupid ones will grab up TVs, cars, jewels, and such. They will feel on cloud nine for a week or so. This is already in evidence when there is a temporary collapse of the system. Some will grab up food, candles, and survival gear. The time will come when the needy will note who has stockpiled the goods and conduct raids. Nothing is yours unless you can protect it, defend it. The goods will end up all over. People will be killing for food. This time might last a few weeks to a year. Some people could be out in the wilderness with everything they need for a year. There will be those who run to the wilderness. Without proper supplies, they will drop like flies. Some wilderness people would be found, killed, cleaned out. Yet, some might not be found.

Those in town would live in total chaos. Those who panic first will fall first. Those who steal the most will themselves be robbed by the following masses. The smart and the strong will tend to survive. Those who work together with others, and work on cooperation, would tend to survive the longest. Thieves don't trust anyone, or even each other, so they wouldn't survive because they couldn't make plans that involve trusting each other. Half the population would be dead within a few months, I think.

There would be a time of disease, rotten food, and fires out of control. It would be a mess and not a good time to be around. After this time, there would be groups who look over the situation and take stock of things. Individuals will have learned what is important and what is not. This would be the beginning of Anarchy. No government, just small groups struggling to stay alive, finding out that cooperation works. Discovering the basic truth, that honesty pays, as well as loyalty, and being trustworthy. Those who survive might be 'good,' not because they will be hit by a big stick, but because 'it works,' 'it's survival.' This would be the time for those in the wilderness who rode it out to come out and see who has survived and see who there was to work with. A person would have to be armed and be no fool. There would still be groups that live off violence and force, bushwhacking travelers.

When it comes down to 'Do you want to work together, or do you want to die!' I think at least some will try to work together. It is smart to get the guy who knows how to hunt in the group with the guy who knows how to build, along with the doctor. I think groups would form that would resemble primitive groups of long ago. I'd guess family groups and groups with no more than twenty or so people in them. Big enough to defend the group, but small enough to where everyone knows everyone else well. There would be no specific form of government, maybe just temporary cooperation, to perform specific jobs, and then the group might break up again. I think there would be a time, on the other side of chaos, with peace. A situation with a lot fewer people and a group made up of the best of society, like a natural selection process. My view, I think, is 'optimistic' and is based on the premise that people are basically 'good,' and that, without government, the scum would get skimmed off the top, the bottom feeders would sink, and what was left, would be healthy."

"So Miles, is this why you believe in stockpiling against hard times?"

"Partly. More because I think the prices of goods will go up, while the quality of goods will go down. I wonder if, as a civilization, we have 'peaked out' or, maybe just our country has seen its best days, and a time will come when we don't have the power we once had. We despise war now, haven't outrightly won a war in a while. We never won in Korea or Viet Nam. Never had our continent invaded, and so seem not to comprehend the reality of war. If we fall as a world power, even are invaded, our quality of life will fall. Americans tend to forget how the rest of the world lives. Many cultures scowl at us for keeping, and controlling the goods of the world, while we Americans sweetly talk about democracy, freedom, and peace in one sentence. In fact, we are not a democratic society, never were. We began as a republic. We are now even further from democracy and individual rights. We live high on the hog and lose our sense of needing to defend and protect what we have. Stronger people are coming along who want what we have, are willing to fight for it, and willing to sacrifice and work. Americans are becoming soft and lazy, as the Romans did.

This is part of my rabbit cycle theory and adds to the idea it might be good to stockpile goods. Even if products remain available, it might be hard to get the job and money in the future to buy what is needed. Today's quality may not be available in the future at any price. The laws may even get more restrictive. We are becoming more communistic over time. Which means no one is 'allowed' to be different.[1]

The concept of free enterprise is getting lost. Those who get ahead are taxed at a higher rate and forced to support the needy. The rich get richer, the poor get poorer. The smart rich take their money and business to other countries. The middle class is becoming more uniform and closer to the poor than to the rich. In this way, too, we are much like the days of the serfs where the majority support the few. Right now, people like you and I still have a chance to get ahead and be free. This time could last longer for us if we store the things we need most, while these necessities are still available, legal, affordable, and built with some quality and pride, so they work when needed. Why put money in the bank? Why not put it in 'goods' that have real value, that are tradable, useful? Money in the bank is very dependent on the survival and strength of our country. 'Goods' can be traded to anyone, anywhere. 'Dry food' will always have value, even if gold becomes useless. Maybe nothing will ever happen to civilization as we know it, but it is easy enough to prepare, just in case. An ace in the hole. Why not? Personally, I feel a lot richer with a lifetime of firewood than I do, depending on those "A-rabs" for oil heat! Suppose those who now supply our country with oil decide to sell it to someone else, or raise the price, or keep it for themselves? Do I personally want to be at the mercy of a country that hates us?"

"We better get some sleep, Miles."

On that note, we both drift off into light snoring.

As an afterthought, I add, "Remind me to tell you about my 'rabbit cycle theory' of civilization." We both laugh. *That should be a good conversation!*

In the morning, the rain has turned into a wet fog. "You ready to do some boating Will?"

"Umm. Coffee. Umm."

He's still half asleep and wants coffee. I'm one of these people that wake up wide-awake, ready to start my day within five minutes, and usually by 6:00 am. Maybe it is one reason I've never been a very social person. My thoughts drift as I wait for Will to remember where he is. We make coffee over an open fire by the truck, and eat sandwiches we brought with us. The boat is in the water by noon. Will's all excited to be boating. The outboard gives us a little trouble, and it is Will who knows enough about them to fiddle with it. I watch and get my first lessons on how to get a cranky engine to get its horses in harness.

Will turns to me, "All engines run on air, fuel, and spark. Those are the three categories to think about, Miles."

I listen.

"If it doesn't run, the easiest thing, and the first thing to check, is to see if it has spark. Pull a plug wire and hold it on the frame. If you got spark, see if you got fuel. Pull a fuel line off if you have to." He gives me a run down on the basics. Nothing is ever that 'simple,' but I have a place to start learning on my own now.

We 'putt-putt' on down the mighty Yukon. The wet fog chills us to the bone. There are big chunks of ice on the riverbank from break up, which was only a week ago. We have seen no one, not on the road, not at the landing, not on the river.

"This is pretty nice Miles, we are out in the wilderness, and it's like a hundred years ago!" It takes us maybe four hours to get to my cabin.

"Pretty small, Miles!"

"Yea, well, it's bigger than the first one I built. I knew I wouldn't be staying, so didn't try to do anything fancy." We find my bow saw in a tree outside. *I must have forgotten to put it inside when I left.* The boat is ok, but maybe some ice has pushed it further in the woods. The motor was further up and is fine. Tucky hadn't found all my furs, some of which got damp but not spoiled because it is still cold. I'm lucky about this. Tucky had brought most of the furs in for me, but there is a wolverine, and some marten left here. Maybe Tucky hadn't seen them when the snow was deep.

I pick up my sourdough starter. "Mountain men can't be separated from their sourdough Will!"

The cabin brings a lot of memories, but I don't talk to Will about it much.

"You cut a lot of firewood here, Miles." There are many tree stumps that represent a lot of work and time. We spend a night in the cabin. One of us has to sleep on the floor.

"I'll take the floor. Will, you didn't sleep so good last night in the truck."

In the morning, we get my boat in the water and the outboard motor on the transom. It doesn't take long to load the boat with my things. There is my camping tent, gun, ax, some clothes, the sourdough, a few dishes. The tin stove is not worth taking now. The weather is still damp. We just do not feel like hanging around. The trip back is uneventful, but now Will and I have shared an adventure together and have bonded as 'friends.'

Unemployment office.

"You set up to live in the boat at Alaskaland now, Miles?" Sam is at the unemployment office.

I fill him in on the boat trip. "Yeah, but the engine doesn't run good, so can't go anywhere. No money anyway, got to get some good work. I'm sort of thinking about a houseboat, but I'll see how the money goes. I know about steam from my military experience and think I might put a steam engine in with a paddle wheel. Fuel is always a problem when going remote. I could use the wood along the beach. This is a setup I could fix myself on the river too. I have a book with plans, and there is a company still selling new steam engines and boilers." Sam is not very impressed with the idea and is only politely listening. Hanging out at the unemployment office is boring and depressing and is the only reason he listens at all. This is my own private plan, with no one else helping to feed the fire. No one else but maybe Will is even remotely interested. Anyone I talk to thinks I'm either insane or a pipe dreamer.

"Sam, the paddle is only forty percent use of engine horsepower, and a prop is closer to sixty. That paddle's forty percent is for the best-feathered paddles. Getting a paddle to feather is a complicated, expensive design problem. Steam engines weigh an amazing amount. A thousand pounds only delivers twenty horses! Then there is the boiler, weight of the water, the pipes, and it can burn a hundred pounds of wood an hour. It's all a lot to overcome, but I think I could make it work."

"Well, Miles, sounds like you researched it a lot anyway. Be seeing you later!" He steps up to the desk, next in line to mow a lawn or wash dishes for someone.

Will and I are driving along in his truck. All I can talk about to anyone is steam. "Imagine Will! She could draw as little as four inches and haul a ton of goods!"

"Yeah, the part I like, Miles is no dependency on gas. You could go out for the whole summer and never need a gas station, and go truly remote. The river sandbars are full of driftwood. It wouldn't matter how much wood you needed. It's also such a simple system you could fix it out in the remote. It would be very forgiving and not so high Tech as modern transportation. In a modern engine, one speck of dust in the carb and you're down, a few drops of water in the fuel, one small wire jiggles loose, there's just so much that can go wrong, and usually does, especially with all the dampness, and—"

"Hey, Will! Pull over! A dead porky-pine in the road. We could bring it back to the fire! This is a chance to eat some wild game. Aren't you as hungry as I am?" As usual, times are pretty lean at the camp.

"Miles, we are the only ones here by the fire! Where is everyone?" I'm busy cleaning the porcupine and haven't taken notice. With a 'swish,' my hunting knife comes out in practiced motion without looking. I only nod at Will's comment. I set the carcass on a tree stump and cut the hide off.

"Miles, that skinned porcupine looks a lot like someone's pet dog, doesn't it?" We both laugh at how much it resembles a little dog. I talk more about 'steam' as the meat fries on a stick over the campfire.

Squatting by the fire, blade of grass in my mouth, I explain. "Will, sometimes chemicals have to get added to the boiler water to balance out the PH. I cannot decide if I want a more simple open system or an efficient closed system. I kind of like the closed system, where I have a condenser and re-use the water. This way, I start with almost boiling water. In an open system, I have to fill the boiler with cold water, close it up, and when I run out of water, have to shut down and open the system to put more cold water in."

"Miles, how do you get the hot water back into a pressurized closed system?"

"That's the feed pump's job, and it's an expensive part, has to work at pressures over 200 pounds. I could even go super-heated steam if I wanted, at higher pressures, and dry steam." Will turns the meat on the stick as I'm talking.

When it is finally time to eat, we feel famished. Just as we get the first mouthful, we hear the other guys who camp here coming up the path toward us. Will and I both think the same thing that there is not much meat on a porcupine, and if we share it, we will still be hungry. If we do not share, we will be selfish, so we are in a dilemma!

"Let me handle it, Will," I whisper as the guys come in sight.

I pretend Will and I have been engaged in a conversational argument and that I do not hear the guys. "Darn it, Will! Next time we do this, we need to perfect our routine! You grab the dog, and I work the collar off! We have to do it quicker. The way that little girl hollered, 'Oh cuddles!' and her mother coming at us, and you couldn't get the collar off, almost got us caught this time!" I turn and pretend this is the first I know the guys are around, "Oh, Hi guys! Anyone hungry? We got some real good fresh meat here!"

Everyone answers, "Umm, no thanks, but thanks for asking, that's ok, we already ate." They all gulp and look at each other, and I pretend I don't notice the awkwardness.

"Are you sure now? We got plenty to go around. We'd be glad to share it, right, Will?" Will is trying hard to keep a straight face and only gets out a "uh-huh." Will and I eat the whole thing ourselves. The guys whisper over in the corner as we eat, and they never are told we are not going through town collecting little girls' dogs to cook for dinner. The people look discouraged at how hard times seem to be getting. They hope they will never have to stoop to eating people's pets to stay alive. 😀 :)

"MILES! Your names up next, you want to hear about the latest job opportunity?"

The secretary is one of my friends and is trying to help me get a good summer job. I get up to the desk for my interview.

"There is a BLM firefighting position available. It looks like a janitor position, but I think it's more like 'maintenance.' This would be civil service on the base—long term, probably lots of bennies."

"Well, I worked on the base, civil service before, at the power plant—but out at Eielson."

"That experience should help you get this job, and you're a Vet, so that helps. Let's give a call and see what they say!"

AT THE MILITARY BASE.

"Don, what are you doing here? You work here?"

"Yea, Miles, have to do something in the summer when I'm not buying furs. Looks like I'll be your boss." This turns out to be good work for me. I stay on the base, keep my boat on the Chena River out back, eat, and live cheap here. The pay is good, with overtime and a chance to come back each year. I learn a lot of skills that will be useful in my life. We do carpentry work, fixing doors and windows. We do electrical, putting in switches, and lights. We do sheetrock and plumbing work; just about anything that can go wrong with a building, we fix it. There are five to six guys on the job. Sometimes we get to go out on a forest fire when there is an emergency, but mostly we take care of the barracks where the crews stay. I get to meet people from every village on the river as they come in off a fire and talk to them about their area. I get to work with the fur buyer, and we become friends. All of this turns out to be a lucky break for me.

"Toot, toot" Don gives his usual 'arm pulling the steam whistle cord' imitation and keeps on walking. He turns around and comes back. "You know, Miles, if you cut your hair, you could become president." He says all this almost every day. On weekends, when I'm not doing overtime work for BLM, I hang out at Alaskaland.

"Hello, Nora!"

"Miles, have you worked on the story yet?" I thought she had been just joking.

"You think I should write up the Survival Story?"

"Well, Miles, look at some of the stories in the magazine! They aren't half as interesting as yours are. I think you might even be paid to do it. You have nothing to lose if you try it."

I spend a few hours writing up my story. Without Nora's prompting, I wouldn't try it. This was an embarrassing time in my life. Mountain men don't get rescued; they do the rescuing! I sigh. I'm sitting at an Alaskaland picnic bench out in the sun, off to the side where not much is going on. A policeman off in the distance starts to stroll my way, but I pay him no mind, just part of the scenery, as I get absorbed in my story.

A tap on my shoulder interrupts my thoughts.

"You'll have to be moving on, kid. Got a complaint against you. You're loitering."

My mouth opens to express my indignation and questions. A scowl comes on his face as he reaches for his baton.

"You're not going to give me any trouble, are you?"

My conscience talks in my head, Like, do I have any choice but to listen to you?

The rest of me keeps a blank face, and the policeman adds, "I don't want to see you around Alaskaland again, now move along, and be glad I don't put you in jail!"

I'm not sure what the problem is, and there's no way to really find out. I suspect it is 'stuff' hinted at around here by some. I have long hair. I wear a knife. I dress funny. I don't always take a bath. I don't 'fit in' according to the opinion of some. This place is set up to represent the old times, the trappers, miners, homesteaders. Shops sell furs to the tourists. There is the old-time photo shop where you can dress up like me and get your picture taken. There are the 'old stories,' told in the shops to tourists, readings from Robert Service about people like me who used to live like I live now, dress as I do now. As long as it's 'the past,' *thank God we still don't live like that, huh? Thank God, it's behind us!* We sell the tourists the dreams, but the truth is a bit much. The truth isn't welcome here. Not even from the Alaskan locals. What a joke.

Bill and Nora hear about the trouble. They get a few of the shop owners who like me, the can-can girls, and others who will speak up for me at the next meeting of shop owners. There is no problem with me coming back, but I'm aware there are some who have very strong feelings against me.

I complain to Nora, "Am I hurting anyone, bothering anyone? Aren't I always in a good mood, full of jokes, and entertaining to the tourists? Don't I bring in business to Alaskaland? Look at all the people who want to have a picture taken next to me. Wherever I go, 'customers' follow me..." and I realize I'm rambling and going on about something I can't do much about, so stop talking. "Oh well—whatever!"

When I have time, I hunt for some pictures taken with the new camera I got. I send my story and pictures to the address on the inside cover of the Alaska magazine. I don't proofread or type it. "That's what editors are for! They spend their time learning how to spell. Anyone can learn how to spell. Someone has to live the stories worth writing about!" It would take me ten times longer to look up all the words, and locate a typewriter, and re-do the whole thing a dozen times. It would still be the same story. I don't want to have a lot invested in it in case it gets turned down.

The Underhill's encourage me as usual. "Hey! The Leather Man, how's it hanging?"

"To the left side. I hear you had quite an experience this winter, huh? Hope it wasn't the Indians we had trouble with that got your goods! If you need any help culling the Indians, let me know!"

"No, nothing so drastic is called for. My problem was just some woman passing through with her kids if you can believe it. Would have made it otherwise, 'cept she took my supplies—thought about fixing her clock, but she's in Steven's village, a ways away. Might be hard to get in and out and keep my scalp. Wouldn't mind going in with a swat team, all right, but you know she has to live her life knowing what she is. It is better for me to get on with my life and not dwell in the valley of death."

"Well, whatever. You always was good for the words, not really an action man. Hey, you know, there never was a thing in the paper about the tourists and the bear. They must have lucked out."

We both laugh about that memory we share. I say, "Well, glad to see you back again, hope it's a good season for you!" I'm already turning away, greeting others with, "Hey! The can-can cuties! Fancy meeting you girls here."

"Miles! Don't be silly, you know we are here at this time every day, and I bet you make sure you are here just to see us!"

"What!? To see skin and leg? Perish the thought! By the way, Janny, did I ever tell you the dream I had?" I take her aside. I make up a story as we walk alone, just to explore the power of words. Love, Romance, and forever. Janny is breathing hard and wants me to tell her more. The story becomes almost a kidnap-rape story. I'm getting my cues from her. I decide this has gone far enough. I'm a little afraid of where this is going and make a mental note to keep away from her. I pause for a while, letting her think. I add as a parting thought, "I learn a lot from animals." The rest of the cuties come along. I watch them practice their skit. They are used to having me around and talk very openly in front of me.

The ice cream shop is part of my routine. "Strawberry ice cream, please!" The usual grass blade is hanging from my mouth. My tongue moves it aside whenever I talk. The young girl squeals at my voice, turns, and runs from around the counter to give me a very big hug.

"Miles! I heard you had quite an adventure this past winter, are you OK? I'm sure glad to see you! Miles, could you watch the shop for a few minutes? I have to go potty. The change is in the drawer, prices are on the board." She takes her time, and I sell a few cones to people I know, who laugh at me, being behind a counter working a regular job.

"Only for a few minutes, don't worry!"

"Uh-huh." My bearskin hat, torn plaid shirt, blade at my side, grass in my mouth that fits right in with the costumes. The tourists love it. I tell the story of how I got the bear this hat is made of a hundred times. *It gets better with each telling.* "...And then I kicked him in the butt, thought he was my dog getting in the smoked fish. I took care of him all right, and he never got any more of my fish! Afraid? The bear had reason to be afraid, not me!" I fondle the hat appropriately as if going over the memory of it all. I, of course, never killed that bear.

I walk around some more. A tourist asks to have a picture taken with me. We pose for the camera. One of the shop owners scowls and tells me not to come in his shop or hang around anymore because I'm bad for business. I shrug my shoulders, "Sure." I amble on over to the dock where I have my boat parked. I can run the boat from here at Alaskaland to the military base where I work.

"Hey, Will! You still living in your car here? No work yet?"

"Yea, I got work. Just saving money living here. I got a camp in the woods."

"I'd be there too, but I got such a good deal for a place to stay on the base, and cheap meals, that it's not worth coming here to stay. I have a room to store my supplies in too."

Will asks, "So you want to go to some garage sales? You got money to do that?" Happily, I chime in, "Sure, sounds good. Maybe we can find some stuff to stockpile!" We run around and find some traps, a tarp, an old pair of snowshoes, a few books to read.

Will gives me a ride back to the boat and to where he stays. "See you next weekend probably. Maybe we can go out for pizza and garage sales again."

"Catch ya later then."

"Toot, toot," Don walks by me again. I'm trying to cut a piece of glass the right size for a small window. Don had just shown me how to do it the day before. All the guys are in the shop working on various aspects of the same project. One guy works on the broken latch, another is doing something with wood filler, but mostly we just wait, glancing at each other and the clock and not saying anything.

"Shit!"

That's the signal. We all know what's going to happen now, but we all have a straight face, don't say a thing. Don stops in mid-stride as he yells 'that signal.' He scowls, moves his tobacco cud to the other side of his mouth, and holds it there in deep concentration.

He repeats again, "Shit!"

Now it's appropriate to ask what's wrong. Someone speaks up, "What's wrong, Don?"

"Did anyone remember to pick up the paperwork on this job from the office?" We all know if Don didn't do it, no one did; it's his job. "We need more wood, it looks like, anyway, need a new work order. God Damn it. I hate inefficiency!" Everyone pauses and looks properly concerned. Don acts as if he is not paying attention to us as he roars on, "Guess we'll have to stop somewhere for lunch, head on out to the office and the lumber yard. I hate government waste!" Don looks around to see if anyone has a solution to this dilemma, of all of us having to go out to lunch on government money. We all need to work together on this project since we all do aspects of the same job. None of us (sadly) has a solution. Guess we will have to knock off early for lunch, go out to dinner, and maybe even get back late. It sure is sad. Don scowls again, swears, as he waves all of us grinning kids into the truck.

A lot of this job is sitting around waiting, looking busy, and being ready and willing to work hard when there is an emergency. It is important to stay out of the suit and tie people's way, and not get caught goofing off. Sometimes we have to dash around running, doing nothing, but in a hurry, over something or other. Other times, there really is hard work, and we miss lunch and stay in after-hours until someone's furnace is fixed, or the door is re-hung, or whatever. When there is a big fire, there is more work to do, and more money is appropriated to the department, and we are allowed overtime. *It's not good to send money back, saying we couldn't spend it.* None of this is really my business, but it's not hard to figure out. No one comes right out and says this is the reality! I hasten to add, "This is only my opinion, quite a false one, I'm sure! Perish the thought that government would tolerate inefficiency."

This is why the job is great seasonal work, but take it seriously, as a way of life? You have to be kidding! I take work seriously, and this job is just too funny. *Well, not exactly 'funny,' but I just like to keep honestly busy, or else be free to do something else.* This is the time I start to develop my metal artwork. My job involves a lot of desk work. There are days when my job is to issue rooms, take dirty linen, and replace lost keys. This job sees most of its activity when everyone firefighting gets back from a fire. There are spells where only a few people come in all day, and there I am at a desk. I buy a small vice, a handsaw, and some other tools. It all fits in a shoebox and sets up on the edge of the desk. I start sawing out animals, birds, and simple scenery.

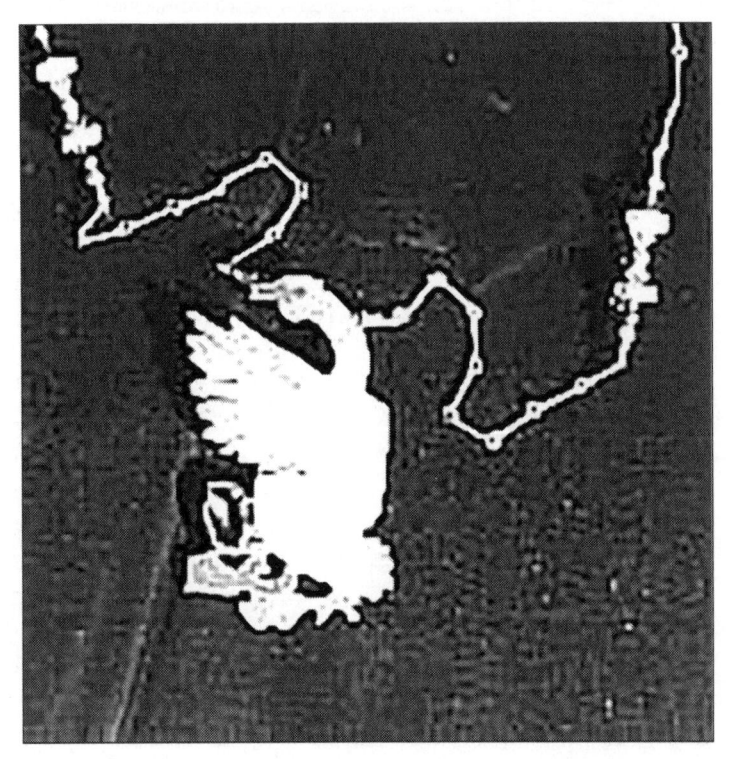

A Necklace I made. Silver, copper, and brass.

A secretary I flirt with at the front desk says, "Miles! That's so pretty! I love the way the swan bends his neck as he flies. You can tell he's trying to go fast! Such a simple design, but so beautiful! You know Miles, you could make money doing this!"

This is the first time I take my artwork seriously. I am just fooling around, passing boring hours, doing something just to do something, maybe to use as gifts. I had sort of thought about 'art' when I moved to Canada, but suddenly I was fed up with it. All those paintings I did, thrown away by the locals after I was deported. That nice sculpture and 'all that.' Why take it seriously? Why get involved with people? The secretary buys this necklace on jade. Her friends sees it, and I start getting orders. Before long, I'm running a little side business.

Some of the honchos in charge get wind of this little 'side business' and get all excited. My attitude about my job is that sometimes we have to work especially hard. For this, I am willing and able. There are never any excuses about "Can't put any overtime in, things to do." I am 100% 'there.' Other times, there is work, but it goes along pretty easy. There are those times when there is absolutely nothing to do, and everyone knows it, so why run around pretending to be busy? As long as I'm available, not asleep, not away from the phone, and not neglecting my responsibility, what I do when there is nothing to do is my own business.

If I was taking some course in school, that would be fine. But it's not fine that I'm busy making extra money. Things are OK, but Don has to speak up for me sometimes to the bosses. I tell Don what a bunch of a hooey it all is, and he may even agree (but better not say so). I notice he, himself, isn't exactly in good standing with everyone in the main office. But anyhow, I do a little messing around with artwork on the side so I don't fall asleep. I don't really fit in, though—just fooling myself. There is no way I could make this my life.

"This is Alaska House, the gallery? Hi, I'm Miles." My hand goes out awkwardly.

"Yes, Miles, someone has already told us about your work, let's see."

I get out about a dozen pieces I have done, all differently. One is on the hoof of a moose, another on a piece of Alaska jade, and another is on a bear claw. They all have scenes of many metals, fit together like a puzzle. I don't know of anyone else doing work like this. I just thought it up.

"This is really nice Miles, I'm sure we can sell it. We do consignment, which means we keep it here, and when we sell it, you are paid a percent of what we sell it for. Usually, we keep thirty-five percent, and you keep the rest." We agree on some prices for the pieces, make up some labels, and I'm in the jewelry business.

A couple of the shops at Alaskaland buy my work, but mostly I just trade. I trade for my ice cream and some raw materials to do more artwork later. Weekends now find me hanging around with a little bag full of my necklaces and making my trades at Alaska land. Some of the people I trade and sell to, I do not remember. Most of my business is wholesale to the shops here. It takes time to realize I'm doing a regular business with the same people, and as more time passes, it is hard to remember just who I met when. I'm still stuck in the upbringing where 'artists' are like beatniks, bums, and art is 'fun' but not something to do as a serious occupation. Even though people are calling my work 'good,' it is to me, like saying, I'm a good card player, dance well, and cook a nice burger. That is all well and fine, but a very long way from saying you are doing something 'worthy' of being a member of society, deserving to be taken into society's fold and protection, but I'm not going to dwell on it.

"Hey Miles! I'm going out to see my dad at the pipeline camp by Delta. Want to come out the road with me?" Will is hailing me, and I decide it would be nice to go out the road in that direction. There are four main roads across Alaska, and this is one of them. Will's dad is making good pipeline money now and takes us both out for lunch, where we eat big buffalo burgers made from the Delta Bison. They are good and advertised as the biggest burgers in the state. I enjoy talking to Will's dad, and they are both good people. Will and I start to come out to see his Dad for lunch as a regular thing.

We get to talking about women, as Will and I are both alone, thinking how 'not to be.' I explain how the magazine ads work, "You see the ads in the Mother Earth? There's some pretty outdoor sounding women in here. Take a look."

I read some of them, and Will and his dad joke about what these women would really be like. I put in my opinion, "Maybe I can find one that would like to live on a houseboat and travel around!" I'm pretty serious about the boat and am getting the money saved to do it. I don't say much more to Will about the ads but decide to put one out myself.

GOING WILD

Under 'Classified' Ads'
Dynamite—lacking detonator.
Bow—Missing string somewhere.
Hunter—Needs a female critter,
(ah! So!, and what have we here!?)
(snicker).
Artist—Trapper—Explorer
(infrequent town visitor)
Would like a female partner,
to share a cabin in the wilderness,
its hardships and its pleasures.
Something of myself should be here,
but my opinion is bias,
and even 'generalities."
I can answer, "It varies."
French, Indian, Creole's my race,
and Hawaii is my birthplace.'
in '52', one of the good years.
Personality? "Mellow," say my friends,
But there are exceptions here,
(If you care to ask a certain bear.)
But if you want to find out more—
Heck, I can send a picture.
(Beard, buckskins, rifle, hat of fur.)
Other words—only one way,
got to write to get a reply!

This isn't exactly how the ad reads! Ha! But wrote this poem while thinking about what to say.

Will and I are on one of our regular trips to visit his dad. "Hey, Miles. Look, a boat shop and half-finished custom boats in the lot. You want to stop in." Will also is interested in 'boats,' and maybe this guy can help me on my boat project. I had been thinking of building it myself, but am stumped with 'no place to do it' and 'no tools, except hand tools.' Dare I admit, maybe it takes more skill to build a boat than I have?

"Steamer," a small, thin-built, white-haired older guy puts his hand out and tells us he's a boat builder. This is on the upper Tanana River just before the Delta Junction Bridge. We talk about boats in general.

Then I ask about my own project. "So, do you think it could be designed and built here? Do you know about paddle boats, steam engines?"

"I've spent my life building boats. I used to race them. I worked with steam. I could do a hull for a steam engine." We discuss some basic ideas. Steamer brings up some things I didn't consider. "If you can keep it under eight feet wide, it can go on a trailer to be moved, and if it is exactly twenty-four feet long, I can special order marine plywood in that length, and it will be structurally sounder, with no splice in the bottom." I had hoped to have it longer, but this makes sense. Steamer wants the work, saying, "Let me look over your plans, and I'll give you a price." He didn't mind that I'm no draftsman, and all he wanted were some artistic drawings.

I'm really excited. "This is going to be for real, Will!" He's almost as excited as I am. "Just think, Will, a home that floats. No owning land to live on, no building a cabin every place you want to check out, or paying rent. A portable trapping camp, moving where the fur is, and never depleting one area." There are all sorts of other things I mention. I've given it a lot of thought.

"Nora? Hello! Guess what! The story was accepted. I got $300 in the mail. For only an hour's work. Not bad, huh? Pretty exciting! It will come out next June."

"I knew they would take it, Miles, it's an interesting story, and you have a good writing style." I don't think it has much to do with my writing, just a different sort of story, but it's pretty slick to make $300 an hour.

Will doesn't understand how someone can be paid for just writing a simple story. "If you can get away with a scam like that, what the heck!"

"I got this kind of idea, Will, that a person could figure out what they like to do the most, find a money angle, and earn a living doing what you love, almost like being retired or getting paid to have fun!"

"What a concept, Miles!" We both laugh. "Miles, do you think you can get the houseboat done in time for this winter's trapping season?"

This is a big thing for me. I hope very much to get out for this winter in a new boat I can live in.

"Will, there are more than two months left in the boating season. There is time. Mostly it will be a matter of money, I think." I pause and talk about the place on the Yukon. "I'm not sure I want to spend another winter in the area I was in. The cabins are not so great, and the people do not want me there. I could stay and fit in if I worked at it, but I don't want to be beholden to anyone, forced to fit in if I don't feel like it. The game there comes and goes, I'm told. There might be better places to trap." I think about Tucky and his family, Piper Wright, and these are good people, but the Yukon seems crowded and sought after. Surely, I can find a place no one is fighting over. My desire is to get away, avoid trouble, and avoid people. This past incident was too much like Canada. Once could be a mistake, but twice is a pattern. I want very much to be mobile, able to move around and find someplace I can belong, call home, maybe just be alone, and sort out my life, while I regroup. Maybe, though, it will just be plain fun!

GOING WILD

AT AN ART GALLERY.

"Miles. We sold something of yours. Let me go check the bookwork. Oh yes, here it is, the bull moose on the shell." Alaska House pays me. It's not a lot of money, but it is enough to think about. I chat with the owner for a while. There are no customers, and things are slow right now. I mention my magazine ad for a woman to the owner. We talk about life in the wilderness and being alone.

Karen adds, "Oh? Well, I met my husband on a spur of the moment thing. He is a state senator. He was passing through a hotel where I was working. He saw me and told his companions he would marry me someday. That was it, one glance. He introduced himself, we went out." She shrugs her shoulders. "That was twenty years ago. We are still happily married."

This has me thinking. *It must be possible to meet someone then and know you will get along with them.* Getting along, meeting someone is such a complex thing; I am surprised people ever get along at all! We both laugh at all the things people go through in relationships.

"Miles, your art shows a unique person. You will find someone, I think; she will just have to be special." I leave some more art on consignment.

An older Eskimo artist comes in to leave his work in the gallery. He is with his son and seems to need the son to interpret for him. He must only know his native language. His dress and look is very 'up north.' He has a parka on with a big wolverine ruff. His footgear is a set of beaded fur mukluk boots. He stands bowlegged, as so many of the older Eskimos do. The old man looks at the work I'm leaving and says something to the son.

The son turns to me, "My father says to tell you he likes your artwork." This seems like a nice compliment to me, because this is an elder who has spent a lot of years doing art, and is a well-respected carver. His work sells well in galleries across the state.

I ask to see what he has brought. The son interprets for the father as the old man gets his work out of a paper bag. I see a very interesting walrus ivory tusk carving. The design is very simple. There is only a little bit of scrimshaw on it. The work is delicate and smooth. The highly polished piece of white ivory has a detailed man in a kayak with the paddle resting. The man is staring from his kayak at the vast expanse of white space in front of him. The ocean stretches out full of ice forever, so overwhelming and powerful. The style is very unique, unlike anything I've ever seen. I ask the son where the father gets his ideas from, since this is so unique and, but more, so 'modern' looking. The son translates to the father. The old man smiles and looks at me, and nods, and explains, through the son, that he is not the artist. I look puzzled. The old man says that the ivory tells him what it wants to be, and it is his job to release the spirit trapped within the ivory.

I am very struck by this concept. It makes sense, but more, I realize this old man cannot speak or understand English, yet here is a form of communication that bridges all cultural and language barriers. We appreciate each other's work and understand each other's deepest thoughts. I realize that it is not just 'us.' I understand at this moment, *this is what art is about!* This is a lesson in art I wouldn't, hadn't learned in school. I Am reminded once again. *In school, Art was like study hall or gym, something you took when you wanted to goof off and couldn't handle the pressure of real classes.* The compliment from this old man meant more to me than any 'A' I ever got on a test in school. This is 'real-life' and having 'effect.' This encounter is one I will remember the rest of my life.

> **Dear Miles**—I got your plans and looked them over. I think I can do this for $5,000. This would just be the hull. When we are done with that, we can get into the house, but my guess would be it could be done for another $2,000. We would use the best materials, marine plywood, clear lumber, and bronze screws. Let me know what you want to do. I'll need a down payment to order the first materials, a couple of thousand dollars.
> Steamer, Aug. 1, 74.

When Will and I go to see his dad again, we stop by the boat shop.

"I've got the down payment, so you can order material and get started. I want to have the boat by winter, so I have a place to live this winter."

Steamer tells me, "As long as things go well, it shouldn't be a problem. You might have to put alternate power in for the first year or two. We can adapt the boat later for the steam. That engine will cost you a bundle, and putting it in will take time." I'm not happy about compromising my original plans, but he is right. There is no way I can pay all that off in one year. It might be better to have a place to stay. The winter's rent saved will pay for the engine and putting it in. The main thing right now is to have a place to stay this winter and be able to go out to the wilderness.

"I'm getting fed up with town life, Steamer! I've tasted the freedom of the wilderness, and I'll never look back."

BACK TO WORK.

"Toot, toot!" Don walks by again.

"Hey Don, I put a down payment on the steamboat. I hope to have it by the end of the season."

In a serious voice, Don replies, "How much will the whistle cost? When you boat into these villages, you have to have a steam whistle to toot you know Miles?!" He pauses and studies me. "If you cut your hair, you could be president." Someone is telling a joke of some kind as I talk to Don. I don't know exactly what is going on, but guess that the joke involves me. The joke has something to do with a bar, a buffalo, and someone being or looking like a buffalo. I never do get the whole joke.

Someone says, "Wild Miles!" and everyone laughs. They look over at me. From then on, all I hear is 'buzz buzz—'Wild Miles!' and a lot of laughing.

I decide the joke is on them. They know little about 'being wild.' From what I know about animals, there is nothing to be ashamed of in being like one of them. I rather respect them. The people talking see animals as crude, crazy, savage, and uncouth. I think animals are sane, quiet, caring to each other, and, in most cases, fairly non-violent. When they are violent, the reason why seems understandable. I think it is these guys making the jokes who are rude, crude, and savage. This is a private joke to me, and I smile, and they think I am stupid, to smile and not understand I am being made fun of, being insulted. I have a look that says I think they insult themselves.

Don tells me there is a bet going around on how many days or weeks I will survive in the wilderness. This is a real bet, real money is collected, and it's a pretty big pot, I hear. Don never tells me which way he is betting. I feel sorry for these people with their dull lives, who will never see a world beyond 'BLM and retirement in twenty years.' These are people whose great thrill in life is to bet on the outcome of someone else's life. I see myself as someone who is climbing in the ring with the bull, win or lose. Not someone in the bleachers throwing rotten apples. I decide *I'd rather live my life for a year and die; than live the life these people have for 80 years.* But who understands this? It is a quiet, private thought. I go by the name "Wild Miles." The barroom joke is turned into the symbol of what I believe in and stand for. Everyone pretty much figures I'm either dense, bragging or need attention. All negative things.

I hope these people will eat their words, but try not to make this my reason for going on. I try to be understanding. They might even be right. "Pobody's Nerfect." If I fail, I will have at least dared to dream! Even so, it hurts that these people I work with choose to make fun of me. Crueler than any animal I ever met. I'm just stuck in that thought right now, for in truth, I have seen animals tear each other up or reject each other for similar reasons, and it is just nature's way of making sure anything different is good for the species and well tested.

"Nora, maybe these people are afraid. It seems odd, but I see society as a herd, and the safety of the herd is in the strength of the number of its members and in the conviction of the rules they follow. When a member of the group decides to leave and talks about other possible alternatives to living, like another set of morals, another way to skin the cat, this threatens the strength of the herd and makes the herd nervous. What would happen if everyone just took off and decided to do what pleased them! If people decided they wouldn't punch the time clock anymore, decided to question the rules we live by, question lifestyles, there would be mass confusion. So only a few people are loners, those that leave the herd, but it makes the rest nervous because it weakens the weave of the fabric."

"Could be, Miles! I know people look at Bill and me strangely, too! We don't do the ordinary things. Here we are with all the pipeline money and still running a small wood shop that barely pays for itself. We still believe in simple ways, don't spend our money on vacations or fancy cars. Our religious beliefs are very simple. We get a lot of looks from snooty people. The truth is, we love working with wood, love the people here, and love talking to the tourists and sharing Alaska with them."

On the job.

One of the office guys in a tie comes up to me with a nervous smile. "We were wondering why you guys wear those knives! To kill all the bears here?" A nervous chuckle follows.

I'm dumbfounded by the question and never really thought about it. *This guy is not being snooty or judgmental. He honestly wants to know.* It is part of the over-all nervousness I pick up on, the hushed whispers, the twitter laughs.

I take the time to explain it as I see it. "Well, I could ask why 'you guys' wear ties. They perform no useful purpose, do they? But you wear them to maybe identify yourselves?" I think this has a lot to do with why I wear my knife. I find a lot of uses for the knife on my job, opening boxes, cutting things like wire. Shaving doors and an emergency screwdriver. I read once that 'a man with a knife is master of a thousand tasks.'

My conscience reviews the knife, *This says something to me, means a lot to me. It is the symbol of what I stand for, simplicity, ruggedness, being functional, and being an outdoor person.* I think when I go to get in line somewhere, I like to know something about the people around me, so I can feel comfortable and so I do not make any social blunders. If the person in front of me is wearing a suit and tie, carries a briefcase, is clean-shaven, then I ignore this person. I do not make eye contact. I keep a social distance and give this person polite space. This person and I will have little in common. *To talk to such a person of another tribe could get me in trouble.* Such a person, for example, might turn me in to the law for poaching a duck in spring if I happen to mention my last meal. Likewise, this 'high finance person' might reveal a tribal secret meant only for 'one of us.' That 'they' (me) would not understand and might get the entire tribe in trouble.

My unconscious turns to more of a reply to myself. If I see someone with a sheath knife, long hair, who needs a bath, I will introduce myself as a member of the sub-group 'bush person.' We probably have things in common, know people in common, have stories to exchange and can have a social interaction. Such a person probably understands the concept of eating spring ducks. I suppose we all can spot those around us that we might be able to count on, side with if there is trouble or an emergency. It can mean a chance to meet a potential friend. We all feel 'safe' around fellow tribe members. *How do we identify members of our tribe? By how we dress! It is, in fact, a very big deal!*

I explain all this in the best way I can but do not fully understand myself, having never thought about it before now.

I go on by saying, "I assure you I do not wear this knife to be threatening to anyone! I'm sorry if that's how you feel! Think of it as no different than your tie!"

The guy gives a 'Yeah right!' look, and I know he hasn't heard a word I said. My guess now is, this guy had hoped the question would be intimidating and cause me to feel guilty and stop carrying a knife. This seems to me to be a clue to why I end up in trouble with people. I see us all as actors playing parts, wearing costumes. I find it exciting to see people dressed every which way. I think it speaks a great deal about how we perceive ourselves, who we would like to be, or be seen as. Watching how a person dresses is like reading a book. I know I dress as I do, very proudly. I imagine most people do. How we dress might say, "I am a well to do businessman, with lots of money and power!"

"I am not concerned with material goods and answer to no one!"

"I am a hippie—"

"I am a policeman—"

"Farmer—"

"Trapper—"

Possibly, however, I am simply in the wrong setting, acting in the wrong movie. I mention the conversation to Nora.

"Well, Miles, you must remember you are a well-traveled person who has seen many kinds of people. Your father is a college professor. You had people from all over the world in your home; people from India, China. You moved almost every year, so you were exposed to different fads, stuck with no one group. Then the military, and all those countries. Not everyone can be so accepting of others' ways as you, Miles."

Letters start coming in. Yes, in response to my Mother Earth ad. At first, just a few. It is fun answering people from all over the country, from all walks of life. I am impressed by the quality of some of the women. I had thought that maybe the women would be desperate, or poor, or crazy. I thought, though, that maybe there would be women who thought like me. I am busy working and do not wish to spend my money or time going out to watering holes to find a partner. I do not find what I am looking for there in the bar anyway. It takes a while to get to know if someone is on drugs, sane, loyal, etc. Bar hours tend to be late in the evening, past my bedtime. If I know what I want, why not just say so, and ask if you want the same thing and if so, let's meet! There are not a lot of people who can, or wish, to live in the wilderness, so what are my chances of just running into such a person, randomly? Why not reach a bigger crowd through the mail, and introduce myself to those who might have a like interest. This is my thinking.

There is a letter from an airline stewardess, who is very pretty and wishes to meet people from all walks of life. She travels, could see me on her way through Alaska. There is an Olympic skier who is looking for a place and situation to ski. Some women send naked photos of themselves and ask what I think. Some women are looking for marriage, a father for a child, fun, and some for a close friend. It is all very interesting and full of possibilities.

One gal who writes works right here where I do! She fights fires. She loves the outdoors. She finds out I have an ad out and I'm 'looking.'

She writes—
"**Miles**! Why look across the fence, do you expect the grass to be any greener? Why not look in your own back yard?"

We start to date. She likes to dance at the Howling Dog. She's short, long blonde hair, blue eyes, stocky build, but not fat. She's very attractive and has an outgoing personality.

"I broke up with my boyfriend when I came here to work from Montana. I had been going with him for three years. He had odd sexual preferences, and it just got more odd the longer I knew him. I felt very degraded. I don't know about having another relationship. Maybe I just want to be friends. I don't know."

WE ARE in her room talking way into the night. It's my turn to talk about myself. I explain about Nancy, and how I miss her, and maybe how I should have paid more attention to her needs instead of dwelling so much on my own. I change the subject, knowing it is not good to talk about other women. "So My life went through a lot of changes out in the wilderness, and even though you say you'd like to live there, I'm not sure you understand what it means. Remember I said I ate foods that most civilized people wouldn't. It is more than this; it has to do with the way the mind works. I would forget to put the lid on the peanut butter, and the mice would get in and poop in it."

"Yuck, Miles! Well, I just wouldn't forget; how could you possibly 'forget!' After the first time, I'd think you'd smarten up!"

I have no answer that is logical. I'm just having trouble picturing this personality out there on the planet I was on. I sigh. She is so darn sure she would—could—handle the life better than I did. Maybe, but I feel confident what I'm doing is not easy. [2]

She wants to know why my hair is long and untamed. I haven't cut it since I got out of the navy several years ago now.

"When I was young, I did what I was told. I never grew my hair long or took up the modern fads. All the adults thought I was grand. What happened?"

She comes over to brush my hair, sits down next to me. I have actually had very little experience with women. This seems interesting. I know animals engage in hair cleaning of each other. (I know more about animals than people in some ways).

"Yuck, Miles! There is a spruce cone tangled in your hair!"

"Huh, imagine that! It must have been in there since winter several months ago." She did not find this at all humorous. This seemed to be the turning point of our relationship. (Hmm). She politely made up excuses when I asked her out, and I got the hint.

Dear Trapper Friend—How are you doing? Your stories are so interesting. I should like to meet you. When the stars are right we will meet. I feel it in my heart and soul...

Hmm, (sniff, sniff). I stop reading. I can smell her perfume on the letter. Such a body. (Looking at her picture again)

Dear Miles—You already wrote me! Don't you even remember! I don't need this crap! How rude!...

Sigh, should I even write her and apologize? Maybe I should keep a file.

Dear Wild Miles—I like...

No, I'm not going to answer this one. It's on blue paper.

Dear Miles—What a lovely...

No, not this one either. It's written in pencil.

I am spending five dollars a day on stamps and answering hundreds of letters. They arrive in the mail by the shopping bag full. We do not give them a chance!? Well, the reasoning goes, *We should recognize our other half maybe easily, maybe right away. God would give us a sign.* It's true, so often, my very first impression I get in ten seconds is the same conclusion I come to months, years, and decades later. It's not dozens or hundreds of women that matter, just the one I am looking for or who is looking for me. *Will we recognize each other??* One reason I do not slow dance is because it is something I want to do only with my wife. *The only one I ever slow danced with.* Stupid. Who cares and Oh well. No one said our hormones make us do logical things.

"Toot, toot."

I look up as Don goes by.

"You're daydreaming again, Wild Miles!" He pauses dramatically and spins around. "Miles, was anyone in the sauna today?" He wants the latest story. We have a sauna that is meant for the workers, but it is not locked up. Some of the folks in town, the 'hippies,' have discovered it and have been using it. The other day I caught a room full of naked women in there. It has become part of my job description to kick the invaders out. I temporarily get the nickname "Took-a-look," which has an Eskimo sound to it. The rest of the guys have questions.

"So Took-a- look, tell me again how old they were and what they were like. Any under age? Were they watermelons—or small and pointy?"

I close my eyes and make with my two hands as if I'm exploring, to give an accurate answer. "Like grapefruits with nipples." This provides an interruption in the day. "Oops! Gotta go check the Sauna! Hate to do it, guys, but you know how it is, anything for BLM!"

"So I can get gas in Tanana? Is there a store, too?" I get a chance to talk to the firefighting crew from the Athabascan village of Tanana. I expect I'll be passing by there when I get my boat going. I find out about Fort Yukon, but think I will not likely go upstream for a while. No firefighters from Ruby? Tanana people know about Ruby?

I ask, "So what happens when I go to Ruby? Do I get scalped or what?" My native friend chuckles but adds, "There are some white people there. Be sure to look up Emit. He won the Iditarod dog sled race and is a friend of mine."

I find out about a lot of the villages and get some contact names. I'm learning it's not polite to visit these villages unless you know someone or are invited. The maps start to look familiar, and place names have stories to go with them along with contact people to mention.

"Will, you getting things together to where you can hole up out in the wilderness?"

Will gives a cheerful reply, "Been working steady, got some money saved up. You going to get another gun, Miles?"

"I got a 270 at the pawnshop at a good price. That's the necked down ought six. I got the lee loader so I can do my own reloading. It will be only a little more expensive than the twenty-two to shoot. Sure be a better moose and bear gun."

Will wants to know about the boat. "How's the boat coming, Miles. You heard from Steamer yet?" I've been waiting to hear from the builder and wondering what the holdup is. Most weekends, I go down to see how it goes and to work on it with him. Little is done during the week when I'm gone—always some excuse or other. He seems to be designing one of his own boats for me that is no different from any of the others in his lot. If I'd wanted a standard hull, I could have just got an existing one already built! And Cheaper! Christ! The price I'm paying is for a custom boat, not a standard hull. He's barely got started, has other projects on his mind, "but not to worry, it will go fast once it gets going!" (So he says).

I explain it to Will. "We don't have a contract, Will, and don't seem to agree on what we agreed to." I sigh, "And now that he has my down payment, I'm on the back burner, it looks like to me."

Will wants to know if it is even started yet. "You seen the beginnings yet?"

Shaking my head, "No, only the pile of wood he ordered."

Will changes the subject. "You going to the fair?"

"You bet! Haven't missed one yet!"

Dear Trapper Friend—I see the mountains reflected in your eyes. I think about you every day. I think it is in the stars that we will one day meet. My job is boring and I wish I had time to be with nature as you live! - **Love, Your Tigress**

Dear Tigress—The trapper has put his bait out and patiently waits for the Tigress. 😊 :)

She is playing coy? Sorry work is not much fun. I have a job now too, just to get supplies and pay for the Houseboat. It would be easy to be caught up in the rat race. I believe 'life' is a precious thing, and comes but once around, so we have to grab it while it is here. If we cannot enjoy and experience life, what good is it? I hope one day then, to have my trapping and various interests pay for my material needs. Etc., etc. **Sunshine, Wild Miles**

I have a talk with my conscience. I think we have to write this gal off, huh? We have been writing a while now, and all she talks about is, depending on the stars.

"We make our own destiny, and if we wait on the stars to tell us what to do, it will be a long wait! But for sure, she is attractive, and maybe we can get her to wake up, but I wouldn't count on it!"

Dear Wild Miles: My husband left me. I have three kids, and I need a man to take care of me. Enclosed is my picture. I need someone kind and gentle, and no drinking! Do you like children?

Good luck! Dream on! She tells all about 'what she wants,' but how's she gonna pay for it? Ya! what's she offering? She's only so-so looking; she doesn't sound smart, interesting, kind, or giving; actually, she sounds rather demanding. I can understand why she's in a bind looking for Mr. Perfect.

I reply—
Dear Woman and Three Kids—Yes, you are very pretty and seem like a nice person, but I don't think I am the right person for you. I don't make a lot of money or have a lot of room. If I live on this houseboat I'm building, it will be overly cramped if there will be children!! I'm sorry about your husband leaving you, but try not to give up on men! Not all of them would do that, and somewhere out there is the man who will treat you right and who needs you and the children! Good luck! **Sunshine, Wild Miles**

I get a long waited for letter from my childhood sweetheart Maggie. Not answering any ad I put out.

Dear Miles—
All is well with me! I got a new dress I have wanted for a long time, and my car is back from the shop...(etc. etc.)...Miles, you tell me about all these letters you get in response to your ad and tell me what it is like and how you reply. Well I think, Miles, you are not saying exactly everything. Men, I find, tend to have this macho thing they put on when they speak to others. I know you are very respectful to women, kind, and understanding and sweet—but if you don't want that to show, I understand! Ha! Men! So have you settled on one yet?? **Love, Maggie**

"Oh Hi, Nora! Yes, it's a nice day to be sitting out. Yes, I'm answering today's mail. It's hard to keep up with all the letters. Sometimes I don't know if I already wrote this person or not! It can be embarrassing. I wish, in a way, that there was only one to concentrate on. This is a lot like flock busting!"

"Flock, Busting Miles?"

"Yea! That's when you're out goose hunting. A whole flock comes by, and you cannot single any one out, so you just point the shotgun up in the air and pull the trigger. You'd think, with all those geese in the air, at least one would fall out of the sky, but usually, none do. You're better off having one come along; you can pace it, lead it, and know what it's gonna do, so when you blast, it comes down."

"Ha, ha, you're funny, Miles. But you better not talk like that to these women; they don't like to be shotgunned."

"Yea, well, I joke around, but I'm pretty serious, really, if anyone gets through to that."

Nora gets serious herself. "Miles, I had a dream the other night. A dream that you find someone. You are heading out in your houseboat, and she is there waiting for you, ready to go. I don't know if it's someone you already know or not. I'm serious, Miles. When I have these dreams, they come true. Ask Bill about it. I see things all the time. The future."

"That'd be pretty nice, all right."

She changes the subject. "How's the boat coming along, Miles? I haven't heard you talk about it in a while. It must be almost done by now?"

I give a disgusted, "No. I don't know what's going on. I gave him the money, and nothing is happening, just excuses. He said he'd have it done in time to go out and live in it this winter, but I don't see how that can happen now. I'm depressed about it. I'm writing these women, too, and what do I tell them? Where will I even be living this winter! Invite them to the Salvation Army! I have nothing to offer them! Hopefully, that will change. Maybe then, when I launch the boat, this woman you speak of will be there to join me. It would be nice to share life with someone."
☺ :)

"Toot, toot."

"Oh hi, Don, What's up?"

"Hey Miles, you ever going to get back to the wilderness? That little 'event' didn't scare you, did it? Everyone still has a bet, you know. Some say you are totally full of hot air. All this houseboat talk is bullshit."

"Well, Don, what can I say? Little minds have little dreams. When you want big things, it takes time, work, and there are going to be setbacks to overcome. The difference between those who accomplish and those who do not is in who gives up and who doesn't."

Don just gives me a look, thinking, Yea, I know, and you are a good talker, but where's the houseboat. That's what I want to know too!

Working with Don is going OK, I guess. I like the actual work, anyway. It's often interesting with all the various aspects of keeping a barracks going. We are digging a sewer ditch now. There's one guy working with us who is older than the rest and a college professor. He likes to do manual labor in the summer. He is a big game hunter who hunts all over the world. We get into conversations about big game and trophy hunting. There is another guy who big game hunts, but more locally, and is an assistant guide for Dall sheep and Grizzly hunting. The hunters, Don, and I, often talk long hours on the subject. I was raised to be against trophy hunting, just on basic principle. It bothers me to think of animals being killed to satisfy someone's ego. Hunting for food is different, or for protection. I admit though that my opinion is based on no facts. It is also apparent to me that most people are not separating 'killing' into categories. If the animal is dead, it's dead. The fine details of why, how, are a moot point, maybe. Perhaps these people have a point. I do ask myself how I'd feel if a loved one was killed in a car accident. How much would it matter if the driver was drunk or not, or did it on purpose and liked it, or was sorry, or if it was even a loved one's doing? Loss is loss.

"Miles, the animal dies, if all the meat is used, and someone wants the antlers to hang up, does that animal know or care? What's the difference if you take the meat and leave the antlers on the ground, or I give the meat to someone and keep the antlers?"

After thinking, I give my view, "Well, the number of animals I kill will be self-limiting. I can only eat so much. But a desire for antlers has no such limit."

The trophy hunter replies, "I can't afford that many hunts! They are very expensive. Lots of people make money off it!"

"Money off of death!"

"Miles, you trap! That is money off of death too!"

"Yea, but it is a minimal amount, and I just buy basic needs. It's not to support luxuries. There are few ways to make a living in the wilderness. I see what you're saying, though. I just have this image of big game hunters out there killing everything they see, not taking care of the meat, and wiping out endangered species and all that." Everyone else laughs as if I am dense.

The guide replies, "Well, don't you think the public has the same exact image of you and your trapping?"

Some of what these guys say makes sense, but I'm hard to change. Certainly, these guys seem nice enough, and not monsters.

The guide replies, "Miles, a trophy animal is usually one that is past its prime and not breeding much anymore. Often it is one that will not live that many more years. I work with a guide, and we book only a few hunts a year. Only four to five animals are killed a year by our business. This number of animals dying supports two Alaska families for a full year. Some of the money, paid in the form of permits and insurance, goes right back into animal habitat enhancement. Hunters and trappers put more money back into the environment than all the animal rights groups combined."

I'd heard this before and think it is the truth. I've heard that a good percent of animal rights funding money goes into things like neutering cats and dogs and other domestic animal stuff that is not directed toward wild animals. I think people should be responsible for their own pets. This issue should not be society's responsibility. There has also been enough in the news to leave doubt in my mind about the entire purpose of collecting money to save animals. It is possible many of these groups are about fleecing the public and a scheme to make a few people rich. 'Friends of the Animals' is in the news for investing its profits into a chemical factory, then justified it, 'As a way to raise more money for our cause.' Just what is the cause? If money is used to support activities that harm wildlife, why is it different from any other cause that hurts the environment for the sake of higher profits? Old beliefs my society has taught die hard. I am reluctant to embrace ideas against Walt Disney, the source of most of my dreams.

I reply to the guys, "Well, what you are saying sounds good, but I have trouble believing that only the old and non-breeders are killed, there is no waste, and all that."

Don speaks up, "A few people give it all a bad name. This is what makes the news, not the people who are doing the right thing and being respectful."

I think this might possibly be so. I know the animal rights people talk about how kind and wonderful wolves are. I myself have come to understand and respect them, but I also saw where wolves turned on their own kind, and it was memorably gruesome. I bet not many goodie-goodies could see that and still love wolves. Each 'side' tends to gloss over its negative side and glorify its positive side. I hear enough stories of wolves that tear a moose open, eat only a little, walk away, and never come back. Talk about waste! I see for myself, all the trees beaver cut down. I bet they only use a hundredth of what they cut. Anyone who says animals are not wasteful is out to lunch. The situation is not like the animals are so much better than us—or that we are so different. If there is 'waste' going on, surely, it is not just the hunters. Hunters might be used as the scapegoat. I also notice many people want change, as long as it is not them who has to change, but someone else. It seems to also be true that people are either for or against, so either pro-hunting or pro preservationist. These two concepts do not seem to blend together in the same mind.

Don tells me, "Miles, I once saw where a wolf ate a meal off of a live moose who was bogged down in deep snow. The wolf left, the moose got up, and is still alive, with twenty-five pounds of its flesh gone! The moose survived."

I have seen enough to think this is happening. Nature, which few people see or accept, can be crueler than man. Society likes to blame the hunters for all the woes of the wilderness. It is hard to know exactly what to think about it all or who is correct. I begin to see it is a more complicated issue than I first thought! *Certainly, a lot of the things I was raised to believe are being questioned. I think now that not all hunters get drunk first—have no respect for people or animals—and love to kill and do not care if they leave it all behind.* The redneck who bombs around on a noisy four-wheeler down public roads, killing deer willy-nilly on private property and leaving them lay, is the image many perceive and notice. The true hunter is not seen or heard, for he is quiet and off the beaten path. I do not agree with my friends, but am willing to admit there is much to think about.

At work.

"Are you busy Miles, you look like you're deep in thought. I can come back later. I wondered if you still had the earrings you were showing Marsha."

Looking up from my desk while issuing linen to firefighters, I say, "No, I'm not busy, just thinking. I sold those earrings yesterday but have another similar pair. They are smaller, but the whale with the crystal as the water spouting out the blowhole is a good idea, huh?"

"Oh yes, I like these even better, how much? It's payday, and I have wanted to get something of yours for a long time."

"Well, I was going to ask $45, but I'll sell them for $35."

The secretary from the front office tries them on and likes them.

Fair time!

It's state fair time, but all I can really think about is my houseboat. The Fire Fighting job is still on, and I'm saving money for the boat. This is the time of year to get out to the woods for winter. The first freeze can come any time after this, even though it is only August. I have the weekend off to be at the fair. I recognize a few more of the vendors. There are the herb lady and the dry fruit guy. Here is that same pottery woman.

I get her attention when she is done with a customer. "I've always loved your work. I have some of my art with me this year. Would you like to trade?" We make a trade, and I get my first ceramic plate with soft blues and earth browns. There is a Salmon on this plate.

As usual, I trade for food with some of the same vendors I traded with last year. I recognize the crabmeat pocket bread guy and his wife. They remember me, and we trade. I make a couple of sales to people who recognize me as the guy who does the metal scene jewelry. I don't outright advertise, but when I get asked, we stop at the nearest picnic table, and I get out my bag.

"Heidi? Weren't you working the grounds last year? Didn't we dance here last year? You going to be at the concert again this year?"

"I sort of remember you, Wild Miles, right? Sure, I'll be at the dance." "See you there then."

My conscience has a bright idea. *Here's a guy selling jewelry. Maybe he would buy some of ours wholesale?* I get out my work, and the shop owner looks at it. One of his customers standing next to us likes one piece, and this encourages the vendor to buy from me. The vendor spends $100. I sell my work wholesale to the vendor at half price. This type of wholesale is called 'keystone' and is the common split between the artist and a vendor.

The mushroom lady is still here. I test my mushroom identity skills again. I check out the record cabbage, turnips, beets, and other root crops. With my ever-present blade of greenery in my mouth bobbing to my swagger walk, I make a pass through the children's section to see what they have been up to with poetry, art, and 4-H animal raising.

"Hey! Wild Miles, haven't seen you around, you got your houseboat yet?"

I don't know who this is or where they know me from, but I smile and ask how they are, and explain about the boat situation. "I still hope to get it in time for this winter, though!"

"So Will, you're going to see your dad? Be a good time for me to stop and see Steamer then, huh? How's your job doing? You going out this winter?"

"I'd like to, but my dad wants me to help him build a shop out the road. My brother's coming up soon, and we'll all work together on it."

Will's too close to his family to ever go out in the wilderness, maybe. "Keep saving your money Will, and stockpiling supplies. If you don't get out this year, you'll at least be set up good for next year, huh!"

We've been talking while he drives, and he reminds me, "Here's the boat shop, Miles. I'll drop you off and pick you up in a few hours on my way back. Good luck!"

"So Steamer, what's going on? I gave you my down payment a couple of months ago, and all I see is a pile of supplies. This is supposed to be done for this winter, and you said I'd have it to live in. If I have to pay rent somewhere, it will put a crimp on my money that's supposed to go toward this boat!"

MILES MARTIN

"Miles, I never promised I would; I said I'd see what I could do! You keep pestering me, and it will take even longer. I have other boats due, besides yours, you know!"

"Well, the reason I came to you in the first place to have it done was because you said you could get it done for this winter, and you said you could set it up for a steam engine. Now it looks like I'm not going to have it this winter, and it isn't being set up for steam. The design you have is the same as the standard boat you sell for $2,000 less. I could have just got one off your lot and put a house on it! I feel like I'm getting the run around here. I don't have time to keep coming down here to check up on things. I expected to turn it over to you, and it should be a done deal."

"You want your money back so you can go somewhere else!? No one else can do it any faster, Miles! This design is not like the other boats. It has more ribs in the back for later conversion to steam as you requested, and it has all clear lumber and bronze screws in its design. It will be one tough boat when you get it, and you'll be happy. I've just had some things come up. The weather hasn't been good to work outside. Too dusty to do the fiberglass work on these other boats, so I'm backed up for space. I'm trying to expand and insulate the shop so I can work in the winter. What I can do is have you come and live here. I have a trailer, and you can work on your own boat in the shop, save money, and have a place to stay. I need security here, and if you live here, that would help me, so I won't charge you any rent."

I ask, "Is there any place to trap around here?" "Sure, all kinds of winter trails. I sell snowmachines in winter. We could work out a deal, and you would have a snowmachine and could run these trails. Quartz Lake is not far, with trails over to Goodpasture River and the Bonneville trail beyond."

I sigh. I had hoped for it to be different. There is little to say, so may as well go along, as he has me between a rock and a hard place.

"Well, my job should end in a few weeks, so I can come then. It would be nice, anyway, to work on my own boat."

Will pulls in on his way back from seeing his Dad.

"Oh hi, Will. Has it been a couple of hours already? How's your dad?"

"Making big money. Looks forward to some time off when winter comes! You ready to go?" Will's Dad has one of those thirty dollar an hour jobs, while most in the country are working for four to five dollars an hour.

Pretty sweet! I could be doing the same if I had taken the Pipe Fitter Union offer.

On the way back, we talk about the coming trapping season, winter, and what we are each going to do.

"I don't know, Miles, you were going to try and disconnect from Steamer, and now it looks like you are even more entrenched! Moving in over there, a snowmachine deal, and all this. Hope it works out OK, but I think he's jacking you around. Why did he take more boat orders after yours and asks you to wait? Why not let the other people wait? Probably because they don't pay him until after he's done, that's why! Because you are the only one paying him ahead of time!"

"Yea, well, whatever. I'm just not that good with people."

"Toot, toot. Hey Miles, you look a little down in the gills. What's wrong? You worried I might lose my bet?"

In his own way, Don is trying to get me to hang in there, so I rib him back, "Thought you bet against me!"

"Well, someone has to bet on the other side, or there's no money to collect!"

I tell him what is going on. "Yeah, well, I'm depressed because there hasn't been anyone in the sauna in a while to kick out." Don, of course, always asks for the latest news on naked women in the sauna, from me, 'took-a-look.'

So on a similar subject, he asks, "Reminds me, are you still seeing that fire fighting gal, the blonde with the big tits?"

"Don, sometimes you are crude. How'd you ever find a wife being that way?"

"That's different, that's love. First, there is lust, then there is love, but ya gotta lust first."

I smile. Certainly, I'm not the one to know about such things. He's the one who has a woman, not me. "Don't marry an Indian though, Miles."

"How's that, Don?"

"Well, you marry her, and you married all her kinfolk, too. They all come and want to move in with you. They all come over and want to borrow money and borrow the truck."

"Don! You're supposed to say it's all worth it! How love is worth all that." I rib him about being married, and he ribs me about being single.

"Hey Don, are the dies to the pipe threader in the truck? I got the wrong size here, I think. You need anything from the truck while I'm out there?" Work slows down a little as there are fewer fires, and the funding for the season starts to run dry. I hang out more at the library and Alaskaland as my hours at work get cut back.

"Miles, I might think about going out for the winter with you." The librarian speaks to me about this. I hardly know her. I've been coming here regularly and talking to her as I do with lots of people. She seems nice enough, very attractive, quiet, shy maybe. I didn't even know she liked the outdoors. She's tall and thin with brown hair. I notice she keeps her dog between her and me when I visit. My conscience notices too. *Doesn't trust men very much, I see. Must have been abused in her past because of how she acts.*

"Well, sure, I'd like to talk about that more. You wouldn't want to go out in the woods with someone you didn't know enough. I'll probably be working on the houseboat all winter in Delta Junction. It's a real pretty area. Maybe you could do your crafts, quilting, and some cross-country skiing. I think we should get together and talk some more. Would that be good?"

"Yes, Miles, why not come over again for dinner tomorrow?" I tell her I'd like that. She asks, "Why do you go out alone as you do into the wilderness?"

I get asked that a lot, of course. I never really know how to answer, and think maybe if you have to ask, you'll never understand. *Wouldn't it be an odd question to be asked what motivates you to live in such a dangerous civilization?* I try to answer.

DING, ding. "Hey, Wild Miles calling. I'm here with a suitcase to collect all the money from work of mine you sold!"

From somewhere in the back, Karen hollers back and laughs. Alaska House is an old historic log cabin with a private living space in the back. When she gets up front, she says, "Only a couple of things sold Miles, but nice to see you so optimistic! Ha, ha."

"Well, I'm practicing for when I'm rich and famous, getting strength in my arms for carrying my briefcase of money."

She chuckles. "Tourist season is winding down Miles, I don't expect much to be going on now till next season. There will be some Christmas business, but that will be it probably. We had a good season, though. Maybe next year we can do a show for you. There has been quite an interest in your work."

"NORA! BILL! ANYONE HERE?" From out back of the Alaska land shop, I hear them talking, so go around to the back.

"Oh, Hi Miles! The season is about over. We are glad enough and look forward to a more quiet winter. Thank God for Alaska winters!"

I say 'A-men' to that and, "I haven't spent a winter in town yet. I expect to be in Delta Junction working on the boat, but I'll get in sometimes maybe, or give a call on the phone. Thanks again for helping me out this spring. It made my whole summer go better."

"Sam, what you been up to, scout?"

"Oh, Hi Miles."

He looks all glassy-eyed, head bobbing. *He must be high on something."*

"Hey, Miles?" He looks around to see if anyone sees us together. I know what he's going to ask. "You got a dollar, man?"

I reach in my pocket and give him five dollars.

"You helped me out when I needed help, gave me a ride and all that. I appreciate it, so now it's my turn to help you out. Hey! I'm hungry, what about you? You want to go out for Pizza? I got the money, don't worry about it."

"No, no thanks, man, I got to meet somebody."

Needs his drugs, no money, no time to even have a free meal with a friend, what a life.

"Well, OK, see you around. Hope you get some buffler put up for winter. Going to be cold soon! See ya!"

"Sue? Who used to work here? A prostitute now? Who'd a thunk it! I imagine it's good money about now with the pipeline going on. Her man Jim is up on the slope. Geez. Well, good for him. Nice to see people succeed. I hear a lot of the old crowd is up on the slope. *Looks like Sam didn't make it through. He was looking pretty run down.*

"Hey, Wild Miles, why aren't you out in the woods yet! How ya doing?"

I don't know who this is, so I just say, "Hi," warmly. "Bla, bla, bla, fair, bla, bla." *We must know him from the fair!*

"And my wife just loved the metal puffin you made."

Must have sold him something at the fair.

"See you next year at the fair. I'll save money and get something else from you!" He shakes my hand warmly and walks on.

Dearest Maggie—Hello! I haven't written a while, but hope you are OK. I've been working with the fire fighters. Oh, yes, to answer your question, umm ahh, I did sort of kind of meet one of the mail order women (I'm still getting letters, but it has slowed down). She was from Alaska! She misrepresented herself I thought. Her picture was in a very loose dress. She turned out to be over 200 pounds and not very attractive. I never told anyone the entire story of how I met her. We were together a few days, but she wanted me to move to another state, and I told her I had plans for here, (the houseboat, and my job). She took off, which is just as well. It wasn't exactly a rewarding experience, but she was nice enough, and it wasn't as if we parted as unhappy people. But, I see I have to be a little careful about what I'm getting into. The one I told you of — blond, big tits, nice smile? Well, we are just friends, and that is nice. I think partly she is not ready for anything because she sort of 'ran away' to be here on her own and work and forget relationships. Some realities of my lifestyle (or dare I say 'me'?) didn't seem to attract her either, hmmm.

I saw someone else, another librarian! She works at the local library, and I talk to her when I go there. I didn't know she was interested in me. She told me she was interested in going out in the wilderness with me, and I told her maybe we should get to know each other first. She had her dog always between us, and the dog didn't like men. This hinted she was uneasy around men. The dog is protective, with a focus only on men. and She didn't notice or say anything to the dog and seemed glad to have the dog between us. Anyhow, we made a date to see each other the next day. No! Nothing happened! She called me up and broke the date; told me she was moving in with a friend and for me not to feel bad, and she's sorry. She sounded very defensive, didn't want to see me in person to tell me, and was like 'afraid.' I got the impression she had some fantasy, and when the reality was about to confront her, she froze up. I sigh. There are a few others talking about coming up. It seems, though, that as soon as I meet someone, I tell the rest not to come up, or that I met someone, and then, when it doesn't work out, I cannot write again and say "false alarm! Please come up!" I end up losing touch and answering only new letters. I'm still optimistic, and I'll keep you posted. 'Love' is right around the corner!

LATER: **September.**

Didn't get this sent off, so will add to it. Summer is pretty much over here. I feel bad that I didn't get outdoors to enjoy it, but at least I made the money to pay for the hull of my boat. I'm going to be working on it this winter myself under the boat builder. The guy might be a little hard to deal with, but I think he will see a good job is done on the boat anyway. The BLM job went OK, and I think I can come back next year even though it is only seasonal work. Winter is a big thing here. Everyone's routine is affected by it. Jobs change, tourists leave, cold and dark come. Most of us look forward to it! I'm excited about building the houseboat! Write when you can, oh yea, forgot to answer your question about my rabbit cycle theory of civilization, maybe next time!
Sunshine, Wild Miles.

Walrus Ivory box. The bottom and lid are mammoth ivory, I found myself. The bird is hand-carved, hand-fitted, and many pieces of ivory. The head is carved opal, eye is copper, feet beak is brass.

CHAPTER NINE

HOUSEBOAT BUILDING, BLM JOB, MORE WOMEN, BIG PLANS

Steamer, the Boatman, is telling me about the job. "The wood doesn't want to go this way. We'll have to adjust the plans."

"That's an interesting concept Steamer, I feel a little that way myself about my artwork. The material tells us what it wants to be."

"Yes, Miles, in a way, it is true with my boat building. Boats 'wish to be', and it is my job to see what it wishes to be.

I have moved into his small trailer parked on the lot. I have followed the boat builder's instructions on cutting and assembling the houseboat framework. It is time now to steam the wood, get it to bend into the bow. Our design seems to be too restrictive for the wood. It stresses the wood too much.

"Miles, if the wood has to make a bend, it doesn't wish to, the water over the hull will not wish to make this bend either. This is a bend nature doesn't like, but it's not a problem. I'll just have to take time out to do some more math." He pauses and adds before he turns, "There are some salmon in the river out back. Maybe you could get some with the gig and have some frozen fish for the winter."

I take the pronged gig on down to the river, but the day is getting dark because winter wants to come. A puzzled conscience notices, *There are lights bobbing around at the water. What's going on?* I never heard anyone come down here, and what would they be doing anyway? My conscience and I slowly and quietly approach the river to see what these people might be up to. As I approach, one light goes out. *Hmmm.* When I take another step, another light goes out, and then all the lights go out. There hadn't been a sound. I pause, wondering what is going on. I wait a long time in silence, straining my ears to hear anything that would tell me what this is about.

A voice out of the dark—

"I think it's ok, just another poacher." One light comes back on, then another. Now I can see about fifteen people in the shallow water with gigs like mine, spearing salmon and putting them in tote bags.

Before I move, I answer, "Yes, just another poacher, like you guys—nothing to worry about."

All the lights come back on to the sound of splashing, laughing, and fish flopping. The salmon here are thick enough to walk on. We stand in the water, watching hundreds and thousands of salmon swirl around our feet. Nothing but fins break the surface of the river as far as the eye can see. This is especially interesting to me because of my experience with nets on the Yukon River. The fish is smaller than the king salmon, but with firmer meat. These 'silvers' weigh about ten pounds each, compared to thirty pounds for the 'kings.'

It looks to me like everyone here could take a thousand fish and never put a dent in the population. I take about twenty Salmon in that many minutes and decide I have as many as I want for the winter (about 200 pounds). In the morning, the salmon are all cleaned and hung in the freezing air on poles, where they will stay frozen throughout the eight-month winter.

In the daylight, I spend time watching salmon spawning in the shallow, clear gravel bottom river. The river bottom is covered with freshly dug holes where the eggs are deposited. These holes are made by the salmon using tail and fin to stir up the gravel. I lay on the riverbank, staring into the water for hours. This is very special to watch. In a screwed up world, it is wonderful to see something doing well, being healthy, and prospering. I feel very lucky to be here and very 'rich' to have this food available.

There is no special rush on the boat now because it will be spring, and many months from now before we can put it in the water. There seems to be only a few hours of work a day available to get boat work done before there is a waiting period. Glue is mixed and applied, but then we have to wait for it to cure. Sometimes there is a new pattern to be designed by Steamer. There always seems to be something to wait for, and I feel impatient.

Will has talked me into signing up for unemployment. I have never thought of it before. I reason that I've paid into it over the years. It's money I've paid. I'm only collecting it back. Since the boat work is only part-time, I'm available for work if any is offered. Steamer has no money to pay me. What I do for him just gives me a place to stay or a discount on the boat price. The unemployment money takes care of my food and basic needs.

"Is this the snow machine you want to sell Steamer? I'd rather just own one than to run the ones you're trying to sell." I buy the ski-doo Olympic that had been set up to run a race. "Do I understand right that you want $200 for this?" I pay the money, and now I can get away when I wish. I am not pleased with this arrangement at Steamer's, but it will be better now that I can leave when I need to escape.

The trailer Steamer has me stay in is not insulated for the winter. It has propane heat, which I discover is a very damp heat. Sometimes my head touches the wall, and my hair freezes to the wall! There is frost forming in a lot of places. Propane is costing me a lot of money. Even though there is no 'rush' on my boat, progress seems slower than it need be. Meanwhile, Steamer worries about building his shop, fixing people's snow machines, taking care of 'whatever,' and not letting me know what needs to be done next on the boat. Steamer is also not ordering the things we need to continue working on the boat, so I cannot just continue working on it on my own. Meanwhile, Steamer is putting me to work on his projects fixing snow machines and not paying me. The deal was for me to work on my own boat and be security, not work for him, with no work on the boat. My conscience expresses my concerns. *If it keeps going like this, we may not even be done with the boat by spring!* The builder is constantly saying, "Don't worry, it will get done after this," then "After that," but never once saying, "Ok, I'm giving this my full attention now. Let's do it!" Always there is pressure, no time, and being swamped with a million other things he'd rather be doing. "It's not like I planned it this way, Miles. Things just come up!"

The snow machine.

I'm on my snow machine. Start the slide into the turn, steering into it, keeping the throttle on, going into a controlled skid around the bend in the snow-covered road. I back off the throttle just enough to straighten out and then punch it again. The snow machine screams to the lake. Out on the lake, people are ice fishing from shacks hauled out by trucks. They fish through holes in the ice for rainbow trout. The lake is maybe a mile long, not as wide, surrounded by hills, and having easy access from Fairbanks. A person can drive out in a couple of hours, so it is a perfect weekend retreat. Not many people come out considering what the lake offers. Sometimes I ice fish, but I enjoy the snow machine more and trapping.

Today I head across the lake to 'Hippie Hill' to go visit some people I just met. Hippie Hill has an empty cabin overlooking the lake. This cabin is on state land. No one owns it. Over the years, different people have moved in for a year or so at a time, usually hippies looking for a free place to stay. This year Bob and Karen are here. They live a simple life together, melting snow for water, having no electricity, and living by kerosene and propane. Bob has a few traps out that he checks on snowshoes. I think they both collect unemployment from summer work.

In the cabin, I answer the question on how the mail-order woman thing is going. "Yea, still getting letters from the tigress who is waiting for the stars to line up. I'm still getting new letters. Some are promising. One gal in Oregon lives in a remote village and is a schoolteacher. She's written me four to five times now. There is a gal, Angie, who writes from Georgia that looks yummy pretty, wants to live in the wilderness, and has dreamed about Alaska all her life. How is a person to know if any of these women will take to the reality or not? They not only have to get used to a relationship with me but a completely new place and lifestyle. I think it would be overwhelmingly hard. I know it happens, though. Didn't you two meet through the mail?"

Karen squeezes Bob's hand. "Yeah." But they don't want to talk about it. Karen tells me she is different from most women, and maybe only one in a thousand who thinks they would like this life and really does.

"So Karen, I might have to go through a thousand women? There must be another way!"

"Find one that's already here?"

"Yeah, sounds good, Karen, but you know how it is. Few women are here long on their own in this lifestyle. There are quite a few more men doing this than women. Not to put women down, but it seems more of a man's world here. There is the lifting of heavy things, dealing with guns, bears, basic mechanical things. It's possible for women to do all this, too, just less likely. Few women even arrive here alone. There are ten times more men than women in the state. Many of the women repeat a joke, 'The odds are good, but the goods are odd.' This implies to me, they are looking for a kind of man that is hard to find here, and they are disillusioned."

Karen laughs, "Good men are hard to find, Miles, you have to admit!"

"Maybe, but so are good women. Why not just say, times are changing, and good people are hard to find. Our whole society seems an angry one to me with an attitude of 'sue' and 'screw thy neighbor first before he screws you.' A world where people who are kind and trusting are seen as suckers. Few people seem at peace."

Karen looks at me with a look like she wonders about me. I'm about to have an 'attitude problem' and start a lecture. I catch myself before I get started. She doesn't want to hear it. I'm in a mood where I'm tired of hearing how tough women these days have it and how their problems are all the fault of men, with the implication that somehow women are better than men are. How are men and women ever going to get together if they insult each other? Karen and I have talked about such things before. I often hear the lines from women like, 'Men and their toys!' 'Men are just overgrown children,' 'Being macho, how stupid,' and other similar comments—not just from her, but also from a majority of women. I see the differences between men and women all right. God created us differently for a reason, and I try to understand the 'why' and prefer to smile about it. Sometimes though, it does get to me, and I wonder if God is just mean or finds it very funny, watching us trying to get along.

"Miles! You look lost in thought! I have wanted to go out on a snow machine ride. We don't have one, you know, cannot afford one. Would you take me out on a ride, just so I can see what it's like?"

I think Karen is going out of her way to try to be nice and cheer me up, being sorry she made an insulting remark about 'men.' I'm not mad at her. I just do not understand the attitude I pick up on.

"Sure! Let's go!" I tell her. It will be fun to go out with someone other than my other-self.

We explore some new trails I've never been on before and always wanted to check out. One has never been broken open, so we have a little trouble making headway in the deep snow, but the Olympic chugs through, plowing snow up over its hood.

"Karen, I see an old cabin across this lake. Let's run over and look at it!" No one has been here in a long time.

"Miles, this looks like it used to be an old homestead. Look at the farm equipment in the grass here!"

A tractor that looks like it came from about the 1940s is all rusty and buried in grass and short willows. The tires are solid rubber with no tubes. The steering wheel is all metal and never had padding. The peddles are big, awkward, solid metal, and have that '40s' look I've seen before. There is an old horse-drawn wagon with hand-forged wheel hubs. I find all sorts of smaller tools like shovels, rakes, and hoes, all hand-forged and untouched for many years.

"Let's take a look in the cabin itself, Karen!" The door is open, so we just walk in, to the creaking of old wood. There are dishes in the cupboards, and some magazines on a table from the '40s, like there had been an unplanned departure.

"Miles, I wonder what happened and why these people left. What story is told here?"

It is hard to tell. Did the work get too hard, no money anymore, market dry up? Did some member of the family die? Did the people just get fed up? Someone just walked away and never came back, not even to pick up their belongings. The place must not have been sold. No one else took it over, and here it sits. One newspaper is from 1914 and has headlines about the opening of the new Suez Canal.

"Karen, check out the ad in here for a new car. Listen to this! ' In most cars, when you reach thirty miles an hour, you notice high vibration. This car will do thirty-five miles an hour and maintain it!'"

She is looking over my shoulder at the picture of the new Ford.

"Look at these other ads for corsets and magic medicines and these old-time pictures!"

We have a lot of fun trying to put together the life of whoever lived here. There is a doll and children's things. There are farmer clothes. There is no longer a road into here, nor any clearings where farming might have been done. I'm sure that back then, the main road to Quartz Lake would have been a one-lane dirt rut.

"There is so much history to find here in Alaska, don't you think, Miles? I mean, it's only been one generation that white people were here, and less than that since the gold rush. Not so long ago, there was very primitive living, and not that many people have arrived since those days, so there is still a lot to find and wonder about. You'd never find an old place like this so easily in the other states!"

We have a fun ride back, and it is not so far to the lake, maybe a twenty-minute ride. It is nice to be with a woman and share something like this. I sigh when she says, "Thanks, Miles, for the good time. Bob and I will have to get a snow machine now, I think!"

She is spoken for, so "Oh well." It is time to try another ad, maybe.

I think about my trips out around the lake on my way back to Steamers. Out on the lake edge, I am able to hunt grouse and set some traps. This isn't the wilderness, so there are no wolverine and few wolves. There are wild bison, though, and I have to avoid them sometimes out on the snowmachine trail. I think they do not like the snow machine. The herd is crossing as I come upon them. I only slow down but do not stop. There is one bigger one, weighing maybe a ton, that seems to be in charge. This one thinks I am not far enough back, so suddenly turns and charges me. My snow machine has no reverse. This big Bison stops short and lowers its head, paws the ground, turns, and looks after the herd crossing the trail, making sure they all get across. The show is impressive, the message clear. The image of the hot breath making ice fog in the winter air and the soft thunder in the snowdrifts of a crossing herd of bison is a scene not many will ever know.

The snow machine, as a form of transportation, is fun and exciting, getting me out further and faster than I could snowshoe. I understand, however, that the machine is only 'nice' when it runs, and it is necessary to maintain it and have access to parts, tools, and a shop. This machine would do me little good at a place like the Yukon where I was. The machine works for Tucky only because he keeps in contact with Fairbanks regularly.

Paul lives across the lake and around the corner from Hippie Hill. He's young and alone, and some of us wonder what he's up to. We think he's stealing from the local people. Some cabins have been dynamited up the Goodpasture River. I'm sure it is Paul that has done the deed. He told me he had dynamite and wanted to blow something up. There is no one else living on the lake.

"You want to go to town, Miles? I'm headed in. Karen and I need some groceries, and a check just arrived."

I'm visiting Bob and Karen again, and guess I may as well go into town to get a few things myself. It's been a few weeks since I went in with Will. There's an hour wait while we use the propane weed burner and stovepipe to warm up the truck's engine and oil pan. The truck has been parked in the lot by the public launch on the lake where the road ends. The windows are still frosted up as we drive out, but I keep scraping so he can at least have a hole in the frost big enough to see out of until the truck heater warms the cab up. It takes about two hours to drive in.

"So, where do you need to stop at Miles? Did you say you needed propane? Did you toss your bottle in the back? Hey, there's a cop behind us flashing his lights! Wonder what he wants? Hold on, let's see if it's us."

I crane my neck to look out the back window, but it's still pretty frosted. The cop pulls us over.

"Ok, let's see some registration and driver's license!" The cop looks suspiciously into the truck and glowers at both of us.

"What's the problem, officer?" We both wonder what is going on.

"Your tail light is busted out." The cop responds as he checks Bob's papers. He takes his time as Bob, and I look at each other with a question. The cop strolls back to his car as traffic slows, gawks, and goes on by.

The cop takes his time strolling back. "Ok, out of the truck, now! You're under arrest!" The cop handcuffs Bob as he gets out.

Bob is asking what is going on, what the problem is. "Where are we going? What about my truck?" The cop has no reply as Bob adds, "But I have a woman back in the wilderness depending on me to get home tonight with food!" The cop could care less. I wasn't sure what to do, didn't know if I was under arrest too. I don't know how to drive, so I cannot take care of the truck for Bob. I find out he'll be at the jail. The truck isn't even locked up; Bob cannot even give me the keys. There the truck sits on the highway, unlocked. Who knows how long it will be sitting here, hours? Days? Weeks? Months? I have to hitchhike to the jail to find out what's going on. The cop wouldn't give me a ride. I wonder all the while what Bob did. It looks serious. My conscience agrees, commenting, *Probably killed someone, the way this is being handled.*

At the jail, I find out Bob is there because he killed a duck out of season the year before down by Anchorage. My mouth falls open. My conscience is as shocked as I am. *Holy Cow! A duck? What would they do to me then? I've killed more ducks than I can count and a hundred other things besides that!* I find out that there is more to it. He was supposed to pay a fine and didn't. *Who knows, maybe he resisted arrest, used a stolen gun. I'm sure there is a reason for all this. Still, Bob seemed like such a nice guy.* It's hard to believe he's a wanted criminal. There's no word on when this will be over or when he'll get out. For sure, it will be a few days at least. So I'm stuck in town and have to find a way home now, and what about Karen, waiting for him, without much food, money, or transportation?

I remember how people in the remote areas joke about how it's less of a crime to kill the game warden than to poach. It was always a 'joke.' This seems odd to me, this over the duck. Christ, the neighbor was dynamiting empty cabins and isn't in as much trouble. *Society is surely very odd.* I just don't understand the situation. *What am I missing here?* I'm puzzled.

Diary: November 21—Will stops by to visit. I am putting together a black powder rifle I traded my artwork for in Fairbanks. I thought Will would be excited about it, but he thinks it will not be useful and is a waste of time to put together. Not much done on the boat, but the framework is there to see the outline of the hull. Still eating the salmon I gigged out back. There is no place I can do my artwork, miss doing it. **Diary ends**

There is an incident at the Steamer shop. Some kids come at night to borrow a snow machine, claiming to be friends of Steamer's son. I think all the kids are with the son and are all going out and coming back. It turns out they did not have permission, and Steamer blames me.

Steamer isn't especially pleased with me, so work on the boat slows to a crawl. I failed to do my job. So now he's not concerned with doing his, or so his logic seems to be going. It's not like I can go stay somewhere else and get out of this situation either. If the Hippie Hill cabin was empty, I could move in there, but it will be spring before Karen and Bob leave. "Oh well."

There is escape in the scream of the machine. Some of the country I get into is storybook nice. Out behind Quartz Lake, the trails go on forever, without cabins or people. Map and compass work seems useless here in the flat country. The snow goes forever and ever. The sun plays on the drifts, turning them into sculptures. There are tracks to see of grouse, Moose, Bison, and caribou. None of the trails are on maps, and there are no reference points. There is my own machine trail to follow back, but no way to know where I'm headed or where I've been. No one I talk to knows the country here.

Dear Maggie--How's life in the fast lane? You sounded pretty busy last time you wrote. I have a snow machine now and it is a lot of fun to run around. This helps with the frustration with the slow progress on the steamboat. I know you think 'steam' is a stupid idea! Ha! But remember, I worked on steam in the navy and understand it. I think it might be good when I wish to be very remote where I cannot haul enough fuel (or afford it!) There is plenty of driftwood along the river. I don't have the engine lined up yet, mostly a 'money' problem. I may have to put in a temporary 'other' source of power. Maybe this could be emergency power when I get the steam engine and boiler. The weight problem is bothering me, at a thousand pounds. This is about all I have on my mind; sorry to be talking stuff you have so little interest in. The problems with

'Steamer' are pretty much the same. No use going into it. I only sigh. As long as I get my boat, it will be OK.

Steamer is teaching me to work with fiberglass resin. This is something that interests me. I do snowmachine cowling repairs in the shop. I enjoy making a wrecked cover look new again. This is the artist in me perhaps. I have to blend the color when the resin and cloth work is done, and it has to be built for strength. This is very interesting work. Should I add it to any work history qualification resume? Ha! Not the sort of stuff you learn in school, huh?

I'm still writing a few gals I met through the magazine. I will put another ad out, maybe because I went out with another guy's girlfriend, and had such a good time a week ago! We found some antiques in an old cabin and had a lot of fun. I'm thinking I need a companion. The Tiger is still waiting for the stars to line up properly (roll my eyes up). The one from Georgia sounds interesting still, but it seems so far away. Right now, I don't feel like I have anything to offer a woman. When I get the houseboat done I'll feel better about that. (Hopefully, this spring!) Wouldn't it be fun to take a woman on a date by boat? You know I don't drive, and that makes it hard to go out with anyone, but with a boat, I could offer a woman something different. I think it will be cool to travel around on the boat with a nice woman. Think of the things we will see! Can you picture the evenings on the boat deck out in the sunset? I doubt I'd be looking at the sunset much! Well, I have seen a lot of sunsets, but not much of women.

Do you know what you want to be when you grow up yet? I think sometimes one of your classes will leap out at you and you'll know what you like most. I feel lucky in this way, that I know what I want. How's 'what's his name'? Any toads turned to princes yet? Don't settle for less than you want, you deserve a good man, and it will be he who is 'lucky.' Write when you can, and know I think of you often! Oh! Merry Christmas! It's a little early, but want you to have this necklace I made and don't want it to arrive late! (Sometimes our mail is messed up), take care, **Sunshine, Miles.**

Dear Dad---Hello! Christmas is here again. I hope you are doing well. As I work on and look upon my boat, it reminds me of sailing with you and your boat from England. Do you still think about boats? I would guess so! This is a riverboat though, and looks a lot different. I don't expect to run into any forty-foot waves as we did! Your thirty-foot boat did all right though. Mine is only twenty four feet. I had a boat this summer, but used it and the outboard as partial down payment on this new boat.

What have you been up to? Still teaching? It's nice that you get to change the classes you teach from year to year, less boring that way. Have you started your joint ventures yet? Last you wrote, you told me you might start up a company between several countries, Russia, Egypt, and China? I have no idea what they all have in common. You would visit these countries in your business? How would you keep your position with the University? You said they would let you have a leave of absence. It sounds interesting anyway. Just wanted to let you know how I am, and hope you are well! Have a good Christmas! **Sunshine, Miles.**

Once again, I sigh after writing Dad. I never know what to say. I think he is lonely and sad that I'm not closer. I didn't go on in school. I think Dad had hopes we would work together in a partnership. I know he is only politely interested in what I have to say about my life, and there seems to be no real genuine interest or excitement for what I'm doing. Mostly, I feel guilty. The good news is, most Alaskans have problems with parents, *or do most people?"*

My Dear Trapper-- Thanks for the early Christmas present, and the lovely painted card. You have so many talents! Your poetry, painting, metalwork, trapping, boat building! It sounds so romantic and exciting! I shall cherish this silver swan on ivory necklace you made, and will wear it forever! I hope you enjoy these cookies I made just for you. I wish I were there to help keep you warm during this long dark winter of yours. You sound depressed about the boat situation, but I know it will be done and you will be glad you stuck it out! My work is boring as ever, and I would like some time and space for myself. This pace is too much for me, so I long for the peace you know! Be patient, the stars will line up! Love, **Your Tigress**

Dear Miles---Thanks for the lovely watercolor and necklace. What kind of duck is this? The shell looks like the water! How did you cut all those small pieces of metal out to fit so well! You are very talented! It is so expressive and shows such passion! I guess I'm doing OK. My father is sick and I need to take care of him and so don't think I will be able to come to Alaska any time soon, but wish I could. This life here is so crazy, and you are so lucky to be out of the rat race, and away from bills, and working for someone else, and I could just scream. Your letters smell like wood smoke, and my cat goes crazy smelling your letter, it must be the woods and wild animal smells. Life on a houseboat sounds like a wonderful dream come true. You make it sound so great; sometimes I could just drop everything and run off with you! Eating salmon every day? Wow! Do you know what we pay for just a small cat-food size can of Salmon here? I can't even imagine 200 pounds of it! You are rich beyond what anyone I ever met has, and not with money Miles, but things that matter! Take care **'Georgia.'**

Dear Miles—How are you doing? Merry Christmas! Remember when we were five, and I got the big doll, and you got the electric train? Things are sure different now, aren't they! I wish we could go back to those times. I sure miss you. Yes, I'm doing all right. Maine is a lot like Alaska right now with the weather. One of the other girls was raped by a doctor here. Nothing we can do about it, though. It almost happened to me. They had me on medication. When you are like that, they can do whatever they want.

Other than that, everything is fine. I've been making things in leather shop. I'm working on a belt for you, but it isn't quite done yet. Thanks for remembering me at Christmas. Your art is coming along nicely. I don't hear from anyone else much, just Dad sometimes. I don't even know where Mom is now, do you know? I wish you could come visit me. **Love, Your sister.**

"Hey, Will! What brings you out this way, your Dad working again at the pipeline camp?"

"Yeah, he called and said he has a day off and wants me to come visit. Thought I'd stop and see how your boat is coming along. What you working on there, you building that black powder rifle?"

"Well, sort of. Someone wanted art from me for Christmas and didn't have any money. I traded for this black powder kit. Looks like it might be fun to put together. You told me you thought it would be impractical, but I look forward to firing it. I just got the parts out to see if it's all here. Looks like it might be nice looking, with all this brass furniture."

"Well, Miles, it might look all right, but I wouldn't bother, not very practical or functional. But maybe you can sell it when you're done."

"Let's go in the shop and check on the boat Will. It looks like a boat now anyway, but I'm not sure it will be done by spring."

Will looks over the boat and says, "The transom looks good and strong. The stringers are notched in. Has a nice line. That quarter-inch marine ply bottom and a full single sheet is impressive. You told me about that. Should be strong, all right. Nothing's gonna bust through that! Will it draw a lot of water, though?"

"Steamer says it will draw four inches. Pretty hard to believe, huh, but sure sounds nice. A canoe draws that much."

Will laughs. "Yeah, you should be able to travel any river you want. What about the steam engine?"

"I've been in touch with Semple Engine Company, got prices and advice. Money is the big hold up. Steamer too. He wants to sell me one of his Chrysler outboard engines and is giving me a hard time about installing a steam power plant."

Will is shocked and says, "But he told you he knew all about steam and was excited about putting a steamboat together. I was there when he said all that. And anyhow, whoever heard about a Chrysler outboard? Could you even get parts? Are they any good?"

"Yeah, I feel the same. I overheard him on the phone trying to get a mercury dealership and couldn't. As for his talk of steam—I think it was only to get me hooked. Now that he's got my money, he thinks steam is a crazy idea. The weight of the steam set up bothers me, and I cannot find anyone who really knows if it will be enough power. The set up I'm looking at is only twenty horses. I know what boiler I need. I hate to spend five grand or so and then not have it work, or spend a year putting it together, and then find out I need something more for another few thousand. If Steamer had the knowledge and desire to help, as I thought he did, I'd probably go for it. Right now, all I want is to get my boat done and away from here! Maybe I can do a temporary deal with outboards and do the steam at another time. Maybe I'll run into someone who knows something about actual installation or has run one of these to know what twenty horses actually looks like in terms of ability to move a load on the water. I still haven't decided between a paddlewheel or prop. I think prop, though."

Will excitedly says, "Paddle would be pretty cool, though!"

"Yeah, but 'cool' isn't what's going to get me places. I'd do it if I thought it would even work, but there's too much waste of horsepower. The more I read about paddles; well, I prefer efficiency to looks if it comes down to a big difference. With the prop, I'd go in a tunnel. That would give me less draft. Steam, with its low rpm, requires swinging a big wheel, at least a foot in diameter. With a four-inch draft, it doesn't make sense to draw a foot more below the bottom of the hull, just for the prop. Sucking it into a tunnel is the answer unless I go with a flex shaft, but that's pricey, maybe not as strong, or reliable. Paddles are only like twenty-five percent use of horsepower. That's pretty bad, Will, if I'm looking at five usable horses off a twenty horse engine."

"You'll need rudders then, probably. A set? I could build them for you, Miles. I got some fittings and could use some sheet metal I have."

"Maybe a marine transmission, too, if you keep your eyes out for one, Will. Velvet drive, if you can find that in your wanderings through salvage yards. I'm almost sure the way to go is through a transmission. Building tunnels is an art in itself. I don't know Will, I'm into this pretty deep for the little knowledge I have."

Will looks again at the hull and says, "Your hull is looking good, and it's extra beefy in the back for the steam engine and boiler weight, I see. I'll stop back when I come out this way again."

"Say 'Hi' to your father for me. Have a nice drive."

Dear Miles--Sorry I missed contacting you at Christmas, I was out of the country. I've got something set up in China with a deal on a trainload of steel. This joint venture business might work out well. We have a government contract we are negotiating on, and I have partners in three countries now. The teaching at the university is going well. It would be nice to see you. You should think about a trip here. I'd be glad to pay for it. It would be easier for you to come here, as I cannot get away to visit you. I'm glad you are doing well and good luck on your boat project. **Love, Dad**

"Hi Will! Time to see your Dad again?"

Getting out of his old truck Will replies, "Yeah! I see you're working on that gun again."

I defensively say, "It's coming along. I could get into this black powder thing. I like the idea of being able to make my own powder and bullets. This would shoot about anything, too; nuts and bolts if you had to. If hard times come, and we see more gun restrictions or can't buy bullets, this would be a handy thing to have, 'just in case.' At least a person could go hunting for food. It's cheap to shoot too. I haven't shot it yet, not ready, but the more I work on it, the more I get into it."

We have talked about hard times being possible, so Will says, "Yeah, well, I guess if hard times come, it could be handy, but I'd rather just buy modern guns and stockpile ammunition. That's what I'm doing. You can buy a lifetime supply of ammo, you know, and then not worry about it! Black powder is just too outdated to be taken seriously. It's much too slow and inaccurate for my interest, and I think you're wasting your time, but anyway, how's the boat thing going?"

I give up on this age-old conversation about weapons. Will forgot we considered what we heard, that the government might demand ammunition have a shelf life, to prevent exactly what Will and I wish to do, stockpile our ability to get food and defend ourselves. Also, we both know what happens to stashes of useful stuff we try to hide someplace, it gets stolen. Knowledge is worth the most. I even know how to build a bow and arrows in the event we end up in a situation we have to run for our lives because the British are coming, as happened once before in American history. Anyhow…

"Steamer's hard up for money and hasn't been working on the boat. He's trying to talk me into buying some land he has for sale, as well as buying outboards through his new dealership. He promised me mercury motors, which I understand, but he cannot get the dealership. He got the dealership for Chrysler outboards, which I never heard of. It's possible the only way I'm going to get my boat out of here is to play along. I have no other place to keep the boat or work on it and no way to move it, and he knows it. He's screwing with my head."

Will chuckles, "Yea, and your bank account. It's not as if he's done something illegal, so there's no way you can do anything. He's got you by the short hairs, Miles. A piece of land here would be nice. This is a nice part of the country. That's a nice lake, full of fish and easy access from Fairbanks. You know Harding Lake is closer to Fairbanks, but land there sells by the square inch practically."

"How you doing on your preparations to move out, Will?"

"I'll get there. Every time I save up some money, something seems to come up I need to spend it on! I can't seem to get ahead enough to make the move, but I'm trying!"

Dear Miles--Yes, I'm ok. Sometimes I think you worry about me too much! It is funny because it seems to me it is you who needs worrying about, out there in the wilds with all those animals, the cold, so far from the comforts of real civilization. I guess I understand your feelings, that you love the lifestyle. I'm not sure I agree with your outlook, but guess yours is based on a different set of experiences than mine. I mean, this thing with your boat. You should have got a contract Miles! What do you expect without a contract! You'll be robbed blind every time! Smarten up! You should have seen it coming Miles. You are just so naive about things! I love you though, but just worry about you. If you had a contract you could take him to court, make him live up to his agreement!

I got a new apartment so my boyfriend can live with me. We both go to school. He wants to be a Banker. He's good with numbers all right. His father is head of one of the banks here so he'll have a job when he gets out of school. He likes to party a lot though, and is into drugs, but I'm helping him slow down. He treats me reasonably well, and I confess, it's nice to have lots of money. Nothing else new with me. Haven't heard from you in a while though, hope the boat is going OK for you. That boat sounds like more trouble than a woman! Ha! Take care, **Love Maggie**

STEAMER and I are in the shop talking about land, and I get to the point, "Well, let's set it up and do-er John. I got the $2,000 down payment, you are talking $9,000 for three lots of waterfront age—$200 a month payments. Sounds like an investment to me."

"All right, Miles, I knew you'd come around and know a good deal when you had the chance. You're pretty smart! Now we can get your boat done!"

"Uh-huh."

Not long after this, Will comes by again. "Miles, what you up to, looks like the black powder is done. You shot it yet?"

"Hi, Will didn't see you pull up. Yea, the rifle is done. A nice fifty caliber. Look at the size of the lead. You can tell if it is loaded by picking it up! I haven't fired it yet, should be ready in a bit if you want to hang around."

We get to talking about this and that as I finish the rifle. Firearms becomes the topic of conversation, naturally. The right to bear arms and all this.

"Miles, my family is from Czechoslovakia, and my parents were there during a revolution when the Communists took over. You know how we were taken over? My parents were there and tell me. Officials went to every town and to the police stations. They got a list of everyone who had a gun and what they had from the registration forms. The Communists went door to door, and at gunpoint, demanded the guns. They had the list, the addresses. It did not take long to take over, and hardly a shot was fired. That's how we became communist."

"Yeah, Will, I can see how that was a bitch of a time, but it's an event not likely to ever happen here. I agree, sort of, with your thinking. I at least agree that people should be able to talk about it, read about it, discuss it, and where the heck would I be in the wilderness not having a gun?"

"The rifle's ready Will, you want to take the first shot?" We go through the ritual of 'loading,' pouring the powder we measure with the cool powder horn. Getting the ramrod out (just like in the civil war movies!), driving the patched lead ball down and tamping it, followed by the cap on the nipple.

"Sure takes a long time to load, Miles!"

"I think it could be done faster with practice. The old 'buffler' hunters did it on the run, can you believe it? Doing this sure is a lesson in history, isn't it?"

"What should I shoot at?" Will is looking around for a suitable target.

I point, saying, "There's an old wretched dump truck over there. See if it will go through the door. Here let me put the cap on first. There's no safety but for the half-cock, so be careful, and there's no way to unload it without firing it, so once it's loaded, that's that."

"Regular open sights, huh? Ok. I wonder if I should hold high or not. What do you suppose the drop would be at this distance?"

"I'd hold right on, and we can see."

I wonder if Will likes the way this rifle balances, and I wonder, as he holds, what the bullet drop will be at this distance, and if the ball will go through the door. While Will takes his time getting the feel of it, I almost hold my breath with anticipation. Once again, I notice how Will's arm is the size of my waist. I'm just about to ask when he is going to shoot when he pulls the trigger and torches it off.

The blast is not the instant explosion of a modern powder. The sound is more like a 'Whump!' of a stick of dynamite. There is a separate 'snap' of the primer going off an instant before the main charge goes off. Six feet of flame shoots out the end of the barrel, followed by a cloud of blue smoke that makes the world disappear in its blanket. The smell that follows would gag a maggot, with its odor of rotten eggs. I noticed the rifle did not seem to kick, so much as 'draw into' Will. The discharge pushed Will back, more than 'kicked' him. I wonder what Will thinks. I cannot read his expression. He is still standing there, holding the rifle up, with nothing written on his face, 'unreadable.'

A smile slowly crosses his face, and he says, "I got to get me one of these." With a tone of voice, I'll remember all my life. So much for 'being practical' so much for efficiency. In the end? What is it that truly matters? "How a person feels about something." All else is 'only words.' I have to hold back a smile and stop myself from making any comment about past opinions.

"What did it do to the truck Will; did it go through the door? Did the bullet drop?"

"Did you see the whole truck shake when the bullet hit? Son of a bitch. Hey, looks like the bullet didn't drop at all! Right through the door. Check out the size of the hole and what it did to the back!"

"Son of a bitch!"

"Yeah, that's what I said."

"It'd blow the whole other side of a Grizzly to hell, and back I think." We're both excitedly talking at once.

We shoot at the river's mud bank and blow a hole in it the diameter of a bowling ball and as deep as an arm is long.

"Geez," Will says.

"Son of a Bitch" I say.

"Those must have been the days!" Will says.

"The days a man could hold one of these suckers over his head and yell, Charge!" I reply, and Will nods in awe.

We both sigh. We think about the days a man used one of these to get his food, 'making meat' they called it. Now, we buy it in a store in a plastic wrapper, 'pretend' nothing died. No blood, no screams, no butchering. We both sigh again. Part of me is angry that I feel I wasted the first twenty years of my life! That only when I came to Alaska was I born!

The duck finds water.

Will asks me, "Hey Miles, you were going to tell me about the rabbit cycle theory of civilization!"

"Yeah, right, forgot about that. It's very simple. You know how animals live in cycles? Rabbits especially. Every seven years, they have a peak, then the population crashes! We really do not know why, but other animals cycle around the rabbit, like the lynx that depends on the rabbit for food. Studies show that even the trees the rabbit feeds on live in the rabbit cycle. They put poison in the bark that makes the rabbit sick. When rabbits peak, they act crazy. Fox, too, get crazy, and want to be caught in traps, are easy to catch, and are prone to disease.

My theory is that 'Man' also lives on a cycle, the same as rabbits, only maybe our cycle is longer, perhaps every 2,000 years. If we made a timeline and looked at it, maybe we would follow its ups and downs. There were the Romans, the Aztecs, and Egyptians, who all had their days in the sun and seem to have crashed. Civilizations crash for reasons we do not understand. I mean, we try to explain it, but it is only theory. There was a time we called 'the dark ages' in which so much knowledge was lost. Maybe there were other dark ages that all lasted about the same length of time, and the fall is simply part of nature, programmed in the system, a sort of check and balance of nature. Think about it. There are many things about civilization set up for us to self-destruct."

This is a lot to digest, so I pause while we both gather the information we have on the subject to see if it fits the theory. I go on. "We tend to move in a direction of consuming faster than we produce. We tend to pollute our own nest."

Another pause and then add, "One of the best examples I can think of is the eating of meat. The subject at hand. What part of the animal do we pay the most for; desire the most, want, if we can get it?"

"Tenderloins!" Will is quick to say.

I nod that I agree and say, "If we name the other most expensive, most desirable slices, they all have one thing in common! They are nutritionally the worse part of the animal! Isn't that interesting? That we wouldn't desire the healthiest parts? And the healthiest parts are? Oh, like the organ meats, like the liver, the brain, the heart, and kidney. Are any of those parts as expensive and desired as the most favorite? Mostly poor people eat these, because it's all they can get, right? Maybe it's nature's way to make sure the rich and well-off fall by the wayside to make room for the poor. For as society gets more and more well-off, we eat what we want and can afford, and that eventually kills us. Most of us eat foods with sugar, preservatives, processed expensive foods that give us cancer, make us fat and diabetic. What we desire is killing us off. What we need, the fresh garden vegetables we can grow ourselves is not getting done except in unpopulated areas.

As we overpopulate, we also tend to not pair up successfully. We are less happy, less likely to build a quality nest or raise young that survive well. We behave a great deal like overpopulated rats or rabbits in experiments. Many other self-destructive symptoms in society are seen elsewhere in nature. Strange diseases crop up—unaccountably insane individual behavior.

The point is, we, as a civilization, have seen our time in the sun, and it might be 'crash time' now. The lemming goes off the cliff. We have people going off the deep end right and left, people climbing towers and mowing us down with guns, poison put in the food, bombs sent in the mail, people killing each other in fights over parking places. When you understand the rabbit cycle theory, it all makes sense. All is happening as it was planned to be. Past civilizations may have figured it out, and is one reason a bible, a book, could predict a series of events on a timeline. Doesn't surprise me a bit.

It does mean, Will, that if you don't feel like self-destructing with civilization, it might be wise to tippy-toe on out of here into the toolies, let it all crash, and see what's left to salvage from the smoke and debris. Don't forget, a few people did survive the Dark ages. Some Romans survived, and they started over. Some rabbits manage to make it, so it can all start over again."

"I don't know Miles, sounds pretty farfetched to me. I never heard such a thing before. Maybe it's you who is the nut case, and not the rest of the world, know what I mean?"

"Yea, that's why I don't really talk about it much. Just keep it in mind, look around you, and give it some thought. Even if true, I have no idea how long a cycle would be or how long a crash takes. It might be a few years, it might be 100. I just don't see any harm in a few people looking at alternative lifestyles for fun, also as a backup in case the doo-doo gets in the fan, and we have to make quick changes. I think it's healthy for a society to have a few members off 'experimenting' in both old and new directions. I think it is healthy for a few to consider another energy source besides fuel oil, alternatives to using electricity, plastic, steel, cotton, chemicals, and such modern things. What harm does that do? It makes the sheep nervous, but someone has to look for new grass, or find out something new about the old grass, for the herd to survive."

Will looks like he can go along with that part of what I say, and I add, "I know it sounds farfetched, and who am I to come up with some theory on my own. I do not ask that you agree. I'm just saying what works for me. By that, I mean it helps me feel less afraid, worried, or that I have no clue why things happen. I'm not happy about it, but the good news is that the planet has been through this before, and it will go through it again and again and survive. I do not believe we will totally destroy the planet! We will simply make it less hospitable for the majority. I think of a sourdough pot. It's a jar, limited space. At first, there is plenty of flour and sugar, so the yeast is happy and begins to multiply. Then it has an ideal peak condition and multiplies like crazy. Until it begins to run out of sugar and flour and puts out poison. The multiplying and quality of life for yeast slows, almost comes to a halt, and goes dormant. Not much going on. Like a dead zone. Waiting for another influx of sugar and flour. That partly describes civilization. It's possible to predict how long it all takes. For rabbits, it is seven years."

"Yea Miles, I'd agree with that part about a need to go out away from civilization. You lost me on the rest! Anyhow, I gotta go. Take care, and keep me informed on how the boat's doing."

> **Diary:** May 7 --74--Depressed on my birthday. Spring and boat still not done. I really looked forward to living on the houseboat on the Chena behind the barracks while working for BLM this summer. It would be a great way to meet women, and a nice way to show all those people who laughed about the boat--and my ideas about how to live-- that I am seeing it through and not just a talker! **Diary ends.**

I'm lonesome for the woods. I miss the sound of running water, the feel of the wind in my face, and the smell of green things. The need for quiet and lack of civilized noises occupies my mind. My time at Quartz Lake is all right, but there is the scream of the snow machine. I do not mind the noise, but it is a different kind of enjoyment than the quiet wilderness pleasures. I feel lonesome for a woman, too. It is not fun to see pretty women on the streets and see my friends with their women and seeing what I don't have in my life. In winter, women are bundled up, go unnoticed. Somehow, spring brings out the legs and the flirting smiles. I briefly wonder if it's related to birds and bees—spring and mating season.

I wonder if, nine months after spring, there are more children born. Hmmm.

Summer work.

"Hey, Don! Looks like Déjà vu back at work together again for another wonderful BLM season. Hello Sarkis, you get to go big game hunting this winter? Before any of you ask, the answer is no, I do not have the steamboat yet. The hull is almost done, but it takes warm weather to do the fiberglass work, then the house has to be built."

"Miles, did you get the check for the fur all right? You did better than last year. Your fur looks a little better now."

"Yea, Don, I wasn't seriously trapping, but it was nice to get out trapping, and the money was nice to get!"

The work is more familiar, so it may be easier this year. I start to go dancing at the howling dog most weekend evenings. Most weekend days, I hang at Alaskaland again. I have no boat this summer, though, to keep at the dock. (Sigh) I sold my running boat and motor to help pay for the houseboat. I am embarrassed talking about my boat dreams because I know most people think I'm bullshitting them, and I will never have a houseboat.

Some say aloud, "Yeah! Right!" Others politely indulge me, pretending to listen. The dream remains a very private one. The world is so filled with people who talk about what they want—and that's as far as it goes. Could have, would have, should have, but do not, and never have, or ever will.

"Miles! What you thinking about?"

"Oh, hi Nora. How's the shop doing? This looking like a good season? Where's Bill?"

"He went to get ice-cream. You can see him over there. How was the Howling Dog last night? I'm surprised to see you out this early!"

"I'm always an early riser! 😊 :)

I'm going to see Bill and get an ice-cream. Pretty hot today."

Along the way to the ice cream shop, I shift the new blade of spring grass thoughtfully to the other side of my mouth, saying, "The can-can cuties, huh? You girls got a new routine to try on me?" I'm passing the replica gold rush saloon. The costume-clad girls are on a break on the wooden boardwalk of the honky-tonk saloon.

"Hi Miles! How was your winter? When will we see your houseboat? Stop by when you can, Alice wants to talk to you!"

I wave an acknowledgment and keep on going toward the ice-cream shop. Everywhere I go, I walk fast, eyes taking in everything, with that blade of grass waving in my mouth. Bill and I talk about the usual things. Tourism, the wilderness, women, relationships, government, working for yourself, and the weather. My blade of grass shifts to the side when I talk.

"Gotta go see a can-can girl, love to stay and chat, but it's spring." I stop by to see Alice and a couple of the other girls who are now friends.

"Sure, Miles, the Howling Dog sounds like a blast! I'll be there!"

I go to the library on the way back to the military base where I stay, as I did last summer. Mostly, it's the same as last summer, I want to save money, and do not do very much besides work, and hang out where it doesn't cost me anything. I run into Will a lot, sometimes see Sam on the street. The routine becomes familiar, and I look forward to each day.

"We have money for you Miles, your work is getting more popular, it seems. You might want to leave more art with us."

There are not a lot of places selling my art, but a few, and enough to wonder if I should get serious. My mind is occupied with my wilderness lifestyle. I need to think about making serious money for the houseboat and supplies for the upcoming winter. My upbringing has me convinced there is no serious money in the art trade.

Back at the boat.

"So today's the big fiberglass day on the boat Steamer? That day we've long waited for?"

"That's it, Miles, sorry it's taken so long, but I had trouble with the shipment of resin, and then it's been windy. We can't work when the river silt is in the air; it would get in the sticky resin before it sets up." Steamer has me cut the matting for the bottom first before we deal with the resin. The bottom will have thicker glass on it.

"Miles, we want to wait till the sun is on the hull before we put a coat of resin on it. The sun helps it soak in and helps the resin set. We don't put much hardener in the first coat. This is one of my secrets you don't read about. This first coat soaks in for a whole day. It will get sticky but not set up. This also helps hold the glass cloth in place before we put the real resin on." This is something I would never have known to do, so right now, I am glad to be working under someone else who knows such things. The resin soaks in overnight, and the next day we are ready to lay glass.

"Don't leave any bubbled up. You have to take this back off, Miles. Start from one end, and work it down, and don't go faster than the glass wants to go."

I don't mind having to do it again. I want it to come out the best it can. We still have to work fast, though, because we have mixed hardener in the resin, and we are on a time limit before it sets up. Once it starts to set, there is little we can do to fix anything. We'd have to let it harden and sand it off. We only have an hour or two per section. This is a critical part, knowing how much hardener, how much resin to mix, what the temperature of it will be.

The layers go down well. The resin from the day before has soaked way into the wood. The new resin in the cloth will help harden the soaked in resin, even though it will take days. The end result will be a permanent bond of wood and cloth that will not de-laminate. I enjoy this work very much. We work out in the sun as the birds sing. The smell of the river is in the air. An Eagle screams overhead as I take time to glance up. I love the look of the grain in the wood. I love the sense of doing a good job that will last a long time. I love the feeling of seeing a dream coming true after all the struggle, heartache, waiting, frustration, and hold-ups. Maybe a lesser person would have given up! I feel good that I did not give up, did not cave into so many people's jokes about my empty dreams. "They will not be empty!" I like the pressure of a time limit and knowing I can do it. Knowing I have the hand-eye coordination it takes to do it right.

"Ok, the color and wax goes in the last layer of resin, Miles. This wax helps the hull slide in the water better. There is no strength in this layer, and it scratches easily, but don't pay any mind to that. It's just for looks and slickness in the water and helps protect the stronger but more brittle layers underneath."

This makes sense to me, and again, probably I wouldn't have understood if I had to do this on my own with no instruction, and I'd screw it up. I find out it is important to do all the glasswork at once and not wait between layers.

John informs me, "We want the previous layer to still be tacky when the next layer goes on it, so there is a good chemical bond."

Again, this is something you wouldn't read on the package or in a book.

We put in a hard, long, but satisfying day. We have been working for seventeen straight hours. I understand better why we had to wait until the heat of summer and a very sunny, calm day with no wind. I feel a little guilty about my anger at Steamer.

Some of my feelings were justified, some not, and I do not know where that line is. Part of the problem is mine. I simply do not trust anyone else with anything important in my life.

"Steamer, thanks for waiting on the glasswork. I should have listened to you better. You did a good job here, the whole thing looks good, and I'm confident I have a sound hull."

"That's all right, Miles. I'm used to dealing with punk kids who think they know better. But at least you hung in there, and that's more than I can say for some kids." I smile. Steamer goes on, "Next weekend, we can do a final sand and turn the hull over. This will be a boat you'll like, Miles. This hull can take a lot of abuse and will do everything I say it will, you will see!"

> **Dear Wild Miles**--Saw your ad in Mother Earth. Hey, how'd you get that nickname anyway? Your life sounds interesting! I know my age of 18 might turn you away, but I'm old enough to know what I want, and young enough to adapt to your ways...

Enclosed is a photo of an eighteen-year-old sweet thing with long brown hair blowing in the wind, dressed in a denim jacket and jeans. She's smiling against a wilderness backdrop on a lake in a Minnesota logging camp where she says there are not a lot of decent men to meet. She was born and raised there. She loves the water and is used to hard work. She's very pretty, which of course we all know isn't everything, but which we also know counts for everything. Hmmm.

I often think *someone who was raised as a 'farm girl' or some outdoor lifestyle type would be safer to depend on than some town type.* Only I myself came from 'town,' so I think that if I did it, made the change, then there is my counterpart in a woman somewhere. I'm still a combination 'town thinker' but 'wilderness type.' Many 'raised in the backwoods' types are too narrow-minded for my taste, and a well-traveled, educated person seems to attract me, so, 'hmmm.'

> **Dear 18**--Old enough to know what you want, huh? Hmm. I can believe it's possible. I knew what I wanted when I was five years old. I'm building a houseboat and am excited about it. I built two cabins before that and decided I wanted to travel more. I want to live on the boat in the winter too, so it is being well insulated and will have a woodstove. You ask about the weather? Summers are really warm. Sometimes we have months straight of nothing but blue sky and calm hot days. The sun never sets and things grow like crazy.
>
> There are hundreds of lakes with no names and thousands of miles of river with no roads, all full of fish and wildlife. If there is a heaven on earth, this is it. These lakes are pretty when frozen with the tan sedge grass sticking up through the snowdrifts. The wolves pack up and howl, as northern lights flicker. The kerosene

light is so simple and such a soft light. There are lazy times to read and do projects. You can lose track of time with no boss telling you what to do. Wood has to be cut for the stove, snow has to be melted for water, and there are a few simple chores that need doing, but no real 'pressures.' Life can be harsh all right, but also simple, as are the pleasures.

The cold? Well, a person doesn't have to go out in it unless you want to. You come in when it gets cold! The air is dry and crisp. It is another planet really. You get used to the cold. The snow is dry like powdered soap, and not wet. I have been colder in a summer rain on the windy river, then at fifty below in winter.

Nothing is 'free' I think. There will be no wonderful life that hasn't got some price to pay. The bugs get bad in summer and winter can be cold, but they are things a person can deal with. I think these things are easier to deal with, and easier to solve, than a town's problems of pollution, high prices, job stress, crazy people, crowded conditions. Not much can be done about these things! I feel in the wilderness a person has more control over their life, and more freedoms! Sometimes money gets tight for supplies, but I always get by, there is work to be found here anyway, and wages are good. I think a person has to decide what it is they want out of life. This life isn't for everyone, maybe not even for many, but if what I say sounds good to you, maybe this is the life for you? Sounds like you already know about the cold and snow, and also the wilderness. (?)...**Sunshine, Miles**

I write on for quite a while and have a thirty-page letter ready to send out. $200 is spent on a phone call to her in just one evening. This looks serious.

Dear Wild Miles---How did you get that nickname anyway? Your life sounds so wonderful! Life on a houseboat! That would be great for the kids. My 'X' never did anything with us, and we had no money. It would be nice being married to someone who could take care of my children...

Dear Wild Miles---Is that your real name? How'd you get to be called that? I hope you are not crazy! Ha ha! I don't like crazy abusive men. My last boyfriend is in jail now. I need to get away from him and have always dreamed of Alaska, and it is very far away, and I could start over there! I haven't got any money though. If you paid my way up, I'd make it worth your while...

Her written words look laboriously done, one at a time, by someone who cannot spell well. Enclosed is a photo of a tired-looking woman, nice enough looking, with no clothes on.

GOING WILD

Dear Wild Miles—What a cool name! I just saw that movie, Jeremiah Johnson, about the mountain man, and I want to live just like that! I like tall strong men, with big…etc.

I note that this movie must have just shown on the east coast. I start a pile of letters that come from that part of the country and address that movie. I don't think liking a movie is wrong. I only think that if this is the very first time it occurs to them to go 'wow!' over the wilderness, then maybe this is just a passing whim, and the next movie will have them wanting to be… 'whatever.'

Dear Wild Miles—How'd you get that…etc. and anyhow I need a job real bad, could you find work there for me?…etc.

Dear Wild Miles—I believe in marriage, how do you feel about marriage? etc.

Dear Wild Miles—Do you drink -smoke -swear? Are you a good Christian? etc.

Once again, I'm spending three to five dollars a day on stamps answering letters. Some are easy to decide about. From my experience with the last ad, I know more about what to expect and spot 'ways of thinking' easier. Instead of sorting by paper color and perfume odor, I learn to spot several other categories. There are women looking for money or work, with no interest in 'me.' There are women looking for an escape, who might be jumping from the frying pan into the fire if they came here. There are women looking for fathers for their children who aren't particular about the 'who.' There are women looking for marriage or children—more than a man or love. There are users, crazies, pipe dreamers, religious fanatics. Maybe ten percent seem worth looking into. In some ways, I'm more critical when I read a letter than I was, and not just excited to get any letter at all. Of course, I could always be wrong about my opinion from a first letter. Sometimes it takes a few letters to know where someone is coming from, so I answer most of them with a positive note. I understand we all have faults or glitches, and any one of these attributes could be overcome or change in time.

My attitude to all can be summed up this way—Yes, I'll pay your way up here if it sounds like we might get along. However, if you wish to leave, you can pay your own way back. Yes, marriage is fine, but not exactly, what I want to talk about in a first letter, because I believe marriage comes after love. A sexual arrangement might be acceptable in exchange for something you specifically want if it's open and honest and we seem compatible, and all is upfront. Sometimes relationships can start out as business, pleasure, friends, and as you get to know each other, grow into something else. I'm just guessing. Sure I like children and am not against other people's children, but I haven't much money, and the life is hard. Maybe you really wouldn't want children here. We need to discuss just what that means. Sure, it's nice to dream, nothing wrong with that! Surely, I have a dream! I wish you to have a concept of the reality a little bit, so you know what you are getting into. I don't mind seducing someone and wooing someone to a certain extent, but I do not want to deal with someone totally out to lunch. I can accept a religious woman all right; just don't cram it down my throat. 'Fanatics' of any type bothers me. I'm not into 300 pounds of love or paper bag over the head types. I believe seventy-five percent of the female population between eighteen and thirty would be fine, 'looks-wise.' But there is twenty-five percent it would be hard to snuggle up to. Some women are sorry they are women and wish they were men. I'm glad I want to be what and who I am. I do not look down on, or up to, women.

God created us differently for a reason. If I had been created a woman, I would be happy about it and appreciate it. I don't like to clean, but I enjoy cooking. I like to sew and see nothing wrong, inherently, in the role of the woman. Stay home, clean, cook, raise kids, and not be involved in the stress of where the money comes from and how the bills are paid could be ok. Yet, when I ask for a woman, I want a woman, not a man in a woman's body. I'm not looking for a macho woman, someone to compete with. I like a feminine woman who sees the wisdom in God's creating us different and equal, and so does not wish to be a man, yet appreciates men for what they are. Being angry sometimes is normal, but I do not wish to be around people who live in it all the time.

Experience has shown, I hardly ever change my opinion from the impression I get in the first letter from, or the first meeting of, people. I just don't always know what to do about what I think. I feel I am coming closer, though, to knowing what I do and do not want in a woman. I think I cannot just rely on 'instinct' as I once thought. I always assumed these things would be natural! 'Love at first sight' and all that. Instinct serves me so well in other areas, so why not in love? Instincts can go wrong. Then you have to use your head!

Dear Wild Miles—I'm a guy in Hawaii looking for someone to tie me up and give me what I deserve…etc.

Dear Wild Miles—I'm a guy who wants to share the wilderness with you…etc.

I reply to some.

Dear Bonkers—Your needs sound very interesting. I'm not really into that though, sorry. I hope you find what you are looking for, good luck!

No! We do not really address them as Mr. or Miss Bonkers! But yeah, that could show up between the lies. I mean lines.
Sometimes I reply—

Dear—My ad said, "Looking for a woman." Sorry to embarrass you, but I wrote what I meant. I understand that men sometimes pair up with men, and I'm open minded enough to accept the ways of the world, but it's not my interest! Hope good things happen in your life, bye!

The stars are still not lined up for the Tiger woman, and the Georgia gal is still hemming and hawing. I still write both, but life goes on. Have I covered them all? My piles, divisions, categories grow. In truth, I cannot cover the probably 300 letters I get, and dozen maybe interested that I exchange personal information and feelings with.
"Next!"

Dear Miles—How are you doing? The banker's son is out the door, the jerk! He was running around on me. I thought I treated him so well too! How come I can't spot these guys?? I feel like such an idiot. I have no one in my life, but you know I don't like to stay that way, so I'll find someone, and maybe it will be the right one this time! How is it going with your ad? I could never do that! It seems like a last resort! Surely, there are better ways to meet someone!? I hope you find someone this time though, you sound lonely in your letters.

I get letters from longtime friends, women I simply trust, like, and share with, but we have nothing intimate going on. One gal is heavier than I like physically and writes about Sasquatch and aliens enough I understand these subjects are her passion. She has written books on the subject. I can discuss such subjects objectively, argue either side in a debate. But being awakened up in the middle of the night to, "Ddddid yyyou hear that? I think it was a spaceship" is not what I can live with.

Dearest Maggie—Asking, "Who are you again" just doesn't cut it, I found out. Ha, ha and the man's pat reply of "huh?" is only a little better. Some of these women I'm writing I mix up. Can you believe, some write three-four times before I remember ever having written them before! Twenty letters a day is hard to keep track of. Want to be my secretary? 😊 :)

I got a whole box of naked pictures now. Not all of the naked pictures I get are women! Ya! I get some guy ones (takes all kinds huh?) Should I send the pictures to you? Would you like to convert someone? Show em what they are missing? Anyway, as for the women and the pictures, it looks like these women see themselves as being on the meat market. It makes me sigh.

Some are nice looking all right. There are a few that seem promising that I write the most. The 18 year old said she was coming up, so I wrote everyone else not to come up. Then she didn't come up, and I didn't think it was right to inform the other women it was a false alarm. "You're number two now, keep writing!" This is a hard way to do things. Why she didn't come up is a long story. I sent her the money to come up.

Some of my friends told me what a fool I am to send some woman I do not even know, money! I look at it differently. My woman is my other half. I have to trust her absolutely and completely. I'd rather find out right away she can't be trusted! How much more awful it would be to marry someone, and then find this out that you couldn't trust her! (I shudder at the thought!) Anyway, I read her right, she at least returned the money. She gave some excuse or other, but I think really, she just got cold feet. Sounded like her family and friends protested. "You don't know a thing about this man! He might be a murderer, you can't go up there!" Something like that. I notice no one ever figures the guy has as much of a chance to be screwed over as the woman. At some point you have to do what you want, and go for it! But anyhow.

Some women are writing of how they like to go on picnics, and feel this qualifies them for my lifestyle. I see a lot of pictures of women in dresses with high heels, make-up, long painted nails, teased hair, false eyelashes, telling me about 'being natural', their love of the outdoors, and well, you get the picture, I guess. Most of my own relatives think my life is one long picnic, or extended camping trip, so what can I say. Sometimes I do feel like all these bags of letters are sifting through my fingers as just so much wasted ink.

One woman I was very interested in, who writes nice poetry for a living, was really upset when I wrote her that this other woman didn't show up and I'd like to keep writing. She went on and on about not settling for being number two, and to send all her pictures back and all this. I feel bad. I think this time though, I will find someone. I am in a better position than I was in the past--once this houseboat is done--so I (we) would have a place to stay and a way to get around. I hope I know enough about Alaska now to offer a more pleasant life then I had my first year up here! Anyhow, take care! **Sunshine, Miles**

Hi Miles!--We've written a couple of times now and I like your honesty and fresh outlook on life. I'm flying to England in a week and am on a flight after that which takes me to Alaska! I hope we can meet then. I hope to get my own plane soon with floats. I like your independence, and maybe, while you are out trapping, I could be doing my flying--maybe a local airline job. Like I said, I can cook about anything over an open fire, love the outdoors, and would like a place to settle and someone to settle with. See you soon, **Jan**

This is one of the women who spoke at first of a simple friend business thing. Let's get together, have fun, make no commitments. I'd be one of her stopping places in a longish list of places she frequents when she flies. *Her guy in Alaska.* That does not bother me. I could sleep with a friend. *Makes more sense than sleeping with a stranger.* Nothing wrong with 'practice.' Learning how to give and take, share, communicate. She's dreaming a little ahead of herself, it seems to me. She forgets I have no phone, no electric. How would she know of upcoming jobs and flights and changes in schedules? She can be off the grid for a week. I can see that working instead. Call it stress relief. *Glad to help.* ☺ :)

Dear Wild Miles—I know you said this was not a good time to come up, and someone else might be coming up, but maybe if I met you first, you might change your mind, so I'll be coming up in a week…

Dear Trapper—How are you My Trapper? Keeping warm? Yes you are right, I do need a vacation and the clock demands my time. This rat race gets to me. The boat trip you speak of sounds like just what I need. What should I bring you? I know it is hard for you to get certain things. I can take about two weeks off; maybe I'll see you soon then. Anyway, take care. **Love, Your Tigress**

Dear Miles—We've been talking by mail enough, I need you in my arms, I'll be coming up…

"Holy moldy." I'm at my BLM job, and the guys I work with are around.
"Did you say something, Miles? You got a pile of letters there. Maybe you need to spread some of these women around and let us have some. If it gets sore and needs to be rested up, just let me know!"
I laugh. Then we all laugh.
"Hey, most of these women, you wouldn't want to put it in! Yet some are pretty nice. I haven't really met any yet. Well, I met two. You know how it is with these women who have never been to Alaska. They might be good for about a weekend, but I'm not really looking for that. It's hard to sort it all out, but now I got a bunch that want to come up all at once. Oh well, never mind."
"Sounds like a serious problem, Miles! Ha, ha."
I reply, "Hey! Here's one from a religious nut! You ready to be saved?"
"Very funny, Miles!" My co-worker walks away.

"Son of a bitch!" There goes Don again at the top of his voice. *Here we go.* Nobody even looks up.

"God damn it, ran out of wire. Hell of a time to run out of wire! Trying to do a rush job here too!"

There's a pause while he tries to think of another solution, *as usual.*

All of us in the shop hold our breath, and yup, he is right on cue. "Welp! No help for it, can't get anything done till we go get wire, no use everyone just standing around, wouldn't look good, guess we may as well all go."

I glance at the clock, yes, usual time, an hour before lunch. We will be caught out at lunch and have to eat somewhere, *gosh that's terrible.* Five workers pile in the truck to go into town to spend three hours getting five feet of wire, with a boss who hates inefficiency. This is all right, even funny, but *how can people live like this? How awful.* (I laugh to myself). I'm glad enough it's only summer work, and I'm not very involved.

I learn more about wiring, running conduit, bending it. I learn about switches, ground wires. Then there is sheetrock work; how to cut it, get it to fit, then mudding. This is all good stuff to know, and I like working with my hands. When I get into it, I really don't want to take three hours out for lunch to go get wire with five other guys. I really want to get into my work. Sometimes though, there really isn't much to do as we wait for something to break or wait for a big forest fire.

I remember this from last year. "78, leave the line." The guy I work with on this job scribes the line. "78 and a half, take the line." The guy I work with scribes the line. Our accuracy is down to the width of a pencil line, and we take pride in our work. "A perfect fit!" We slap each other's hand.

"Lunchtime, guys, let's get out of here!" Don calls out the time.

I'm not satisfied with the work. "Don, I'm going to stay. There's a glitch in the wall here, so this sheet needs to be adjusted. I don't want to leave it. I'll be along later, maybe." I stay behind as the guys take off to the cafeteria. We all stay late on our projects at different times, so this is nothing new.

"All right! Who took the furniture from the rooms over the weekend?"

All the workers are assembled in a gathering, being addressed by one of the office honchos. This reminds me of 'assembly' in high school. Apparently, someone ran off with the furniture. *Imagine that! I'm not the least surprised.*

"We have to crack down on theft here. It will not be tolerated!"

We all bow our heads solemnly. I almost burst out laughing, but I know I'd be fired, so I play along. It's what this guy deserves. Yeah, well, I happen to know, along with three other guys here, which one ran off with the furniture and sold it. This guy in charge here, talking to us, stole the furniture. I know because we were ordered to load it into a truck, not knowing at the time what was going on.

My conscience has the same thoughts as I do. This isn't high school. I was mistaken. It's kindergarten! I manage to sigh loudly, enough to get a scowl, but not enough to be reprimanded. Spare us your bullshit, will you, and let's just all get on with our job. Say something? To who? Why? The crookedness starts at the top. I'm just a peon. I'm smart enough now to keep my damn mouth shut and keep my job. But live like this? Ha! I'd sooner go to hell to live. I'll be damn glad when I can live without having to work for someone else. I zone out of the lecture as my conscience rambles on in my head. The military was exactly like this, only then it was some multimillion-dollar satellite dish. That was amazingly hilarious, too, the same speech. Probably sold it to the Russians.

"Hey. Remember when Sam played musical chair with the leather jackets?" Ha, ha.

At least he was one of our peers, and we got a cut of the action.

The speech ends. The honcho scowls at me again. I smile and wink. He hates my guts. Good. I hate him and what he stands for, the stealing son of a bitch. Not for the theft totally, but all this bullshit speech involving others—a play-act, the whole bit. Nothing ruins morale more than this. This man cares nothing about our work, has no pride. I respect Sam a hell of a lot more. At least he admits what he is. *Which one will end up in jail first! This guy here will get promoted. Christ, he could be president of the United States if he's slick enough! Damn, I wish the revolution would come!* Damn, I wish the people would take their country back! Something in civilization gives me a bad attitude. It must be me. I only know that when I am in the wilderness, I have patience, do not get upset.

After lunch, Don walks by, stops briefly, stands like he's on the runners of his dog sled. He pauses long enough for me to get the mental image, says "under the stars," and walks away.

I smile to myself. No one would figure red neck swearing Don would have a romantic side. Or a moral side. He, too, wishes he could escape, and in this way, tells me what his escape is. I notice every day, without fail, he calls his wife at lunchtime. *He doesn't want the guys to overhear him.*

"You ok, Honey?" He always starts off that way. Hands are over the phone, looking to see if anyone is overhearing him. He always ends with "I love you."

I don't say anything. What's to say? I think that's what love is, married twenty years and still calling every day at lunch like that.

Don says, "You know Miles, if you cut your hair, you could be president!" He walks away again. I don't pay attention because, like last year, he says this every day. He has a thing about long hair hippies. It bugs the heck out of him that I have long hair. *The real problem is, he likes me a lot and cannot stand that he likes someone with long hair!*

Don is telling us we have to make up for lost time and get things done today. "Shit!" Don throws a hammer down.

I look at the clock. It seems a bit early. Hmmm.

Don mumbles, "We could use a staple gun here, make this go faster." 15 minutes later, Cursing at the top of his voice, "Shit!"

I look at the clock again. It's about time now. Another string of curses after a pause, as he tries to think of another solution, letting us know how upset he is that there is no solution other than going to lunch early.

"Out of God damn screws, can you believe it! Who ordered screws? God damn it!" Nobody says anything. "Well, we'll have to go pick up screws and a staple gun, I guess, no help for it, no use everyone standing around, God damn it, I hate to see wasted time, son of a bitch anyway!"

A truckload of happy puppies bounces off down the road, whistling at all the pretty women who turn and laugh. It's a hot day. We have our shirts off flexing our muscles and…

"I love you!" one guy hangs out the window to yell at a gorgeous redhead in a miniskirt, off on her lunch break from a nearby office building. He blows her a kiss as she turns. She giggles and walks into a telephone pole. She and all of us burst out laughing, and we all scream how gorgeous she is—and how we all want to marry her. *Isn't life grand? Isn't summer wonderful?* We all think we are God's gift to women. *As women are God's gift to us!*

The very next day, there is a forest fire taking off on a windy day. The crews are called in from the villages. I'm up until after midnight every day issuing linen, and up and at it at 8:00 am fixing doors, dealing with plugged toilets, and everything else that comes up when a hundred people are in a hurry and tired, and drop in. The whole crew is running ten to fifteen hour days for the next week with no bullshit going on. I like these times best. I just wish I was where the action is, dropping in on a fire from a plane or something. The smokejumpers come in for their linen, all tired and covered in soot. They tell me how it's going. They are a group unto themselves, and all know each other. They have to go to a special smoke jumping school and pass strict health and physical fitness tests. This isn't something I want to do badly enough to go through all the hoop-la.

There are more 'assemblies' about damage in the rooms, linen, and towels missing, light fixtures used as ashtrays, shaving cream words on the walls with rude diagrams of various people in charge. The people in charge do not understand why and are appalled. More rules to keep everyone in line. (She-it). It's my job to enforce the new rules in the barracks since I'm the barracks manager.

The suit and tie boss asks, "Miles! Why is this all happening?"

I look at what is going on and only sigh. One of the workers had just said this morning about the bosses, "Those assholes are lucky this is all that's going on. Wait until the lynch mobs form. What do the bosses think we are? Stupid?"

Why is it that so often, those high up have so little comprehension of what they have done? Why is the answer always "More rules! That'll teach em!"

I answer, "I have no idea what the problem is, sir." The big cheese doesn't quite believe me—maybe there's just the faintest hint of a smirk on my face. This is the asshole who stole the furniture. Had us load it onto his truck and then had the gall to give a speech about theft. Now he is too stupid to see the problem. If I knew who to go to, thought anyone cared, or would listen, I'd see this guy went to jail. Or no, not jail, but quietly given a different job, transferred. *Telling him the truth about upset workers would get me fired and accomplish nothing.*

Dearest Maggie—Work got hectic all of a sudden. None of the women who said they were coming has showed up (yet). Just as well I suppose. It's not exactly a good time as I'm working fifteen hour days. Lots of overtime though, but "no" in answer to your question. Keeping busy helps, and I am making the money to finish the boat and, hopefully, get supplies for winter so I can head out into the wilderness.

I find something curious. I notice how I change over time, between what I'm like in the wilderness, and what I'm like in civilization. I understand, in a way, what happens to primitive people when they meet civilization and get absorbed into it. It is like being sucked into the buzzing of a swarm of bees. It is easy to 'become' what is around you. I find myself getting angry, uptight, stressed, impatient. It's so easy to lose touch with nature and things that were once important. Well, they still remain important, but well, never mind. Only, I lose my sense of humor, sense of peace.

I've been looking over maps and think I will go downriver and up the Koyukuk. This would be hundreds of miles by the houseboat and would get me into some remote country. My friend Nora Underhill had a dream in which I meet a woman, as I get ready to leave. This woman is packed and ready to go on the boat with me. Perhaps it will be like this. Perhaps too, I am only looking for a simple answer to a complicated situation. You know, I still think about Nancy. Remember her?

I'll have put about $12,000 into the boat project, mostly within the past year, by the time I take possession. I'm not doing so badly, really, but I want to get going as soon as I can. I will be able to get work done on the boat and get it finished soon. (!)

I was dancing at the howling dog every weekend until the fire season got going. I sure like to dance! I've met a couple of gals there, and see women friends that I dance with, also the can-can cuties at Alaska land dance with me sometimes, (I told you about that already).

So are you able to keep up with the rent on this nice apartment now that 'what's his name' is gone? Are you going to move? I know you like the place a lot. You got a new roommate yet? (So you don't have to move). I hope your classes are going well. You should be pretty smart by now! Is school a good place to meet men? Or, are they too busy studying to be looking at the women? Is it like school was for us? I don't feel like I learned much that was relevant to my life when I was in school. Hmm. I understand how 'school' can have meaning, and what is learned there can be rewarding for the right kind of person. My father for example! He went a long way in school for sure--made a career out of going to school. I am uncertain it is meant for you though. I wonder if you do it 'because it is the thing to do.' I want you to look at your life and ask what it is you love to do most, and then find a way to do it. I want you to be happy. Anyway, gotta go, work to do! **Sunshine, Miles**

Will and I on a trip with the houseboat.

CHAPTER TEN

FALL, JOBS END, FINISH BOAT, LIFE ON A HOUSEBOAT

Dear Trapper—We have been writing each other a long time now, so I feel I know you. I don't think we would get along Miles. I thought you would be at peace because of your lifestyle! You are so clever with your words, but so often I see anger, problems and hurt. I think you get your own self in trouble! Should I feel sorry for you? All this interest in guns! I love the animals Miles, and do not like to see them hurt, and I love the outdoors, and I thought you did too!

I don't like macho men, always out to prove something, talking guns, putting other people down, testing themselves, others, nature all the time. What is wrong, Miles, with just living in peace!? Instead of looking at and judging other people, you should try looking into yourself for a change!

I met a medicine man who will show me a better way! He is kind and sweet to me and is full of peace. I am moving to Arizona to live in the desert with him, and we are leaving our worldly possessions behind. He wants to start a commune and has asked me to help him. We will help people find their totem animals, and get back to nature... etc. **No longer your tigress!**

This guy sounds like a nut, but I think I'm only jealous. Years later, there are a series of events concerning similar groups of people lead by gurus like this who commit mass suicide and other odd goings ons, and I wonder whatever happened to this woman and if they ever got a following. Or is she one of the ones who drank the poison cool-aid?

"Looks like you got another letter, Miles!" Steamer shakes his head in wonder as he continues, "You sure have a way with words and women. How do you do it? How many letters have you had now? Hundreds for sure!"

I sadly reply, "Yeah, well. This is another 'Dear John' one, and it seems I've disappointed hundreds of women. This one doesn't like guns and wants peace."

Steamers shocked reply, "Miles! You surprise me! You don't mention those things to women! Good grief! You tell 'em what they want to hear until they are yours. Women expect to be conned. It's what it's all about, Miles! Women don't want reality!"

My dumbfounded reply, "Then how come they say they do? I'm puzzled."

A chuckling Steamer, "You don't listen to a woman's words Miles, that's not how women work. You appeal to their emotions! You tell 'em you love 'em, and you dress nice, give 'em flowers, buy 'em things, be polite. Promise to protect 'em, bullshit 'em, say how you couldn't live without them and all that."

I don't believe him, saying, "Then, at what point do you introduce them to the real world?"

"You never do, Miles! That's the secret."

My shocked, dubious reply, "I just thought I could give women more credit than that, then to fall for that shit."

I am depressed, even though I knew for a long time, this 'waiting for the stars to line up' woman wouldn't be happy with me. Maybe I'm depressed because I should have got out of that wasted wordy relationship a long time ago instead of setting myself up for this. I shake my head to clear it. My conscience tries to console me. *Sometimes you have to just let the lemming go off the cliff.*

I'm ready to change the subject. "Well, let's get some work done on the boat. I got a lot of overtime on the summer work, and they let me off early, so now I can devote full time to the finishing of the boat."

"Ok, Miles, the twin twenty-five horse Chryslers came in, and I still need to put the riffle runners on them. You should see what they look like. I think the riffle runners will let it run shallow and not take away much power. We need a duel steering set up now, and I'll have to order that."

At least he is thinking about the boat now and on track, but I want to know what I should be doing, so I ask, "What do I do on the house part now? Is that clear lumber you ordered here?"

"Yes, that came in a week ago after I got your money in the mail for the engines and the next batch of wood."

I ask, "Will we use the two-foot centers? I know you said we needed different, closer spacing."

"Yeah, Miles, but it would mess up the paneling and other things inside. The clear lumber's extra strength will compensate."

I speak over the sound of hammering. "I still want to put the steering console up on the roof, even though you don't think it's a good idea, so best order the longer cables." I have to yell so he can hear me as I continue, "I just want to be up high so I can see the water ahead, and I don't want all the steering things in the cabin with me when I'm living in there. It will be crowded enough as it is, with only fourteen feet of length and seven-foot width to the house."

Steamer still does not agree and explains once again, "But Miles—as I said before, it will expose you to the weather, why not steer in out of the rain and wind! You got this nice house, and you will not be putting it to use. Up high like that, it will look like shit and make you top-heavy in the wind."

We go over some of the same ground on how to set this up. We go over design ideas, keeping in mind what I want to use the boat for, how I want to run it, and all the factors to take into account. As we work, we go over our idea.

"Miles, there's four inches of bilge space. Hold on, the phone is ringing."

There's a long pause as he leaves.

"Phone for you, Miles!"

I wipe the paint from my hands on an old shirt rag before I touch the phone. "Miles here, speak to me."

"Will here, Miles, you're boat done yet? I was thinking, I have time off work and could help you on the trip down as far as Fairbanks. I know Steamer promised a trailer trip to here because the water is so skinny from Delta, but it looks like that fell through, and you'll have to boat here. Maybe you could use a hand!"

I'm glad Will has got my interest in mind and am grateful he is such a friend. After a pause, I reply, "Sure, that'd be great. Should be ready in a few days. We plan to launch her in a couple of days, test the engines, make any adjustments on things, and then I'll be ready to go! I'll give a call to confirm a date!"

A final coat of paint goes on, but the color isn't what I expected it to look like. I wanted water blue and sandbar brown, ideally, so when the boat is stopped, I blend right in. Conscience, *A person never knows when they might need to blend in. Like about the time I shoot a duck dinner, and the game warden happens by.*

"What are you doing sleeping in the hull, Miles?"

"Oh, Hi John, I was just...um checking it out." He shakes his head at the lunatic he has on his hands. My conscience reminds me with good cheer since I'm depressed now, being thought of as a nut. *The bed and tables get put in today.!*

I holler out, "Two inches of foam goes in tomorrow, John!" As if he didn't know. I sleep in the boat again.

"I think it likes me." The wind blows, and all is peace in here. The new wood smells so wonderful. The two small windows put a lot of light in. It is easy to understand how men can name their boats. I will call this one 'Sable.' This is the Russian animal related to the 'marten,' the animal I trap, live by, and am named after. Our name is Martin, with an I, after the bird! Not the animal! We can pretend. The Sable is a faraway, exotic, and not quite a water animal (like my boat, which I shall live on ashore in winters), but is related to the water animals in the weasel family (the otter and mink). It is an unusual name for an unusual boat and unusual captain. 'Sable' is sort of a feminine name too, as boats are supposed to be, which reminds me of dreams and riches, (furs of course). Which reminds me of 'pirates,' sneaking around in shallow waters, looking for treasures, avoiding governments, sitting by open fires, and…I drift off to sleep.

I'm awake way before Steamer in the morning since I know what to do now and can do it on my own. I'm up at 4 a.m. installing the foam, putting touches on the paint job, putting steering cable brackets in. If I'm away from my boat even an hour these days, I miss it. I don't want anyone else near it and get jealous if anyone touches her. I didn't know I had these feelings in me.

In the River.

"So untie us Will, the engines are warmed up!"

The houseboat rocks gently in the water, happy to be here. As anxious as we are to get underway. We get a late start because Steamer and I had to make some adjustments on the steering, engine, and carbs. Will unties, tosses the rope on the front deck, jumps aboard, and gives another shove off the muddy bank with the boat pole. I let the boat drift out into the eddy, which swings the nose around downstream where I want it. Some people might have gunned the engines, powered into the turn. With a big houseboat, I know already by instinct that everything needs to go slow and easy, let the river do your work, think ahead. I put the engines in gear when the nose is downriver, and the boat slowly goes forward until we are under our own power. The landing and bridge disappear. There is no one to see us off but a grumpy Steamer.

Will doesn't say much, but I know him, and see his eyes taking everything in, and know he's pretty excited too. The current is about five miles an hour. Water depth is about two to three feet in the braided main channel. Up ahead, the river splits into so many fingers it looks like a hand, a mile across. The water is shallow enough to have trees stuck in its main channel. This is not a good way to learn the boat. Few people run this stretch, not even experienced boaters. We don't belong here in a houseboat, but I'm stuck with this situation Steamer put me into.

GOING WILD

Conscience, So much for his promise to haul me to Fairbanks when the boat is done, to launch it from there—

Will interrupts my private thoughts. "This will be easy Miles, relax. This is a shallow draft boat!"

But I'm not experienced, and I'm really in over my head here, so I'm nervous. "Which channel has the water Will, can you find the water?"

He goes upfront and uses a pole in the water as I slow down, but the current sucks us along. It is difficult to go slower than the current when going downstream, even in reverse. The transom has a lot of water resistance from behind, and steering is lost going this slow.

"The deepest we got is six inches, Miles!" We hold our breath as the boat goes into six inches. The engine protests as the props suck silt into the riffle runners, grind sticks, but keeps going.

I have the engines in neutral now, with the riffles just bouncing off the bottom. At the currents five miles an hour, we thread the needle.

Will hollers, "Hard right!"

With a pole, I shove us out, and we miss the arms of an upturned tree root that beckons to us like a ghost. "ffffffffff," the sound of the silt on the hull in the quiet.

"A creek up ahead, Will, good place to spend the night, getting dark." We are in deeper water now, engines running, and I 'eeeeease' us up the creek, just far enough to get the boat out of the main current.

A nervous conscience, I don't want any trees coming downriver to slam into the boat in the night. This creek is calm and safe looking.

A fire is started in the woodstove.

"Will, you want to get some firewood and cut it up from the sandbar while I get some chow ready? Unless you want to cook!"

"Naw, I'll get wood." Will is only a silhouette now, against a setting sun, as he gathers wood. The sucking sound of his boots in the river silt fades in the distance, and I'm left with an utter silence I have missed since I was last in the wilderness.

The houseboat is toasty warm as Will and I gaze out the window into the cold, windy dark. The kerosene lantern gives a nice orange glow to the boat.

"I saw a mink slide under the boat Miles when I went to get a basin of water."

I only yawn in response. My adrenaline has run out, leaving me drained, like coming off a drug. Basically, the house part is a seven by sixteen foot box set on a twenty-four-foot flat bottom boat hull. There is a back door leading to the five feet of open space for storage in the back. There can be room for the steam engine, but also room for barrels of gas and things not wanted indoors. There is another door out front leading to a small three-foot bow deck that comes to a blunt point. There are only three windows, two-foot big on the sides.

"I'm going to bed, Will. You can have the bunk. I'm sleeping on the roof."

I like to be out in the elements. The stars are overhead, and we are out on the river somewhere, on a creek with no name, and only a few hours out of Delta. I'm amazed once again, how quickly civilization turns into wilderness. People in town lose perspective of this and only see the bright lights man makes, not grasping that 99% of the earth hasn't got man's lights. I had been out on the sailboat with my father on his trip bringing it from England to the U.S. I had been amazed how much of the earth is covered with water. Hearing a statistic isn't the same as sailing thirty days and never seeing land. On this thought, I drift off to peaceful dreamland.

In the morning, I see the water has dropped overnight. The river's water is dependent on a lot of factors, like local rain, sun on distant glaciers, and how much snow we had over the past winter. It is normal for the water level to change by as much as a foot overnight in the bigger rivers, and for reasons not predictable to the novice. I had forgotten this when I parked in the shallow creek here for the night. Now the creek has only two inches of water, and the houseboat is stuck fast in the mud!

"What are we going to do, Miles?"

Another wilderness problem to solve. Just part of life out here. I pause to think. I have an idea. "Let's see if we can get some slippery green willows under it."

We end up having to use the handyman jack. The back of the house is lifted so the poles can go under. Standing knee-deep in the mud, shoving with all our might, we are able to get the houseboat into the water.

"Just one day, and already deep into an adventure Will!"

He laughs. "Didn't you tell me that an adventure is usually a mistake? Guess you are right!"

I laughingly admit, "Yeah, people who know what they are doing don't have adventures. So we are a couple of bozo's, right?" We both laugh. We have to wash off in the cold river, and it is nice to have the warm fire going in the boat's woodstove.

"So Miles, how far did you say it is to Fairbanks?" "I'm not sure, Will, but around 200 twisty miles. I don't know how long it will take. I don't want to be in too much of a hurry. I did that with the last boat and almost sank it, so I want to take my time, especially since this water is so shallow and braided." My conscience, *The boat itself is drawing only three inches of water, but I need six to run with the props, but even so, that's not bad. It was just as Steamer had said it would be.*

"Will, guess I'll stop in Fairbanks a few days. I need a few more supplies I want to transfer directly to the boat, like a lot of gas. I want to go up the Koyukuk River, I think. That's off the Yukon and maybe 1,000 miles from here. I hope to be there by winter."

Will asks, "Did you make enough money this summer to do all this?"

"It will be tight, but think I can get by. I got a lot of overtime in with the fires going on this dry summer."

Will's sunning himself on the roof, black powder rifle across his bare belly, snoring. The woodstove smoke sends Indian signals in puffs that lazily drift across the river. The smell of birch wood from this smoke wafts my way. I take a deep breath and smile. Mount McKinley stands out like a vanilla ice-cream cone in the heatwave distance. Hours of listening to the purring twin engines lull me into boredom. Not quite, though, because there are always decisions to make about water depth. A sweeper under water scrapes the hull and rocks the boat, causing me to hold my breath. The underwater spruce tree pops to the surface after being disturbed by the boat. I'm glad the props miss it. Will must feel the boat rock as his snoring does a few more 'inward air' before 'outward air' sounds.

The sweepers on the bank have to be avoided. These spruce trees hang out forty feet parallel to the river and form an impenetrable rampart of spears. I try to steer just off the tips because the deep water is actually under them, but there is no room to fit.

I misjudge a corner. The river current changes direction and takes control of the bow before I can compensate with the steering. The houseboat gets crossways between two sweepers. The trees hold the boat and stop it. The current pushes on the hull. The boat leans. The heavy top wants to roll us over. Will wakes up record-fast, and almost drops the rifle in the river, then almost gets swept off as the boat leans. I'm thinking, *Here we go!* The gunwale comes even with the water, and I have three-foot-high sides. The whole river wants to rush in on top of us. The boat slowly pivots on the downstream sweeper, out into the stronger current and a more dangerous place.

"Will, see if you can reach that sweeper with the handsaw from the bow!" I yell. "I'll use the engines in reverse!" Will is able to reach the sweeper, but there is so much pressure on it that the saw blade binds. I give full throttle in reverse, but this sucks the stern toward the cut bank, and it could mean ruining the engines if I pick up a log or the bank in the props. The riffle runners do not allow much power for reverse since they are made to suck the water from one direction only in a funnel shape. The backwash of the reversed engines causes a large wave behind us. This wave wants to come over the stern, so I have to back off the throttle. I cannot hear Will over the scream of the engines, and I can't see him through the house. I hope I caused enough slack, and for a long enough time for him to get the saw free cut the tree.

I feel the boat shudder, then a loud "snap!" The stern swings out into the main river, and we spin end for end until I gain control with the engines.

"That was close, Miles! What happened!?"

"I need to keep more power on Will. Seems like if I go too slow, the current takes over when we hit the change in current in a turn. I'll just have to get used to it. I don't like to run under too much power going downstream. It seems like we are going fast enough already and want to save on fuel!"

"Miles, the sweeper got your fishing pole and chair."

"Shit. Oh well, at least it didn't get us, huh!" Things settle down again, but I am aware how fast things can go from 'honky dory' to 'hunk in the drink' while the 'D' words turn to 'Dork.' Trying to save a dollar on fuel, and as a result, lose equipment worth ten times as much is not good thinking.

"Have I got water still coming out the weep holes?" Will goes back to the engines and checks to see they are spraying water, which tells me the engine water pumps are working. "Steering from the roof is working out good, Will. I can look around good, and up here, I can read the water better. I'm glad I decided to set it up this way."

"Boaters ahead Miles!"

I'm wondering what other boaters would be doing in this shallow area until I see it is two canoes headed downstream. When we catch up to them, I see they are walking their canoes with a rope over the shoulder. Under power, I bring the boat right up alongside them, wave hello, and pass them. Everyone's mouth just hangs open at the sight of this twenty-four-foot houseboat passing them in water only ankle deep, where they cannot even paddle the canoes. I just smile calmly, as if I do it every day, ask them if they need any help.

With mouths still open, they can only shake their heads "No."

We disappear around a bend, still under power. I wish I could have yelled back, "It gets shallower up ahead here, hope you don't get stuck! You sure you don't want a lift?" They are too far away now, and the engines are too loud.

"That was something Miles! This is one hell of a boat; to pass through water a canoe can't go in!"

"So Will, you still think fifteen grand is too much to pay?"

Will compliments the boat and explains, "This is a heck of a boat all right. I'm just telling you what other people in Delta were saying, that Steamer stiffed you."

"Maybe Will, but then most of those people don't know the facts about the marine plywood at $300 a sheet, and the bronze screws, clear lumber, and that kind of quality materials that make this a better boat than it first appears."

I spot a landmark and tell Will, "Looks like the Salcha River ahead, and this should be about halfway. I see a road that we come close to. I remember this spot when we drive to Delta."

Will focuses up ahead and says, "Yeah, I recognize it too. The water should get deeper with the Salcha water being added to the Tanana." The current looks swifter, though, judging by the waves. The color of the water changes from the color of a cardboard box to the color of the duct tape wrapping the box. This is the first time I have passed a river coming in and seeing how that main river is affected by it.

Night finds us on the river in flatland again. I choose an eddy to park in.

"This looks protected, Will. You see how all the drift avoids the eddy here? There's kind of a whirlpool with slow water."

I have to jump down off the roof to grab the rope to tie us up. The boat settles in its night spot without tugging on the reins. The sound of the engines remains in my head as I run my fingers through my hair, shift the ever-present blade of grass in my mouth to the other side.

"There's a duck trying to blend in against the cut bank Miles, see, over there? Looks like a male mallard."

"Dinner Will, fetch me the smoke pole!"

"Have to take his head off. A body shot would make a pile of feathers from here to Fairbanks."

"Uh-huh," I mumble through my grass blade as I try to line up on the 'sitting duck.'

"Whump!" The sound of dynamite going off. The six-foot of flame is now familiar. The practice has paid off. After we stop gagging on the smoke, and it clears away, the duck is floating in the river eddy, and there is a hole behind him in the bank I could bury one of my engines in, left by the lead ball. Mud is still falling from the sky as we speak.

"Damn," we both say at once, as usual. I sigh as I pick the duck up.

With a straight face, I say, "Damn, missed." Will looks at me in puzzlement. I explain, "I wanted to take the neck. I got the head. I'll have to practice more. Must have missed by a good quarter of an inch!"

We both laugh. This is less than the diameter of the bullet, and it was a good shot.

The duck is cleaned in the river as the fire in the boat is stoked up. We stuff the duck with rice, add some spices, and put it in the stove to cook.

I show Will how I figured out how to use the stove itself for an oven. "Get a bed of coals, put green logs on, and set the roast pan on the leveled logs in the stove. Be sure to shut the stove down, so it will not flame up. It's about 400 degrees." The duck has a strong smoked flavor, which we like. The rice has kept the bird moist.

We sit on the front deck with our feet in the water as we eat our wild duck.

"You look like Tom Sawyer Will!"

"Yeah? Well, you don't look like Jim, his black sidekick! Ha!"

"Well, almost! We are very dirty, Will. Hey, don't wiggle your toes like that; a pike might think they are worms."

"Do you think there are fish in here?"

"We could find out if we still had the pole. Guess there would be. Why not?"

"Did you see the Grizzly tracks on the sandbar, Miles?" "She-it Will they weren't Grizz. That was only a small black bear!"

"Yea, right! Did you see the size of 'em?"

I laugh. "Wait till you see real Griz tracks, Will."

I see Will look around in the darkness and see he's nervous. "Well, nothing should come around while we are in the boat, huh? It's pretty stout, and a bear would be nervous about this boat, wouldn't figure out how to get in." Will wants to sleep by the rifle, though.

I sleep on the roof without any gun, but I know it would be hard for a bear to get to me here. "I'll just wake you up Will, you can shoot it, ok?"

He doesn't answer but checks the cap on the rifle. We both sleep soundly, though.

Pancakes are our breakfast, cooked on the morning fire in the stove. I have a Coleman camp gas stove, but we don't use it. There is a fog on the water until the sun comes up.

"We should get into Fairbanks today Will. I look forward to that. Maybe I'll run this houseboat on up to the barracks where I stayed all summer. Like a knight in armor, rescue one of those damsels in distress in the front office."

"Yea, that'd be nice, all right, take one of them out for a picnic on the river. Be a nice way to make some points. Maybe love at first sight, Miles?"

"Hey, you never can tell! I have been talking about this boat since I showed up there, and a lot of people don't believe I got it done. Be nice to just pop in and show it off, huh?"

We talk about all the cool things that might happen, and what the boat can be used for, and how envious everyone will be.

The morning fog lifts. "Let's get a move on, Will. Places to go, things to do. I'm not really sure how long I want to stay in Town. I've had my fill. I just want to get going on down the river with my winter supplies. This fog reminds me, cold weather can come any time now, and the water will start dropping."

Will reflects on this and adds, "Well, at least you won't have to build a cabin for winter anymore, huh! You should be able to get a moose with this boat too, just sit somewhere on the water and look out the window every now and then as you read your book, nice and warm!"

This is a positive thought to start the day off.

The engines warm up nicely, and we are on our way. There are no problems. I only want to be sure I'll recognize the Chena river when we get to it. We see airplanes coming into the airport, flaps down, ready to touch the runway, and we know that the airport is by the Chena River, so we can't be too far.

"That's it, Miles, over to the right."

We are surprised we have seen no other boats out, except the canoe. We have to go up the Chena to get to Fairbanks. The boat handles differently going upstream. I have to give more throttle and read the channel differently. When I come downstream into a turn, I allow for current drift, so I hug the inside turn, knowing the current will drift me out. Now, I still hug the inside turn but am slower and can back off the throttle and drift back to get another angle if I want. The Chena has little current, but I do have manmade walls and docks to deal with that stick out from the bank. I figure it out well enough and have only two to three miles to go to get into downtown, where I hope to park at the Alaska land dock where I have parked before.

My conscience has women on his mind reminding us. *Maybe take a spin up to the barracks tomorrow.*

"There's rocks on the bottom here, Miles, not just silt. Better stay off the bottom!"

There are wrecked cars and other junk in the river too. I go slowly to avoid these things. There are a few people on the riverbank that wave at my strange boat. I've never seen a houseboat around here before, nor have they. My 'dreamboat' does not look like what other people would call the answer to their dream. This does not look like a luxury yacht. This boat does not have nice lines but is more like a pig in the water. Women will not scream and swoon or beg for a ride in it, as I once fantasized. I feel more like the knight in dull armor who falls off his horse when he goes to lift his visor to view the damsel in distress. The women wave all right, but swoon? It is more like 'titter' behind the hands.

I ask Will, as I put my cupped hand to my ear, "Hark! Do I hear a damsel screaming— Take us! —on yonder shore, asking for a ride in this sexy houseboat?"

"No, Miles, I think she's yelling at us all right, but it's, 'You ass!' not 'take us.'"

Will and I both laugh, but it bothers me very much that once again, there is no one who understands the dream and sees what I do in this boat, except maybe Will.

The town power plant is on our right, and I hug this side in the turn coming up. As I get into the turn, there is a submerged car I do not see. Some of these things were put in the water as erosion control, but some parts are out into the current where I need the deep water. "Clunk" I feel the prop hit something, but we have hit the branches before, so I am not so concerned. The engines start to run rough. I ease over to the bank so we can stop and check it out. Before we get there, one engine locks up.

"Miles looks like the prop is dinged up and will not turn by hand." Will is the mechanic, so I leave it up to him. He tilts the outboard up, locks it, and plays with the shifter while trying to turn the prop. I watch what he does and learn. The prop comes off, the prop nut put back on, another turn tried, another frown. "Something inside Miles, not good. I hoped it might be a bent shifter rod. It's in your lower unit because the engine turns over. Your gears are jammed up."

I comment, "A delay of a few days. I suspect the warranty covers it. The engine is only a few days old. We didn't hit anything hard enough, did we? I'm not sure when it went tits up, but maybe the gears locked up due to mechanical failure. Nothing was going on when we heard the grinding sounds."

"Hard to say, Miles, but you better get it back to Steamer."

There is little I can do with one engine, though I could drift downstream with it if I had to, but it wouldn't be safe, not being able to move back upstream. "Will, I have to hang around a few days anyway, to load up winter supplies, and get a few more things done. Probably by the time the engine gets fixed, it will be time to leave." I'm only a little upset by the delay.

Not much I can do but park here. I'm not sure what the 'law' is on parking 'wherever,' but am told that the rivers come under the marine laws (any navigable waterway). There is a fifty-foot easement on all shores that belong to the public to allow pulling over, even camping. This is similar to the emergency lane along a road and easements along roads to allow plows to pile snow and allow for road expansion. Most people respect private property down to the water, and it's simply 'not polite' to camp in front of someone's house. (And who would want to, if there is a better place to camp!) This is a business district of town, and the bank is steep, so I'm a little out of the way, though people can look down and see me from the road. I think and hope I'm not going to be in the way here. Will is consulted, and he agrees with my thinking. I can't make it to Alaska land.

Will calls his brother to come pick him up while I stay with the boat. Will takes the engine. The lighter weight of running two engines at least allows an engine to be removed by hand.

"I'll get it to Steamer."

"Will, you need gas money or anything? I feel bad, you having to make that long trip over this."

"No problem, Miles, you paid for the gas on the boat trip and all its costs. I had a nice trip with you that would have cost me a bundle if it wasn't with you, so I'll help you out."

I just don't want Will to be doing too much for me and thinking he's being used. As he leaves, I tell him, "I'll just stay here then. Looks like I have a lot of driftwood for the stove, and this is as good a spot as any to sit tight."

I have time to contemplate the future. I'm sure I will have lots of adventures! I don't have to go to work for another eight months. I'll have a place to live rent-free-with enough food to last a year. I'm sure I'll get a moose for winter meat—1,000 pounds. How could I not with this houseboat to hunt from? There will be villages to see, wild, untamed, unmapped country to travel and trap in. Does life get any better than this? I must be in heaven.

THE END OF BOOK 1

A personal note—

Reviews help! If you enjoyed this book, please leave a review where you purchased it—it would be greatly appreciated!

Sign up for my newsletter, "Keeping Up With Miles," @ www.milesofalaska.com Deals, new books, comments, links to YouTube. Stay updated!

The Alaska Off Grid Survival Series Summary

Book 1 - Going Wild (This Book)

In 1973, I am 22 years old, and a city kid. I enlisted in the Navy and got out after the Vietnam War.

I travel to interior Alaska, a 'Cheechako' (Greenhorn) by Alaskan standards. But I have been raised on Walt Disney and feel qualified to be a mountain man!

I arranged with a pilot to drop me off in the wilds of Alaska. I do not have everything I need and have things I do not need. I learn about guns, trapping, and the loneliness of living in the vast wilderness with no other humans around.

I do not see anyone for many months, then walk out of the wilds to civilization in the spring. After working odd jobs to make supply money, I return to the wilds in the fall and have a hard time my second winter. I almost die, and need to be rescued.

I decide to build a houseboat so I can travel around without having to build another cabin. I have to accept summer work in Fairbanks to pay for the boat materials and work under a builder. The boat takes much longer to build than expected.

I live as a street person much of the time to keep expenses down.

Book 2 - Gone Wild

I have many adventures on the houseboat and acquire a dog team. There are issues with the police, a bear on my boat, and a trip to see my family who live a civilized life.

My houseboat sinks. I get lost and learn other hard lessons. I start doing artwork and end up on TV. I win a land lottery and start my first homestead.

There are mail order women, and I live with a woman and her kids. Ten people are murdered in a village we visit, and myself and the family are almost among them. Family life is more difficult than I imagined.

Fish and Game becomes a concern.

I head back into the wilderness, which leads into book 3.

Book 3 - Still Wild

I acquire a couple more homesteads and cut more trapline.

I give up sled dogs and enter the world of snow machine adventures.

I winter in Galena and visit many native villages. There are bear encounters, and many survival situations to learn about.

I become a serious mammoth hunter and find fossils as part of my living. I work with a land surveyor specializing in homesteads and wilderness surveys, getting paid to use my boat.

My art sells well, so I do some big shows. I become more social and understand

ABOUT THE ALASKA OFF GRID SURVIVAL SERIES

civilization better. I see the wisdom of being accepted by others. I learn. I grow. I try to change, as the world does.

The economy changes. It is less acceptable to be a trapper. I never become totally civilized as a city person defines it, but maybe I do, relative to the life I had in book one.

Book 4 - Beyond Wild

I am getting past just survival and doing well, even prospering. I own more than the houseboat can easily haul. Gas gets expensive. I need a new houseboat engine.

There is a homestead and trapline that keeps me in one place now. There are more bear stories and adventures into the wilds, including a 300-mile boat trip looking for mammoth tusks, which has disastrous consequences.

I find where I want to live on the Kantishna River. A river 300 miles long with about five people on it. I hang out in the native village of Nenana, spending a lot of time here.

I get my first computer and learn to build a website. People are looking at the pictures and buying my raw materials and art. This is a chance to make a difference.

Life is beautiful. Life is precious. I Dare to live it.

Book 5 - Back To Wild

I acquire a home in Nenana and start a web store. I am forced out of my subsistence lifestyle, partly because of changes in the laws. I do some serious mammoth hunting.

Unstable power causes a lot of computer data loss. I learn by punching keys to see what happens. It takes a long time to get good enough to create a book.

I continue the Mammoth hunts. The Tucson fossil gem show and State fair do well for me.

This period of 'being civilized' that I am trying out, has advantages, but also a price to pay—a big change from the wilderness life and being alone!

I am a suspect in a murder investigation. Another trapper tries to move in on my territory. There are neighbors and infringements on my property.

I fear I cannot change who I am. There is difficulty blending the two lives and ways of thinking. There are mail-order women coming and going, as well as the usual adventures and situations I manage to get myself into.

Book 6 - Surviving Wild

Iris is my partner. Business grows, with money coming in, but causes 'complications.' I understand why I left for the wilds in the first place.

I get better at fossil hunting and have some exciting trips getting mammoth tusks and other ancient treasures. I am viewed as an expert on a few subjects and Discovery TV and reality shows contact me several times.

The new life in town causes legal issues that have been nipping at my heels off and on throughout my time in Alaska. Fish and Wildlife ask, "Why are you alone out here where we cannot keep an eye on you? We know you are up to something. What is it you have to hide? We will find out!" This mentality is that different is bad and of concern. I end up being investigated. A SWAT team shows up at my property with a dozen cars and 20 cops.

My arrest makes headlines. I'm sentenced to Federal Prison for six months as a felon. This is a stark contrast to 'Book 1-Going Wild,' where I have as much freedom as it is possible to have.

How did I get from there to here?

Book 7 - Secretly Wild

I am a convicted felon, describing life in prison from the viewpoint of someone used to freedom and the wilderness life. The same feather in the hat I wore on the cover of Ruralite magazine in 1979, is now worth five years in prison.

What do I need to do to survive here? There are classes to take, books to read, farm work to do, and people to help. There are interesting felon stories.

I observe more crime within the prison system by the system than I am accused of committing. "The prison could not survive if we operated legally," I am told by officials. I do my time. Now what? Am I a better person? I see the error of my ways. I am saved. Society is safer now.

Book 8 - Retiring Wild

I talk about news relevant to living off the grid as an individual in the wilderness that few citizens are aware of. I adapt my business, and still have adventures, depending as much as I can on the subsistence life I love and understand that is now becoming illegal as a white man.

I ponder whether the end of my life is in agreement with the views I held dear from the beginning. I have hope that even in times of control and suppression, I can still focus on the plus side, and continue to find ways to enjoy personal freedoms and individuality.

I continue to explore choices, how to have better control of my destiny, happiness, and success. I refer to this as 'Survival.' I have few regrets, and hope my life's path as written can provide entertainment and insight.

As someone who is interested in being different, not one of the sheep, I look realistically at the rewards that choice offers, but also the price that has to be paid.

Please visit www.alaskadp.com for links to the books.

Visit www.milesofalaska.com to find a bio of Miles, additional photos, stories, how-to videos, handmade artwork, and raw materials for sale.

AFTERWORD

THOUGHTS ADDED IN 2021

My early books were written when I was very young. I'm socially naïve, not very street-wise, or bush-wise. I know more about dreams and heroes than reality. I'm not someone whose shoes you'd want to walk in. In 2021, I realize these early works is 'me,' with no writing training. The value is in rawness, as a diary. With over thirty years more writing experience and eight books completed, I see major edit issues and express my past experiences using a better-developed style.

Only one person in a thousand who dreams of going off the grid into a wilderness life even tries it. Of those who try, one in a hundred lasts more than a year. That's just simple homesteading. There are less than twenty-five people in the USA per decade successfully living as I do. Of those, who is capable of writing about it? I learn that 'special' does not mean 'better.' Many of my heroes are tweaked. Few talk about that.

While many people read, talk, and dream, it might be useful to see some reality. Civilization creates roles to strive for, with heroes to emulate! Bill Cosby comes to mind, the image of the perfect family man for decades. Who was he, really?[1] The football hero is someone we envy yet know only when he runs the touchdown. What is the truth of his life? Important if you wish to walk his walk. It is easy to comment from the peanut gallery but very different in the ring with the bull.

I believed Walt Disney was the only view of the wild offered to a civilized young lad. The truth of Mr. Disney is not much like the movies. My heroes happened to be mountain men, as I understood them from TV series like Daniel Boone, Davy Crocket and movies like Jeremiah Johnson. I live as close to this lifestyle as possible.

AFTERWORD

I'm later described as, "Among the best there is at what he does." There can be no higher compliment.

The highest level of excitement and adventure as is possible, and still be alive. This can be following my dream or an addiction. A good thing to learn from or something to avoid. It's my story as it unfolds, to be entertained by, but also to learn from.

"What is it that you believe in, and what are you doing about it?"

The series began as a single book about wilderness survival. At eighteen, survival was defined as the ability to build a fire and kill bears. Through the series, survival changes! To survive, we must get ahead, be happy, be adaptable. Survival in the wilds requires many of the same skills necessary to live at the cutting edge of civilization!

Understand your surroundings, figure out what controls your life, and have an influence on these controls. Balance reality with the thrill of a dream and passion. A Zen outlook works better than a Clint Eastwood view of the world. Think and ponder before saying, "Make my day!" All the biggest, meanest, baddest creatures of the wild are endangered. There is a reason for that I had to learn.

My writing began as my mountain man story. It evolves and ends up, a lifetime later, cutting edge future science fiction.

I do not know what it is called; I just live it. I call it my biography. It is not outside the box because I do not recognize there is a box to stay within. I live and do the impossible. Do I do it well? Am I an idiot, seeking attention by exaggerating, telling fish stories, even lying? This may not matter. Let it be the story of such a person.

If asked, I say, "Extremely gifted!" But least I am bragging and stuck up, I add, "But tweaked!" Said with a proud smile. I wish to inspire others to not be ashamed of who you are, to go for your dream, whatever that is. Turn a weakness into a strength. For me, it was to be a mountain man, but it could have been wishing to be a football star, a fireman, or a garbage man.

Do it well, be proud and happy. It's you. If I can do it, so can you. I make an amazing number of mistakes and am not ashamed to speak of that. I think of Edison. 9,999 failed lightbulbs, what an idiot. One lights up, and this is all we get told about. Where would we be if he gave up after 9,998 failures? No, not all of us are Edison! Let this be a story of not giving up. Along the way, I teach many bears how to lay down, rollover, and play dead. Does it take more courage to drink from the same pond, take turns, leave the bears alone, greet each other in passing? I did kick that one bear. Wow, what a lesson.

Visit my website at www.milesofalaska.com to link to the rest of the books in the series, my art, custom knives, pictures, videos, and more info. A life as self-sufficient as it can get. I cut the wood, build my own dog sled, build my own team from puppies.

No ID, bank account, rent, utility bills of any kind. No missing or needing credit. No electricity, timepiece, or alarm clock. I eat when I am hungry, sleep when I am tired. No boss, taxes, address, insurance, permits, being counted in a census, or jury duty. Feeling rich, lucky, and blessed.

Of course, it all has a price! Da! Part of the adventure!

"If it was easy, everyone would be doing it!"

Yes, this becomes illegal, but not until books five and six, past midlife. Another set of adventures.

With my favorite lead sled dog Kenai.

Magazine and News Stories

Alaska Magazine

Alaska Magazine July 77—Survive by Miles Martin two pages, Photos. By Miles about my rescue, walk out on the Yukon River, five days at 50 below zero.

Nomadic House Boater Have Cabin Will Travel January 81—by Miles. Three pages, four color photos, a map. About life living on a houseboat, trapping and selling art (photo of my art), and all the adventures I have had on the river.

Would You Make A Good Bush Homesteader? June 86—by Miles four pages, six color pictures (One shows my custom knives.) A story I wrote about what it takes to be a homesteader.

Surviving The Big Lonesome— March 98—by Jim Rearden five pages, two color photos, one double page photo of Miles. Photos by world-famous photographer Jean Erick Pasquier. Describes life in the wilderness.

GEO Magazine

GEO in Germany is like "National Geographic" in the US.

Life in The Wilderness Alaska Special—87 by Miles Martin ten pages, sixteen color photos, a map

Photos by Jean Erick, one of the best photographers in the world, I Wrote it myself, winter life in the wilderness.

Alaska Special - 95 Einer gegen den Rest der Welt

Eight pages, seven color photos, three are double page. A follow up story to the first, written by New York Times reporter Ted Morgan, with Brigitte Helbing, photos by New York Times photographer Rex Rystedt. My fight for a lifestyle.

The New York Times

New York Times Magazine an insert to the paper, April 17, 1994, section six, The Vexing Adventures of the Last Alaskan Bushrat.

Six pages, four color photos, one is a double page Written by New York Times writer and bestselling author Ted Morgan. Photos by Rex Rystedt (World-renowned photographer). Facing twenty years in jail and a $10,000 fine for putting artwork on a bear claw and selling it.

Book-- A Shovel Full of Stars 95—Published by Simon and Schuster — New York

MAGAZINE AND NEWS STORIES

By Ted Morgan about ten pages with Miles. About one of the last homesteaders, and the lifestyle I live, of a Subsistence person.

Ruralite Magazine

Put out by Golden Valley 180,000 circulation
Wild Miles August 79, two pages, four black and white photos, Full cover page photo of Miles doing artwork. Story and photos by Margaret Van Cleve — Mostly about my artwork, some about my lifestyle on a houseboat

Newspaper, Daily Newsminer, Fairbanks Alaska

Associated Press, date unreadable, think a Thursday, and think spring of circa 74 **'Trapper rescued by Chopper**; Vows to Return to the Bush' headline, one column, National news, about my rescue after five days walking at 50 below.

Alaska Trapper Magazine

Put out by Alaska Trappers Association, a cover photo of me with Wolf. Five-page story by Miles comparing snowmachine and snowshoe trapping Nov. 99—four pages. Over the years, another six-seven articles on various trapping and related issues. Contact organization for exact issues.

Me in 1975.

OTHER TITLES AVAILABLE FROM ALASKA DREAMS PUBLISHING

Visit www.alaskadp.com to see these titles.

Books by Miles Martin:

- Going Wild
- Gone Wild
- Still Wild
- Beyond Wild
- Back To Wild
- Surviving Wild
- Secretly Wild
- Retiring Wild

Titles by other ADP authors:

- Rookie
- Alaska Freedom Brigade
- Apache Snow
- In Search of Honor
- A Coming Storm
- Arizona Rangers Series – Blake's War
- Legend of Silene
- Inspiring Special Needs Stories
- My Life In The Wilderness
- All Over The Road
- Ghost Cave Mountain
- Inside the Circle
- The Silver Horn of Robin Hood
- Alaskan Troll Eggs
- Through My Eyes
- The Professional Ghost Investigator
- The Adventures of Jason and Bo
- Seeds Of The Pirate Rebels

FOOT NOTES

CHAPTER 1

1. 'Flash past' taken from the music industry "Knock out nifties of the past, golden oldies" Spinning us back in time to when we first heard that song 'so very long ago' spinning me back in time. A word I make up, so you understand I am not speaking about 'present time'
2. I arrive with city values. Here, someone as stupid as me doesn't deserve help. In fact the policy is to let stupid people cull themselves from the gene pool. This is the world of 'survival of the fittest.' Wilderness people are kind and helpful to each other. For now I am still 'one of them.' Not 'us'.
3. Very little I purchase on the advice of others proves useful. Though I do not know much, I seem to know more than the people I'm talking to! There was a movement in the early 70's in Alaska, of hippies showing up to tune in drop out, and form communes in the wilderness. Starry eyed free love flower children without a clue what reality is. Some 'made it' most did not. Knowing what the correct supplies to get are, is one of the tests. The true trappers, mountain men, skilled people, capable of helping me with a list were 'out there,' not hanging around the Salvation Army, bar, or on the street.

CHAPTER 2

1. If you make it to book 7 decades from now, I become a felon and do prison time over these very issues.
2. The 44 magnum hasn't come out yet, nor the series of even bigger magnums. The 357 is the next step above the 38 special, and compared to it, this is a cannon, and is the rave of the gun world. Clint Eastwood as 'Dirty Harry' carried one. Once the 44 came out, the 357 got talked down a lot. But oh! you should have heard the first words about a 357! It was the cat's meow. Over the years I stuck with 357, as a caliber I understand. It leaves a hole in flesh you could drop a bowling ball in. That's good enough for me. Many experts say "It is best to use what you understand and know." Accuracy is more important than power.
3. In 2014 a customer sends me a book 'Descent Into Madness.' The diary of a killer by Vernon Frolick. I recognize the picture as 'one of us'. He never gives us his real name. This 'character' ends up in remote Canada. (where my story begins, and where I wanted to live). A story I suppose, about what can happen when we spend too much time alone. Or cultures collide. Or personal views, do not mix with social views. Ultimately the guy kills a Mountie. Much like 'The Mad Trapper of Rat River" story.
4. My upbringing has to be remembered. If I saw a policeman, he was my friend. I believe we are all treated equal. I don't notice I have changed. If so, why would it matter, if we are all equal? My hair is long. I'm dirty, scruffy, and hanging out with those who look the same, for the first time in my life. I expected a smile and "We'll straighten all this out, now what is your side of the story Sir?" As would have happened as the son of a professor.

CHAPTER 3

1. This is a critical time period in Alaska history. The concept of 'wilderness' is changed forever due to legislation in the works. The Native Settlement Act is getting sorted out. Natives are forming corporations and acquiring vast tracts of land to control. Prime real-estate along waterways. So at this time in my life, the 70's through the 80's and part of the 90's a local could find a piece of ground and build a fish camp, trapline home, and not much was said. Still true today perhaps, but "if, if, and if." I am used to, "no if and or buts."

FOOT NOTES

2. Saws before electronic ignition, and other modern improvements were hard starting and cumbersome, so it wasn't totally my lack of knowledge. A lot of people still preferred handsaws in the 70's. There is other technology that comes along to keep in mind, that I did not have. Time was told by wind up watches. There were no cell phones. Solar power is new and expensive. There is no google search, and there are fewer books in print, so hard to get reliable information on wilderness survival. These are just a few examples of changing times to keep in mind.
3. I discover years later, quality products can be had, but it takes a lifetime to collect the contacts for reputable specialty companies, and it may cost ten times the going rate, and is usually handmade, and must be ordered, so suppliers come and go. If something is labeled 'survival use" That means the maker hopes you never need to depend on it, but keep it with your other survival gear. The hope is you never discover it will not hold up. It's made at best for 'one time' use.

CHAPTER 4

1. It is not so common for wolves to eat each other, but I find out later this is an unusual year for wolves. In Fairbanks this season, wolves came into town and ate dogs off the chain. There was a very high population, and not much around to eat. There are also social, dominant reasons a wolf might kill and tear apart another, if caught in a weak situation, like in a trap.
2. Years from now I notice this same phenomena among many civilized people. The weather report says in the news, the weather will be sunny. Therefore that is the weather. That is reality. If I comment it is raining, the reply is, no, it is not. No I am not wet, no those are not rainclouds over our head. If I comment, or ask about the weather, heads tend to go into the newspaper, not up at the sky. The news weather used to say, "The prediction is…" Now I hear "It's going to be." No longer a prediction, a sunny hot fact.

CHAPTER 5

1. This road is later renamed the Dalton Highway. In the beginning it was built as 'the haul road' to haul pipe for the pipeline, privately built. The concern at the time was this is the first road to cross the Yukon. What will the impact be on this vast country if the road becomes public? Hunters trappers and other human impact would drastically alter this wilderness. The public approved only on the promise this would never, ever, cross your heart and hope to die, become a public road. Many , including myself said "You cannot be trusted, and will break this promise."
2. While 'past flash' is about the knock out nifty memories of the past, the 'future flash' is about running the time line the other direction. Why not! I do it, because I can. If my story reads somewhat like science fiction, why not time travel?

CHAPTER 6

1. I see this same guy off and on over the years, and in 97 we strike up a conversation, discussing a business deal. He remembers me, the crazy hippie from the wilderness selling furs. He seems an all right honest guy. Probably I skinned the fur badly, stretched them on the board wrong, dried them poorly, and basically 'ruined' good fur. He gave me a 'low,' but honest price. In this way I learn to wait on feelings. Sometimes a situation is my mistake. From my perspective it seems unjust. It's easy for problems to be someone else's fault.
2. I'm unaware at the time but these conversations, small jobs, people I meet have a big influence on my later life. The ski resort people who hired me meet me years later, collect my art, and remember me as good hard honest worker. Talks of art, business, how to sell, how to buy, helps me one day run my own business.
3. I didn't realize it at the time, but maybe these days were not 'normal' times. The pipeline days were hectic. There was big money, short seasons, temporary companies. A big pie that everyone seemed to

FOOT NOTES

want a slice of. More crime and corruption may have been around then would be normal. I later do not feel all unions are corrupt or act this way. For now I only have this, my first introduction to unions.
4. True friendship takes time. Some of these people are there for me later on. I'm a loner, slow to get really involved with people. five years to remember who you are, fifteen to be friends, twenty to trust you. But down the road it happens.
5. If I had thought about it, or been taught, I could have asked for money in exchange for my help, and thus used that money to buy my ticket in. Or the Fair could allow free admittance to volunteer workers. Later in life I myself, as a vendor, offer free tickets to the poor, in exchange for help, or as a community service. Partly to pay back, or make up for, these years of being slick, and sneaking in free.

CHAPTER 7

1. I've overloaded the boat, and got it to front heavy. I barely know that my gas needs oil in it, probably don't even know what ratio, and have no tools, don't know what the water pump is. But I only have thirty miles downstream to go.
2. I Learn in years ahead, there are, in fact, specific 'rules' about such places. Nothing in writing, but understood by 'bush people,' This is very like town life where, if you want privileges, you have to know someone, have an in, be part of the group. I run into Bill again when it is time for me to have sled dogs of my own. I end up with a couple of the very dogs I see here on the Yukon. No he never returns with food. I did not specifically ask him to. Just "If you happen to come back this way." Partly not wanting to be a burden on anyone. Party I think in my 20's I have no concept what death is. I had never lost a loved one, not even a pet, not been close to anyone who had. Death is an abstract concept hard for the young to grasp. likewise ultimate defeat. Something will always work out, because it always has.
3. I find out almost a year later that a bulldozer got stolen from the pipeline camp at the Yukon, and no one knows how it was gotten out, or where it went. I conclude this was that cat. So it is as well I didn't show myself to the thieves.
4. Years from now, I get a routine health check and find out that at some point I had hepatitis. I do not know when that could have been (they can tell from liver damage scars). The time in my life I felt the most 'sick' is this time, when I couldn't understand why I feel so weak. Though I remember, it was 'the first year' that I had the yellow eyes, a symptom of hepatitis.
5. Years later, as a senior I come to understand "No, I was not 'ok,' though probably nothing anyone could do about it. I learned a simple truth. It all cost. I ponder at movies when our hero gets shot, and two days later is up and running, saving the day again. Injuries never end, yet always heal completely. It is said every boxer has only so many punches, so many knock outs in him. A body can only take so many near death experiences before saying 'Halt! Enough!" Only in fairy tales can a body take unlimited punches without ending up like Muhammad Ali.
6. I'm speaking here from the viewpoint of someone in their 20's. I am meeting a lot of poor and street people that were not a part of my upbringing. I've turned down a lot of 'golden opportunities' by civilized standards. I do not recognize I am probably scared. I have social issues I feel will get me in serious trouble if I spend a lot of time in civilization. As you follow my life in future books, I am the number one suspect in a murder, have my home burned down more than once, and end up a felon as a senior.

CHAPTER 8

1. Much of what I say here has come to pass. This was written before '9/11' before WACO, before the ENRON events where a majority of the banking-lending system was exposed as a Ponzi scheme. Before China came into power. Before a recession began. Before police brutality is proven through digital picture recording with phone cameras, because this was written before the computer age. This was written before the Arab nations conflicts, before Bin Ladin even. Not an "I told you so," to civilization, more of a, "So what is wrong with a handful of disillusioned people wanting to drop out and

FOOT NOTES

tune in to something else besides the rat race? Why is that so scary, weird, illegal, unfathomable to the average citizen?" I'm expecting a "Wow, well I wouldn't want to do it, but have at it, I can understand why!" Instead I and 'my kind' get smacked with a stick. Why? Pictures Will and I took of each other posing as wild mountain men at twenty four years old in the early 70's on this trip ended up getting digitized. They were found in my computer by 'the Feds' and used as evidence that I need to be locked up in 2013.

2. Statistically one in a thousand who dream of such a life actually get into the wilds. Of these, one in a hundred lasts a year. In any given year there are less than 25 people in Alaska living as I do. They all have certain things in common.

AFTERWORD

1. This book was written well before his now well know legal issues.

Printed in Great Britain
by Amazon